The Gospel of John

The Gospel of John

A New History

HUGO MÉNDEZ

OXFORD
UNIVERSITY PRESS

OXFORD
UNIVERSITY PRESS

Oxford University Press is a department of the University of Oxford.
It furthers the University's objective of excellence in research, scholarship,
and education by publishing worldwide. Oxford is a registered trade mark of
Oxford University Press in the UK and in certain other countries.

Published in the United States of America by Oxford University Press
198 Madison Avenue, New York, NY 10016, United States of America.

© Oxford University Press 2025

All rights reserved. No part of this publication may be reproduced, stored in a retrieval system, transmitted, used for text and data mining, or used for training artificial intelligence, in any form or by any means, without the prior permission in writing of Oxford University Press, or as expressly permitted by law, by license or under terms agreed with the appropriate reprographics rights organization. Inquiries concerning reproduction outside the scope of the above should be sent to the Rights Department, Oxford University Press, at the address above.

You must not circulate this work in any other form
and you must impose this same condition on any acquirer.

Library of Congress Cataloging-in-Publication Data
Names: Méndez, Hugo author.
Title: The gospel of John : a new history / Hugo Méndez.
Description: New York, NY : Oxford University Press, [2025] |
Includes bibliographical references. |
Identifiers: LCCN 2025007036 (print) | LCCN 2025007037 (ebook) |
ISBN 9780197686126 (hardback) | ISBN 9780197686157 | ISBN 9780197686133 (epub)
Subjects: LCSH: Bible. John—Criticism, interpretation, etc.
Classification: LCC BS2615.52 .M43 2025 (print) | LCC BS2615.52 (ebook) |
DDC 226.5/066—dc23/eng/20250428
LC record available at https://lccn.loc.gov/2025007036
LC ebook record available at https://lccn.loc.gov/2025007037

DOI: 10.1093/9780197686157.001.0001

Printed by Marquis Book Printing, Canada

The manufacturer's authorised representative in the EU for product safety is Oxford University Press España S.A. of El Parque Empresarial San Fernando de Henares, Avenida de Castilla, 2 – 28830 Madrid (www.oup.es/en or product.safety@oup.com). OUP España S.A. also acts as importer into Spain of products made by the manufacturer.

*To Roman,
the very best one.*

Contents

List of Abbreviations   ix
Preface and Acknowledgments   xiii
Introduction   xvii

PART I. THE GOSPEL

1. The Hidden Author   3
2. Why John Was Written   26
3. Symbols and Signs   63
4. An Apocryphal Gospel   103

PART II. AFTERLIVES

5. Invented Letters   141
6. Becoming John   163

Notes   187
Bibliography   221
Index of Bible References   247
Index of Subjects   259

Abbreviations

Scholarly Works

AB	The Anchor (Yale) Bible
ABRL	The Anchor (Yale) Bible Reference Library
AG	Bart D. Ehrman and Zlatko Pleše, *The Apocryphal Gospels: Texts and Translations* (New York: Oxford University Press, 2011).
AM	Herbert Musurillo, ed., *The Acts of the Christian Martyrs* (Oxford: Clarendon, 1972).
ANT	J. K. Elliott, ed., *The Apocryphal New Testament: A Collection of Apocryphal Christian Literature in an English Translation* (Oxford: Clarendon, 1993).
BETL	Bibliotheca Ephemeridum Theologicarum Lovaniensium
BINS	Biblical Interpretation Series
BMSEC	Baylor-Mohr Siebeck Studies in Early Christianity
BZNW	Beihefte zur Zeitschrift für die neutestamentliche Wissenschaft
CBQ	*Catholic Biblical Quarterly*
CBR	*Currents in Biblical Research*
CCSA	Corpus Christianorum, Series Apocryphorum (Turnhout: Brepols, 1983–).
CCSL	Corpus Christianorum, Series Latina (Turnout: Brepols, 1954–).
EKK	Evangelisch-Katholischer Kommentar zum Neuen Testament
GCS	Die griechischen christlichen Schriftsteller der ersten drei Jahrhunderte (Leipzig, J.C. Hinrichs, 1897–).
GS	Bentley Layton and David Brakke, *The Gnostic Scriptures*, 2nd edition (New Haven, CT: Yale University Press, 2021).
HBS	Herders Biblische Studien
HNT	Handbuch zum Neuen Testament
HTR	*Harvard Theological Review*
ICC	International Critical Commentary
JBL	*Journal of Biblical Literature*
JSJ	*Journal for the Study of Judaism*
JSJSupp	Journal for the Study of Judaism Supplemental Series
JSNT	*Journal for the Study of the New Testament*
JSNTSupp	Journal for the Study of the New Testament Supplement Series
JTS	*Journal of Theological Studies*

LCL	Loeb Classical Library
LNTS	Library of New Testament Studies
LXX	Septuagint
MNTA	*New Testament Apocrypha: More Noncanonical Scriptures*, 3 vols. (Grand Rapids, MI: Eerdmans, 2016–20).
Neot	*Neotestamentica*
NICNT	New International Commentary on the New Testament
NovT	*Novum Testamentum*
NovTSupp	Novum Testamentum Supplements
NTS	*New Testament Studies*
OECS	Oxford Early Christian Studies
OECT	Oxford Early Christian Texts
OTP	James H. Charlesworth, ed., *Old Testament Pseudepigrapha*, 2 vols. (New York: Doubleday, 1983–85).
PG	J.-P. Migne, ed., Patrologiae Cursus Completus: Series Graeca (Paris, 1857–66).
PL	J.-P. Migne, ed., Patrologiae Cursus Completus: Series Latina (Paris, 1878–90).
SBLECL	Society of Biblical Literature Early Christianity and Its Literature
SBLRBS	Society of Biblical Literature Resources for Biblical Study
SBLSymS	Society of Biblical Literature Symposium Series
SC	Sources Chrétiennes (Paris: Cerf, 1942–).
SNTSMS	Society for New Testament Studies Monograph Series
SP	Sacra Pagina
SPhilo	*Studia Philonica Annual*
SVTQ	*St. Vladimir's Theological Quarterly*
TENT	Texts and Editions for New Testament Study
THKNT	Theologischer Handkommentar zum Neuen Testament
ValC	Geoffrey S. Smith, ed., *Valentinian Christianity: Texts and Translations* (Oakland: University of California Press, 2020).
WUNT	Wissenschaftliche Untersuchungen zum Neuen Testament
ZNW	*Zeitschrift für die neutestamentliche Wissenschaft*

Ancient Authors and Works

Apoc. John	*Apocryphon of John*
Aug.	Augustine of Hippo
Tract.	Tractate
Cic.	Cicero
Att.	*Epistula ad Atticum*
Clem.	Clement of Alexandria

Ad. II Joh.	Adumbrationes in Ep. II Ioannis
Strom.	Stromateis
Diog. Laert.	Diogenes Laertius
Vit.	De vita moribus philosophorum
ep. (All authors)	Epistle/Letter
Ep. Ap.	Epistula Apostolorum
Eus.	Eusebius
h.e.	Historia Ecclesiastica
GMary	Gospel of Mary
GThom.	Gospel of Thomas
Ign.	Ignatius of Antioch
Eph.	Epistula ad Ephesios
Smyrn.	Epistula ad Smyrnaeos
Iren.	Irenaeus of Lyons
haer.	Adversus Haereses
Joseph.	Josephus
Ap. Contra	Apionem
A.J.	Antiquitates Judaicae
Just.	Justin Martyr
dial.	Dialogue with Trypho
Lucian	Lucian of Samosata
Dem.	Demonax
Mur. Frag.	Muratorian Fragment
Paus.	Pausanias
Graec. desc.	Descriptio Graeciae
Or.	Origen
Comm. Matt.	Commentarium in evangelium Matthaei
Comm. Rom.	Commentarium in Romanos
Hom. Luc.	Homiliae in Lucam
Philo	Philo Judaeus
Abr.	De Abrahamo
Agr.	De agricultura
Conf.	De confusione linguarum
Det.	Quod deterius potiori insidari soleat
Fug.	De fuga et inventione
Her.	Quis rerum divinarum heres sit
Leg.	Legum allegoriae
Legat.	Legatio ad Gaium
Migr.	De migratione Abrahami
Mos.	De vita Moysis
Opif.	De opificio mundi
Post.	De posteritate Caini

QE	*Quaestiones et solutiones in Exodum*
QG	*Quaestiones et solutiones in Genesim*
Sacr.	*De sacrificiis Abelis et Caini*
Somn.	*De somniis*
Spec.	*De specialibus legibus*
Virt.	*De virtutibus*
Polyb.	Polybius
Hist.	*Historia*
Tat.	Tatian
orat.	*Oratio ad Graecos*
Tert.	Tertullian
Bapt.	*De Baptismo*
Cult. fem.	*De cultu feminarum*
Marc.	*Adversus Marcionem*
Res.	*De resurrectione carnis*

Preface and Acknowledgments

This book reimagines how the Gospel of John came to be and how it ignited an entire literary tradition in its wake. Its own origins are a simpler tale to tell. This book grew out of my courses at Yale University and at the University of North Carolina at Chapel Hill. Every time I have taught John, my engagement with the text has deepened thanks to the incisive questions, deep curiosity, and infectious enthusiasm of my students. In many ways, I am publishing this book to them and for them, precisely as a crystallization of all we have learned together over the past decade.

To complete a book, however, one needs at least a little time away from the classroom. In my case, I was fortunate to be gifted ample time in the form of two scholarly residencies. The first was a year-long research leave sponsored in part by UNC's Institute for the Arts and Humanities, where I had the privilege of being a Borden Faculty Fellow (2022). I am deeply grateful to the IAH's director, Patricia Parker, for allowing me to take that fellowship remotely to be present for my young son at home—an accommodation I wish more corners of the academy would offer parents and caregivers. The second of these opportunities was a Summer Residency at the National Humanities Center (2023)—by far the most intense and rewarding research experience of my life. For that unexpected gift, I must thank Elizabeth Englehardt, senior associate dean of humanities and fine arts at UNC. Two more investment were critical to bringing this project to completion. One was a generous grant from the Catholic Biblical Association, awarded in 2023. The other was an Arts and Humanities Publication Grant awarded by the IAH and UNC's Office of Research Development.

As I developed this text, I had the privilege of workshopping parts of it in different settings. I am especially appreciative of the feedback I received after invited talks at Duke University, the University of Birmingham, and Australian Catholic University, after workshops at Durham University and the Jesuit School of Theology, and after presentations for the Society of Biblical Literature's "Johannine Literature" unit and the Catholic Biblical Association's "Gospel and Epistles of John" task force. I also received many helpful comments—some truly critical—when sharing individual chapters of the book at the UNC-Duke "Christianity in Antiquity" reading group.

Many colleagues in the field have made decisive contributions to my thinking and to this manuscript in these and other settings. First and foremost are Harold Attridge and Bart Ehrman, both towering figures in the study of the New Testament and incredible mentors. Others include James Barker, Douglas Campbell, Stephen Carlson, Jeremiah Coogan, Wayne Coppins, Elizabeth Crosar, Susan Hylen, Jared Klein, Julia Lindenlaub, Joel Marcus, Candida Moss, Alicia Myers, Adele Reinhartz, Christopher Skinner, Jason Staples, Matthew Thiessen, Ross Wagner, and Robyn Faith Walsh. I am grateful to my editor, Steve Wiggins, for his enthusiasm for this project and guidance through its development.

Among so many scholars, however, I'd like to spotlight one figure for special thanks: Mark Goodacre. Mark's work on the Synoptic Gospels, the *Gospel of Thomas*, and John has transformed how a generation of scholars, including me, think about all these texts. Traces of his thought and, undoubtedly, some of his iconoclastic spirit run deep in this work. More important, Mark has been an exceptionally generous mentor and friend, always ready to lend his wisdom and encouragement. I am incredibly privileged to count him as a colleague across our local UNC-Duke community.

The contributions of loved ones may be less intangible in a work such as this, but they are no less vital. I owe everything in my life to the sacrifices of my parents, Hugo and Ida, and to the kindness of so many family members and friends. Names such as Andres Hernandez, Rachel Elovitz, Fr. Philip Scott, Fr. David Hyman, Mitchell Esswein, Kaitlyn Gray, Alex Brown, Kevin Sevcik, Hank Tarlton, the Martinez family, Ruben Mendez, Pedro Mendez, and Camila Cribb-Fabersunne are but a few of those etched across my heart. And there are no words to express the full debt I owe to my partner, Divya—my loving companion through the entire journey of composing this manuscript.

In the end, however, this book is dedicated, quite appropriately, to the most important person in my life: my son, Roman. We spend our evenings talking about astronomy, plants, countries, electricity, ancient Egypt, and yes, even the Bible. And I have written so many words of this book beside him or waiting to pick him up from preschool, school, theater company—always thinking of him, always imagining what it would be like for him to one day read this text. Roman, this book is yours.

Since this book took shape over several years, it was informed by multiple pieces I published in that period, incorporating text from several. Specifically, the book's fifth chapter reproduces sections of my 2020 article, "Did the Johannine Community Exist?," and the book's second and third chapters incorporate text from my 2025 article, "The 'Last Day' in John: Future or Realized?" Additionally, a segment of chapter 4 emerged from a conference whose proceedings are forthcoming.

Since this book was written for a broad audience, including undergraduates and general readers, I have limited the amount of ancient language material reproduced in the text, preferring English translations and limited Greek transliterations. To avoid idiosyncrasy in those translations, I utilize contemporary editions. Biblical quotations in the text are my own, with the RSV and NRSVue as models. My scholarly citations are also guided by a principle of selectivity, balancing a range of factors to the best of my ability.

Introduction

The Gospel of John is one of the central scriptures of the Christian tradition—a book invested with immense spiritual, historical, and cultural significance. The purported author of the book, a mysterious figure who identifies himself only as the "disciple whom Jesus loved," sits beside Jesus in Leonardo's *Last Supper* and is depicted on a dedicated leaf of the Book of Kells. He is the orator of Bach's most beloved *Passion*, and the introductory words of his Gospel were the last lines of the Roman Catholic Mass for centuries.

But who was this figure, and why did he write this text? In this book, I argue that he was not the disciple of tradition and memory. Rather, he was a literary fiction—the mask of a disguised author, living and writing around the beginning of the second century.[1] The text's real author believed in a startling vision of human exaltation—one casting Jesus as a divine being who came to earth to transform humans into divine beings. To encourage others to embrace his vision, the author composed a gospel in which Jesus himself communicates this vision across so many cryptic dialogues. In turn, he set these speeches within a reimagined narrative of Jesus's life, populated with symbolic episodes that communicate the same ideas. Finally, to make this revisionary portrait of Jesus plausible, the author disguised his identity, attributing his Gospel to an invented, shadowy disciple of Jesus—a supposed eyewitness to his life. In this frame, the Gospel of John is a text quite comparable to other so-called apocryphal gospels produced in the second century—works such as the *Gospel of Thomas* and the *Gospel of Peter*.

The most distinctive contribution of this book, however, is the idea that the invention of this disciple was not a self-contained event but the genesis of a new and dynamic literary tradition. In the period in which the Gospel of John was written, other writers were actively co-opting the identities of well-known disciples of Jesus in new narratives, visionary texts, treatises, and letters. As the Gospel gained acceptance as a historical account, its invented author became a viable mask for these sorts of projects. And in time, others did take up that mask. Three such authors composed the works we know as 1 John, 2 John, and 3 John. As I argue here, these letters position themselves as works of the same narrator as John—a figure who has "touched," "seen," and heard" Jesus, who alternates "we" and "I" language, and who deliberately takes up the distinctive speech patterns of John's narrator.[2] They are a chain of falsely authored works built on another falsely authored work.

The literary tradition represented in the Epistles flourished in other forms as well. In the same period, some Christians had begun identifying the invented disciple of the Gospel with a known disciple of Jesus: John, the son of Zebedee. Unsurprisingly, then, one also finds various writings written in the persona of the implied author of the Gospel, but which call this author "John"—among them, the *Secret Book* (*Apocryphon*) *of John*. Scholars often marginalize these texts as late interlopers in the tradition, reserving the term "Johannine literature" for the Gospel and Epistles of John alone. But if the Gospel and Epistles are also falsely authored works, we have no reason to privilege them over later texts. All of the above works participate in the same literary practice, and all of them deserve an equal place in the "Johannine" family.

This book, then, weaves together a new history of John and of the Johannine literature more broadly. It reveals how a gospel beloved by billions came to be. And it explains how a single act of disguised authorship inadvertently sparked an entire literary tradition, transforming twenty centuries of Christian culture.

I. Key Terms and Concepts

The terms "disguised authorship" and "invention" carry significant weight across this study. Before setting out on this new hisory, then, a brief word about these terms is in order.

A. "Disguised Authorship" or "False Authorship"

As I use the phrase, "disguised authorship" is when a real author suggests to readers that some other person wrote their work. Most narratives—even anonymous works—give readers some impression of who their real author is, either directly within the work or paratextually (through titles and other framing materials). This projection is the text's "authorial claim" or "implied author."[3] In examples of "disguised authorship," however, the author projects a false authorial claim. That real author does not merely mischaracterize the text's true author—for example, modifying minor traits or accentuating certain features. Instead, the author suggests that a different person altogether wrote the text.

There are several ways to construct and project a false authorial claim.[4] One can do this explicitly by assuming a name other than one's own (pseudonymity). But one can also do this implicitly, imbuing even a nameless implied author with a set of traits that would make them a fundamentally different person than the text's real author. One can, for example, suggest a different age, gender, background, or set of experiences for the implied author. Whatever strategy they employ, such works make a "false authorial claim" and construct a "false implied author." They are "falsely authored works" or "authorial impostures."

1. Motivations

Scholars suggest a wide range of reasons why ancient writers chose to produce falsely authored works, none of which are mutually exclusive. As the historian David Hackett Fisher observes, historical motives and justifications "are usually pluralistic, in both their number and their nature," so that even "conscious and unconscious motives tend to coexist and interact," and "motive sets are never, ever, inalterably fixed in a living individual."[5] Some persons adopted false authorial personas to enhance the authority of their literary products, often within polemical contexts.[6] Other authors seem to have engaged in disguised authorship to turn a profit, exploiting motivated buyers who were eager to buy supposedly lost or obscure works.[7] More recently, classicists have speculated that some such works reflect the arcane interests of ancient literati who were eager to supplement fragmentary historical memories (so Patricia Rosenmeyer) or to playfully experiment with ideas of authorial authenticity as part of a "sophisticated game" (so Irene Peirano on Latin literary fakes).[8] Following different paths, recent studies from the field of religious studies have speculated that some programs of disguised authorship might have represented a kind of spiritual practice, perhaps within a spirituality of self-effacement (so Charles Stang on the Pseudo-Dionysian corpus), or from a desire to restore or update the teachings of a founding figure (so Hindy Najman on Jewish pseudepigrapha).[9] False authorship might also have offered a path for certain marginalized writers to circulate their works, including women and enslaved persons.[10] This range of motivations, of course, is subject to a range of ethical assessments.

In this book, I link the works I explore to several possible motivations. I argue, for example, that the Gospel of John probably uses disguised authorship to authorize its innovative ideas and position itself more competitively in a crowded field of gospels. But I also speculate that the author of John might have understood his project through other lenses, including a charismatic spirituality. In one chapter, I suggest that 3 John might have been written by an author with a very different aim—namely, to augment existing traditions about the eyewitness narrator of the Gospel of John. I offer these possibilities not to close off other possible interpretations but as a starting point for new debates over these works.

2. Alternative Terms ("Literary Fake," "Forgery," "Pseudepigrapha")
The terms I have chosen to use in this study—"disguised authorship," "false authorship," "false authorial claims," and "falsely authored works"—can be coordinated with others in use among scholars. What I call "falsely authored works" are essentially equivalent to what the classicist Irene Peirano Garrison calls "literary fakes," that is, "texts which self-consciously purport either to be the work of the author to whom they are attributed or to be written at a different time from that in which they were composed."[11] What I call "falsely authored works" can also be called "pseudepigrapha"—a term popular with classicists and biblical scholars—but only when the meaning of that term is carefully delimited.

As Najman and Peirano observe, "pseudepigrapha" is a term fraught with potential ambiguities, all of which potentially touch on this study. The term first surfaces within Hellenistic literary criticism, where it was used for texts whose real authors were not identical to their presumed authors. The problem is that those Hellenistic literary critics applied the term to both (a) texts that disguise their real authorship (primary pseudepigraphy) and (b) texts that later editors, scribes, and readers misattributed to other authors (secondary pseudepigraphy).[12] Both of these processes shaped the Gospel and Epistles of John. As I will show here, these texts were both falsely authored and later misattributed to John, the son of Zebedee. A second issue is that the term "pseudepigrapha" is built from the prefix "pseudo-" (false, deceitful) and the word "epigraph" (title), suiting the fact that the Hellenistic literary critics who coined the term were primarily engaged in a bibliographic exercise, evaluating the titles affixed to works by their primary authors or by later editors. And yet the many works I will explore, beginning with the Gospel of John, did not initially carry titles or epigraphs. Here again, the term "pseudepigraphy" does not offer the precision or clarity needed in this study. Third, in some sectors of biblical studies, the term "pseudepigrapha" is also an umbrella term for a particular set of (Jewish) noncanonical works—a category to which none of the texts I explore in this book belongs. And last, the term "pseudepigrapha" is typically applied only to ancient literature despite the fact that practices of disguised authorship have persisted into the medieval, early modern, and modern periods. In this way, the term "pseudepigrapha" suggests an exceptional status for ancient (and especially canonical) works that they may not deserve, raising serious issues of scholarly objectivity and ethics.[13] For all these reasons, I use the term "pseudepigrapha" sparingly but always with reference to primary pseudepigraphy—that is, disguised or false authorship. In turn, I use the term "pseudepigrapher" to describe one who produces a falsely authored text.

One other term commonly appears in scholarship on pseudepigraphy: "forgeries" (in German, *Fälschungen*).[14] In my usage, this term describes only a particular subset of falsely authored texts—specifically, those produced with deceptive intent, following Bruce Metzger's definition: "a literary forgery is essentially a piece of work created or modified with the intention to deceive."[15] Several works I discuss arguably fit this label.

3. Beyond "Authenticity"

Even though I identify John and related texts as falsely authored works, I do not regard the question of authenticity to be the first, only, or best way to analyze such works. That question is, rather, one of many possible entry points into this literature—one that can and will occasion related explorations.[16] In this study, the idea that the Gospel of John is a falsely authored work will occasion new ways of reflecting on the Gospel's penchant for cryptic discourses and its tendency to situate those discourses in unrecorded moments of the life of Jesus and private exchanges between Jesus and different confidants. It will also connect to deeper reflections on John's narrative design and symbolism. As I hope to demonstrate, the authorial deception woven into John adds to the literary depth and complexity of the work, and it was critical in shaping the eventual afterlives of the text.

B. "Invention"

Across this text, I argue that the Gospel of John constructs not merely a false implied author but an "invented" author. I also suggest that many elements of the Gospel's in-text world are similarly "invented," "pseudo-historical," "imagined," "fabricated," and "fictionalized." In my usage, all these terms are interchangeable, indicating that an in-text element does not have a one-to-one correspondence with an external person, place, event, or thing, but that it represents a literary creation of the author.

In practice, I alternate between these terms both for literary variety (a necessity in a study of this length) and to exploit the particular shades of meaning implicit in each. The term "pseudo-historical" captures the fact that the elements in question are ahistorical but presented as if they were historical. The word "fictionalized" recognizes that the element is no more concrete than a given element of a strictly fictional work. The terms "invented," "fabricated," and "imagined," in turn, place emphasis on the intention and agency of the author who develops these elements. Each finds its origins in different metaphors of conscious creation and construction (the invention of technology, the fabrication or manufacturing of objects, and the use of imagination to develop stories). Still, their semantics largely overlap, and I use them to capture the same reality.

II. A New History

This work is "a new history" of the Gospel of John since it departs from traditional conceptions of the authorship of John as well as from popular scholarly approaches to this text. Over the past half-century, scholars have generally interpreted John as a work produced publicly over several generations by multiple hands living and working in a hypothetical network of ancient churches called the "Johannine Community."[17] In this view, a series of writers composed the Gospel to condense the community's memories and traditions of Jesus in written form, doing so independently of similar projects emerging around the same time (e.g., the gospels of Matthew, Mark, and Luke). Scholars have also generally assumed that the letters of 1 John, 2 John, and 3 John were written within the same network as real communications between members of the group.[18] Viewed in this way, the Gospel and the Epistles become ready soil from which to excavate the intellectual and social history of the community in so many approaches (tradition-critical, source-critical, redaction-critical).

The past quarter-century of scholarship, however, has seen dramatic changes to the study of the Gospel of John—changes that inform the reconstruction offered here. In keeping with recent scholarly trends, I argue that John is mostly the work of a single author rather than multiple authors. I question the extent to which one can reconstruct a "community" with purely and specifically "Johannine" traits around that author. I also question whether one can assign the Epistles to the same social matrix as the Gospel. My book weaves critical discussions of the community hypothesis into various sections, but I have deliberately avoided framing this entire book as a response to that hypothesis. (I critique it in other publications.)[19] In the end, my book is not so much a discussion of twentieth-century scholarship on the Johannine literature as a reintroduction to the Johannine works themselves—one that sets out a new, coherent vision of their origins from their internal data.

III. Chapter Plan

This study unfolds in two parts, spanning six total chapters. Part I explores the first and central work in this tradition: the Gospel of John. Part II explores the origins and projects of later works derived from the Gospel, among them, the epistles of 1 John, 2 John, and 3 John, the *Secret Book of John*, and the *Epistula Apostolorum*.

Chapter 1, "The Hidden Author," probes what we can know about the authorship of the Gospel, laying the starting premises for later chapters. In it, I argue that the core of the Gospel is the product of a single pen. I also isolate the intellectual and literary contexts that informed that author. As I note, the mind that produced John probably knew all three of the Synoptic Gospels—that is, Mark, Matthew, and Luke. That author also seems to have developed his worldview in conversation with the thought of Paul and with streams of Hellenistic Jewish philosophy related to those found in the writings of Philo.

In Chapter 2, "Why John Was Written," I contend that the author of John composed his Gospel to press a revisionary vision of Jesus. The Gospel presents a series of invented discourses, in which John's Jesus articulates a complex system of ideas unlike those in earlier gospels. He reveals that he is a divine being who has come to earth to transform humans into divine beings like himself: the celestial man who creates celestial humans. In this chapter, I outline this vision of human exaltation in detail, centering it as the critical intervention of the Gospel.

Chapter 3, "Symbols and Signs," argues that the author of John not only invented new teachings for Jesus; he also modified, tailored, reshaped, or invented narratives to supplement those teachings. To demonstrate this point, I survey the Gospel scene by scene, highlighting the hidden symbolism of individual episodes and accumulating evidence of the text's contrived nature. The Gospel's symbolism can be difficult to detect for readers who do not grasp the author's vision of human exaltation in all its proportions. When those teachings are understood, it becomes clear that a symbolic program pervades every corner of the text, structuring its larger narrative arcs and penetrating even supposedly minor episodes.

In Chapter 4, "An Apocryphal Gospel," I explore the question of how John gained acceptance beside Mark, Matthew, and Luke despite its innovations. I conclude that the author of John won over potentially skeptical readers by taking up various authorizing strategies—strategies also seen in other apocryphal gospels of the period. Crucially, the author of John positioned his text as an eyewitness account: the memoir of an imagined "disciple whom Jesus loved." But the author also wove in other supporting devices, among them, cryptic speech and suggestions that the teachings of Jesus were meant to be supernaturally recalled and interpreted after his death. The chapter ends by assembling a tentative profile of how the author of John composed and disseminated his text.

After the publication of John, other writers were inspired to create texts in its image. In Chapter 5, "Invented Letters," I identify 1, 2, and 3 John as falsely authored works in the same tradition. That chapter begins by condensing the evidence that the author(s) of the Epistles knew and imitated the language of the Gospel. I argue that these parallels were meant to support a common, false authorial claim. Although 1, 2, and 3 John were not written by the author of the Gospel, they were meant to look as if they were. As the chapter concludes, I reinterpret these works in light of this analysis, isolating new possible motivations for their production.

Finally, Chapter 6, "Becoming John," explores other branches of this literary tradition. By the mid-second century, the eyewitness author of the Gospel had become conflated with a known disciple of Jesus: John, the son of Zebedee. This chapter explores the basis for that attribution. It also canvasses second-century works that claim the Gospel's narrator as their author under the name "John," including the *Secret Book of John*, the *Epistula Apostolorum*, and the book of Revelation, arguing that all these continue the same literary practice that forged the Gospel and Epistles. In this constellation of texts, we can see the broader imagined corpus of the invented disciple of Jesus—a rich and dynamic tradition of disguised authorship.

PART I
THE GOSPEL

But there are also many other things that Jesus did.
—John 21:25

1
The Hidden Author

Tracing the origins of the Gospel of John is no easy task. The text keeps its beginnings shrouded in the deepest darkness. John is strictly anonymous; it never names its author.[1] Although it now bears the title "The Gospel according to John," this title is not original to the work; it was added later, evidently by a scribe attempting to distinguish multiple early such accounts of the life of Jesus.[2] For that matter, the text also does not name its original addressees, nor does it indicate where or when it was written.

As thick as this darkness might seem, however, it is not impenetrable. Between the lines of the text are faint clues, subtle indications of the origins of this enigmatic work. Increasingly, scholars believe that the Gospel was the project of a single primary author.[3] Around the turn of the second century, an unknown figure conceptualized the project and structure of the work we now know as John, directing its complex drafting over an extended period.[4] Additionally, contemporary scholars are increasingly confident that this individual drew inspiration from previous accounts of the life of Jesus, basing his work on the still extant gospels of Mark, Matthew, and Luke.[5]

In this chapter, I will outline the basis for these two insights—insights critical for any comprehensive understanding of the text. Only when we recognize the unity of the Gospel of John can we map out its primary intervention, multifaceted theology, and careful literary design. And only when we set the Gospel in its literary world—when we understand its position relative to related works such as Mark, Matthew, and Luke—can we begin to comprehend the text's unique place and contributions to early Christian literature. To appreciate all that makes this Gospel unique and to trace its later legacy, we must return to the hidden author, the creative mind, at its beginning.

I. A Single Author

It may seem intuitive to attribute the Gospel of John to a single pen. Scholars attribute most other ancient works, even most ancient gospels, to individual authors. And yet, through much of the twentieth century most critical scholars conceptualized John as a different kind of work: a communal product, "composed in two or more successive editions by a School of Johannine writers who felt free to write, and to rewrite the Gospel."[6] Today, however, this view is in retreat, and for good reason.

A. The Problem of the Aporiae

For many scholars, the first reason to posit that the Gospel of John was the product of multiple hands was the presence of so many aporiae—inconsistencies, skips, or seams—in the text. For example, in chapter 2, the narrator identifies a particular sign as "the first of [Jesus's] signs" (2:11), and in chapter 4, the narrative enumerates another miracle as "the second sign Jesus did after coming from Judea to Galilee" (4:54). Between these two verses, however, the text mentions multiple "signs" performed by Jesus, disrupting the numbering scheme (2:23, 3:2).[7] Similarly, the Gospel sets the events of chapter 6 on "the other side of the sea of Galilee" (6:1)—ostensibly "the other side" from the location where the events of chapter 5 occurred. The problem is that chapter 5 is set in Jerusalem, nowhere near the Sea of Galilee (5:1). And in 14:30, Jesus claims, "I will no longer talk much with you," but he continues speaking for another three chapters (chapters 15–17).

There are multiple ways of making sense of these inconsistencies, and it is not clear that all of them require the same explanation. Some might reflect a single author's inconsistent use of sources, though as Jörg Frey writes, "interpreters today are more skeptical vis-à-vis the reconstruction of continuous sources behind the work of the evangelist."[8] Other aporiae might indicate that John is, in the words of Martinus de Boer, "the product of a long and complex process of composition by one or more (Johannine) authors."[9] But as de Boer concedes in this line, that complex composition process does not require multiple authors; it could be the product of only one. In fact, by Occam's razor, we should prefer positing a single author unless we absolutely must posit others.

In this case, there is no need to posit a separate author. We can easily imagine a single author working, reworking, and tinkering with the same draft over an extended period, and we can easily imagine a few careless mistakes or inconsistencies slipping into the draft that way. We can also imagine an author failing to recognize those inconsistencies because he had a poor editorial eye or from a rushed publication process. More recent scholarship has called on scholars to avoid contemporary (that is, post–printing press) assumptions about the quality and coherence of ancient texts, stressing that many ancient writers noted that texts could be circulated in a state that was raw, disorderly, or unpolished.[10]

As it stands, two features of John make it especially likely that a single individual produced the text. First, unlike the aporiae in texts developed by multiple authors, most of the aporiae in John are relatively isolated; they do not point to larger layers or divisions in the text. Consider, as a point of contrast, a section of the Bible that has long been understood as incorporating distinctly authored documents or editorial layers: the books of the Pentateuch. Echoing Richard Elliott Friedman, "the strongest evidence establishing" the presence of multiple layers in the collection "is that several different lines of evidence converge," especially around certain stories that are found twice in the Pentateuch in different versions (doublets):[11]

> When we separate the doublets, this also results in the resolution of nearly all the contradictions. And when we separate the doublets, the name of God divides consistently.... And when we separate the doublets, the terminology of each source remains consistent with that source.... And when we separate the source, this produces continuous narratives that follow with only a rare break. And when we separate the sources, this fits with the linguistic evidence.... The name of God and the doublets were the starting-points of the investigation.... But they were not, and are not, major arguments or evidence in themselves.[12]

None of the aporiae in chapters 1–20 open up these sorts of coincidences. For example, we can recognize what appears to be an inconsistent pattern of trying to number the "signs" in John across chapters 2–4 of the text, but this numbering system does not correlate with other features that would indicate multiple hands working on the same draft (e.g., other distinctive linguistic patterns or ideological agendas). Similarly, the geographical error at 6:1 is unusual, but it is the only peculiarity in that segment of the text. The material on both sides of that verse shows no other discontinuities.[13] The same is true of the material surrounding 14:30; that material is also remarkably consistent in theme and development.[14] It is no surprise, then, that, despite many efforts, the field has never coalesced around a single reconstruction of the text's supposed redactional layers.

The primary reason to posit a single mind behind most of John, however, is the overwhelming impression of unity and coherence in the text as we have it.[15] As we will see in later chapters, John has a single, focused theological vision that it presses with remarkable consistency from its prologue on and across both its discourse and narrative materials.[16] Along the same lines, literary critics of the Gospel have also uncovered significant evidence of the text's unity. On a macro level, Alan Culpepper notes, "the Fourth Gospel develops narration, themes, characterization, ironies, and symbolism with a great deal of internal consistency"—a claim supported by dozens of studies.[17] Similarly, Harold Attridge observes that "the general uniformity of the Gospel's style and its intricate cross-referencing suggests that a uniform literary vision governed most of the text's development."[18] And on the linguistic plane, Craig Koester recognizes that "a clear and simple style of Greek is used throughout the book."[19] For all these reasons, we can confidently approach the book as a literary whole. As for the literary tensions remaining in the text, we can address these on a case-by-case basis, searching out probable causes for each inconsistency.

B. "We" Language

Another reason why many scholars have claimed that the Gospel of John was the product of not one but several hands is that, in their view, the Gospel itself suggests as much. In the text's prologue, John's narrator speaks in the first-person plural (we): "we have seen his glory" (1:14). More important, in the conclusion to chapter 21, the voice of the narrator claims that a certain disciple "is testifying to these things and has written them," adding, "and we know that his testimony is true" (21:24). De Boer insists that "the closing verses of the Gospel (21:24–25) attest multiple hands in the composition of the Gospel."[20]

Nevertheless, this simplistic appeal to the Gospel's use of "we" language is problematic for several reasons. For one, "we" language does not necessarily indicate multiple authors. As I will detail later in this study, many single authors in antiquity adopted a "we" voice in their works, some alternating it with a singular "I" voice. (I will suggest that 21:24–25 alternates its forms in this very way.) Second, there is compelling evidence that 21:24, the verse that carries most of the weight of this appeal, was added to the Gospel later by a later scribe; in that case, it cannot be a reliable guide to the composition of chapters 1–20.[21]

There is, however, one other reason to dismiss the "we" language of the Gospel as an appropriate basis to reconstruct who wrote the text. Simply put, the text has a false authorial cast. If the author of John deliberately disguises his identity, as I will argue in subsequent chapters, then we cannot trust that any verse, including these, will faithfully reveal the actual hand(s) behind the text. A single hand could hide behind the façade of a plural "we" narrator voice as easily as behind an "I" voice. The possibility of disguised authorship changes the evidence available to us and the ways in which we can use it, and rightfully so.

C. Later Scribal Additions

Despite my view that the Gospel was the product of a single primary author, later scribes often altered texts in significant ways. As it stands, there is good evidence that two passages in the Gospel represent major scribal additions to John. The first is the *Pericope Adulterae* (7:53–8:11).[22] The second is the final chapter of the text (21:1–25).[23]

1. *Pericope Adulterae* (7:53–8:11)

No critical scholar today doubts that the *Pericope Adulterae*—a story in which Jesus saves a woman caught in adultery from stoning—is a later addition to the Gospel of John. The section is not attested in any extant manuscript of John predating the fifth century. It seems to have been slow to gain a foothold.[24] It also lacks the signature linguistic and literary features of other sections of John.[25] We do not know who inserted the story, though it was undoubtedly a copyist or scribe, someone with the ability and opportunity to manipulate and alter the text. The motivations of that scribe, however, are also unclear.

2. The Final Chapter (21:1–25)

Another section of the Gospel, chapter 21, is also likely to be secondary, though the evidence in this case is more contested.[26] One issue is that the passage is attested in all known manuscripts that contain the concluding chapters of John. If it was introduced into the Gospel later, it must not have been too much later.[27] Nevertheless, the passage is a site at which several unusual features converge—precisely what we need to determine the limits of an editorial layer.

The first reason for considering the passage a later addition to the Gospel is that it occurs immediately after a line that reads like a suitable conclusion or epilogue to the book: "Jesus did many other signs in the presence of his disciples that are not written in this book, but these are written that you might believe" (20:30–31). As Armin Baum notes, many ancient works ended with lines in which authors explained their purpose in writing.[28] Take, for example, the following line from the *Testament of Solomon*: "For this reason I have written out this, my testament, in order that those who here might pray about, and pay attention to, the last things and not the first things, in order that they might finally find grace forever. Amen."[29]

Some such conclusions are even more similar to John 20:31, pairing statements of purpose with implicit acknowledgments that the author has left unnecessary materials out:

> These are a very few things out of many which I might have mentioned, but they will suffice to give my readers a notion of the sort of man he was.[30]
>
> I have given an exact account of our laws and constitutions in my previous work on our *Antiquities*. Here I have alluded to them only so far as was necessary for my purpose.... I have, I think, in the present work adequately fulfilled the promise made at the outset.... Upon the laws it was unnecessary to expatiate.... To you, Epaphroditus, who are a devoted lover of the truth and for your sake to any who, like you may wish to know the facts about our race, I beg to dedicate this and the preceding book.[31]

The clearest sign that 20:30–31 should be seen as a conclusion, however, is that our current text of John ends with precisely this sort of conclusion, in a redundant line: "But there are also many other things that Jesus did; if every one of them were written down, I suppose that the world itself could not contain the books that would be written" (21:25).

What we have in chapter 21, then, is not only (a) extra text after an apparent ending but (b) a doublet in the text—the very feature used to distinguish layers in the Pentateuch. The redundancy of 20:30–31 and 21:24–25 also gives us what every other aporia in the Gospel does not: (c) a clear indication of where an editorial layer in the text might begin and end. If 20:30–31 is the original ending of the text, then whatever follows it—that is, chapter 21—is likely a later addition to the text. For that matter, 20:30–31 (d) sits immediately before the most plausible, even expected place for such an interpolation. The blank space after the conclusion of a text was a soft spot in manuscripts, vulnerable to the introduction of new materials. In this place, such additions are neither difficult to insert nor disruptive to the original text. Famously, the Gospel of Mark has had multiple endings added to it following its concluding verse (16:8).

Other peculiarities contained within chapter 21 also point to its secondary status. The most significant is (e) the unusual and unexpected content of the passage. Whereas 20:30–31 seems to imply no further "signs" would be narrated, the chapter depicts yet another supernatural deed Jesus performed after his resurrection. Still more unusually, the miracle occurs while Jesus's disciples were fishing (21:3), but it is not clear why the disciples are fishing in the scene.[32] In the noncanonical *Gospel of Peter*, the resurrected Jesus appears to a group of disciples fishing because those disciples had grown despondent over Jesus's death, returned to Galilee, and resumed their former careers as fishermen, unaware that Jesus had risen from the dead. By contrast, chapter 21 situates a fishing scene in an unusual and less likely context: after the disciples' climactic encounters with Jesus and reception of the Spirit. For that matter, scholars have also noted (f) other un-Johannine features in the passage. Raymond Brown observes that 21:1 is different from other transitions in the Gospel and marked by "awkwardness" in its phrasing: "Jesus revealed himself again to his disciples, and he revealed himself in this way."[33] Baum highlights the unusual and sudden introduction of "the sons of Zebedee," figures no other verse in the Gospel mentions either by name or under this title.[34] The idea that Jesus will "come" in the future (21:22) also sits uneasily with the way earlier chapters predict Jesus would "come" to his disciples precisely through the Spirit (14:23).[35]

It might be possible to explain away a few of these curious features of the passage, and some authors offer valiant attempts.[36] With each stacked peculiarity, however, the probabilistic load against seeing chapters 1–20 and chapter 21 as parts of a single, unitary work becomes too great. The latter must be a secondary addition to the text.[37] In turn, the differences in phrasing and thought across these chapters also make it unlikely that the same author who composed chapters 1–20 also composed chapter 21. The added chapter is the work of a later copyist or scribe.[38] Evidently, that scribe inserted this new material reasonably early—no more than a few decades after the text entered into circulation—since "surviving witnesses to Tatian's Diatessaron, originally compiled in the late second century C.E., contain John 21" and since no extant manuscript of John attests a version without chapter 21.[39]

The motivations of this scribe are unclear. Perhaps he wanted to reconcile John with other gospels by including a Galilean appearance of Jesus, adapting one circulating in the period.[40] He was clearly aware of traditions concerning Peter's crucifixion (21:18–19), and he apparently believed it was helpful to allude to those traditions, perhaps to resolve Peter's storyline.[41] Another fold in the story—a dialogue in which the narrator resists rumors that the "disciple whom Jesus loved" would never die—might address concerns about the delay of the return of Jesus or later speculations arising around the figure of John.[42] To fully integrate his new material into the Gospel, the scribe fashioned an ending for it modeled after the work's original ending.[43]

3. Author and Redactor as Community

For some scholars, the model I have just outlined—the idea that the Gospel was composed by an author but edited by a later redactor—is often confused or conflated with the hypothesis that John might have been composed by multiple, connected members of a single "school" or "community."[44] The idea of a "Johannine Community" has significantly impacted scholarship on the Gospel. This model, however, presses the limited data of the Gospel too far.

There is good evidence that the Gospel had an author and a later redactor (or multiple redactors), but an author and a redactor do not, in and of themselves, point to the existence of a coherent school, circle, or community. These terms, after all, are not neutral descriptors but further layers of hypothetical that require additional evidence. The terms "school," "circle," and "community" assume or entail personal relationships between the author or redactor (X knows Y), lines of succession (X had Y as a pupil or disciple), or mechanisms of authorization or coordination (X allowed or charged Y to modify his work), but we have no evidence for these sorts of relationships in the case of John. We do not know where and when John's author and later redactor(s) were alive and active. They could have lived decades apart in locales hundreds of miles away.

By way of comparison, in the second century a redactor added endings to the Gospel of Mark. And yet scholars generally do not integrate the author of Mark and that scribe into a Markan school.[45] In short, it takes much more than edits to a common text to demonstrate that sort of complex social structure. It takes evidence we do not have for the author and redactor of John.

More to the point, there are compelling reasons for assuming that the author and redactor of John were not directly connected. For one, most interpolations of ancient texts were made by unconnected or unauthorized actors—later copyists, scribes, or interpolators with no clear links to the original author.[46] From the standpoint of probability, then, single authorship and later unauthorized interpolation should be our default assumption.[47] Second, scholars determine that John 21 is an appendix, at least in part, due to subtle differences in thought between it and earlier sections. The same differences, however, also point away from continuity and authorization, suggesting that the author and redactor came from different (intellectual, social, and/or geographical) locations.

In the end, however, the most compelling reason not to apply the terms "school," "circle," and "community" to the author and redactors of John is the fact that John was written by a disguised author—a point I will elaborate in a later chapter. If the author of the Gospel deliberately concealed his true identity when writing the book, it is significantly less likely that the redactor knew him personally and worked in coordination with him. For that matter, the redactor of the Gospel also engaged in the same practice of disguised authorship, concealing his own identity (21:24–25). What we have in the Gospel of John, then, is evidence of the intervention of a (disguised) author and a (disguised) redactor—no more, no less.[48]

II. Contexts and Influences

Even though we cannot attribute the Gospel of John to multiple authors, that does not mean the author of John was writing in social isolation. Humans are social animals embedded in concrete social contexts; in fact, humans are embedded in multiple such contexts. To better understand the author of John, it is helpful to piece together at least some part of the world around him: the groups with whom he was connected and that shaped his thought.

A. Initial Readers

One way to explore the social contexts of the author of John is to determine, as far as possible, the shape of the initial, intended audience of the Gospel, that is, the persons the author thought would read his work. Ostensibly, these implied readers represent the persons and networks with which the author himself was connected.[49] Examined closely, it seems that the Gospel was directed toward an initial audience that was composed at least partly of (a) persons already familiar with Jesus tradition (b) who were non-Jews.

1. Readers Devoted to Jesus

The author of John seems to have envisioned a readership already familiar with Jesus—probably one already devoted to Jesus. The clearest evidence of this is the fact that the narrator cites events connected to the life of Jesus as if his readers are already familiar with them.[50] For example, the narrator tells his readers that John the Baptist "was baptizing at Aenon near Salim ... for John had not yet been thrown into prison" (3:23–24). In so doing, he presupposes knowledge of a detail found in other gospels (Mark 1:14, 6:17–29; Matt. 11:2–7, 14:3–12; Luke 3:19–20) but which does not appear in John itself. John's readers, Richard Bauckham writes, "seem to be expected already to know that John's ministry came to an end when he was imprisoned."[51] Similarly, when introducing Mary and her siblings, the narrator explains that "it was Mary who anointed the Lord with ointment and wiped his feet with her hair, whose brother Lazarus was ill" (11:2). At this point in his narrative, a reader would depend on their prior knowledge of Jesus's life to interpret this detail. (John goes on to narrate this episode, but a chapter later.) The author also seems to assume that his audience possesses other basic literacies typical of members of the Jesus movement. For example, he freely cites biblical texts and traditions without explanation, evidently trusting that his readers are familiar with these.[52]

2. Non-Jewish Readers

There is also good evidence that the author assumed that some, if not most, of his readers were ethnically non-Jews. Scholars assume a similar sort of audience for the Gospel of Mark on the basis of Mark 7. There, the author interrupts his narrative to gloss a particular Jewish practice for his readers:[53] "(For the Pharisees and all the Jews do not eat unless they wash their hands, observing the tradition of the elders. And they do not eat anything from the market unless they wash. And there are also many other traditions they observe: the washing of cups, pitchers, and kettles)" (Mark 7:3–4). Evidently, the author of Mark expected that a significant segment of his readers were unfamiliar with these customs and would need some context to understand the narrative, supplying that information in this parenthetical statement.[54]

Interestingly, John makes similar kinds of glosses. In two places, the author highlights or explains some lesser-known Jewish cultural mores to his readers, as if his implied readers would not necessarily know of these customs:[55]

> The Samaritan woman said to him, "How is it that you, a Jew, ask a drink of me, a woman of Samaria?" (since Jews do not share things in common with Samaritans). (John 4:9)[56]

> They took the body of Jesus and wrapped it with the spices in linen cloths, according to the burial custom of the Jews. (John 19:40)[57]

The author's apparent sensitivity to non-Jewish readers may also explain why he glosses many of the rituals mentioned in the Gospel as "of the Jews," for example, "the Passover, the festival of the Jews" (6:4; cf. 2:13, 11:55), "the festival of the Jews, Tabernacles [*Sukkot*]" (7:2); "the day of Preparation of the Jews" (19:42), and "the [rites of] purification of the Jews" (2:6). Here again one might detect a desire to contextualize certain practices for an audience composed of many non-Jews.[58]

B. Literary Networks and Worlds

Of the many contexts we can imagine for the author of John, we can reconstruct at least one other with certainty. Our author, whoever he was, participated in at least some network of elite, literate writers. As Stanley Stowers writes, "in antiquity, where only a tiny fraction of the population was literate at all and a much smaller fraction literate enough to write and interpret literature, networks or fields of writers, interpreters of writings and readers educated into particular niches of the fields formed highly specialized social arenas that produced and contested their own norms, forms of power, practices and products of literacy."[59] Some such networks were close-knit; our extant sources demonstrate that many authors knew and corresponded with one another, exchanged and critiqued one another's drafts, or helped to publicize one another's works. But ancient authors could also be linked less directly, that is, as unconnected readers of one another's works. As they received, stored, and helped circulate books, ancient authors were knit into a broader field of writers who consumed, influenced, and challenged one another's ideas.[60]

Undoubtedly, the author of John was integrated into at least one such field, circulating and consuming various works accessible to him. When we study his text closely, it seems that he was acquainted with at least some accounts of Jesus's life circulating in his day, among them the Gospels of Mark, Matthew, and Luke. It would also seem that the author had at least some familiarity with the thought, if not the writings, of Paul as well as Alexandrian Jewish philosophers.

1. The Synoptic Gospels

In the search for the literary influences behind John, it makes sense to begin with the texts most like John in genre and content: the earliest known gospels, including Mark, Matthew, and Luke. And yet for much of the twentieth century, "a broad scholarly consensus (at least in North America) . . . tended to regard John's Gospel as quite independent of the other gospels and related to them only on the level of prior tradition (whether oral, written or some combination of both)."[61] For such scholars, the issue was that while Mark, Matthew, and Luke share extensive verbatim overlap, including hundreds of verses of shared material, John lacks parallels of this kind.

Today, however, an increasing number of scholars—now a majority—have arrived at a different view. They recognize that the author of John likely used many oral or written sources when composing his Gospel.[62] Still, they find no reason to exclude the Synoptic Gospels from among these sources. While it is true that John shares few instances of verbatim overlap with the Synoptics, the extensive overlap one finds in the Synoptics is atypical in ancient literature.[63] Other early gospels—works such as the *Gospel of Thomas* and the *Gospel of Mary*—clearly know earlier gospels, and yet they differ in dramatic and creative ways from those earlier works.[64] Second, there are positive reasons to suspect that the author of John had been exposed to one or more of the Synoptic Gospels, at least to some degree.[65]

Generic Similarities
The first reason to suspect that John knows the Synoptics is that it is too similar to them in length, structure, and literary elements to have arisen without any awareness of their existence and shape. John is roughly the same size as

those works—a little longer than Mark but shorter than Matthew and Luke. It is also a narrative text, something not all early Jesus sources/gospels are (contrast the *Gospel of Thomas*). John also follows the same basic narrative skeleton as Mark, Matthew, and Luke, a structure which, as Mark Goodacre reminds us, was hardly inevitable, as seen by the fact that many noncanonical Jesus sources/gospels do not follow the same plan:

> Who told Mark and John, independently of one another, to begin their works with John the Baptist's testimony to Jesus, to go on with the calling of the disciples, and to devote half of their gospels to the Passion Narrative? This is not a question of individual "traditions" but of narrative direction and overall literary structure. The generic constraints of writing a *bios* do not account for this specific way of configuring the Jesus story. Our failure to find the similarities striking may say more about our innate canonical bias than anything else; our presumption of the normativity of telling the story in this way not only ignores countless other "non-canonical" ways of telling Jesus' story, but it assumes that there is something inevitable about the Synoptic and Johannine constructions.[66]

For that matter, John mirrors the Synoptics in how it constructs individual segments of this plan. For example, Frey points out that "the Johannine account of the Baptist in John 1:19–34 features three sayings of the Baptist (vv. 23, 26–27, 33) in the exact same sequence in which the corresponding textual elements occur in Mark 1:3, 7, 8, though with significant modification and expansion."[67]

When we juxtapose these features, it is hard to believe that the author of John could have independently struck on all of them by coincidence, as if he reinvented the Gospel "wheel." Rather, literary parallels as global as the ones listed above deserve a literary explanation. It is easy to imagine that, like the author of Luke (Luke 1:1–4), whoever wrote John was aware that other figures were composing texts of the same kind, and he consciously set out to fashion a text within this developing tradition or (sub)genre. But how many earlier gospels, and precisely which gospels, did the author of John know? I suspect he knew all three of the Synoptic Gospels: Mark, Matthew, and Luke. The reason is that when John tells stories in parallel with these works, he fuses elements found in all of them, including some redactional details. One cannot explain the shape of his materials without referencing all three gospels.

Mark

Scholars are in broadest agreement on John's knowledge of Mark. This makes a priori sense; Mark seems to have been the earliest gospel, and it was known widely in the late first century, as is evident by its use by the authors of Matthew and Luke. It seems unlikely that John could have been exposed to other early gospels without at least some exposure to the earlier Mark.[68] More to the point, Mark and John also share other tantalizing parallels that evince a direct relationship between them.

One especially striking concentration of verbal similarities appears in an episode shared by Mark and John: an account of Jesus being anointed by a woman before his crucifixion. As Goodacre writes, these episodes contain a "close agreement in structure and wording—an agreement that Mark does not share with other cognate episodes in Matthew (26:6–13) and (the still more distant) Luke (7:36–50). One can, in fact, line up the Markan and Johannine episodes in a synoptic comparison:

Mark 14:4–7	John 12:4–8
But some were there who said to one another in anger,	But Judas Iscariot, one of his disciples (the one who was about to betray him), said,
'Why was the ointment wasted in this way? For this ointment could have been sold for more than three hundred denarii, and the money given to the poor.'	'Why was this ointment not sold for three hundred denarii and the money given to the poor?'
...	...
But Jesus said, 'Leave her alone; why do you trouble her? She has performed a good service for me. For you always have the poor with you, and you can show kindness to them whenever you wish, but you will not always have me.'	So Jesus said, 'Leave her alone. She bought it so that she might keep it for the day of my burial. For you always have the poor with you, but you will not always have me.'"[69]

The overlap visible here is comparable to the overlap one finds in pericopes shared by any two or three of the Synoptics.

Mark also has other minor verbal agreements with John, including some exclusive turns of phrase that increase the probability of a connection between these texts. For example, only Mark and John specify that it would have taken "200 denarii" to feed the crowd of five thousand men (John 6:7; Mark 6:37). Similarly, only Mark and John identify the oil used to anoint Jesus on the week of his death as a "costly ointment of pure nard" (John 12:3; Mark 14:3). Even more strikingly, only those two gospels depict Jesus saying, "rise, take up your mat and walk" (John 5:8, 11–12; Mark 2:9, 11), and in two different stories.[70] As B. H. Streeter observed, "the close agreement of John with Mark in these particular passages is the more noticeable since the phrases used in the parallels in both Matthew and Luke happen on all these occasions to be quite different from Mark's."[71]

For that matter, John seems to know the specific contours of Mark's Passion Narrative. In Mark alone, one finds Jesus saying all three of the following things in the garden of Gethsemane: (a) a request that "the hour might pass from him" (14:35), a prayer for God to "remove this cup from me" (14:36), and a brief instruction to his disciples, "Rise, let us be going" (14:42). Interestingly, John contains sayings of Jesus that parallel each of these quotes (12:27, 18:11, 14:31). Two of them implicitly critique Mark's materials: "Should I say, 'Save me from this hour?' No! For this reason I have come to this hour" (12:27–28) and "Should I not drink the cup that my Father has given me?" (18:11).[72]

Admittedly, we cannot rule out the possibility that John acquired these Markan features from another source, either a lost oral or written channel also informing the author of Mark or a lost gospel that incorporated Mark's materials. Nevertheless, Occam's razor cautions us against multiplying hypothetical entities unnecessarily. On balance, then, we should credit these materials to the only ancient work that we know for sure existed and contained these details and that we know was widely utilized by other writers of the period: Mark.[73]

Matthew
A widely accepted principle for establishing literary dependence indicates that when two texts show the same edits to a shared source, we should presume a literary relationship between them.[74] It is, after all, less probable that two authors would coincidentally edit a given text in the same ways—an improbability that grows with each parallel feature we find. Tellingly, the extant Gospel we call Matthew and the Gospel of John are bound by precisely this sort of relationship. They both presuppose Mark as a source, but they both modify Mark's materials in ways that Luke, the only other known gospel from the same period, does not.

Consider a few examples. Although Mark depicts Jesus miraculously feeding over five thousand persons, both Matthew and John add that Jesus did so after he "sat" on a "hill/mountain" by "the Sea of Galilee" (Matt. 15:29; John 6:3).[75] More striking, while the canonical gospels mention Jesus entering Jerusalem riding a colt, only Matthew and John explicitly quote Zechariah 9:9 and also mention a "donkey" using the same Greek word (*onos*) not found in the Old Greek text of Zechariah (Matt 21:5; John 12:15).[76] These gospels are also the only ones to suggest that it was customary to release a prisoner at Passover (John 18:39; Matt. 27:15) and to describe Joseph of Arimathea as a "disciple" of Jesus and to relate that he buried Jesus in his "new tomb" (Matt. 27:57, 60; John 19:38, 41).[77] And only these two narrate Jesus appearing to women near his empty tomb and instructing them to "go" and "announce" what they had seen to his "brothers" (Matt. 28:9–10; John 20:14–18).[78]

Matthew and John also agree in passages not derived from Mark. Consider, for example, the following sayings of Jesus, parallel across multiple gospels:

Matthew 10:24–25	Luke 6:40	John 13:14–16 (cf. 15:20)	John 15:20
"A disciple is not above the teacher nor an enslaved person above the master; it is enough for the disciple to be like the teacher and the enslaved person like the master. If they have called the master of the house Beelzebul, how much more will they malign those of his household!"	"A disciple is not above the teacher, but every disciple who is fully qualified will be like the teacher."	"So if I, your master and teacher, have washed your feet, you also ought to wash one another's feet.... Amen, amen, I say to you: enslaved persons are not superior to their master, nor is one sent superior to the one who sent him."	"Remember the word I said to you: 'A slave is not superior to his master.' If they persecuted me, they will persecute you also. If they kept my word, they will keep yours also."

As Dale Allison observes, (a) only the versions of the saying found in Matthew and John incorporate both teacher/disciple and enslaved person/master analogies (Luke has only the former); (b) only Matthew and John pair two analogies, bound by "not . . . nor" language [*ouk . . . oude*]); and (c) only Matthew and John relate this teaching to the problem of persecution.[79]

The specificity and number of these parallels suggest some relationship between John and the various textual forms of Matthew in antiquity.[80] (Once again, Occam's razor cautions us against positing additional, hypothetical entities mediating that relationship.) Most likely, the line of dependence runs from Matthew to John. The key reason is that several of these parallels suit Matthew's redactional profile rather than John's. For example, Matthew has a noted penchant for situating events on hills or mountains (e.g., Matt. 5:1).[81] Matthew also has a well-known investment in identifying fulfillments of biblical prophecy in his work.

Luke

Luke contains some of the deepest links to John.[82] For example, only these two incorporate Martha and Mary as characters, each depicting Martha as one who "serves" family meals while Mary attends to Jesus (Luke 10:38–42; John 12:1–8).[83] Likewise, only these gospels indicate that a woman anointed Jesus while wiping his feet with her hair (Luke 7:38, 44; John 12:3; cf. 11:2). Only these two show Jesus positioning himself as one who serves his disciples at the final meal before his death (Luke 22:26–27; John 13:1–17). Only these two narrate that Satan entered into Judas Iscariot, provoking him to betray Jesus (Luke 22:3; John 13:2, 27). Only these claim that Peter cut off the right ear of the high priest's slave, and only these texts place this event before Jesus's arrest rather than after it (Luke 22:50–54; John 18:10–12). Only these claim that Jesus was buried in a previously unoccupied tomb (Luke 23:53; John 19:41). Only these place two angels at Jesus's tomb on the morning of the resurrection (Luke 24:4, 23; John 20:12) rather than a single one, as in Mark (16:5) and Matthew (28:2–5). Only these indicate that some disciples inspected the tomb after the women's report (Luke 24:24; John 20:3–10).[84] And only Luke and John report that Jesus appeared to his disciples in and around Jerusalem on the night after his resurrection (Luke 24:13–49; John 20:19–29).[85] To these details, Streeter notes, "certain infinitesimal points of contact, which if they stood alone would prove nothing, carry weight as confirmatory evidence"—among them the use of a double "crucify him" formula in Luke 23:21 and John 19:6.[86]

These examples indicate at least some literary relationship, some direct line of knowledge and use, between these works.[87] Most likely, Luke was written before John, and the author of John utilized Luke as a source.[88] First, John sometimes presupposes his readers' knowledge of the stories Luke contains. For example, the narrator says that Lazarus hailed from "the village of Mary and Martha"—figures known only from Luke—before he has even introduced the sisters into his narrative (11:1; cf. Luke 10:38). John also describes Mary as "the one who anointed the Lord with perfume and wiped his feet with her hair"—details from Luke—before it narrates that event (11:2; cf. Luke 7:38). In each case, it would seem that the author of John expected his readers to come in with a knowledge of Jesus gained from at least one other source. (Luke, tellingly, does not.) Assuming Luke is the source of these episodes, then Luke must predate John.

More evidence of John's dependence on Luke appears in its account of Jesus being anointed by a woman. This scene finds cognates in Mark (14:3-11) and Luke (7:36-50). But as Goodacre observes, John's version lacks the internal coherence of either Mark's or Luke's version, blending their features in an unusual way that exposes John's story as derivative from these accounts:

> The anointing in each of the Synoptic accounts makes sense. In Mark and Matthew, Jesus' head is anointed with perfume. No hair is mentioned; no feet are mentioned. In Luke, the woman wets Jesus' feet with her tears, an act of repentance, and she wipes them with her loose "sinner's" hair before she anoints them with perfume. But John's reminiscence of the Lucan detail about the wiping of Jesus' feet with her hair creates an anomaly. First, there is no reason for Mary, in John, to be wearing her hair like Luke's "sinner," which is the point of the Lucan story. Second, because there are no tears in John, Mary's wiping of Jesus' feet with her hair means that the perfume ends up on her hair and not on Jesus. Jesus is the one who is supposed to be being anointed. The most plausible explanation here is that John has drawn a favourite Lucan detail into a narrative in which it no longer makes sense.[89]

In this case, we can safely assume that Luke was written first and that John utilized Luke as a source.

Third, John incorporates a critical in-text character never attested in Luke—a "disciple whom Jesus loved"—across several scenes common to the texts (i.e., at Jesus's final meal, crucifixion, and inspection of the tomb). It is easy to understand why John would insert the character into these scenes; as I will argue later, the character gives John's account eyewitness credibility. It is harder to understand why Luke would systemically excise so central a character from John's work.

Finally, the idea that Luke used John is inconsistent with the authorial practices of Luke. We know that the author of Luke utilized other gospels when writing his own. We also know how he utilized these texts: he incorporated entire sections of these texts into his own, word for word.[90] And yet Luke has virtually no verbatim overlap with John. In other words, if the author of Luke knew and used John, he would have used John in a peculiar, atypical way vis-à-vis his use of other gospels. By contrast, avoiding verbatim overlap is perfectly in line with how the author of John uses other known gospels. It makes more sense, then, to assume that John used Luke.

A Different Project
Although John knows Matthew, Mark, and Luke, it is clear that John did not use those texts in the same way as they used one another. Since the Synoptic gospels have such extensive word-for-word overlap, it is clear that the Synoptic authors consulted one another's work in a sustained and close way when writing their own texts. John, on the other hand, seems to have used previous gospels more loosely. At times, the author of John probably consulted these earlier works, perhaps taking notes on individual passages in them or copying down key lines on waxed tablets as templates for his own accounts.[91] On other occasions, however, the author might not have directly consulted these texts, relying instead on his mental recall of their contents.[92]

In this case, we can also say that the author of John was not engaged in the same sort of project as the Synoptic authors. His aim was not to write an expanded or revised version of Mark, as perhaps Matthew conceived his project to be. His aim was also not to harmonize or aggregate materials from previous gospels like Luke, Tatian's *Diatessaron*, or the many fragmentary papyri that seem to combine materials from earlier accounts of the life of Jesus. Instead, Frey is correct when he imagines the author of John using other gospels "in a much more eclectic and critical way."[93] According to Attridge, John's author "selected and reworked stories and sayings to create a new kind of narrative," one suited to his specific vision.[94] But again, John would not be alone in this respect; many second-century gospels that know the Synoptics—works such as the *Gospel of Thomas* and the *Gospel of Mary*— also utilize these sources eclectically and creatively.

2. Other Influences
Besides the Synoptic Gospels, which served as the templates for his work, the author of John was undoubtedly steeped in other literatures of the period.

These literatures might well have included (a) Pauline and Deutero-Pauline works and (b) Hellenistic Jewish philosophical texts closely related to the writings of Philo.

Paul

Paul was the most significant writer in the first generation of the Jesus movement. His letters were likely in broad circulation, perhaps already as a developing collection, by the end of the first century.[95] It is hard to find literate Christians of the first and second centuries whose writings do not engage his thought to some extent, in either sympathetic, resistant, or hostile postures.[96] And yet, constrained by the hypothesis that John was written by a separate, even isolated group, many scholars have overlooked possible connections between the Gospel and Pauline works.[97] Nevertheless, several features of John suggest that its author stood "on the shoulders of Paul," that is, that he was deeply conversant with the ideas of the apostle and of his second- and third-generation interpreters.[98]

First, John contains ideas strikingly similar to those contained in Paul's extant epistles. Like Paul, the author of John assumes that Jesus was a preexistent, celestial being (John 1:1; cf. Phil. 2:6).[99] He also expresses ideas about spirit (*pneuma*) very similar to Paul's. For example, he communicates the notion, elaborated across the Pauline corpus, that Jesus seeds a new "inner nature" of Spirit into a person (John 14:16–17; cf. Rom. 8:10; 2 Cor. 4:16), allowing one to be spiritually "in" Jesus, that is, integrated into his glorified "body" (John 2:21, 14:20; cf. Rom. 8:1, 9–11, 12:4–5; 1 Cor. 12:12–30). Like Paul, he uses the image of drinking "the Spirit" (1 Cor. 12:13; cf. John 7:37–39, 4:7–14). He also claims that humans cannot attain the kingdom in the flesh but only in or as spirit (*pneuma*) (John 3:3–7; cf. 1 Cor. 15:35–57). John certainly evokes Paul in its initial (though unsustained) contrast of "law" and "grace" (John 1:17; cf. Rom. 6:14). He evokes Paul by gradually centering the command to "love" as the supreme and all-encompassing ethical command (John 13:34; cf. Gal. 5:6, 14; Rom. 13:9–10; 1 Cor. 13). He shares a common interest with Paul in the question of who can be counted as Abraham's children, insisting with Paul that only those who believe can claim this descent (John 8:39–40, 45–47; cf. Gal 3:6–7, 2:16). He also evokes Paul by casting Christ's death as an act of "love" (John 15:13; cf. Rom. 5:8).

John also contains ideas that are not explicitly attested in the genuine letters of Paul but which do find cognates in the later pseudonymous letters attributed to him. For example, like the author of Colossians, the author of John asserts that those who believe in Jesus experience a spiritual resurrection (John 5:24-25; cf. Col. 3:1). And like the author of Ephesians, John expresses the idea that humans can, even now, enjoy access to heavenly places through Jesus (John 14; cf. Eph. 1:3, 2:6) and that their participation in him places them in a spiritual "temple" or "dwelling place for God" (John 2:21, 14:2-3; cf. Eph. 2:21-22). And like the author of Hebrews—a text that does not expressly co-opt the name of Paul but that falsely implies its Pauline authorship—the author of John embraces a Christology that recognizes Jesus's participation in creation (John 1:3; cf. Heb. 1:2).[100]

These points of contact strengthen the impression that the author was perhaps formed, at least at some earlier point in his career, in what we might conceptualize as a "post-Pauline" movement, that is, a group that stood within Paul's legacy and continued elaborating or modifying this thought into the second century. Other features of John support this reconstruction. For one, we saw that the author seems to direct his work to a readership that included gentile Christians—a demographic largely committed to the Pauline tradition in this period. Similarly, John's Pauline/post-Pauline pedigree may also be apparent in its unflattering characterizations of some of Paul's chief peers and rivals. John casts "the brothers of Jesus"—including, presumably, James, a figure with a tensive relationship with Paul (Gal. 2:12)—as unbelieving (7:5).[101] Interestingly, the text also subtly demotes Cephas/Peter—another figure with a complex relationship with Paul (Gal. 2:11-14)—in ways the Synoptic Gospels do not.[102]

Hellenistic Jewish Philosophy
For centuries, Jews in Egypt synthesized biblical tradition with ideas derived from such Greco-Roman philosophical traditions as Middle Platonism and Stoicism. By the end of the first century CE, these syntheses represented longstanding interpretive traditions in their own right, influencing a wide range of Jewish and Christian works. Paul's writings contain evidence of some sampling of philosophical thought: "a Platonic mixture ... along with the clearly Stoic elements."[103]

Today, scholars are confident that the author of John was also deeply integrated into one such interpretive tradition.[104] Some find even more specific coordinates for John's ideas, observing that John contains features highly evocative of the writings of the first-century Jewish philosopher Philo (c. 20 BCE-50 CE).[105] We will explore these parallels in detail in the next chapter. These connections may not rise to the level "of a direct connection"—of

John's direct use of Philo's works—but as David Runia writes, "the hypothesis of a 'common background'" for John and Philo is "confirmed" by a careful examination of their writings, such that "if Philo had never existed . . . we would know a lot less about the background of the Gospel's thought."[106] The two literatures seem to sit within a common, branching intellectual tradition, likely connected by one or more lost literary or oral nodes.

Interestingly, several Deutero-Pauline works contain intriguing parallels with ideas articulated in the works of Philo.[107] Runia, for one, comments that Colossians 1:15–18 includes several traits "very close to what is found in Philo" and also observes that Hebrews and Philo share "impressive" "linguistic, hermeneutical, and thematic correspondence."[108] Although some scholars cite these parallels to claim an Alexandrian provenance for these works, Attridge correctly points out that "neither rhetoric, philosophy, nor the Greek scriptures were confined to Alexandria."[109] Theoretically, Philonic or Philonic-adjacent ideas were circulating within networks of post-Pauline Christians. There, they could have easily found the author of John and shaped his reflection on Jesus—a reflection ultimately condensed in his Gospel.[110]

III. Conclusion

In this chapter, I have argued that the core materials in the Gospel of John were penned by a single author. That author was connected to gentile readers and was familiar with the Synoptic Gospels, Pauline thought, and Hellenistic Jewish Philosophy, among other corpora and traditions. That author was probably male; in the deeply patriarchal society of the ancient Roman Empire, literacy was more commonly associated with men.[111] That author was also clearly a native Greek speaker who wrote to native Greek speakers. John depends on gospels written in Greek. It was also written in Greek, with no signs of translation or interference from a language other than Greek.[112] And it translates common Hebrew terms into Greek for its audience (John 1:38, 41–42).

Unfortunately, we have no secure grounds to establish where this author lived.[113] Greek was spoken across much of the empire, and the literature our author likely read—for example, the writings of Paul and the Synoptic Gospels—also circulated widely. It may be revealing that certain sections of John reflect a surprisingly accurate knowledge of the topography of Palestine, and of Jerusalem in particular (e.g., John 1:28, 2:1, 3:23, 4:5, 5:2, 9:7, 18:1).

That knowledge could indicate the author's past or present experience in the region, perhaps as a resident of nearby Greek-speaking centers in the Levant such as Caesarea, Damascus, certain towns of the Transjordan, or even the city of Antioch.[114] Then again, John Kloppenborg argues that the author of Luke utilized existing maps or descriptions of Palestine to construct his gospel.[115] The author of John might have done the same, drawing his knowledge from maps, written descriptions of the city, pilgrim itineraries, the oral memories of Jewish refugees, or even earlier Jesus traditions.[116]

We do not have sufficient data to determine the author's ethnicity, though there are reasons to suspect that he might have been non-Jewish.[117] Admittedly, the author's knowledge of Jewish customs is compatible with the idea that he was Jewish. Then again, many non-Jews—especially those in direct or indirect contact with Jewish persons and sources—also knew of these customs. Meanwhile, other facts about the Gospel of John—especially its post-Pauline outlook—may indicate the author's gentile extraction. Above all, the extent to which the author persistently speaks of Jews and Jewish customs in seemingly distant and otherizing ways, as well as the text's more problematic statements about Jews (e.g., 8:44, 9:22, 16:2), make it difficult to imagine his Jewish positionality.[118]

Finally, the dating of the Gospel is also difficult to narrow.[119] The text certainly dates no earlier than the First Jewish-Roman War and the destruction of the Jewish Temple in 70 CE. As Frey observes, the Gospel alludes "to the Jewish war, to the disempowering of the Jewish leaders by the Romans, and to the loss of the temple," especially in 11:48.[120] The Gospel also dates no earlier than the Synoptics—texts that also presuppose the same events (Mark 13:2; Matt. 22:7, 24:2; Luke 21:6, 20). Unfortunately, there is no way to find absolute dates for these texts and thus to clarify the date of John. At the other extreme, one cannot date John later than the mid-second century since references to the Gospel appear in various works dating to that period, if not earlier.[121] In the opinion of most scholars, then, "the period of 90–110 constitutes a reasonable framework for the work's composition."[122]

For all that we cannot know regarding John's author, however, we can access one dimension of this figure: his thought. The Gospel of John provides a wealth of data to reconstruct the ideas and outlook of the individual who penned it. To understand this author more fully, then, we must explore his only known literary product in detail, drawing out its essential message and purpose.

2
Why John Was Written

Why did the author of John write his Gospel? There were, after all, other narratives of Jesus's life already in circulation—among them, the Gospels of Mark, Matthew, and Luke. To begin to answer this question, one must appreciate what makes the Gospel of John distinct or novel vis-à-vis earlier accounts of the life of Jesus. As it stands, one specific feature, one novelty of the text stands out above all others: in John, Jesus pronounces entire discourses whose style, tone, and contents differ so radically from those preserved in the Synoptics as to indicate what Andrew Lincoln deems "creativity . . . on a large scale."[1] The Gospel, in short, is a revisionary presentation of Jesus, which recasts him as the mouthpiece of a set of ideas different from those he articulated in his lifetime.

That system of ideas is, on the one hand, eclectic. It reflects a robust engagement with various intellectual streams coursing through second-century Christian circles—among them, Hellenistic Jewish philosophical speculations, apocalyptic traditions, and the teachings of Paul. But it also shows the unity of a single, creative mind, which selectively synthesized all these influences into a distinctive but coherent theology communicated throughout the text. That theology can be condensed into a single, dramatic thesis: that Jesus is a godlike being who has come to transform humans into beings like himself. He is the celestial human who makes celestial humans.

In the Synoptics, Jesus never claims to be celestial or divine. In John, however, Jesus never ceases to insist on this point. He explains with unparalleled clarity that his origins and destiny lie in a different realm, a realm "above." He is a preexistent, immortal, and divine being—the *Logos* or "Word"—who descended from above and assumed human flesh. But John's discourses are not only a revelation about Jesus; they are also a revelation of the destiny of a select set of humans: those who apprehend Jesus's extraordinary origins and respond to his message. According to the Gospel, those humans, though "born of flesh," can now receive the celestial, undying nature of "spirit" (*pneuma*). Through that new nature, they now also enjoy secret, spiritual access to celestial realms and the ability to "see" God. And through their

The Gospel of John. Hugo Méndez, Oxford University Press. © Oxford University Press 2025.
DOI: 10.1093/9780197686157.003.0002

new access to God, they are exalted into a new state, becoming divine beings themselves. The author of John wrote his Gospel to condense this startling vision in written form, words that testify to "the Word."

I. The Celestial Man

To understand John, one must first appreciate the text's teachings about Jesus himself. The Gospel, after all, is framed as an account of Jesus's earthly life; any understanding of the text must flow from what the text discloses about Jesus. Even at a cursory glance, it is clear that those teachings include sophisticated propositions foreign to the Synoptics. In John, Jesus is a divine being: the creative *Logos*, the very intellect of God, now become human flesh.

A. Divinity in Early Jewish and Christian Thought

John assumes a monotheistic view of the universe, in which there is one "only true God" (17:3). And yet, as Paula Fredriksen has argued, ancient monotheists did not assume that divinity was an attribute exclusive to the one God.[2] Rather, divinity was a communicable attribute that could be shared with or transmitted to other entities to various degrees.[3] This was true even in Second Temple Judaism, segments of which imagined the existence of various subordinates for God, mediating his divine activities, presence, and attributes to the created universe. In one such segment, represented by thinkers such as Aristobulus and Philo, the chief subordinate of God was the *Logos* or "Word," a concept taken from contemporary streams of Greek philosophical thought but transformed in conversation with Jewish biblical texts that reflect on the power and agency of God's "word."

The concept of the *Logos* lays bare the fluid ways Philo conceptualizes God, especially in his interactions with the world. In his writings, Philo affirms the existence of "one God," who alone is "truly God" and who stands at the pinnacle of life.[4] Nevertheless, this God operates through his *Logos*. As Deborah Forger writes, for Philo, "the *logos* is not separate from Israel's supreme God, but rather functions as an essential and constitutive element of that God's very identity."[5] It is his Reason, Intellect, Mind, or (mental/spoken) Word hypostasized, that is, conceptualized as a distinct entity: "Just as a person cannot exist without his or her cognitive abilities, so too Philo claims that

God cannot exist without God's *logos*. This is because, as the semantic range of the word *logos* implies, the *logos* functions as the very 'thoughts,' 'rationality,' 'creative logic,' and 'mind' of Israel's supreme God. By participating in the divinity of Israel's supreme God ... the *logos* too, like Israel's high God, is also fully divine. Yet Philo further reifies the link between God and the *logos* by indiscriminately employing the same words to describe the two."[6]

For Philo, then, it is natural to attribute divinity to both God and the *Logos* while preserving a distinction between them. Philo places "the most high One and Father of the universe" on a rank "above the *Logos*." And yet he hails the *Logos* as the "image of God," the "vice-regent" of God, and thus, loosely, "the second god."[7] In another passage, he freely assumes that both God and the *Logos* can be called "god," but he distinguishes God and the *Logos* by the presence and absence of a definite article, respectively (*ho theos* vs. *theos*).[8]

No less telling of the close relationship between God and the *Logos* is the link Philo draws between the *Logos* and the divine "Name"—a connection framed by the fact that one entrusted with the "word" of a person speaks "in" their "name" (e.g., Deut. 18:19; 1 Chron. 21:19; Jer. 44:16). For Philo, the *Logos* is the hypostasized "Name" of God. In one passage, he expressly calls the *Logos* the "Name of God."[9] In another, he casts the *Logos* as "the signet" of God, that is, the seal bearing God's name (cf. 1 Kings 21:8; Esther 8:8). In so doing, he constructs an especially close and intimate link between the two entities.

B. God and the *Logos* in John

Like Philo, John assumes the existence of a single "God" (1:1), "the Father" (1:14, 18), "who is greater than all" (10:29; 14:28). The Gospel assumes that this god does not have a corporeality like our own, a corporeality of flesh. Instead, "God is spirit [*pneuma*]" (4:24), a term used in several streams of ancient thought to denote the kind of material from which, in a prescientific worldview, heavenly entities such as the stars or angels are made.[10] And yet, as in Philo, this God is not alone. In the same breath as it introduces God, the Gospel posits the existence of a second entity: a preexistent *Logos*, which also participates in the Father's divinity.[11]

John's concept of the *Logos* parallels the one found in the writings of Philo, and there is good reason to believe it reflects its author's familiarity with genetically related streams of thought; scholars have noted many specific points of contact between their reflections on the *Logos*.[12] For example, though Philo and John recognize the Father as the "true" God, both leave room for assigning the language of divinity or godhood to the *Logos*, albeit in a subordinate manner.[13] In fact, both call the *Logos* "god," and in a similar manner; both distinguish God from the *Logos* by the presence and absence of the article with the word "God/god" (*ho theos* vs. *theos*).[14] As David Runia notes, Philo and John are the only two writers to adopt this distinction.[15] Both Philo and John speak of the *Logos* as a "son," "begotten" of God.[16] Likewise, just as Philo hails the *Logos* as "the Name of God," John seems to conflate or identify Jesus with the "Name" of God.[17] Both place the *Logos* "in the beginning" (*en archē*) and associate the *Logos* with the creation of the world.[18] The two also associate the *Logos* with light imagery.[19] Both associate the Logos with "eternal life."[20] And both connect the language of "paraclete" (advocate) to the *Logos*.[21] More striking still, Harold Attridge observes that Philo and John share a "fundamental conceptual and rhetorical structure" in how they mythologize the *Logos*.[22] Both represent the *Logos* as the house of God and the subject of Jacob's dream,[23] one who offers himself as "wine" to drink in place of water,[24] one who offers "water" to drink that bequeaths eternal life,[25] one set over the "flock" as a shepherd,[26] and one who provides heavenly food/manna.[27] What makes these parallels so compelling is their diversity and specificity.

According to the Gospel, God and the *Logos* dwell in a realm "above" (3:31, 8:23, 19:11), a realm elsewhere also known as "heaven" (6:32, 12:28, 17:1). Nevertheless, there is a second realm "below": "this world" (8:23) or "the earth" (3:31). Both Philo and John also conceive of the Logos as the instrument or agent who created this material world. Philo describes the *Logos* as the one "through whom the whole universe was framed" and who was "making the world."[28] Similarly, John affirms that "all things were made through" the *Logos* (1:3, 10). That world becomes the stage of the central metastory of John—the narrative arc at its core—namely, the descent of the *Logos* into the world and his ascent again.[29]

C. The *Logos* Becomes Flesh

Although the Gospel indicates that the world was created through the *Logos*, the text assumes a stark separation between the realms below and above.

According to the text, those "below" have neither "seen" nor "known" God (1:18). The world above is also closed off to humans; Jesus says that "no one has ascended into heaven" (3:13).[30]

This division is structured, at least in part, by the activity of another agent: an evil figure called "the ruler of this world" (12:31, 14:30, 16:11), a figure equivalent to "the devil" or "Satan" (6:70; 13:2, 27 [cf. 14:30]).[31] The Gospel does not elucidate the origins of this figure or how we came to rule the world, though it appears he assumed control of the world illegitimately (10:1, 10). Nevertheless, his impact is clear. Satan is a liar by nature, who spreads falsehood (8:44). He is able to influence and even possess individual humans (13:27). In his grip, the world is locked in unbelief, which is, evidently, "the sin of the world" (1:29, 16:8–9).[32] And because of this sin, the world below is trapped in "darkness" (3:19) and "death" (5:24).

This alienation between the realms "above" and "below" is the backdrop of the prologue's most remarkable claims about the *Logos*. The Gospel presents the *Logos* as an entity that occasionally bridged the realms above and below, allowing its celestial glory to be seen in visionary glimpses by different persons (8:56, 12:38–41).[33] But these appearances were only a prelude to a pivotal move to resolve the division. According to John, at a definitive point in time, "the *Logos* became flesh and dwelled among us," "coming into the world" (1:14, 9). Another verse clarifies that the *Logos* took the form of an individual "man" (1:30)—a man identified as "Jesus Christ" (1:17).

1. Descent

The Gospel does not clarify the mechanisms that would allow the *Logos* to assume human flesh, leading scholars to propose different possibilities rooted in ancient philosophical thought.[34] Similarly, the Gospel does not delineate the precise relationship between the preexistent *Logos* and the human Jesus, at least not with the same precision attempted by Christian thinkers in later centuries. The text has fostered readings we might think of as "incarnational," "adoptionist," or "posessionist" from the time of its production. The Gospel does not even specify when this "coming" or descent of the *Logos* occurred. Ancient and modern interpreters have mounted cases for associating that event with Jesus's birth (described only in other gospels) or at the descent of "the Spirit" of God upon Jesus (alluded to in 1:32–34).[35]

What the Gospel does make clear is that most humans could not detect the celestial and divine nature of Jesus, leading them to mistake him for a mere human (6:52, 7:15, 27–28, 35, 9:16, 29). The *Logos*, according to the prologue, "was in the world, and the world was made through him, yet the world knew him not" (1:9). Much of the text, however, depicts Jesus revealing his hidden celestial origins and divinity. He reveals these in his teachings (e.g., 8:23). He reveals these in instances in which he utters the words "I am" (*egō eimi*), a phrase used in biblical texts during theophanies, encounters with visible or speaking manifestation of divinity (e.g., 8:58).[36] Jesus also reveals these in the "signs," or miracles, he performs (2:11, 3:2, 5:36, 10:25). Through this patient work, Jesus gradually helps some see his true nature. And in this way, Jesus "takes away the sin of the world"—that is, unbelief—at least from some (1:29).

2. Ascent

Although the *Logos* moved in the world in the person of Jesus, the Gospel is clear that Jesus would not remain in the world forever—at least not in a flesh-and-blood form. In earlier chapters, Jesus repeatedly speaks of an imminent time, an "hour," when he will ascend to the Father, returning to the realm "above":

"I came from the Father and have come into the world; again, I am leaving the world and going to the Father." (16:28; cf. 7:33, 16:5, 14:12, 28)

Jesus knew that his hour had come to depart out of this world to the Father.... he had come from God and was going to God. (13:1, 3)

The Gospel casts this ascent as a complex process, taking shape across the last week of Jesus's life. In the text, the "hour" of Jesus's departure arrives at his entry into Jerusalem and continues unfolding through the rest of the week (12:27, 13:1, 3). On the night before his crucifixion, Jesus speaks as a figure already in transition; addressing the Father, he says, "I am no longer in the world.... I am coming to you" (17:11, 13). The crucifixion marks an important moment in this transition (12:32–33). Nevertheless, this transition is only fully complete even later still—at his ascension. In his first post-resurrection appearance, Jesus tells Mary Magdalene, "I have not yet ascended to the Father; but go to my brothers and say to them, 'I am ascending to my Father and your Father, to my God and your God'" (20:17). In turn, the Gospel casts this ascent as Jesus's "glorification" since it marks his transition into a celestial form characterized by "glory" (12:23, 13:31, 17:1, 5).[37] From then on, he remains hidden from the world (14:19).

According to John, the departure of Jesus from the world coincides with another important event: the sending of the divine "Spirit," also known as the Paraclete (*paraklētos*).[38] The text does not fully parse out the identity and nature of the Spirit.[39] Nevertheless, the text is clear that the Spirit is available to humans only through the departure and glorification of Jesus; as Jesus says, "it is to your advantage that I go away, for if I do not go away, the Paraclete will not come to you; but if I go, I will send him to you" (16:7).

II. The Celestial Humans

Why did the *Logos* descend into the world and ascend from it again? The Gospel layers multiple significances onto this coming, but we can distill these into a single idea, first expressed in the prologue: the *Logos* came to earth to transform humans in its own image: "to all who received him, who believed in his name, he gave power to become children of God," "born . . . of God" (1:12–13).[40] Just as Jesus has a celestial origin and nature—"from above" and "not of this world"—he came to give humans a celestial origin and nature so that they are "not of this world" either. Just as Jesus has a celestial destiny or destination, ascending to heaven, he has come to ensure that humans will "follow" him into the realm "above," where they can live with him forever. Just as Jesus has "life in himself" (5:26), those humans made like him can have "eternal life" in themselves (5:24; cf. 6:53). And just as Jesus enjoys a divine status and attributes, so too will the humans made like him.

A. *Pneumatic* Existence

Central to John is the idea that the *Logos* imparts a new nature to humans. Though "born of flesh," they receive a new nature "not of the world": an existence as "spirit" (3:6, 17:14, 16). This idea was not an unusual one in the ancient world. On the contrary, it was a widely held premise among Jews and Christians of the period that humans were destined to assume a nature like that of stars and angels at the end of time.[41] The bodies humans naturally possess—bodies of earthly materials like flesh, bone, and blood—are intrinsically prone to injury, illness, aging, death, and decay. They are incompatible with an eternal existence. To participate in the "age to come," to live forever, one would need a different sort of existence: an existence akin to that of celestial beings.

1. The Celestial Body in Judaism

In the ancient imagination, the celestial realm was a richly populated place full of sentient beings. Before the advent of modern astronomy, these beings included the stars, which many ancients imagined as intelligent, embodied beings themselves—a higher order of life. Alan Scott explains that "aside from the Epicureans, all the major philosophical schools in the Hellenistic era believed in the divinity of the stars."[42] Likewise, many Jewish and Christian sources assume that the stars are living, sentient beings, with some ranking them among angelic and other quasi-divine beings or linking them to such beings.[43]

In keeping with this outlook, many Jewish texts imagine the righteous assuming bodies like stars—a process of "asterification":

> And many of those who sleep in the dust of the earth shall awake.... Those who are wise shall shine like the brightness of the sky; and those who lead the many to righteousness, like the stars forever and ever. (Dan. 12:2–3)[44]

> But now you shall shine like the lights of heaven. (1 Enoch [Epistle of Enoch] 104:2)[45]

> It is shown to them how their face is to shine like the sun, and how they are to be made like the light of the stars, being incorruptible from then on. (4 Ezra 7:97)[46]

> How happy are the righteous who shall escape the Lord's great judgment; for they will be made to shine seven times brighter than the sun. (2 Enoch 66:7)[47]

Building on the same assumptions, other Jewish works go so far as to imagine the righteous taking on bodies akin to those of celestial beings such as angels, even joining their ranks:[48]

> For [the righteous] shall see that world which is now invisible to them, and they will see a time which is now hidden to them. And time will no longer make them older. For they will live in the heights of that world and they will

be like the angels and be equal to the stars. And they will be changed into any shape which they wished, from beauty to loveliness, and from light to the splendor of glory.... And the excellence of the righteous will then be greater than that of the angels. (2 Bar. 51:8–12)[49]

And there I saw all the righteous from the time of Adam onwards. And there I saw the holy Abel and all the righteous. And there I saw Enoch and all who (were) with him, stripped of (their) robes of the flesh; and I saw them in their robes of above, and they were like the angels who stand there in great glory. (*Asc. Isa.* 9:7–9)[50]

2. Early Christians on Celestial Bodies

These speculations, diffuse across many apocalyptic Jewish sources, were also cultivated in the early Jesus movement. On the one hand, there is evidence that the historical Jesus assumed a future transformation of this kind. The earliest gospels—Mark, Matthew, and Luke—all depict Jesus preaching that humans would attain an existence similar to that of the "angels in heaven" in the "age to come" (Mark 12:25; Matt. 22:30). Interestingly, Luke goes further, with Jesus expressly claiming humans will achieve an existence "equal to angels" and identifying this transformation as the cause of their immortality:[51] "those who are accounted worthy to attain to that age and to the resurrection from the dead neither marry nor are given in marriage, for they cannot die anymore, because they are equal to angels [*isangeloi*] and are sons of God, being sons of the resurrection" (20:35–36).

A more robust discussion of the end-time transformation of human beings appears in the extant writings of Paul. In 1 Corinthians, Paul addresses the questions "How are the dead raised? With what kind of body do they come?" (15:35). He insists that humans will not be raised with the same sorts of bodies—bodies of the same materials—as they possess now: "what you sow is not the body which is to be, but a bare kernel" (15:37). Humans possess a flesh-and-blood body from Adam, a body Paul calls a *psychic* body, recalling Genesis, which claims that Adam "became a *psychē*" when he was created (LXX Gen. 2:7). According to Paul, however, human beings will be resurrected in a different kind of body. That body will not be of "flesh and blood" since, Paul writes, "flesh and blood cannot inherit the kingdom of God, nor does the perishable inherit the imperishable" (1 Cor. 15:50). Rather, in his view, the deceased "*psychic* body" will have to be "changed," converted into something "imperishable" to persist into the next world (15:51–52). It will have to be raised as a *pneumatic* (Gr. *pneumatikos*, "spirit/spiritual") body (15:44), a body composed of *pneuma* (Gk. *pneuma*, "spirit").[52]

Here, Paul draws on the idea, common in ancient philosophical currents, that *pneuma* was an actual, imperishable material—the stuff of celestial bodies.[53] Paul develops this idea in a contrast of celestial and earthly bodies, arguing that "there are also heavenly bodies, and there are earthly bodies; but the glory of the heavenly bodies is one kind, and the glory of the earthly bodies is another" (1 Cor. 15:40). Paul insists that Jesus was raised with the former sort of body: not a body "of dust" or "of flesh" but a body endowed with "glory," that is, a body "of heaven," a *pneumatic* body, being made "spirit": "So it will be with the resurrection of the dead. What is sown is perishable; what is raised is imperishable. It is sown in dishonor; it is raised in glory.... It is sown a *psychic* body; it is raised a *pneumatic* body. If there is a *psychic* body, there is also a *pneumatic* body.... So it is written: 'The first man Adam became a *psyche* [Gen. 2:7]; the last Adam [i.e., Jesus], a life-giving *pneuma* [spirit].... The first man was of the dust of the earth; the second man is of heaven'" (15:42–47). He is equally clear that humans will also undergo the same glorification, assuming *pneumatic*, heavenly bodies:

> As the one of dust, so are those who are of the dust, and as one of heaven, so are those who are of heaven. And just as we have borne the image of the earthly man, so shall we bear the image of the heavenly man. (1 Cor. 15:48–49)
>
> He will transform the body of our humiliation that it may be conformed to the body of his glory. (Phil. 3:21)

According to Paul, those who believe already possess a "guarantee" or "first fruits" of this change (2 Cor. 5:5; cf. Rom. 8:23).[54] Although they exist in bodies that are effectively "dead," they now possess the "Spirit of God," which is "alive" within them as a kernel of their new life (Rom 8:10–11). Even as their "outer nature is wasting away," they possess a new, "inner nature" that "is being renewed every day" (2 Cor. 4:16).[55] Crucially, however, Paul believes this change will be fully realized only at a future point in time: the coming "day of our Lord Jesus Christ" (1 Cor. 1:8, cf. 5:5). On that day, humans will see an entire transformation of their flesh-and-blood bodies into *pneumatic* bodies, endowed with life: "our commonwealth is in heaven, and from it, we await a Savior, the Lord Jesus Christ, who will change our lowly body to be like the body of his glory" (Phil. 3:20–21; cf. 1 Cor. 15:51–53).[56]

3. Flesh and Spirit in John

John takes up the same assumptions about the destiny of the material flesh as Paul, possibly from direct exposure to his writings. Just as Paul claims that "flesh and blood cannot inherit the kingdom of God," John's Jesus says in his very first discourse—a private conversation with Nicodemus—that those who are merely "born of flesh," who are "flesh," "cannot enter the kingdom of God."[57] Only those who have become spirit/*pneuma* can enter the kingdom—a transformation unique to believers:[58] "'Amen, amen, I say to you, unless one is born from above, they cannot see the kingdom of God....' 'Amen, amen, I say to you, unless one is born of water and spirit, they cannot enter the kingdom of God. That which is born of flesh is flesh, and that which is born of spirit is spirit. Do not marvel that I said to you, "You must be born from above"'" (John 3:3–7). By calling the assumption of *pneuma* a birth "from above," Jesus uses language that, as Troels Engberg-Pedersen argues, "should be understood wholly concretely and cosmologically: from heaven," as in 3:31 (cf. 3:12–13, 27).[59] Although humans are by nature "of this world" (8:23), they can receive a nature "from above," so that, as Jesus says, "they are not of the world, even as I am not of the world" (17:16). What Jesus envisions is the assumption of a celestial mode of existence: the very existence of God, who "is spirit" (4:24). Through this new birth, those who are "children of God" (1:12) become "spirit," as he is.[60]

The Gospel, however, casts this change as one that occurs imperceptibly, invisibly, through the hidden movements of the Spirit of God, whom "the world ... neither sees nor knows" (14:17). As Jesus first tells Nicodemus: "the wind/spirit [*pneuma*] blows where it wills, and you hear the sound/voice of it, but you do not know where it comes from or where it is going; so it is with everyone who is born of spirit" (3:8).[61] The world at large cannot discern where those who are "born of spirit" come from—that is, their new, celestial birth and nature. They retain flesh and blood, even though they have become *pneuma* inwardly. They move around the world as Jesus does, whose celestial origins and nature are also opaque to humans (7:28).

The idea that this transformation into spirit occurs imperceptibly is represented in the very first "sign," the first symbolic miracle, depicted in John. In the narrative, Jesus orders men to fill six large stone water jars to the brim with water; Jesus then surreptitiously transforms this water into wine (2:6-9). The narrator writes—in words prefiguring Jesus's later words to Nicodemus—that "the steward of the feast tasted the water now become wine and did not know where it came from" (2:9).[62] Those who receive the Spirit are water become wine. They are invisibly reborn "of spirit" as undying "spirit" in an unseen manner.

B. Celestial Access and Divine Indwelling

In his discourse with Nicodemus, Jesus says that just as humans do not know where those "born of spirit" come from—that is, their celestial origins and nature—they also do not know where those who are "born of spirit" are "going" (3:8). Jesus reveals where his disciples are going later in the text. They are going to the same place to which he is departing: the realm "above," heaven. There, they will dwell with and within the Father (cf. 8:14).

The idea that humans will ascend to celestial realms is also woven into many Jewish and Christian expectations of the afterlife (e.g., 4 Ezra 7:98; Rev. 7:9-10) or the end of time (e.g., 1 Enoch 104:2).[63] Characteristically, John relocates this idea to the present. Humans do not enjoy this celestial access later; rather, those "born from above" now have access to the realm above, precisely in and as spirit—an idea shared by some of Paul's later interpreters.

1. Coming and Going

The teaching that humans, after their rebirth as spirit, can now access the realm "above" is the prevailing theme of the longest and most important discourse in the Gospel, the "Farewell Discourse," which accounts for about one-seventh of the Gospel's contents (13:31-17:26).[64] Jesus had claimed throughout the Gospel that he is departing from the world (16:28; cf. 13:36, 14:12, 28, 16:10, 28). In this discourse, however, Jesus reveals to his disciples that after he leaves, he will make it possible for them to follow him (13:36). He elaborates upon this idea at the beginning of chapter 14: "In my Father's house there are many dwellings/abodes [*monai*]. If it were not so, would I have told you that I go to prepare a place for you? And if I go and prepare a place for you, I will come again and will take you to myself so that where I am, there you may be also. And you know the way where I am going" (14:2-4).

At first glance, this statement reads as a classic prediction of the future, visible, second coming of Jesus, such as one finds in the writings of Paul and the Synoptic Gospels. It would seem to envision Jesus leaving Earth but returning again to lead humans along some physical or spatial path or "way" to heaven. There, ostensibly, they will inhabit new physical/spatial "dwellings" with the Father. But this reading is incorrect. The "coming," "house," "way," and "dwellings" humans are destined to experience are not physical/spatial realities. They are, instead, spiritual, *pneumatic* realities.[65] Jesus is returning in a spiritual manner, opening a spiritual mode of access to the Father and a spiritual mode of dwelling with the Father.

Jesus begins clarifying this point in the lines that follow. After speaking of "the way" to the Father along which he "is going," Jesus tells his disciples, "you know the way where I am going" (14:4). He then states, "I am the way, and the truth, and the life; no one comes to the Father, but by me. If you had known me, you would have known my Father also. From now on, you do know him and have seen him" (14:6–7). After speaking of "the way" to the Father along which he "is going," Jesus announces that he is "the way ... to the Father." At this point, any attempt to interpret Jesus's words in literal and spatial terms breaks down. How can Jesus go to the Father along some "way" and simultaneously be that "way"? The paradoxical nature of Jesus's reply indicates that these images are not meant to be read in a literal sense.

For the disciples, this is a difficult lesson to grasp. Philip, revealing the deep misunderstanding still pervading the group, asks Jesus, "Lord, show us the Father, and we will be satisfied" (14:8). His request doubles down on the idea that there is a literal, spatial gap separating the Father and the disciples. In response, Jesus insists there is no such distance, making the metaphorical force of his opening words that much clearer: "Have I been with you so long, and you still do not know me, Philip? The one who has seen me has seen the Father. How can you say, 'Show us the Father?' Do you not believe that I am in the Father and the Father is in me? The words that I say to you I do not speak on my own, but the Father who dwells/abides [*menōn*] in me does his works. Believe me that I am in the Father, and the Father is in me" (14:9–11). In these lines, Jesus intimates that the "Father's house" is not a far-off reality. Instead, Jesus is the dwelling place of the Father. The Father "dwells" in Jesus; he "is in" Jesus, and Jesus is with him.[66] Not coincidentally, the verb "dwell/abide" here (*menō*; 14:10) is directly related to the noun "dwelling/abode" appearing earlier in the discourse (*monē*; 14:2); the noun is derived from the verb. Across these lines, then, Jesus weaves the idea that the "dwellings" he promised are also spiritual. He will open up a new mode of spiritual dwelling with the Father.

Jesus presses this point even more clearly and directly as the dialogue continues. He restates and elaborates his initial claim that he is "coming," but he does so in more concrete terms, now revealing the form of his return: "I will not leave you orphaned; I am coming to you. Yet a little while and the world will see me no more, but you will see me; because I live, you will also live. On that day, you will know that I am in my Father, and you in me, and I in you. The one who has my commandments and keeps them is the one who loves me; my Father will love the one who loves me, and I will love that one and manifest myself to that one" (14:18–21). Once again, Jesus insists that he is "coming," but this time he clarifies how he is coming: in a way the world cannot see.[67] He will come in, through, or as "the Spirit of truth," an entity the world cannot receive because it "neither sees him nor knows him" (14:17). And through the Spirit, Jesus will be "in" believers and manifest himself to them (14:20–21).

Jesus makes it clear that not only is his "coming" *pneumatic*, but so too are the "dwellings" with the Father he promised to prepare. When another disciple asks, "Lord, how is it that you will manifest yourself to us, and not to the world?" (14:22), Jesus explains, "If a person loves me ... my Father will love that one, and we will come to him and make our dwelling [*monēn*] with that one" (14:23). Jesus takes up the word "dwelling" (*monēn*) from earlier, clarifying its meaning. The "Father's house" and its many "dwellings" (*monai*) are spiritual dwellings. When humans receive the Spirit, the Father and Son manifest themselves to believers, enter into them, and dwell with them (cf. 17:23).

Crucially, however, this indwelling is not one-directional. Just as Jesus "comes" to dwell "in" those who believe, they dwell "in" him: "dwell [*meinate*] in me, and I in you" (15:4; cf. 17:21). In other words, this spiritual indwelling is more than a spiritual descent of Jesus into believers; it is also a spiritual ascent of believers to Jesus. It opens up a form of double presence, whereby those "below" on earth can simultaneously access the realm "above"—the realm where Jesus and the Father are. Several chapters later, Jesus holds these tensive threads together, asking the Father both that those who believe in him not be taken out of the world (17:15) and that the same persons be with him where he is (17:24). Spiritual indwelling makes both options simultaneously possible.

2. Early Christian Context
The ideas outlined in the Farewell Discourse are not ones Jesus develops in the Synoptics. Traces of these ideas, however, are found in the writings of

Paul. For example, the concept of mutual indwelling finds plausible roots in Paul's discussions of the Spirit. In Romans, he notes that those who are inhabited by the "Spirit of God" have "Christ in" them, and they are "in Christ" (Rom. 8:9-10, 1).[68] He conceives of those sharing the Spirit with Christ as incorporated into the "body of Christ" (Rom. 12:4-5; 1 Cor. 10:16-17, 12:12-31). He even implies his ability to project his presence through the Spirit (1 Cor. 5:3-5).

In certain respects, however, the Gospel takes these ideas further than Paul's surviving articulations, albeit along trajectories attested by Paul's later interpreters. Analogous images of a double presence, mediated by the Spirit, appear in Ephesians, a pseudo-historical letter written in the voice of Paul, with other tantalizing parallels to John.[69] In one section, the text claims that "in" Jesus, believers "are built together in the Spirit into a dwelling place of God" (2:22). More pointedly, the letter teaches that God has made those who believe "alive'" and that he has "raised us with [Jesus] and made us sit with him in the heavenly places in Christ Jesus," guaranteeing human "access in one Spirit to the Father" (2:1, 6, 18).[70] In John, we see these ideas placed on the lips of Jesus as if they were Jesus's own.

C. Eternal Life

In the logic of John, these teachings—that humans can now receive an existence as spirit and can now spiritually access heaven—have an important corollary. They indicate that humans can now also possess a true personal immortality, a mode of existence immune to death. Even if their bodies of flesh perish, they survive in the celestial realms in spirit and as spirit.

1. Immortality

As I noted earlier, many ancient Christians conceptualized immortality as a gift received in the future, at a final resurrection and judgment, when human bodies are transformed from earthly into celestial material. In Mark, for example, Jesus specifies that those who follow him will receive "eternal life" "in the age to come" (10:30; cf. Luke 18:30; Matt. 25:31, 46, 18:8). Likewise, Luke claims that humans will "die no more" when they at last "attain to that age and the resurrection from the dead," becoming "children of the resurrection" (20:35-36). Paul operates with similar assumptions. He casts humans, born in bodies of "flesh and blood," as intrinsically "perishable" and "mortal"

(1 Cor. 15:50–54). Nevertheless, he recognizes that those who believe have a Spirit that can impart immortality to their mortal bodies one day (Rom. 8:11), precisely as these bodies are transformed into fully *pneumatic* bodies, bodies of spirit, that are "imperishable" and "immortal" (1 Cor. 15:50–54). Paul, then, consistently speaks of "eternal life" and "immortality" as future gifts, received at "the day of wrath when God's righteous judgment will be revealed" (Rom. 2:5–7; cf. 6:8).

We can map part of John's thought onto the above. The Gospel shares the assumption that those who are merely "flesh" by nature are helplessly mortal. Since they "have no life within" (6:53), they are in a state that can be called "death" (5:24), a state in which they inevitably "die" or "perish" (8:21, 24, 3:16).[71] They are, as Jesus says, "condemned already" (3:18)—in effect, condemned by nature. Other aspects of John do not map onto the above, however. Most notably, John is clear that those who believe possess "eternal life" now, articulating this idea in present-tense verbs—something the Synoptics and Paul never do:

The one who believes in the Son has [*echei*] eternal life. (3:36; cf. 3:16)

Amen, amen, I say to you, the one who believes has [*echei*] eternal life. (6:47)

Even more bluntly and surprisingly, John's Jesus ensures his hearers that all who believe "will never perish," "never die," or "never taste death" (3:16, 10:28, 11:26, 8:51–52)—promises foreign to the Synoptics and Paul.

These verses demonstrate a subtle shift, development, or innovation in perspective. For John, eternal life and immortality are no longer future possibilities. They are accessible—realized—now, precisely through the internal transformation of human beings into spirit/*pneuma*. In chapter 6, Jesus expressly states that "it is the spirit that gives life" (6:63). Elsewhere, Jesus locates "eternal life" "in" the human person (6:53, 4:14); that is, he isolates it in precisely the sphere where the Spirit "dwells" (14:17, 19–20, 7:38–39) and where humans are "born of spirit" (3:3, 6).

If those humans who receive the Spirit are "born of spirit" and thereby are "spirit/*pneuma*" (3:6), then it follows they already partly possess an imperishable nature. For John, then, the dissolution of the body cannot affect that aspect of their being—a part of their being that can and does fully mediate a person's thought, rationality, and personhood. (John's thinking, rational, personal God, after all, is spirit/*pneuma* [4:24].) Processes of decay inexorably overtake the flesh, but they cannot touch the undying spirit in the reborn person. The new life as spirit—that eternal life—persists even through and after death (11:25). This is precisely why Jesus introduces the idea of immortality in the same discourse as he introduces the idea that humans can become *pneuma*: the dialogue with Nicodemus. The two expectations are closely linked.

Celestial Survival
So what becomes of those humans who have *pneuma* when their flesh dies? Their life persists in the other realm "above"—in the celestial realm they already have access to in spirit. John's Jesus lays out precisely this notion of postmortem survival in one of the few verses in which he addresses the death of his followers. In chapter 12, Jesus urges his followers to "hate" their "life in this world" and to be prepared to "follow" him into death—words that evoke Mark 8:34 and Matthew 16:24. But critically, he also claims that if one loses one's life, laying it down as he does, that person nonetheless will be with him: "Amen, amen, I say to you, unless a grain of wheat falls into the earth and dies, it remains alone, but if it dies, it bears much fruit. The one who loves his life loses it, and the one who hates his life in this world will keep it for eternal life. If anyone serves me, that one must follow me, and where I am, there will my servant be also" (John 12:24–26; cf. 13:36–38).[72] Jesus's claim that his followers will be "where I am" alludes to his later revelation that he will provide spiritual "dwellings" for believers so that they can be "where I am"—in the realm above (14:3; cf. 14:23).[73] When one loses one's life "in this world," one continues to dwell, to live, with Jesus in that realm—that is, in the Father's house.[74]

Other verses develop the same teaching. In chapter 8, Jesus tells his opponents that they are "enslaved to sin" (John 8:34), an idiom lifted from Paul (Rom. 6:15–22). He then insists that "the enslaved person . . . does not dwell [*menei*] in the house forever, but the son dwells [*menei*] forever" (John 8:35). Here, Jesus intimates that those freed from sin are permitted to live in the Father's house "forever." Similarly, in chapter 14 Jesus explains that it is precisely in the spiritual indwelling that humans experience "life": "Because I live, you will also live. On that day, you will know that I am in my Father, and you in me, and I in you" (14:19–20). They remain in Jesus, safe from the grip of death. Jesus insists, "I give them eternal life, and they will never perish, and no one will snatch them out of my hand" (10:28; cf. v. 29).

2. Reimagining Resurrection

What the Synoptics promise for a future resurrection, then, John anchors in the present coming of the Spirit. In this respect, John develops what is sometimes called a "present" or "realized eschatology," but which might better be called a "Spirit-realized eschatology"—a system in which events anticipated for the end of time are instead anchored in the present time. Consistent with this view, John depicts Jesus exclaiming, "now is the judgment of this world" (12:31; cf. 3:19), that is, the time of resurrection in conventional apocalyptic interpretations (cf. Matt. 12:36–42; Luke 10:14, 11:31–32). Likewise, John's Jesus casts the rebirth as spirit precisely as a spiritual resurrection, attained at the "hour" of his departure so central to the text (13:1).[75] Consider, for example, the following parallel statements in chapter 5: "Amen, amen, I say to you, the one who hears my word and believes him who sent me has eternal life; that one does not come into judgment but has passed from death to life. Amen, amen, I say to you, the hour is coming and now is when the dead will hear the voice of the Son of God, and those who hear will live" (5:24–25). The "dead" mentioned here are not the physically dead since the physically dead are not capable of "hearing" and "believing." They are, instead, humans in their natural state of mortality, who "have no life within" themselves (6:53). For these individuals, the coming of the Spirit marks a resurrection—a passage "from death to life." Later in the same discourse, Jesus will metaphorically refer to the same experience as "the resurrection of life" (5:29).[76] To quote Jaime Clark Soles, the Gospel of John "has taken the tradition's language of future resurrection and corrected it so that the future is completed not at a second coming but rather at Jesus' resurrection," when he gives the Spirit to humans (20:19–22).[77]

The Fate of the Body

If John rearticulates the promise of resurrection around the transformation of humans into spirit/*pneuma*, then what is the destiny of physical flesh in this schema? What happens to the fleshly body that is buried in the ground? The Gospel does not offer a clear answer to this question, but it operates with a pessimism about the flesh that makes it difficult to imagine any future destiny for that body, at least as such. Echoing Paul's notion that "flesh and blood cannot inherit the kingdom of God," John's Jesus intimates that physical flesh does not see or enter the kingdom of God, implying that earthly materials such as flesh and blood are unsuitable for an eternal existence and destined only for decay (3:3–6; cf. 1 Cor. 15:50). Moreover, in a stark departure from the Synoptics, John's Jesus claims that his kingdom "is not of this world" (18:36). Only in John does Jesus claim that "the flesh is of no avail" (6:63). Jesus is also depicted refusing physical food and acting as if it is unnecessary (4:32; cf. 6:27)—a scene evoking images of humans preparing for a translation to another state of existence in other ancient texts.[78]

One may imagine that John, like Paul, assumes that Jesus will one day return to retrieve the fleshly bodies of believers, causing those bodies to be "changed" or "swallowed up" by the other substance of *pneuma*, as Paul teaches (1 Cor. 15:52; 2 Cor. 5:4). This is possible. For Paul, this sort of swallowing up is necessary to endow the human being with "immortality" (1 Cor. 15:53–55). But John's notion of spiritual resurrection seems to supplant some of the ideas associated with Paul's physical resurrection. Tellingly, John decisively recasts the idea of Jesus coming again as a reference to his coming by the Spirit to indwell believers (14:2–29). Similarly, when the Gospel speaks of Jesus raising humans "on the last day" (i.e., 6:39, 40, 44, 54), it does so in ways open to realized eschatological interpretations.[79] John also insists, in ways Paul never does, that humans fully possess immortality now, even while they are in the flesh. And last, John casts the two physical resurrections depicted in the Gospel—those of Lazarus and Jesus—as "signs," pointing humans to a resurrection of a spiritual nature, received now (11:24–25, 47, 20:30–31).[80] In this case, John may have no need for a future physical resurrection; it might be content with the idea of spiritual resurrection alone.

3. Early Jewish and Christian Comparands

John is hardly an outlier in developing a vocabulary of spiritual resurrection. On the contrary, comparable concepts appear in other Jewish and Christian sources of the period, situating our author in a very plausible intellectual context. Among Jewish texts, one can find a comparable concept in the *Epistle of Enoch* (1 Enoch 91–108), a text that teaches, as John Collins observes, "the resurrection, or exaltation, of the spirit . . . to heaven."[81] According to that text, "the spirits of those who died in righteousness shall live and rejoice; their spirits shall not perish."[82]

We also know that some Christians held these views—not least because certain texts condemn them for doing so. The Pseudo-Pauline 2 Timothy indicts figures "who have swerved from the truth by holding that the resurrection is past already" (2:18)—evidently a reference to a spiritual resurrection. Likewise, 2 Clement warns its readers against claiming "that this flesh is neither judged nor raised," and 3 Corinthians (Acts of Paul) also rebukes those who claim "there is no resurrection of the flesh."[83] Other sources expressly identify certain Christian teachers and groups with this view. Notably, John was a favorite Gospel of the Valentinians, who, according to Hippolytus, do "not want the flesh to be saved, calling it the 'coat of skin' and 'the corrupted human.'"[84] We can also detect resonances between the Gospel of John and the *Gospel of Thomas*. According to *Thomas*, the "kingdom" is not a future reality but a present one "spread out upon the earth, and people do not see it"—that is, a spiritual realm accessible to humans now.[85] For those humans who gain knowledge (*gnosis*) and apprehend that kingdom, physical death marks no more than the removal of the outer flesh, an idea represented through the metaphor of undress.[86] The spirit/soul, in turn, will not "see" or "taste" "death," and it will survive the eventual destruction of the material world: "The heavens and the earth will roll up in your presence, and whoever is living from the living one will not see death."[87]

Although John's vision may not be identical to these or other systems of thought, we can plausibly situate it within the same broad intellectual current. It is also easy to see why the author of John would want to rearticulate at least some ideas of resurrection and eternal life around the present. If that author was active near the turn of the second century, then he lived at a time when many Christ-believers struggled to make sense of the apparent delay or failure of Jesus's predictions regarding the end, including his prediction, related in Mark, that "there are some standing here who will not taste death before they see the kingdom of God come with power" (9:1; cf. 13:30). By his time, presumably all of the disciples had died, and the promised kingdom of God had not come with visible signs.

Some Christian texts urged additional patience in the face of this apparent delay (cf. 2 Peter 3:3–4). Others, such as the *Gospel of Thomas*, reinterpreted the language of future eschatology along spiritualizing lines. This seems to have also been John's approach. John intimates that Jesus's prediction in Mark was true: there were some standing with Jesus who would "not taste death" before seeing the "kingdom" come. But John makes this prediction work by reinterpreting that kingdom and the promise of not tasting death. For John, as for *Thomas*, the "kingdom of God" is a kingdom that is "not of this world" (18:36) but one "seen" and "entered" only by those who become "spirit" (3:3–6; cf. 14:19). For that matter, the promised "judgment" is also not a future judgment but one that occurs "now" (12:31, 16:11). And for John, not tasting death involves acquiring the new life as "spirit," one that bequeaths an immortality experienced now.

D. Exaltation

On their face, the various transformations we have explored so far—the experience of becoming *pneuma*, celestial access, and immortality—would seem to give humans some likeness to celestial beings such as angels, and rightfully so. Ancient Christian literature readily makes these sorts of comparisons, intimating that humans will assume ranks beside or above other heavenly beings. Interpreters find traces of such vocabularies in the writings of Paul.[88] The same ideas also appear in the Synoptics. Luke, in fact, depicts Jesus using especially strong language to communicate this idea: "those who are considered worthy to attain to that age and to the resurrection from the dead ... cannot die anymore, because they are equal to angels [*isangeloi*] and are sons of God, being sons of the resurrection" (Luke 20:35–36).[89]

The Gospel of John shares these vocabularies of exaltation, but characteristically it orients them toward the present. In John, Jesus teaches that humans are taking their place beside other ranks of celestial life even now, in their earthly lives, through a process we can conceptualize as a "deification."[90] In this vision, humans are exalted even to the pinnacle of that ladder of life, sharing the life and attributes of the *Logos*/Son.

1. "Children of God"

As I noted earlier, many ancient Jews and Christians saw divinity as a broad, fluid, and communicable attribute shared down the chain of life through various modes of participation and union. We saw that through such a mode of participation, John casts the *Logos* as an entity worthy of being called "the Son of God" and to be called "god" or divine (1:1). What many easily miss, however, is the fact that the Gospel indicates that other humans will participate in the same status. According to the Gospel, Jesus came to create fellow "children of God," who, like him, are also "born ... of God": "to all who received him, who believed in his name, he gave power to become children of God [*tekna theou*]; who were born, not of blood nor the will of the flesh nor the will of man, but of God" (1:12–13).[91]

It is easy to miss the staggering implications of the language here. As we saw earlier, the Gospel posits a literal, ontological experience of being born of God. God, who is spirit, makes humans into spirit. In that case, we should not underestimate the literal and ontological analogy between "the Son of God" and the other "children of God" who result from this birth. To quote Michael Peppard, "divine sonship is an image that unites Christ with

Christians more than it separates them"—an idea fleshed out in the Gospel.[92] To the extent that Jesus is the "unique son" (*monogenēs*) of God, it may be precisely as he is "uniquely able to empower others to become God's sons and daughters" like himself.[93]

Divine Glory

First, and quite dramatically, John posits that the celestial humans share one of the seemingly exclusive attributes of the preexistent *Logos*/Son: his divine "glory." We saw that in multiple places, the Gospel speaks of a special "glory"—a glory endowed by the Father (cf. 8:54), shared with the Father, and proper to the divine "only/unique son [*monogenēs*] from the Father":

> And the Word became flesh . . . and we have seen his glory—glory as of the Father's only son. (1:14)

> And now, Father, glorify me in your own presence with the glory which I had with you before the world was made. (17:5)

This "glory" was not overtly visible to humans, veiled as it was by Jesus's flesh, though Jesus made that glory manifest in fleeting impressions: the signs he performed (2:11, 11:40, 12:41). Later, however, Jesus reveals that through the indwelling, all those who believe will "see" him (14:19) and behold his glory. In his final and climactic prayer he prays, "I desire that those also, whom you have given me, may be with me where I am, to see my glory which you have given me in your love for me before the foundation of the world" (17:24). But Jesus goes further, indicating that he also imparts that glory—the glory of "the unique Son"—to humans: "the glory that you have given me I have given to them" (17:22).

This juxtaposition—of seeing the glory and receiving the glory—suits an ancient Jewish and Christian assumption that the sight of divine glory is transforming, exalting, and even deifying for humans, that one cannot see the glory proper to divinity without being exalted by it. For ancient Jews, the prototypical example of a human exalted in this way was Moses. In Exodus, Moses asks to see the "glory" of God, and God permits him to behold part of his "glory" passing by (Ex. 24:16–17, 33:18–23). In a subsequent verse, Moses learns that his encounters with God have altered his appearance: "when Moses came down from Mount Sinai . . . Moses did not know that the skin of his face shone because he had been talking with God. And when Aaron and all the people of Israel saw Moses, behold, the skin of his face shone, and they were afraid to come near him" (Ex. 34:29–30). The episode was the focus of Philonic speculations.[94] It also frames a section in 2 Corinthians with especially tantalizing connections to John (2 Cor. 3:12–18). In that passage, Paul indicates that the Spirit indwelling humans communicates the sight of the "glory of the Lord" and that this sight changes humans into the likeness of what they see so that they too acquire the same "glory" he possesses: "The Lord is the Spirit... and we all, with unveiled face, beholding the glory of the Lord, are being changed into his likeness from one degree of glory to another [lit. "from glory to glory"]; for this comes from the Lord who is the Spirit" (2 Cor. 3:17–18).[95]

John works from similar assumptions. In the Gospel, as humans receive the indwelling presence of the unique Son, they "see" him (14:19). The Gospel does not delineate the mode of this "sight," but it is probably not a literal sight, that is, a perception of light through the physical eye or in a hallucination or dream. After all, in John the disciples apprehend the glory of Jesus in actions devoid of any extraordinary visual displays such as brilliance or light, as in his transforming water into wine or raising a dead man from the tomb (2:11; cf. 11:40). Instead, the sight would seem to be akin to the one imagined by those writers with whom the Gospel partly shares a thought world, such as Philo—that is, an intellectual, noetic, rational sight, appropriate for the *Logos* of God.[96] The Gospel, for one, places a clear emphasis on knowledge:

> And this is eternal life, that they may know you, the only true God, and Jesus Christ, whom you have sent. (17:3)

> You will know the truth, and the truth will make you free. (8:32)

It even juxtaposes references to "knowing" and "seeing," intimating an essential link or synonymity of the two concepts (1:18, 14:7, 9, 17). Through this "sight"—this intellectual apprehension and knowledge—of the glory of God, humans acquire that glory.

Oneness with God
The Gospel takes the analogy between the "unique/only Son" and the "children of God" still further. By indwelling those who believe and giving his

"glory" to them, the Son bequeaths another attribute of his to the other "children of God," namely, the oneness with the Father that he enjoys. Jesus makes this point explicitly in his climactic prayer to the Father:

> I ask not only on behalf of these but also on behalf of those who believe in me through their word, that they may all be one. As you, Father, are in me and I in you, may they also be in us, so that the world may believe that you have sent me. The glory that you have given me I have given them, so that they may be one, as we are one—I in them and you in me, that they may be made perfect into one, so that the world may know that you have sent me and have loved them even as you have loved me. (17:20–23)

Humans do not enter merely a oneness like the one the Father and Son enjoy; rather, they enter the very oneness uniting the two. Becoming one with the Son, they experience precisely his unity with the Father.

2. "Gods"

The premise that humans enter the oneness of the Father and Son is even more radical than it appears. In John, the perfect oneness of the Father and Son is closely linked to the claim that the Son is worthy to be regarded as a "god" or "divine." This is already intimated in John 1, which juxtaposes the two ideas: "the Word was with God, and the Word was god/divine" (1:1).[97] It is even clearer in chapter 10, which describes a confrontation between Jesus and the Jews of Jerusalem. When Jesus tells the crowd around him: "I and the Father are one" (10:30), his opponents take up "stones . . . to stone him," claiming, "it is not for a good work that we are going to stone you but for blasphemy; because you, being a man, make yourself god/divine" (10:32–33). The opponents of Jesus understand that the claim of oneness with the Father entails a claim of divine participation and status—a claim Jesus does not dispute but defends in subsequent verses.

If Jesus's oneness with the Father entails participation in his divinity, then humans who participate in that oneness would also seem to attain a god/divine status. And indeed, as Andrew Byers writes, it would appear that "for the Fourth Gospel, oneness means deification."[98] The Gospel does not shy away from the notion of humans being called "gods" in some participatory manner; on the contrary, it lays out this idea in the same scene. When "the Jews" accuse Jesus of blasphemy for making himself "god/divine," Jesus defends his ability to claim divine status even as a human. He does so by citing Psalm 82:6, a verse that uses the expressions "gods" and "sons [of God]" interchangeably, further supporting the idea that these expressions are equivalent in the Gospel: "You are gods, and all are sons of the Most High." Since the verse addresses humans as "gods," Jesus reasons, he is more than justified calling himself "son of God":[99] "Is it not written in your law, 'I said, you are gods' [Ps. 82:6]? If he called those to whom the word of God came 'gods'—and the scripture cannot be broken—can you say 'You are blaspheming' to the one whom the Father has sanctified and sent into the world, because I said, 'I am the Son of God?'" (John 10:35–36). M. David Litwa observes that "the argument works, to be sure, but at the price of Jesus's uniqueness."[100] It implies that it is also appropriate to call some other humans "gods," specifically those "to whom the word of God came." But who are those other "gods"? The Gospel presents Jesus as the "Word" sent from the Father to humans (1:1, 1:14), who speaks the "words of God" to them:

He whom God has sent speaks the words of God. (3:34)

The one who is of God hears the words of God. (8:47)

In this light, it seems inescapable that the one who "hears" and "believes" Jesus, the one who believes, is also "god/divine."[101] In their assimilation to the life and nature of the *Logos*, they are also assimilated to his character as a participant "god."[102]

Admittedly, John's Jesus stops short of using more direct language, for example, an express claim that those who receive him become "gods" (*theoi*). But John's Jesus also refrains from ever directly calling himself "god" (*theos*).[103] Nevertheless, the coded language Jesus uses and the implications of his language are unambiguous. In the Gospel, Jesus claims godlike status and attributes for himself and for those who receive him. The Gospel, in short, works with a true concept of deification, one in which humans are exalted into a derivative, contingent, participatory godhood like the one Jesus enjoys.

In the logic of the narrative, Jesus's reluctance to use more direct language makes sense. Whenever he makes even coded claims, his listeners perceive the dangerous force of his words, casting him as a blasphemer and targeting him for violence, including attempted stonings and a crucifixion (e.g., 8:59, 10:31). It may be no coincidence, then, that John's Jesus tells his disciples in the Farewell Discourse, "I still have many things to say to you, but you cannot bear them now" (16:12). The text indicates that the disciples were not yet able to bear the full implications of Jesus's teachings. It is also telling that Jesus excludes Nicodemus, who is struggling with understanding and believing the "earthly things" he has heard, from learning even more radical "heavenly things" (3:10–12). The Gospel casts Jesus as a teacher who leaves the weightiest things unsaid, implicitly leaving its readers to infer the complete and dramatic implications of his words.[104]

3. "Angels"

As we have seen, Luke's Jesus pairs the idea that humans can be "sons of God" with the idea that they can acquire an existence, form, or position "equal to the angels." This connection was a natural one for many Jews and Christians since, by the first century CE, references to "gods" and "the sons of God" in biblical texts were linked to angelic beings. The Greek Septuagint, for example, translates the Hebrew expression "sons of God" precisely as "angels" in multiple verses (e.g., LXX Job 1:6, 2:1, 38:7).

Angelification was also a popular way of interpreting the final transformation of humans in later Christian texts. In Acts, Stephen's face becomes "like the face of an angel" moments before his death, implying his transition into an angelic state at that time (6:15).[105] Along the same lines, the late second-century writer Tertullian insists that human beings will acquire "angelic substance" (*substantia angelica*), change into an "angelic state" (*in statum angelicum*), and be "refashioned into angels" (*in angelos reformandi*).[106] In the Martyrdom of Polycarp, martyrs confronting their deaths are said to be "no longer humans but angels."[107] The third-century writer Origen taught that "God has graciously bestowed on us the removal from human nature and appointed us for the angelic," with humans possessing "bodies of angels, ethereal and brilliant light."[108] In another place, he writes that "those who will be like angels will thus be angels."[109]

John may sit within the same field of speculation. In the first chapter of the Gospel, Jesus utters a cryptic but suggestive line to his disciples: "You will see greater things than these.... Amen, amen, I say to you: you [pl.] will see heaven opened and the angels of God ascending and descending upon the Son of Man" (1:51). Despite the saying's prominence in the Gospel—it is Jesus's first direct teaching in John—many scholars find it puzzling and marginalize it in their discussions of John's theology. The background of the saying is clear; it adapts imagery from the story of Jacob's Ladder in Genesis

28:10–22, in which Jacob recognizes that he has found the "door of heaven" and the "house of God." The problem is that the saying finds no obvious fulfillment in other lines of John. Raymond Brown calls it "a verse that has caused as much trouble for commentators as any other single verse in the Fourth Gospel."[110] The Gospel never depicts an opening of the heavens, nor do humans see angels move in the text.[111] To what, then, does the saying refer?

As I see it, the saying encapsulates the essential teachings of John, namely, that certain humans will acquire a celestial nature and be granted access to the celestial "Father's house" (14:1–31). The only experience called an "ascension" in John is the path to the Father in the celestial realm (3:13, 6:62, 20:17; cf. 14:2), the journey Jesus intends humans to "follow" (13:36, 14:3, 17:24).[112] Also, the image of beings ascending "on the Son of Man" as a ladder—that is, by means of him—evokes other passages that present Jesus as the "way" or "door" through or by which humans access "the Father's house" above (e.g., 14:6). Most strikingly, one verse in particular speaks of "the sheep" going both "in" and "out" of the "door"—an image that maps perfectly onto the image of angels ascending and descending: "I am the door; if anyone enters by me, that one will be saved and will go in and out and find pasture" (10:9). Last, in other texts, the "greater works" of Jesus are precisely the medium of this celestial access, namely, the coming of the Spirit that transforms human beings into spirit (5:20–25; cf. 14:12).

We could read this image figuratively so that the angels merely stand in for the exalted humans without any notion that humans become angels themselves.[113] But it is also possible that Jesus uses the language of "angels" precisely to signal the new status of these humans. Assuming a celestial nature, these humans take their ranks alongside angelic beings. Either way, Jesus's first teaching in the Gospel proves programmatic for the entire vision of human exaltation articulated throughout it.

III. The "Word" and the "Words"

Across this chapter, we have explored John's vision of human transformation, one that encompasses rebirth as *pneuma*, divine indwelling and celestial access, the reception of eternal life, and an exaltation into the status, attributes, oneness, and divine glory enjoyed by the *Logos*/Son. And yet beneath this multifaceted image lies a single unifying principle. The Gospel attributes all these transformations to a single instrumentality: the "word" (*logos*) or "words" of Jesus. Jesus affirms that those who receive his "word" receive the divine indwelling (14:23). He asserts that the one who hears his "word" will "never taste death" (8:51–52; cf. 5:24–25). And with respect to deification, Jesus says that God calls "those to whom the word of God came 'gods'" (10:35).

But why this emphasis on the "word" or "words" of Jesus? How do mere "words" effect the many changes to human beings envisioned across the text? A compelling answer to this question can be found in other texts with *Logos* speculations similar to those in the Gospel. According to these texts, when the hypostasized Word, or *Logos*, of God comes upon humans, it can transform them into what the *Logos* itself is, drawing a human being into immortality, divine attributes, and oneness with God—a premise tantalizingly close to and possibly influential for the Gospel's presentation.

A. The "Words" as Divine

As we have seen, the Gospel of John sits within currents of Hellenistic Jewish thought that hypostasized the *Logos*—the intellectual Word—of God. Tellingly, some of these streams presupposed that this hypostasized "Word" could be condensed in and mediated as speech acts, a view used by Jewish authors to describe how "the word of the Lord came" to individual prophets, animating their speech. In this framework, "God's thoughts become uttered speech ... [and] the act of speaking itself renders God's incorporeal thoughts into tangible realities; through the medium of sound, an entity perceptible to the senses, they are experienced corporeally."[114]

Various writers have seen evidence of the same ideas in John.[115] Forger notes that "when the Word [*logos*] became flesh [*sarx*] in the person of Jesus (John 1:14, 18), what had previously only been the thoughts or rationality of God could be suddenly spoken and heard" precisely in, through, and as "the words (*logoi*) that Jesus speaks."[116] Those words, then, are not mere human speech acts. They are, instead, something ontologically distinct: expressions, condensations, or mediations of the divine Word. As Forger states elsewhere, John "presents the *logos* ... as embodied in the created world that God has made, through not just the person of Jesus (cf. John 1:14, 18), but also, and perhaps more significantly, through the words (*logoi*) that Jesus speaks."[117]

Along similar lines, Gitte Buch-Hansen claims that "Jesus' organs of speech are at the disposal of the holy [*Logos*], which articulates itself in his words."[118]

This view finds ample support in the fact that the Gospel consistently blurs the identities of the "Word," Jesus, and the "word(s)" Jesus speaks. Just as the "Word," as god/divine, has "life" in himself (1:4, 5:26) and is *pneuma* (cf. 4:24), so Jesus can say, "the words that I have spoken to you are *pneuma* and life" (6:63; cf. 6:68). Moreover, just as Jesus claims he will "dwell" in persons and that humans will "dwell" in him, he speaks of "word" or "words" "dwelling in" persons (5:38, 8:37, 15:7), and he claims that they will "dwell" in "the word" (8:31). The "Word" is communicated in or mediated by his words.[119] To internalize those words, then, is to internalize a hypostasized reality, a divine presence.

B. Immortalization through the *Logos*

The idea that humans encounter and internalize the divine *Logos* in the words of Jesus is more significant than it might appear. Interestingly, Hellenistic Jewish thinkers such as Philo posited that human encounters with the divine *Logos* could transform human nature, allowing humans to become what the *Logos*/Word is: immortal, deified, and one with God. As I will argue here, this premise provides an essential missing link in understanding John, one that reveals the inner, even necessary logic of its multifaceted vision of human exaltation.

1. Immortalization in Philo

As I noted, Philo conceptualizes the *Logos*, Word, or Reason that created the universe as the divine "Mind" (*nous*) or Intellect. He hails the "the divine *Logos* ... above us" as the "Mind ... above us" and "that Mind" who "came and ordered all things."[120] Interestingly, Philo conceptualizes "mind" in other passages precisely as "*pneuma*, hot and on fire."[121] That mind is monadic or simple because it lacks lower nature; thus Philo calls it "the perfectly pure and unsullied Mind of the universe."[122] Angels too are "all mind through and through, pure intelligences, in the likeness of the monad."[123] Elsewhere, they are "divine living beings which are altogether intellectual spirits."[124] And thus "it is customary to call angels" "immortal *logoi*."[125]

By contrast, Philo views humans as dyadic, a combination of mind and body. But according to Philo, certain humans can become so "filled with

God" that their nature changes; they resolve into pure mind and intellect, leaving aside the nonrational parts of their nature: their bodies. These humans become "divine intelligence alone—a monad like God as he is manifest in the Logos" or like "one of these angelic *logoi*."[126] Philo is also frank about what this process entails; through this process, one is "changed into the divine": "For when the prophetic mind becomes divinely inspired and filled with God, it becomes like the unity [*monad*], not being at all mixed with any of those things associated with duality. But he who is resolved into the nature of unity (*monad*), is said to come near God in a kind of family relation, for having given up and left behind all mortal kinds, he is changed into the divine, so that such men become kin to God and truly divine."[127]

Elsewhere, Philo suggests that Moses, the greatest luminary of the Hebrew Bible, experienced a dramatic form of this transformation. The traditional account of Moses's death indicates that his body was never recovered (Deut. 34:6)—a line that invited considerable speculation about his ultimate destiny in ancient Jewish literature. Philo engaged in the same speculations, developing his own solution; in his view, Moses's body was never found because Moses himself was translated into a higher state. In the concluding days of his life, Philo writes, Moses "began to pass over from mortal existence to life immortal and gradually became conscious of the disuniting of the elements of which he was composed. The body, the shell-like growth which encased him, was being stripped away and the soul laid bare and yearning for its natural removal hence."[128]

Crucially, Philo credits this change to the *Logos*: "through the 'Word' of the Supreme Cause [Moses] is translated [cf. Deut. 34:5], even through that Word by which also the whole universe was formed ... for that same Word, by which He made the universe, is that by which He draws the perfect man from things earthly to Himself."[129] No less telling, Philo intimates that this process made Moses into what the *Logos* is: "monad" and "sun-like mind":

> Afterwards the time came when he had to make his pilgrimage from earth to heaven, and leave this mortal life for immortality, summoned thither by the Father who resolved his twofold nature of soul and body into a single monad, transforming his whole being into sun-like mind. Then, indeed, we find him possessed by the spirit, no longer uttering general truths to the whole nation but prophesying to each tribe in particular the things which were to be and hereafter must come to pass.... This was indeed wonderful: but most wonderful of all is the conclusion ... for when he was

already being exalted and stood at the very barrier, ready at the signal to direct his upward flight to heaven, the divine spirit fell upon him and he prophesied with discernment while still alive the story of his own death; told ere the end how the end came; told how he was buried with none present, surely by no mortal hands but by immortal powers.[130]

The characterization of Moses as like "sunlight" evokes Philo's characterization of the *Logos* himself as an entity who has "light" within and is "light," precisely as "*pneuma* hot and fiery": "For the model or pattern was the Word which contained all His fullness—light, in fact; for, as the lawgiver tells us, 'God said, "let light come into being"' (Gen. 1:3), whereas He Himself resembles none of the things which have come into being."[131]

Philo also clarifies that this transformation "divinized" Moses, so he became "truly divine."[132] Admittedly, Philo draws a hard line on the notion that Moses could achieve parity with or participate in the primal God (the Existent).[133] Nevertheless, Litwa argues:

> Philo could (and I argue did) present a form of deification that posed no threat to his primal God (the Existent). In fact, Philo presented a form of deification in which Moses did not even directly participate in the Existent at all.... Moses is deified by participating in the Logos, the Mind of God, and Philo's "second God." In his pre-mortem ascent to heaven, Moses's νοῦς—having temporarily left his body behind—was purified and deified by fuller participation in the Logos. At his death, Moses was permanently resolved into pure nous, the reality of the Logos, and made his enduring ascent to the divine realm. In this way, Moses assimilated to and identified with a divine being (the Logos) and became divine himself.[134]

For Philo, however, the deification of Moses has a necessary result; it culminates in his final retrieval from the world to unity with God. Since God is one, a person who has participated or shared in divine attributes and status must necessarily, inexorably, become one with God because God knows no separation. Thus, citing Exodus 7:1, Philo can say that God "appointed [Moses] as a god."[135] But he adds, "God is not susceptible of addition or diminution, being fully and unchangeably himself. And therefore we are told that no man knows [Moses's] grave [cf. Deut. 34:6]."[136] Rather than say "oneness means deification," Philo seems to understand the relationship in reverse: "deification means oneness." That is, deification impels one toward oneness with God; the draw of like to like, god to God, is irresistible. For Philo, then, their presence in the world is merely as a "loan to the earthly sphere."[137] It is a natural inevitability that those "whom God has advanced even higher" must "soar above species and genus alike," beyond all mortal flesh, "stationing them beside [God] himself."[138]

To the extent that humans are inexorably drawn to a station "beside God himself," they are also necessarily drawn into the realm or sphere associated with God. It makes sense, then, that Philo repeatedly conceptualizes Moses's translation in spatial terms, that is, as an "ascension" (*anabasis*) from the earth to God.[139] He also describes Moses's ascension as an "upward flight to heaven."[140] In another passage, Philo writes that "a holy soul is divinized by ascending not to the air or to the ether or to heaven (which is) higher than all but to (a region) above the heavens. And beyond the world there is no place but God."[141] For Philo, "oneness" with a God "beyond the world" entails at least some sort of spatial translation.

C. Rereading John

In Philo's discussions of the ascension of Moses, we see a constellation of ideas highly evocative of John's vision of human exaltation: the agency of the *Logos*, infusion of Spirit, rebirth as *pneuma*, deification, oneness, celestial access. This likeness confirms that John likely hails from the same intellectual clime behind the thought of Philo. More important, this likeness points to the web of connections and causations that probably underpin John's own concepts. By reading John in conversation with Philo, we can better interpret it within the Hellenistic-Jewish philosophical setting that seems to inform its thought.

Like Philo, John identifies the *Logos* as the rational principle by which all things are created. The *Logos* was "with God" "in the beginning," is god/divine, and contains the "fullness" of God (1:1, 16; cf. Col. 1:19, 2:9). The *Logos* also has "light" within (1:4) and is "light" (1:9, 9:5, 11:9–10, 12:46). As the prologue continues, however, it reveals that this *Logos* came into contact with humans at a distinct time—precisely by assuming flesh, a human body. In this way, the *Logos* was able to speak directly to humans and, in so doing, to condense and communicate itself—that is, the very *Logos*, mind, and intellect of God—to humans. In the Gospel, the words Jesus speaks are the nature of God made into intelligible, human speech; again, as Jesus says, "the words I have spoken, they are *pneuma*, and they are life" (6:63). Against the *Logos* Christology of the prologue, these are not mere metaphors. Instead, they communicate the premise that the speech of the incarnate *Logos* communicates the *Logos*, which is *pneuma* and contains "life" (1:4), to humans. As Jesus states in his prayer to the Father, "I have given them your word [*Logos*]" (17:14).

In later discourses, Jesus reveals the effect of these words. As humans receive the *Logos*, who, as god, is *pneuma* (John 4:24) and who speaks *pneuma* (6:63), they enter into affinity with that *pneuma* and are transformed into it; they become *pneuma*. And as they receive the *Logos* who has "light" in him and is "light," they receive "light in" themselves (cf. 11:10) and become "sons of light" (12:36). These words are no mere metaphor. Rather, in Hellenistic Jewish philosophy the "words spoken by God" are a substance with material properties of brilliance and radiance: "the sacred oracles intimate that the words of God are seen as light is seen; for we are told that 'all the people saw the Voice' (Ex. 20:18), not that they heard it; for what was happening was not an impact on air made by the organs of mouth and tongue, but virtue shining with intense brilliance, wholly resembling a fountain of reason . . . the voice or sound that was not that of verbs and nouns but of God, seen by the eye of the soul, he rightly represents as 'visible.'"[142] By receiving these words within them, humans acquire their substance and nature—a nature with brilliant and radiant properties. They have the "light" and "day" within them—a radiance observed not by the physical senses but by another form of perception (John 11:9–10, 12:35–26). This is the "glory" of the *Logos*, which humans now receive. This change is also, as in Philo, an immortalization. Through it, humans possess an immortal nature, granting them immunity from death.

Above all, however, this assimilation to the nature of the divine *Logos* is a deification. The text means exactly what it says: "those to whom the word [*Logos/logos*] of God came" are "gods" (10:35). But crucially, this deification entails, even necessitates another reality—namely, the "oneness" with God effected by the mutual indwelling: "I in them and you in me, that they may be perfect in one" (17:23). Like Philo, John acknowledges the unity and uniqueness of one God, even while recognizing the existence of other deified beings, other "gods." To accommodate this divine multiplicity, John leverages the same idea as Philo: "oneness."[143] For both writers, God draws all expressions of deity—all derivative, participatory "gods"—into himself because there is no expression of divinity other than, or outside, God. The *Logos* must be "with God" (1:1), "in" God (10:38, 14:10–11, 20), and "one" with God (17:21, 23). So too, those whom the *Logos* assimilates to itself and deifies are inexorably drawn into the Father and "made perfect in one" (17:23). Deification requires oneness, leads to oneness, and effects oneness.

Like Philo, John encodes some part of this in spatial terms. Since John identifies God with a particular realm—the realm "above" or "heaven"—it necessarily casts this process of becoming "one" with the Father as entailing some transposition to that realm. In other words, just as deification entails oneness, oneness entails *pneumatic* ascent and celestial access.[144] That part of human nature that is deified is drawn to the realm above.

For the Gospel, however, this spiritual ascent is not a removal from the world, at least at first. Those who believe have a double existence, above and below. In his climactic prayer, Jesus asks the Father, "I do not pray that you should take them out of this world," even as he asks the Father that they "may be with me where I am" (17:15, 24). In other passages, he imagines that humans will not merely "ascend" to heaven; they will "descend" from it as well (1:51), or better, they "will go in and out" (10:9). The celestial humans access the world above through *pneuma*, but they also move in the world in and as flesh. They live within and between two worlds, like Jesus, who was at once united to the Father (10:30, 14:10) but also removed from him while in the world (13:1); to borrow Philo's metaphor, they are on "loan to the earthly sphere." This double existence is also oriented toward the same ends as Jesus's own; it is necessary so that believers can fulfill their own mission in the world—a mission patterned after that of Jesus. As the Father sent the Son, so now are they sent into the world (17:18, 20:21) to perform "greater works" than the external signs Jesus performed (14:12). Now filled with *pneuma*, they will speak the words that are *pneuma* to others, effecting their *pneumatic* transformation as well. *Pneuma* begets *pneuma* begets *pneuma*.

But their time in this world is limited. Their bodies will inevitably die and decompose since they are intrinsically mortal. Again, in his dialogue with Nicodemus, Jesus casts flesh as a lower nature that does not enter the kingdom of God (3:3–6). But no matter; in a Gospel that posits that "God is *pneuma*" and that assigns personality to the *Logos*, personhood and intellect can be entirely mediated by the substance of *pneuma*. What remains of the individual deceased—the undying *pneuma*, the elevated, rational, deified intelligence—is living, active, personal, immortal, and eternal. Even on earth, then, these individuals have already "passed from death to life"; they already "have eternal life," and they "will not taste death." When they die, the exalted, celestial, deified humans will persist in the heavenly, *pneumatic* realms they also inhabit—one with the God who is *pneuma*.

Not surprisingly, then, John casts this final transition positively, as the full and final consolidation of human oneness with the Father, as it was for Jesus. As Jesus explains in a saying that prefigures his death but that he applies to his followers, it is the grain that falls to the earth and dies that "bears much fruit" (12:24; cf. vv. 25–26). For the Gospel, oneness with the Father will ultimately lead humans to lay down their lives in bodily death (12:26, 13:36–38). Every believer "hates his life in this world," and so orients toward life in a different realm (12:25).

IV. Conclusion

At the outset of this chapter, I asked, "Why was the Gospel of John written?" The answer, it would seem, is that the Gospel was written to press a distinctive theology: a vision of Jesus as the "Word," transforming, exalting, and deifying humans by the "words" he speaks. This is clear from the fact that the prologue—the interpretive key to the text—foregrounds precisely this vision, presenting Jesus as a divine being who gives others "power to become children of God" and be "born . . . of God" (1:12–13).[145] This is also clear from the fact that the author also weaves this theology across all the major dialogues and discourses in the text, embedding it in all of chapters 1, 3, 4, 5, 6, 7–8, 9, 10, 11, 12, 13–17, 18–19, 20. But it is perhaps most obvious from the fact that the author foregrounds this theology in the statement of purpose he incorporates into his text: "these [signs] are written that you may believe that Jesus is the Christ, the Son of God, and that believing you may have life in his name" (20:31). In these lines, the author affirms that he has written the Gospel to guide readers into a belief in Jesus's identity as the "Son of God" (a title which, in John, carries the weight of his vision of Jesus's celestial origins and divine status; e.g., 1:14, 10:30–36) and so that individuals "may have life in his Name" (i.e., that they might share the *pneumatic*, immortal existence Jesus offers throughout the text). The author, in short, casts his text as a vehicle for communicating his distinctive theology of exaltation and seeing its results in his readers.

As central as this message is to the Gospel, however, it presents an obvious problem to the historian. Although the Gospel of John attributes its complex and sophisticated theology to Jesus, this synthesis is unlikely to be Jesus's own. The Jesus depicted in Mark, Matthew, and Luke never expressly claims to be a preexistent being, let alone a divine one. He never claims that he will spiritually "dwell in" his followers, secretly "manifesting" himself to them. He does not teach that his followers can be "born of spirit" and become "spirit" now, endowed with "eternal life," so that death can no longer harm them; on the contrary, the Synoptics depict Jesus associating human transformation and eternal life with the future.[146] For that matter, no other gospel also depicts Jesus teaching his followers that they could ascend with him, in spirit and as spirit, to the celestial realm and "dwell" with the Father. And certainly the Synoptic Jesus never elaborates a complete notion of human deification and oneness with God in this life. If these were points of Jesus's teaching—let alone ones as central and persistent in his teachings as John implies—why are they absent in all earlier accounts of Jesus's life?

In the case of John, it seems more likely that the teachings Jesus proclaims are not his own but those of the text's real author—a literate, highly educated figure able to synthesize Hellenistic Jewish thought and the ideas of Paul. The views of the text fit better in a late first- or early second-century context. More striking still, Jesus's speech bears an uncanny likeness to the speech of the text's narrator. As Alan Culpepper writes, "when Jesus, the literary character, speaks, he speaks the language of the author and his narrator":[147]

Narrator:
He who has seen has testified ... His testimony is true. (19:35)
    Jesus:
    "There is another who testifies ... I know that his testimony to me is true." (5:32)
Narrator:
But these are written so that you may believe that Jesus is the Christ, the Son of God and that by believing you may have life. (20:31)
    Jesus:
    "For God so loved the world that he gave his only Son, that whoever believes in him should not perish but may have eternal life." (3:16)
Narrator:
And the Word became flesh and dwelled among us, and we have seen his glory. (1:14)
    Jesus:

> Jesus said to her, "Did I not tell you that if you believed, you would see the glory of God?" (11:40)

It would seem that the author has commandeered the voice of Jesus, making him the mouthpiece of an intricate system of ideas foreign to his historical teachings. We may not find the historical Jesus in John, then, but we will find something no less compelling: the thought of the text's hidden author—a mind that would profoundly influence the course of later Christian theology.

3
Symbols and Signs

The many speeches and sayings of Jesus in the Gospel of John are invented, the products of a later author who sought to retroject a sophisticated system of ideas—of spiritual birth, celestial access, immortality, and exaltation—onto the lips of Jesus. In earlier Jesus sources, Jesus does not teach his followers that he would spiritually "dwell in" them. He does not teach that believers can be "born of spirit," nor does he claim that in spirit, and as spirit, believers can spiritually "come" and "follow" him to the celestial realm now to "see" the Father and the Son. Nor does Jesus articulate complex visions of human exaltation rooted in Hellenistic-Jewish *Logos* speculations. These ideas and the many dialogues in which Jesus communicates them are the author's own.

The Gospel's inventions do not end with its discourse material, however. It is widely understood that there is no neat distinction, no hermetic seal between discourse and narrative in John. The Gospel blends the two strategically so that its narratives occasion, anticipate, and symbolize adjacent teachings of Jesus.[1] As Craig Koester observes, "the Johannine account of Jesus' ministry is structured around a series of symbolic actions" that stage, anticipate, and signify themes in the discourses that follow them.[2] "Although the [miraculous] signs have a privileged place," Koester writes, "several nonmiraculous actions also contribute" to the same pattern.[3] If the discourses of Jesus are artificial, then the narrative elements linked to them may also include invented elements.

In this chapter, I will shed the same critical light on those narratives as I did on the discourses of Jesus. When one understands the Gospel's vision of human exaltation in all its proportions, the centrality of symbolism in John becomes apparent, and with it, the artificial qualities of many of its narratives. Although the Gospel is undoubtedly rooted in traditional Jesus materials—especially but not exclusively Synoptic materials—nearly every story in the text has been modified, tailored, reshaped, or invented to support the principal points of the Gospel's theology. Together, these scenes bear the unmistakable fingerprints of the text's enigmatic author, laying bare his agenda, his techniques, and, above all, his remarkable creativity.

The Gospel of John. Hugo Méndez, Oxford University Press. © Oxford University Press 2025.
DOI: 10.1093/9780197686157.003.0003

I. Symbolism in John

The Gospels are literature, and as such, they utilize common literary devices found in other Greco-Roman works, including foreshadowing, symbolism, and irony. Mark, the earliest gospel, uses all three to great effect.[4] It makes sense, then, that as a reader of Mark, who composed a gospel in its image, the author of John knew and imitated some of Mark's literary techniques. And yet the author widened the use of one particular device, symbolism, well beyond his template. Whereas Mark uses symbolism occasionally, John uses it on a more dramatic scale.[5] In Sandra Schneiders's words, "symbolism in John is not an element in the Gospel but a dimension of the Gospel as a whole, namely, its characteristic revelatory mode."[6]

Even though many readers are aware of this symbolic program, however, not all appreciate how far that program extends—that is, how many of the Gospel's individual scenes are structured by symbolism and how deeply that device penetrates the details of each passage. The reason is that many readers, even scholarly readers, do not grasp John's startling vision of human exaltation—its vision of spiritual rebirth, spiritual indwelling, celestial access, and deification—in all its proportions. Only with all these themes in focus can one fully discern the more complex structures woven throughout the text. As I will demonstrate below, those structures are far more pervasive than those found in other narrative gospels with similar devices. Most of the text's narratives can be conceptualized as symbolic episodes—that is, scenes that refract and symbolize ideas disclosed in Jesus's speeches.[7]

As we saw in previous chapters, John communicates its themes through a rich but closed-set inventory of keywords and phrases, including "word," "depart," "follow," "live," "see," "dwell/abide." When we explore the narrative with a keen eye toward those key terms, something remarkable appears: we quickly see that the same expressions also appear in—even structure—nearly all of the episodes in John, miraculous and nonmiraculous. These episodes seem to anticipate, allude to, or evoke those themes.[8] This close connection between word and action makes sense. In several places, the text treats Jesus's gestures in the same way it treats its cryptic teachings: as elements to be understood and interpreted (e.g., 12:16, 13:7; cf. 2:21–22, 10:6). Evidently, John's Jesus does not only teach his vision of human exaltation by word, he also teaches by action and gesture.[9] In fact, the narrator himself draws attention to this symbolic layer in his conclusion, insisting that the "signs" contained in his book "are written so that you may believe that Jesus is the

Christ, the Son of God, and that by believing, you may have life in his name" (20:30–31). For the author, the narratives of the text exist to illustrate and advance the central propositions of his theology.

In what follows, I will explore the symbolic episodes found across John, surveying them in the order in which they appear.[10] As we will see, the ideas symbolized by these scenes do not unfold in a linear sequence. Instead, as C. H. Dodd observes, the Gospel's "movement is more like that of a musical fugue," with an individual theme and motif introduced at one time and then successively woven in and developed repeatedly through sequential sections.[11] Some are discernible at a first reading, but others can be appreciated only upon a careful rereading of the Gospel.[12] Together, these structures reveal a sustained plan or design for the entire work. They also suggest that the author designed the Gospel to be an object of careful rereading, extended reflection, and decipherment.[13]

II. Chapters 1–4

The author of John planned a text that was recognizably a work of the same type as Mark, not least to compete with Mark and its derivate texts. Mark begins his narrative by depicting Jesus encountering John the Baptist (1:9–11), calling his first disciples (1:16–20), and beginning a public ministry—a ministry punctuated by so many miracles, teachings, and conflict episodes (1:21–10:52). John opens with cognates to all these events but layers each with symbolic meanings. Together, these scenes focus the reader on several critical themes of the text, especially the ideas of spiritual rebirth and celestial access.

A. 1:19–51: Images of Following and Dwelling with Jesus

The first chapter of John is often a blind spot for studies of its symbolism. Scholars recognize that the Gospel's opening materials serve as a stage for its broader narrative, but they fail to realize that the chapter also sets the Gospel's literary techniques, especially its symbolism, into motion. In fact, the author of John was very intentional about how he structured this section of his account, crafting a narrative that anticipates the most essential ideas of the Farewell Discourse. That narrative reveals that when humans accept the "witness" of those who have seen Jesus, they will "come" and "follow" Jesus to the (celestial) place where he dwells, to "see" him and "dwell" with him there.

As the episode begins, John the Baptist demonstrates the role of a witness. He confesses that he did not know who Jesus was, but that God revealed to him that the one "on whom you see the Spirit descend and dwell" is the one who "baptizes with the Holy Spirit" (1:31–33), that is, the one who helps others receive the Spirit and be "born of spirit." John then testifies of Jesus, "I saw the Spirit descend as a dove from heaven, and it dwelled on him" (1:32), a term evoking the entire system of mutual indwelling developed later in the text (cf. 14:17).

The next scene of the Gospel—the first to involve Jesus—is the first symbolic episode in the Gospel. It is, in effect, a living parable of the central image of the Gospel's Farewell Discourse, illustrating the idea that certain humans will "follow" Jesus to the celestial place where he "dwells" and "dwell" with him there. At the outset of the scene, John the Baptist testifies to Jesus in the presence of two of his disciples. The two men illustrate the ideal response to such testimony: upon "hearing" this message, they "follow" Jesus (1:37). The men ask him, "where are you dwelling [*pou meneis*]?" (1:38), a paradigmatic question, evoking the disciples' later inquiries in the Farewell Discourse as to where Jesus is ultimately going and how they will be able to dwell with him there (13:36, 14:5, 8, 22). In response, Jesus says, "come and see" (1:39), anticipating his later teaching that those who believe will spiritually "come" to him in the Father's House (14:6) and "see" him there (14:19).[14] According to the text, on "that day," at a particular "hour," the men "came" and "saw where he dwells" and "they dwelled/remained" with Jesus (1:39), a line foreshadowing the "day" (14:20, 16:23, 26) and "hour" (5:25) on which certain humans will "follow" Jesus to the celestial realm where he "dwells" and where they will "dwell" with him (13:36, 14:23).

The following scenes extend and enrich the symbolism of "following" Jesus, layering on additional emphases. Andrew, one of the two men "dwelling" with Jesus, goes back out and testifies to his brother Peter that he has "found" Jesus (1:41), a term associated elsewhere with the idea of celestial access to Jesus (cf. 7:34; cf. 14:19). Peter responds to his word and also comes to Jesus (1:42). In this way, the episode represents the idea that those who "follow" Jesus and "dwell" with him are also "sent" out to invite others to the same experience as well (17:20, 20:21). Afterward, Jesus goes to Galilee. There, he encounters a man named Philip and summons him with the words "follow me" (1:43). Philip immediately obeys, illustrating the principle that Jesus's own will "follow" him to celestial realms because they "know" him and recognize his "voice" (cf. 10:3-5, 14-16). Philip then becomes a witness to Jesus himself, testifying to his brother Nathanael that he has "found" the one foretold in earlier scriptures and inviting him to "come and see" (1:46). Nathanael responds to this invitation.

In the next lines, Jesus demonstrates his supernatural power for the first time. When Nathanael approaches him, Jesus reveals his knowledge of Nathanael's character as a "true Israelite" and his earlier location (1:47-48), illustrating the idea that Jesus "knows" those who will "follow" him (10:27).[15] Nathanael is stunned by Jesus's abilities.[16] His response occasions Jesus's first teaching of the Gospel: a single cryptic saying that provides an interpretive key for the preceding scenes; it reveals what those who "follow" Jesus will, at last, climactically, "see." Jesus tells Nathanael that he will "see greater things"—greater demonstrations of Jesus's power—than he has just seen (1:50). Specifically, he "will see heaven opened, and the angels of God ascending and descending upon the Son of Man" (1:51). As we discussed in the previous chapter, the image encapsulates the idea of human exaltation laced throughout the Gospel; those who believe in Jesus will assume the celestial nature of angelic beings and they will have the ability to spiritually "go in and out" of the heavenly realm (cf. 10:9).[17]

B. 2:1-11: Water into Wine, Flesh into Spirit

The second chapter of John depicts "the beginning of [Jesus's] signs," that is, his miracles (2:11).[18] Like so many other chapters in the Gospel, it is articulated around water imagery. As that episode begins, Jesus and his disciples arrive in Cana "on the third day" (2:1) for a wedding. During the wedding, his mother tells him, "they have no wine" (2:3), as if urging him to supply some. At first, Jesus rebuffs his mother's request, cryptically saying, "my hour has not yet come" (2:4). After an initial delay, however, Jesus does precisely what he seems to rule out, albeit in a secret manner: completing a Misdirection-Delay-Secret Action pattern found in other episodes in the Gospel.[19] Jesus instructs others to fill six large jars with water, and he transforms the water into wine (2:6-9). According to the story, when "the steward of the feast" "tasted the water now become wine," he "did not know where it came from" (2:9).

As noted in the previous chapter, the scene illustrates the secret transformation—the rebirth as spirit—Jesus effects in humans through his resurrection and ascension "on the third day" (cf. 2:19; cf. 20:1–2, 17, 22). The narrator's comment that the steward "did not know where it came from" anticipates Jesus's words to Nicodemus: "the spirit blows ... but you do not know where it comes from and where it goes; so it is with everyone who is born of spirit" (3:8).[20] Those born of spirit are the water become wine. They are reborn "of spirit" and become "spirit," but imperceptibly—in this world, in such a way that the world cannot detect their (new) celestial origin or the eternal life they now possess. It is no coincidence, then, that the transformation occurs when "water" is poured into the empty jars, filling them "to the brim" (2:7). The narrator elsewhere glosses "water" as a symbol of the Spirit "welling up to eternal life" (4:14; cf. 7:38–39).[21] In turn, the Misdirection-Delay-Secret Action pattern maps onto Jesus's teaching in the Farewell Discourse that he will obscure his movements from the world so that they will not know where he is (7:34; 8:14), but that, after a "little while," he will secretly come to the disciples alone, in a manner "the world will not see" (14:19; 16:16–24).[22]

Other features of the narrative support this symbolic interpretation. When Jesus's mother invites him to provide wine, Jesus seems to read her reference to "wine" on a different plane of meaning—as a cipher for some spiritual reality—and he responds on that plane, saying, "my hour has not yet come" (2:4). In so doing, he hints that he intends to provide the spiritual benefit symbolized by the earthly sign at "his hour ... to depart from this world to the Father" (13:1). The wine, in short, condenses a transformation fixed at the departure.

Interestingly, after tasting the wine, the steward assumes that the wine has come from the "bridegroom" of the wedding, and he expresses his surprise that the bridegroom has "kept the good wine until now" (2:10). This mention of the "bridegroom" anticipates John the Baptist's identification of Jesus as the "bridegroom" in the next chapter (3:29). Likewise, the word "now" anticipates the climactic hour of Jesus, when he departs to the Father and imparts the Spirit, signaled in several texts by the adverb "now" (*nyn*; 12:27, 31, 13:31, 16:5, 17:5).[23] By thanking the earthly bridegroom for providing wine, the steward symbolizes "the true giver of the wine might also be the true bridegroom."[24] The scene ends quite appropriately with an image that draws together the ultimate result of this transformation: Jesus "dwelling" with his family and disciples (2:12).

C. 2:13-25: Raising the Father's House

The next episode in the Gospel takes up new themes, this time centering the image of the "Father's house" from the Farewell Discourse. As the scene begins, Jesus makes his first of several festal pilgrimages to Jerusalem (2:13).[25] When he arrives at the temple, he drives out those who are selling there, charging them with defiling his "Father's house" (2:14-16). A group of "Jews" confront him over this act, demanding a "sign" to demonstrate that he has the authority to do such a thing (2:18). Jesus responds, "Destroy this temple, and in three days, I will raise it up" (2:19).[26]

The narrator clarifies for the reader that Jesus's words should be interpreted symbolically: "he spoke of the temple of his body" (2:21). In so doing, he hints that the entire scene is a vivid image of the spiritual realities taking shape around Jesus's (post-resurrection, glorified, *pneumatic*) body—the true "Father's house" (14:2), or spiritual temple, in which the Father dwells (14:10, 20).[27] Jesus's claim that he will "raise" this "temple" "in three days" is consistent with the Farewell Discourse's teaching that the resurrection and ascension are necessary for the disciples to obtain dwellings in the "Father's house" (2:19; cf. 12:24, 14:2-3, 16:7).[28] The central image of the temple scene—Jesus chasing out and "taking away" (*airō*) whatever does not belong in the "Father's house" (2:16)—dramatizes another idea in the Farewell Discourse. According to Jesus, the Father "takes away" (*airō*) those who do not "dwell" in him (15:2, 6).[29]

D. 3:1-4:42: Images of the Spirit

The next sections of John consist mostly of discourse or dialogue, but scenes tucked between them also symbolize realities about the new *pneumatic* life.[30] In chapter 3, Jesus speaks to a Jewish leader named Nicodemus, revealing that humans will be able to be "born of water and spirit." This is the higher-order baptism of the Spirit (cf. 1:33), which imparts spirit and transforms humans into spirit (3:3-6). The next scene visualizes this idea. Jesus retreats from Jerusalem to the Judean countryside, to a place with "much water," where people "were coming and were being baptized" (3:22-23). At the end of the chapter, John the Baptist reveals the symbolic import of the episode, explaining that shortly, and "not by measure," Jesus will give "the Spirit" to humans (3:34).

In the next episode, Jesus travels to a site near the ruins of the Samaritan temple (4:5, 20), paralleling his various visits to the Jerusalem Temple (2:14, 5:14, 7:14, 10:23, 11:56, 18:20).[31] When the disciples leave Jesus to buy food, he approaches a woman at a well and offers her "living water" (4:10)—a cipher for the Spirit.[32] The woman embodies those who invite others to receive this "eternal life" (4:36-38). At the end of the scene, she goes out and invites a group of Samaritans to "come" and "see" Jesus (4:29). The Samaritans "believe because of his word" and invite Jesus to "remain/dwell" (*menō*) with them (4:40-41), the same verb for "dwell" in the Farewell Discourse (cf. 15:4).

E. Historical Issues

Symbolism is a central feature of these scenes. But the above episodes also contain a second important element, namely, details that contradict earlier Jesus traditions, dubious details, and anachronisms. It is the combination of these features—the presence of both symbolism and dubious historical details—that suggests the episodes surveyed above are or contain inventions. Evidently, the author felt free to significantly modify, tailor, reshape, or outright invent to suit his ideological aims.

Consider, for example, the first scenes of the text, in which Jesus gathers disciples to himself. Those scenes disagree with the Synoptics in many details. In Matthew, Mark, and Luke, Jesus first encounters Andrew in their native region of Galilee and invites him and Peter to "follow me" as the two are fishing (e.g., Mark 1:16-18; Matt. 4:18-20). The Synoptics never suggest, as John does, that Jesus met Andrew at the Jordan River. Nor do the Synoptic accounts suit a scenario in which Jesus had already invited Andrew to "follow him" at that first encounter. (Did he cease to follow him later?) For that matter, the Synoptics present Jesus calling Peter directly and not through the testimony of his brother. Likewise, Mark locates the house of Andrew and Peter in Capernaum (Mark 1:21, 29), but John claims their home was in Bethsaida (1:44).

Another issue—an idealized and patently artificial element of the scene—is the level of knowledge the disciples display throughout the scene. In the Synoptics, none of the disciples recognizes Jesus as either "Messiah" or "Son of God" until well into their ministry with Jesus in Galilee, Simon (i.e., Peter) being the first disciple to do so (Mark 8:27-29; Matt. 16:13-16).[33] In John, by contrast, Andrew draws Peter with the insistence that Jesus is the "Messiah" (1:41; cf. v. 49), and Nathanael instantly recognizes Jesus as the "Son of God" (1:49).[34] Similarly, John the Baptist displays full knowledge of Jesus's preexistence (1:15, 30). Finally, we cannot ignore the fact that the end product is entirely structured around key Johannine linguistic words: "hour," "come," "see," "follow," and "dwell."

Taken together, these contradictions suggest that the author of John outright invented an alternative account of how Jesus met his disciples, suited to symbolize his distinctive views. That author might have taken his inspiration from Mark's accounts of Jesus calling the disciples with the words "follow me" (Mark 1:16-20)—words John invests with new meanings in later discourses. Working from that starting point, the author of John constructed a new narrative of that call that centers John the Baptist as a witness, one laced with other key Johannine images, terms, and themes.

The materials united in chapters 2-4 present their own historical problems. The origins of the first episode in this section, the Wedding of Cana, are unclear. No such material appears in earlier gospels. The episode could be a story taken over from an earlier oral or written source about Jesus.[35] But it could also be a wholesale invention of the author. As we have seen, the dialogue and narrative framing of the episode are shot through with Johannine elements—among them, mention of the "hour," water imagery, the tantalizing comment that the steward tasting the wine "did not know where it came from," a motif of Misdirection-Delay-Secret Action, and mention of the bridegroom. When one removes these elements, there is hardly a kernel of the episode left to recover.

By contrast, the account of the Cleansing of the Temple is almost certainly modeled on Synoptic materials. Each of the Synoptics also depicts Jesus cleansing the Temple around the time of Passover (Mark 11:15-19; Matt. 21:12-17; Luke 19:45-48). John, however, alters this chronology of the episode, moving the scene closer to the beginning of his Gospel. The move may serve an interpretive purpose. As Mary Coloe observes, the passage "provides the reader with ... an explicit hermeneutical key for interpreting the Johannine Jesus as the new 'Temple'" and, by extension, a "critical key for understanding the rest of the narrative."[36] The move may also undermine Synoptic chronology to establish the superiority of John's account.

John also weaves a separate element into this narrative. In Mark's Passion Narrative, "false witnesses" charge Jesus with the provocative claim that he would destroy the temple and, more bizarre, that he would "construct another, not made with hands" (Mark 14:58; cf. Matt. 26:61). Likewise, in Mark's depiction of the crucifixion, "scoffers" mock Jesus for saying he would "destroy the temple and construct it in three days" (Mark 15:29; cf. Matt. 27:40). The mention of "three days" hints that Jesus's opponents are crassly misinterpreting some prediction of Jesus's crucifixion and resurrection, but neither Mark nor the other Synoptics relates a saying of Jesus open to this sort of (mis)interpretation. John, in effect, supplies that missing saying, placing a cryptic saying on Jesus's lips in the Temple cleansing in which he threatens, "Destroy this temple, and in three days I will raise it up" (2:19).[37]

The dialogues and scenes of chapter 3 are suffused with Johannine language. When one removes those lines, there is hardly anything like an independent story to salvage. The same is true of the dialogues in chapter 4. For that matter, the idea that Jesus engaged in ministry and made "many" converts in the Samaritan heartland (4:41), though not implausible, is difficult to reconcile with the Synoptics. In Matthew, Jesus expressly instructs his disciples to "enter no town of the Samaritans" (10:5) and implies that this was his own pattern of ministry (15:24).[38] The same idea also stands in some tension with Luke, which relates that Jesus was not permitted to enter a Samaritan village when he requested such passage on his way to Jerusalem (9:52–53).[39] Even still, these scenes might have provided the author of John with sufficient ground for inventing a trip Jesus took to the region, ostensibly an unrecorded moment from Jesus's life. In turn, the image of Samaritans coming to believe in Jesus may draw inspiration from positive portrayals of Samaritans in Luke (10:25–37, 17:11–19) and Acts (8:4–25). Here again, the author's creativity is at play.

III. Chapters 4 (Continued) through 6

The next several chapters describe further miraculous deeds of Jesus—further "signs"—that symbolize humans receiving "life" through Jesus. Most of these miracles immediately precede extended dialogues between Jesus and crowds of "Jews" intended to draw out key themes from the miracles (5:16–47, 6:25–71).

A. 4:46–5:47: The Word Saves Humans from Death

Perhaps the most obvious examples of symbolic narrative in the Gospel of John are a pair of healings in chapters 4 and 5. In the first episode—a scene expressly marked as one of the "signs" of Jesus in the text (4:54)—Jesus comes to Capernaum. There, a local official stops him, begging him, "come down and heal my son, for he is at the point of death" (4:46–47). For a moment, as Marianne Meye Thompson observes, Jesus "appears to rebuff or ignore the request" (4:48), prompting the official to plead further (4:49); only after this second request does Jesus intervene, but in a delayed and unseen manner, mirroring how Jesus responds in the Wedding of Cana episode.[40] Specifically, Jesus heals the man's son with the mere directive, "Go, your son will live" (4:50). According to the text, the man "believed the word" (4:50). The miracle occurs even though the man does not see it. Later, however, the father learns that at the very "hour" Jesus uttered the "word," "his son was living" (4:51–53). In the next story, Jesus travels down to Jerusalem. On the Sabbath, he comes to the pool by the "Sheep Gate"—another water setting—and he finds a man lying on the ground, paralyzed from birth (5:1–5). In the following verses, Jesus heals the man by his word, commanding him to "rise, take up your mat, and walk" (5:8). The man rises and walks—an image evocative of the dead rising from their tombs.

The meaning of these episodes is unlocked in Jesus's very next discourse, which picks up vocabulary from these scenes (5:16–47). In that discourse, Jesus claims that he is about to do "greater works" than the ones he just performed. Specifically, he will send out his "word" at a coming "hour," granting "eternal life" to all who "believe":[41] "For as the Father raises the dead and gives them life, so also the Son gives life to whom he will. . . . Amen, amen, I say to you, the one who hears my word and believes him who sent me has eternal life; that one does not come into judgment but has passed from death to life. Amen, amen, I say to you, the hour is coming, and now is when the dead will hear the voice of the Son of God, and those who hear will live" (5:21, 24–25). In these verses, "the dead" are not the physically deceased since corpses are not in a position to "believe." Instead, "the dead" here are the spiritually dead, that is, who have no spiritual life in them (6:53). As Jesus tells the crowds in the same discourse—now in the "dwelling" vocabulary of the Farewell Discourse—"you do not have his word/*Logos* dwelling in you," and "you refuse to come to me to have life" (5:38, 40). According to Jesus, however, an "hour is coming" when some will hear the "word" and the "voice of the Son of God," and they will receive eternal life through that word—a central teaching of the Gospel (3:15, 6:47). That change will occur, as hinted in the story of the official's son, in an unseen manner.

In the genius of the Gospel, then, the two healings that precede this discourse anticipate and dramatize its essential themes. In them, Jesus acts on the physical/temporal plane to illustrate the "greater works" he accomplishes on the spiritual/eternal plane. That is, the episodes demonstrate his supernatural power *a minore ad maius*. In this way, they also reveal his glory (2:11), that is, his divine power and prerogatives as the preexistent Son of God, who possesses and gives "life."

B. 6:1–14: Bread of Life, Words of Life

The next miracle, the feeding of the five thousand, is a true cognate of a miracle story in the Synoptics (6:1–15; cf. Mark 6:31–44; Matt. 14:13–21; Luke 9:12–17). As the episode begins, Jesus and his disciples travel "to the other side of the Sea of Galilee," arriving at a remote, hilly location. There, Jesus sees a crowd of people coming to him who need food (6:1–5). In the following verses, Jesus provides food for the multitude, miraculously multiplying a few loaves and two fish provided by a small boy so that everyone eats their fill (6:8–11). At the end, Jesus instructs his disciples to "gather up the fragments left over, so that nothing may be lost/perish," and they gather twelve baskets full of leftovers (6:12–13).

In later dialogues, Jesus spotlights the symbolic nature of his action (6:25–71). When the same crowds seek Jesus on another day, he reprimands them for seeking physical food—the earthly sign—rather than the spiritual reality it signifies: "do not labor for the food which perishes, but for the food which endures to eternal life" (6:27). Instead, he urges them to consume "the bread of God ... which comes down from heaven and gives life to the world" (6:33). Jesus's language in the passage is cryptic, but he unlocks its meaning at the end; the bread that "gives life" is a cipher for the words of Jesus, which are "spirit and life" (6:63). Through those words, one receives the spiritual indwelling of Jesus within themselves: "the one who eats ... dwells in me, and I in that one" (6:56). (Ingestion is an apt metaphor for receiving Jesus within oneself.)[42] What Jesus speaks of, in short, is the mode of union he effects through his departure—his spiritual presence—as he clarifies to his disciples at the end of the dialogue: "Does this offend you? Then what if you were to see the Son of Man ascending to where he was before? It is the spirit that gives life; the flesh is useless" (6:61–62).

The image of Jesus's disciples "gathering" up the uneaten food so that "nothing may be lost/perish [*apolētai*]" (6:12) is also laden with meaning. It anticipates another thread in the discourse that follows it: Jesus's repeated claim that he will "lose [*apolesō*] nothing" of what the Father has given him

(6:39), an expression that refers to immunity from death in other passages: "I give them eternal life, and they will never be lost/perish [*apolōntai*]. No one will snatch them out of my hand" (10:28; cf. 10:10, 12:25). Likewise, the fact that Jesus invited the disciples to "gather" the uneaten food underscores the participation of the disciples in drawing others to this immortality; Jesus's words echo his earlier command that his disciples "gather fruit for eternal life" (4:36).[43]

C. 6:15–21: Walking on the Sea as Celestial Access

Embedded in the chapter is a second miracle—yet another water-oriented miracle—also attested in the Synoptics in conjunction with the feeding of the five thousand (Mark 6:45–52; Matt. 14:22–33). After Jesus feeds the crowds, he permits his disciples to cross the Sea of Galilee on the only available boat while he withdrew to a nearby mountain (John 6:15–17). The crowds, seeing Jesus retreat to the mountain, might have assumed that he would remain behind (6:22). Jesus does remain behind, but only for a brief period. When night falls, he does precisely the opposite of what the crowds expect. He miraculously traverses the sea, but secretly, under cover of night, completing the Misdirection–Delay–Secret Action pattern (6:19–21).

As the scene continues, Jesus encounters his disciples at sea, fighting hopelessly against a sudden storm. In this moment of turmoil, they suddenly spot "Jesus walking on the sea" and "coming" to them (6:19; cf. v. 17). When Jesus reveals his identity, however, they bring him into the boat (6:20–21). This action produces another miracle, a unique twist to the story, appearing only in John. "Immediately" upon receiving Jesus into the boat, the text concludes, "the boat was at the land to which they were going" (6:21).

The episode symbolizes Jesus's departure and the celestial access he secretly gives some humans. As in other instances, the Misdirection–Delay–Secret Action pattern illustrates Jesus's teaching in the Farewell Discourse that he will obscure his movements from the world so that the people will not know where he is, but that, after a "little while," he will then secretly come to the disciples alone, in a manner "the world will not see" (16:16–24). And indeed, the image of Jesus saving the disciples at sea as he "comes" to them on water and as they take him "into the boat" (6:17, 19) evokes the idea of Jesus saving humans as he "comes" to them upon the living water of the Spirit, and as they "receive" him and his indwelling presence (1:12,

7:37–39, 13:20, 14:17). The only element of the story unique to John—the detail that Jesus's "coming" to the disciples caused the disciples to "immediately" reach the place "to which they were going"—represents another theme from the Farewell Discourse: the idea that when the human person receives Jesus's indwelling presence, they immediately arrive at the destination where Jesus is "going" and where they are "going"; that is, they arrive at the "Father's house" (14:2–3).[44]

D. Historical Issues

The first of these healings is strikingly similar to, and almost certainly an adaptation of, an episode in Matthew and Luke in which Jesus, again in Capernaum, heals a Roman centurion's slave by his "word" alone (Matt. 8:5–13; Luke 7:1–10). The story would have been an attractive one for the author to utilize since, in its Synoptic form, it foregrounds Jesus's power to save a person from "death" (Luke 7:2) by his "word" (Matt. 8:9–10; Luke 7:7–8). The choice to rewrite the story—transforming the "centurion's enslaved person" into the "official's son"—makes sense as a way to give the author greater creative control. The episode in John is just different enough that a reader could interpret it as a distinct episode in the life of Jesus—as indeed most Christians have—freeing the author to deploy or utilize only those elements that suited his purpose. In Matthew and Luke, the healing of the Roman centurion's slave is an episode demonstrating Jesus's embrace of even non-Jews (Matt. 8:10; Luke 7:9). Removing the non-Jewish "centurion" allowed the author of John to orient the story away from this concern. He could also infuse the story with elements that better suited his purpose.[45] The result is "a very Johannine story through and through," suited to a "completely new emphasis."[46]

The second healing also has strong similarities to an episode in the Synoptics, in which Jesus heals a paralyzed man with a very similar formula: "Rise, take up your mat and go home" (Mark 2:1–12; cf. Matt. 9:1–8; Luke 5:17–26). And yet the setting and circumstances of the Synoptic and Johannine stories are different. In the Synoptics, Jesus encounters the man in the Galilean town of Capernaum (Mark 2:1; Matt. 9:1). In John the story occurs at a pool in the Judean city of Jerusalem (5:1–3). The timing of the stories is also different; the Synoptic tale does not take place on the Sabbath. Some unusual features of John's story strengthen the suspicion that the author took the Cana miracle as his inspiration. It may not be a coincidence that, after the story ends—a story set in Jerusalem—the narrator puzzlingly indicates that Jesus "went to the other side of the Sea of Galilee" (6:1; cf. vv. 17, 25, 59). Scholars have long recognized this as an error, an aporia, in the Gospel. (Jerusalem is nowhere near the Sea of Galilee.) That error makes sense if we imagine the author adopted a story originally set in Capernaum. The preceding scene, the healing of the official's son, is set in Galilee, and its action concludes in Capernaum (4:46, 51). The author might well have introduced the healing of the paralyzed man here, originally in a form that set the scene in Capernaum. At a later point, however, the author changed the setting to Jerusalem, forgetting to alter the Capernaum-oriented geographical indications of 6:1.[47] In short, the aporia may reveal the compositional history of the passage.

The new elements of the story served the author's purposes well. By setting the scene on the Sabbath, the author provides a plausible occasion for the heated dialogue that follows, mirroring similar Synoptic episodes (e.g., Mark 2:23–3:6). The Sabbath setting also sets up the theme of Jesus performing "greater works" (John 5:20–21). The choice to place the scene at "the Sheep Gate [*probatikos*]" in Jerusalem (5:2) also invests the passage with symbolism.[48] In a later chapter, Jesus expressly depicts himself as a "door/gate" for "sheep [*probatōn*]": "I am the door; if anyone enters by me, he will be saved and will go in and out" (10:1–2, 7, 9). He also describes himself as "the shepherd" who leads his sheep through a "door" or gate into "eternal life" (10:3–4, 11, 27–28). As we will see, this image anticipates the ideas of celestial access made concrete in the Farewell Discourse. Last, the setting of a pool continues the author's pattern of situating events around water or incorporating water imagery—the primary symbol of the Spirit in the text.

Although the episode is set in a real location, it is not without its historical difficulties. As Jodi Magness points out, one detail of the story seems to be anachronistic:

> After 70, the Sheep's Pool was the site of a healing sanctuary dedicated to Serapis (usually described in scholarly literature as an Asclepeion). Ancient sources describe Asclepius and Serapis as healing patients through a combination of bathing in water and dreaming during incubation. John's description of the Sheep's Pool—surrounded by invalids lying on mats—sounds

more like the incubator of an Asclepeion than pools used for ritual purification as prescribed by biblical law.... John's story better fits a post-70 than pre-70 reality in Jerusalem, and a scene of invalids sleeping on mats by a pool hoping for a miraculous healing would have made more sense to a Gentile than a Jewish audience.[49]

The final two stories—the feeding of the five thousand and the walking on water—present their own difficulties. Since the author of John changes no essential details of these stories, it seems he expected his readers to encounter them as true cognates of the episodes found in those texts (for example, he keeps the boy with the five loaves and two fish, the headcount of the crowds that eat the food, and the link between the two stories in Mark and Matthew). This hypothesis is confirmed by the fact that, before describing the second miracle, the narrator notes, "it was now dark, and Jesus had not yet come to them," as if his readers know the Synoptic story and are anticipating that Jesus will "come" to his disciples by walking on the water (6:17).

Even though the narrator preserves much from these accounts, however, he alters the stories in ways that support his aims. For one, he introduces a finer level of detail into the feeding of the five thousand so that actions credited to "the disciples" in general in the Synoptics are now credited to specific, named characters: Philip, Andrew, and Peter. This suits a broader pattern in the Gospel of introducing specific details to make it seem like an eyewitness account. Second, the author introduces a final twist in the walking-on-water account—effectively, another embedded miracle. Whereas the Synoptics presume that the boat continued to the other shore normally (Mark 6:53; Matt. 14:34), John has the boat "immediately" arrive at the other shore.[50] The move, as we saw, supports the author's distinct theology.

IV. Chapters 7–10

The next few chapters can be understood as a continuous, multipart episode. All the chapters occur in Jerusalem, as if in one single visit to the city. Still, it makes sense to explore each of these scenes separately since new images emerge in each section.

A. 7:1–8:59: Dramatizing the Departure and Hiddenness of Jesus

The opening narrative of this section portrays a confrontation between Jesus and his brothers and a secret journey to Jerusalem. It is easy to miss the symbolism penetrating this episode, and indeed, most commentators cast 7:1–13 as mere "transitional material."[51] To appreciate that symbolism, one must understand the central idea of the dialogue that follows it. There, Jesus reveals for the first time that he must depart from this world to a place where the world will no longer see him: "I go to him who sent me; you will seek me and you will not find me" (7:33–34; cf. 8:14, 21). The opening episode encodes the twin ideas of Jesus's departure and hiddenness from the world.

As the story begins, Jesus's brothers pressure him to "depart" and "go up" to a major feast in Jerusalem, precisely so he can more openly "show" himself "to the world" (7:3–5). The verbs "depart" (*metabainō*) and "go up" (*hypagō*) are used for Jesus's departure from this world elsewhere in the Gospel (13:1–3).[52] Likewise, the insistence of Jesus's brothers that he "show" himself "to the world" (7:4) anticipates, even parodies the Gospel's later claim that, after his departure, Jesus will no longer "show" himself "to the world" (14:22; cf. 14:19). In effect, Jesus's brothers set up an inverted symbol or foil for Jesus's final departure. They pressure him to make an alternative departure to a place where the world can openly see him. But in fact, Jesus is destined to depart to a realm where he will be hidden from the world.

Jesus's subsequent actions in the story dramatize how his actual departure will unfold. After rebuffing his brothers, telling them he will not go to the feast (misdirection), Jesus remains in Galilee (delay) (7:8–9). A little while later, however, he does "go up" to Jerusalem, albeit in a secret manner (secret action), evoking the mode of his future departure and concealment from the world: "after his brethren had gone up to the feast, then he also went up, not publicly but in private" (7:10).[53] He goes in such a way that his unbelieving brothers and the unbelieving world do not know his whereabouts and cannot find him: "the Jews were looking for him at the feast and saying, 'Where is he?'" (7:11). The inability of the Jews to find Jesus foreshadows his later, repeated teaching in the same discourse that the "world" will not know where he is and will not be able to find him once he departs:[54]

> You will seek me, and you will not find me; where I am, you cannot come. (7:34)

> You will seek me and die in your sin; where I am going, you cannot come. (8:21)
>
> You do not know ... where I am going. (8:14)

The image of Jesus moving undetected among the crowds dramatizes the idea that, after a brief delay, he will be present in the world in a secret manner: "in a little while, and you will no longer see me, and again a little while, and you will see me" (16:16; cf. 14:19).

This episode serves a second function: it also reveals why Jesus must at last depart from the world and assume only a secret presence within it. Jesus must depart because the world will never tolerate his public, visible presence; it hates him and will inevitably seek to kill him. Early in the narrative, Jesus explains to his brothers that the world "hates me because I testify of it that its works are evil" (7:7). The next scenes confirm that Jesus is right. Whenever he decides to make his presence visible (7:14), he is met with resistance, even violence. His opponents try to arrest him (7:30, 32; cf. v. 44), and at the climax of the scene, a crowd of Jews take up stones to kill him (8:59). It is only fitting, then, that, as the episode concludes, "Jesus hid himself and went out" (8:59). Having demonstrated why Jesus must depart and hide from the world, the narrative ends with another symbolic image of that departure.

B. 9:1–41: Seeing the Light of Life

The next section of the narrative extends the action of the preceding one. After Jesus escapes from the temple area, he passes by a man who was blind from birth (9:1). After proclaiming himself "the light of the world" (9:5), Jesus heals the man of his blindness in yet another water miracle. He smears mud on the man's eyes and instructs him to "wash in the pool of Siloam, which means 'Sent'" (9:7). The man recovers his sight—and by extension, his access to "light"—in the water.

This episode is also unambiguously symbolic, as Jesus's closing words in the chapter demonstrate: "I came into this world for judgment, that those who do not see may see, and that those who see may become blind" (9:39). Like so many others, this scene symbolizes the reception of the gift of eternal life. The man born blind represents those who "believe" and who are transformed by the Spirit, the "living water" (4:10, 7:37–39) "sent" to humans (14:26), an idea condensed in the pool called "Sent."[55] They receive the ability to "see"—that is, to see God. They also receive "light," an image the Gospel directly links to "life":

In him was life, and the life was the light of humans. (1:4)

The one who follows me ... will have the light of life. (8:12)

Such humans are deified. After acquiring this sight/light, the man presents himself to others, insisting that he is the same person who was formerly blind. Critically, he does so with the words "I am" (*egō eimi*). The statement "I am" is otherwise used only by Jesus as a double entendre, marking him as divine. (God uses the same phrase in biblical texts.)[56] By using the same expression, the man betrays his likeness to the divine Jesus. He is assimilated and exalted to the nature of the one who can say "I am." In short, we can read the scene as a "deification narrative"—a symbol of how humans attain to divinity.[57]

Later twists in the episode enrich this symbolism. After the miracle, Jesus's opponents search for him, asking, "where is he?" (9:12), and they interrogate the formerly blind man and his parents repeatedly. At the end of the story, however, Jesus comes to the man and reveals his presence and identity to him. The man responds, "'Lord, I believe,' and he worshiped him" (9:38). These scenes anticipate the idea that Jesus "comes" to human persons and "manifests" himself to them so that they recognize his divinity (14:21, 23). The world, however, is left in darkness, unable to recognize Jesus's identity (9:24, 29) or find him (9:12; cf. 7:11, 34).

C. 10:1–42: Leading His Own to Eternal Life

As we have seen, other sections of the Gospel begin with symbolic narratives. This section, however, starts with Jesus telling a symbolic story—a cryptic "figure" or "proverb" (*paroimia*; 10:6).[58] The figure is similar to the Synoptic parable of the Lost Sheep (Matt. 18:10–14).[59] And yet it is not an authentic saying of Jesus, at least in its received form. It is, instead, a sort of verbal allegory for the idea of celestial access brought out later in the Farewell Discourse.

The core image of the parable is a shepherd and his sheep entering and exiting through a door or gate. Strangely, however, Jesus identifies himself with two images in the scene. On the one hand, he states that he is "the good shepherd," who leads the sheep through that door/gate (10:11; cf. vv. 15, 17–18, 27–28). But paradoxically, he also identifies himself as "the door/gate of the sheep," by which one is "saved, and will go in and out and find pasture" (10:8–9).

Interpreters have long struggled to make sense of the "figure" because the interpretation of the image is not coherent. How can Jesus be both the shepherd and the gate by which the shepherd enters? Some have gone so far as to dismiss it as "the wreckage of two parables fused into one, the fusion having partly destroyed the original form of both."[60] Nevertheless, the figure's meaning is readily apparent to one who understands the Farewell Discourse. In the Farewell Discourse, Jesus says that he will lead his disciples along a certain "way" to new, spiritual "dwelling places" (13:36, 14:3, 23), but paradoxically he reveals that he is the "way" itself (14:6). The shepherd figure maps onto this paradox, revealing that it is a metaphor for the same realities—namely, the mutual indwelling and celestial access. Jesus is the portal, the "door," connecting the realm below and the realm above (10:7; cf. 1:51). He enters into the realm below to "call" his own (10:2–3). But he then departs, going "ahead of" his sheep to lead them (10:4). This occurs through his death and resurrection; Jesus notes that the shepherd "lays down his life for the sheep," albeit with the intent "to take it up again" (10:17–18; cf. 16:16–24).[61] In turn, those who respond to his "voice"/word "follow" him, and through him they go to the realm above to spiritually be with him where he is (cf. 13:36; 14:3). But as Jesus notes, the sheep "go in and out" of that place (10:9); that is, they can transcend realms, living in earth and heaven, also evoked in the "ascending and descending" language of 1:51.

After this initial discourse, the narrator takes us to a later scene also set in Jerusalem, now on the Feast of the Dedication (Hanukkah). It is unclear if Jesus ever left Jerusalem, or if he remained there for several months, but the dialogue that follows depicts Jesus continuing to explore the image of "sheep" as if hardly any time had passed between the two occasions (10:22–39). Here, Jesus makes it clear that the figure's central image—the leading out of the sheep to pasture—refers precisely to a realized-eschatological reality culminating in "eternal life": "My sheep hear my voice, and I know them, and they follow me; and I give them eternal life" (10:27–28).

Throughout his discussion of the figure, Jesus repeatedly stresses that the sheep are subject to threats: "a wolf," "thief/thieves," and "bandits" who seek to "steal and kill and destroy" (10:1, 8, 10, 12). These agents are ciphers for the threat Jesus anticipates in the Farewell Discourse—namely, the devil, if not also the agents under his control, who seek to "snatch" humans from the possibility of "eternal life," keeping them under the power of death (10:28; cf. 14:30, 15:18–16:4, 17:15).[62] At the end of the second scene, the crowds listening to Jesus embody this response, attempting to kill him (10:39). Jesus, however, evades them; he "goes out" (10:40). In this way, the scene may illustrate the idea that the humans who attain the new life as *pneuma* "shall never perish" as they too "go out," following the shepherd into celestial realms (10:28).

A final scene, a coda to the multipart episode, completes the image. After "going out," Jesus withdraws to a remote place and "dwells" there (10:40). In turn, people "come" to seek Jesus there, "believing" in him (10:41–42). This final vignette illustrates the notion contained in the preceding figure, that Jesus will at last "depart" from this world and that believers (sheep) will "follow" him out and "come" to the place where he dwells.

D. Historical Issues

There is little reason to doubt that the material in chapters 7–8 is almost entirely pseudo-historical. The introductory episode and trip to Jerusalem are attested in no earlier gospel, all of which register only one climactic trip by Jesus to Jerusalem (Mark 10:32–33; Matt. 16:21). Although it is possible that Jesus traveled to Judea more often than the Synoptics report, these chapters would hardly seem the place to extract accurate memories of these journeys. Jesus's dialogue with his brothers is structured around the themes and language of the dialogue that follows it—a dialogue completely shot through with Johannine themes and language (departure, hiddenness).[63] When constructing the scene, the author probably drew inspiration from several sources. The scene evokes the apparent distance between Jesus and his brothers in the Synoptics (e.g., Mark 3:31–35). In turn, the climax of the episode, in which the Jews threaten Jesus's life, mirrors scenes in which Jesus's opponents attempt to kill him for his teaching (Luke 4:28–30).

The remaining scenes present similar problems. The Pool of Siloam scene could reflect an authentic memory of Jesus; it is set at a location excavated by archeologists. But the scene could also be a historical fiction loosely built off similar Synoptic healings (e.g., Mark 8:22–26, 10:46–52).[64] Certainly, the dialogue structuring the episode and extending into chapter 10 is almost entirely reflective of the distinctive outlook of the Gospel. The many narrative transitions woven into that dialogue, then, may also be inventions of the author.

V. Chapters 11–12

The author of John begins turning toward the pivotal movements of his narrative—the death, resurrection, and ascension of Jesus—in two episodes: the raising of Lazarus (11:1–57) and the meal Jesus shares in Lazarus's home (12:1–11).[65] In John's plot, these episodes set Jesus's death in motion as they stir up the jealousy and hostility of his deadliest opponents (11:47–53), a point even Jesus acknowledges in the narrative. At the beginning of the first episode, Jesus tells his disciples that Lazarus's illness has occurred "so that the Son of God may be glorified by means of it," that is, the miracle precipitates his transition into a glorified state (11:4; cf. 17:5, 1).

Like other episodes in the Gospel, however, these are more than elements or transitions of a single plot. They are, instead, symbolic episodes intended to carry the weight of the text's revisionist theology. Each supports threads in the complex theology of John, illustrating and clarifying its vision of eternal life and immortality.

A. 11:1–53: Illustrating the Spiritual Resurrection

In earlier scenes, Jesus claims that those who believe in him "will not perish" (3:16), "never see death" (8:51), or "never taste death" (8:52; cf. Mark 9:1; Matt. 16:28; Luke 9:27). At face value, these claims might seem like promises of immunity from physical death. In one instance, Jesus's audiences understand—or better, misunderstand—his words in precisely this sense (8:51–53). In the Lazarus stories, however, Jesus reveals that the immortality he offers devolves not on the flesh but on the spirit. That life, and that life alone, is eternal and impervious to death, transcending the body's dissolution.

To bring this clarification into focus, the evangelist depicts Jesus displaying a puzzling disregard for fleshly suffering and death. As chapter 11 begins, Mary and Martha inform Jesus that their brother Lazarus is dangerously ill (11:1–3). One might assume that Jesus, who said that those who believe would "never see death," would prevent Lazarus's physical death. But he does not. He bides his time, telling his disciples that "this illness is not unto death" (11:4). The statement seems false on its face; Lazarus dies (11:14).

Jesus's shocking inaction raises an important question: If he has come so that those who believe "will never die," why does he permit his friend's death? The apparent contradiction between Jesus's words and behavior is not lost on the scene's characters, who wrestle with Jesus's behavior in dialogue with his earlier claims. When, for instance, Jesus finally makes his way to Bethany, each of Lazarus's sisters separately protests, "Lord, if you had been here, my brother would not have died" (11:21, 32). Their words evoke Jesus's earlier promise that those who believe "will never die," keeping the apparent tension between Jesus's words and actions firmly in view (cf. 8:52). Similarly, a crowd mourning Lazarus asks, "Could not he who opened the eyes of the blind man have kept this man from dying?" (11:37). At the heart of all these responses is the same misunderstanding seen in other parts of the text: that Jesus's promise that the believer "will not die" is a promise of immunity from physical death.

Jesus begins the difficult work of untangling these ideas in his dialogue with the first of Lazarus's sisters, Martha. When Martha laments that Jesus could have kept her brother from dying, Jesus assures her, "your brother will be resurrected" (11:23). Instinctively, Martha refers Jesus's response to the idea of a future, physical resurrection: "I know that he will be resurrected in the resurrection at the last day" (11:24). In response, Jesus insists that this resurrection—anaphorically, "*the* resurrection," that is, the very same she just referenced—has already come: "I am the resurrection and the life" (11:25). The "resurrection" on "that day" is standing before her; as Jaime Clark-Soles writes, Jesus insists that "the 'last day' has already come."[66] Jesus also reveals himself to be the "life" anticipated on that day. As Jesus tells his disciples in the Farewell Discourse, "the world will not see me, but you will see me; because I live, you will live also; in that day, you will know that I am in my Father, and you in me, and I in you" (14:19–20). As Jesus indwells them, humans now share in his eternal, undying existence.

To consolidate the idea that his promise refers to a resurrection not of flesh but of spirit, Jesus utters another line—in effect, a paradox: "The one who believes in me—even if they should die—will live; and the one who lives and believes in me will never die" (11:25-26). Whereas the first part of the statement assumes that the believer can "die," the second insists the believer can never "die." Both cannot refer to the same kind of "death." Here, Jesus jumps from the physical to the spiritual. "Even if" one "should die" physically, it is possible that they "will live" and "never die" in or as spirit. Jesus reveals a "life" sitting on a plane distinct from the realities of physical life and death. As it stands, each of the lines parallel realized-eschatological statements across the Gospel, many of which are phrased in the future tense since they anticipate the (then) future coming of the Spirit:[67]

> The one who believes in me—even if they should die—will live. (11:25)

> Compare:
> The one who hears my word and believes him who sent me has eternal life. ... those who hear will live. (5:24-25)
> Everyone who sees the Son and believes in him should have eternal life. (6:40)
> The one who believes has eternal life. (6:47)[68]

> The one who lives and believes in me will never die. (11:26)

> Compare:
> If anyone keeps my word, that one will never see death. (8:51)
> This is the bread which comes down from heaven, which one may eat and not die. (6:50)

Even the juxtaposition of the two positive and negative affirmations—one promising that the believer "will live" (11:25) and the other promising that the believer "will never die" (11: 26)—parallels other realized-eschatological texts, which characteristically pair the same ideas (10:28, 3:16, 6:58; cf. 6:50-51). Their juxtaposition is natural; the two are corollary ideas. By definition, the one who possesses eternal life never dies, and the one who never dies possesses eternal life. By juxtaposing these statements, Jesus emphatically stresses the enduring quality of the "life" he promises.

These parallels help us see the passage for what it is, then: a discussion of the *pneumatic* transformation and life articulated elsewhere in John.[69] Here, however, Jesus promises that this "eternal life" is available even after or within physical death. "Even if" the one who believes dies physically, "yet [they] will live." The notion here is postmortem survival as *pneuma* in the celestial realm. As we saw, Jesus elsewhere insists that one who loses one's life will be with him where he is: in the realm above (12:25–26).

In the next scene, Jesus illustrates this process in a startling symbolic gesture: the raising of Lazarus, the friend he "loves" (11:3), from (physical) death. Jesus comes to the tomb of Lazarus and orders those around him to unseal it. When they do so, he calls out to the man decaying within the tomb "with a loud voice," saying, "Lazarus, come out!" (11:43). According to the narrator, "the dead man came out, his hands and feet bound with bandages, and his face wrapped with a cloth"; Jesus then instructs those around him, "Unbind him, and let him go/depart" (11:44). The miracle dramatizes Jesus's earlier teachings about spiritual resurrection, especially that "the dead will hear the voice of the Son of God and those who hear will live" (5:25) and "the hour is coming when all who are in their graves will hear his voice and come out" (5:28–29).[70] It also symbolizes the end of those raised spiritually: they follow Jesus and "depart" themselves (13:36).

The raising of Lazarus, however, is only that: a symbol, a representation. It is not "the resurrection" Jesus reveals in the chapter—the spiritual resurrection—any more than the five loaves Jesus multiplied are the "bread of life." If it were, this resurrection would bequeath the life Jesus promises: the "eternal life" through which one "will never die." But even after the miracle, Lazarus remains mortal, vulnerable to physical death.[71] According to the text, "the chief priests planned to put Lazarus also to death because on account of him many of the Jews were going away and believing in Jesus" (12:10–11). The response of the chief priests, however, is a sign of their ignorance. They believe they can invalidate Jesus's power by killing Lazarus in the flesh again. But Jesus's power to give life is not contingent on Lazarus's physical life, nor is it invalidated by his physical death, as often as it may occur. "The resurrection and the life" Jesus offers transcends life in the flesh; it is a life "above," of and as "spirit." By lifting his friend from physical death, however, Jesus signals to those around him that he has the power to bestow a spiritual resurrection.

B. 11:55–12:11: The Servant and the House

The dinner at Lazarus's home is yet another symbolic episode, constructed as a climax to the first. The episode recounts how Jesus "came" to the "house" of Lazarus (12:1). According to the narrator, Martha "served" Jesus, Lazarus "reclined with" him, and Mary welcomed him by pouring out an extravagant gift: "a pound of costly ointment of pure nard" costing "three hundred denarii" (12:2–5), or ten months' wages. The "house," in turn, is "filled" with the oil's fragrance (12:3). Judas, however, observes the scene with disgust, scolding Mary for pouring out so much wealth on Jesus. The narrator exposes his hidden motives: Judas regularly coveted and stole money from Jesus and his companions. Jesus, however, scolds Judas, telling him to "leave her, so that she may keep it for the day of my burial" (12:7). The wording of this last sentence is highly unusual; as Marianne Meye Thompson asks, "since Mary has just poured [the oil] out on Jesus' feet, how can she also keep it?"[72]

The symbolism of the episode is subtle, but it is easy to trace for someone accustomed to reading each scene in John in light of its neighboring discourses. The scene anticipates a saying of Jesus later in the chapter, in which he articulates the conditions for eternal life: "The one who loves his life loses it, and the one who hates his life in this world will save it for eternal life. If anyone serves me, he must follow me; and where I am, there shall my servant be also; if anyone serves me, the Father will honor him" (12:25–26). Martha, Lazarus, and Mary embody the person destined to "eternal life." That person "serves" Jesus, just as Martha does in the opening scene. (In each case, the verb is *diakoneō*, tying the chapter together linguistically: 12:2, 26.) That person also demonstrates their perfect love for Jesus by laying down all earthly resources for him, even at a staggering personal cost, like Mary (12:3).[73] In so doing, that person will paradoxically "save" or "keep" what they have poured out. (The terms are synonymous elsewhere in the text, as in 12:47; 17:12; cf. 14:15, 23–24.) That person also experiences the union depicted in the scene. Jesus will "come" to where they are, and they will be with him—in the mutual indwelling—just as Jesus "comes to where Lazarus was" and "Lazarus is 'one of those with him'" (12:1–2).

Viewed in this light, the scene typifies the final destiny of the one who "loves" Jesus and whom Jesus "loves": the mutual indwelling. A chapter earlier, the narrator informs his readers that "Jesus loved Martha and her sister and Lazarus" (11:1). Here, we see where that love leads: not only to spiritual resurrection (as in chapter 11) but to Jesus sharing a common "house" (cf. 14:2) or "dwelling" with someone: "If one loves me, that one will keep my word, and my Father will love him, and we will come to him and make our dwelling with him" (14:23). They are, then, "filled" with joy (15:11, 16:24). Not coincidentally, the presence of Jesus in a person draws others to them, who come to believe through them (12:9). Such persons, however, will attract the hostility of the world—a world that will seek to put them to death (12:10; cf. 15:18–16:4).

The perfect foil to these persons, however, is Judas. In his greed, he represents the one who "loves his life" in this world, coveting all it has. He is also the one who refuses to "serve" Jesus. Not coincidentally, when Jesus attempts to share a meal with Judas in the next chapter, Satan enters into Judas, and Judas breaks company with Jesus (13:2, 27).

C. Historical Issues

The first major episode in this section, the raising of Lazarus, has no cognate in the Synoptics. It is also shot through with Johannine ideas and language. What makes this miracle especially unlikely to be historical, however, is its intimate relationship to the account that follows it: the episode of the dinner at Bethany. That second story is more obviously a manipulated Synoptic story.

Both Mark and Matthew depict Jesus attending a dinner in the village of Bethany, a suburb of Jerusalem, on the week of his death (Mark 14:3–11; Matt. 26:6–16). Those gospels, however, claim that the dinner was hosted in "the house of Simon the Leper" (Mark 14:3; Matt. 26:6). They also describe an unnamed woman anointing Jesus's head with myrrh and triggering a negative response from onlookers, immediately before describing Judas's betrayal. Luke too includes a story of Jesus attending a dinner at the house of a man named "Simon" at which a woman anoints him, but the story differs significantly from the Markan and Matthean versions (Luke 7:36–50). First, it appears much earlier in Luke's narrative, during Jesus's ministry in Galilee. Second, it occurs after a story in which Jesus arrives in a city called Nain and raises a widow's son from the dead (Luke 7:11–17). It may even presuppose the same location as that story. In his account of the dinner, Luke writes that a woman "of the city" (7:37)—ostensibly Nain, the most recent city cited—anoints him. In Luke, however, the story has no connection to Judas's betrayal.

John presupposes that his readers know from other sources the account of the woman who anointed Jesus, referencing it a chapter earlier (11:2). Like Mark and Matthew, John places that event at Bethany (12:1) and links it to Judas's betrayal (12:4–6). The Gospel even uses the same distinctive formulae as Mark when describing the ointment poured over Jesus, noting that it was an ointment of "pure nard, very costly" (12:3), costing "three hundred denarii" (12:5). But, as discussed in chapter 1, John blends the above with features of the Lukan account in ways that undermine the basic coherence of the story.[74] The Gospel also changes the characters joining Jesus at the dinner, excising any mention of Simon, identifying the unnamed woman as Mary (11:2, 12:3), introducing Martha as the one who "serves" Jesus, and adding the figure of Lazarus (12:2). Martha and Mary come from a pericope in Luke in which Jesus, who has set out to Jerusalem on a journey that will end in his death, enters "a village" and stays with the two sisters, one of whom, Martha, "serves" him (Luke 10:38–42). That village, however, is probably not the Jerusalem suburb of Bethany since Jesus reaches it before he arrives at Jericho (Luke 18:35) and well before he arrives at Jerusalem (Luke 19:28). This stay also has no connection with the anointing performed by the unnamed woman, which occurs well before Jesus's journey to Jerusalem. John, however, blends these images. The name "Lazarus," in turn, evokes a character from the Lukan parable of the Rich Man and Lazarus (Luke 16:19–31). That parable depicts a reversal of fortune: a wealthy man on earth is cast into an afterlife of torment while a local beggar named Lazarus attains a place with Abraham. At the conclusion of the story, the rich man begs that Lazarus be resurrected to warn his brothers of the fate awaiting them. The man is told that his brothers would not be convinced even "if someone should rise from the dead" (Luke 16:31). It hardly seems coincidental that John, when crafting a new resurrection account, opted to give his resurrected character the same name.[75]

One final parallel between John and Luke is worth noting: John follows Luke in placing the account of the dinner and anointing very near to—and, again, after—a resurrection in the same town (John 11:1–44). This hardly seems coincidental for understanding the origin of John's story. The author of John probably took the story of the raising of the widow's son as a loose inspiration for his new account. In effect, the author exploits the ambiguous relationship between the Markan Bethany and Lukan Galilee versions to justify the invention of a Bethany resurrection before the Bethany dinner.

The complicated and fluid relationships between all these stories reveal the extent and limits of the author's creativity. They betray an author who blended episodes and merged characters when inventing new stories, taking familiar elements but placing them in unfamiliar frames, orders, and juxtapositions to build something new. The result welcomes readers to latch on to what they know while ostensibly introducing them to what they do not know or what the other evangelists might have confused. All the while, the author weaves in his distinctive theology.

VI. Chapters 12 (Continued) through 17

Like the author of Mark, the author of John devotes roughly half his Gospel—all of 12:12 to 20:31—to events in the final week of Jesus's life. In this final cycle of stories, the author of John follows the other gospels more closely than before, assuming the same basic sequence of events. Jesus enters Jerusalem, shares a final meal with his disciples, is arrested, dies by crucifixion, and appears to his disciples after death. But in his characteristic style, the narrator redevelops these stories, weaving an intricate tapestry of symbol and sign, gesture and word.

A. 12:12–50: Leaving the World

The critical moment anticipated throughout the first half of the Gospel, the "hour" of Jesus, the time of his departure, arrives when Jesus enters Jerusalem for the Passover for a final time (12:12–19; cf. Matt. 21:1–11; Mark 11:1–11; Luke 19:28–44). As the scene opens, Jesus comes to Jerusalem, riding upon "a young ass," the animal prophesied in an earlier biblical text to be the transport of the "king" who "is coming" (12:14–15; cf. Zech. 9:9). As Jesus rides into the city, he is greeted with palm branches by crowds of people who proclaim him "the one who comes in the name of the Lord, even the king of Israel" (John 12:13).

As always, the cries of the crowd are saturated in double entendre. The populace of Jerusalem is correct to hail this moment as the time Jesus enters his kingdom. What they do not comprehend, however, is that Jesus's "kingdom is not of this world" (18:36); it is, instead, a kingdom located in the realm "above" (17:11), where Jesus has "glory" awaiting him (17:5). As he enters

Jerusalem, Jesus is taking the first steps of his departure to his otherworldly kingdom. Appropriately, then, from this point on, Jesus speaks in ways that suggest his departure is already underway—as if he is now "coming" to the Father and no longer "in the world" (17:11–13). For the first time, he speaks of the "hour" as a fully present reality: "The hour has come for the Son of Man to be glorified.... Now is the judgment of this world" (12:23, 31). The narrator directs the reader's attention to these hidden meanings of the scene by indicating that Jesus's "disciples did not understand" what was being done to Jesus at his entry into Jerusalem but that they could perceive its significance after "Jesus was glorified," that is, fully ascended (12:16). What the disciples do not grasp is that his departure has begun.

Since the entrance into Jerusalem sets Jesus on his way to celestial glorification, it is only fitting that, immediately afterward, the Gospel details how humans can follow Jesus and share in his exaltation. John expands the Synoptic triumphal entry episode with new material: the first of several lost moments in the last week of Jesus. Upon entering Jerusalem, the disciples tell Jesus that some Greeks are also in the city and want to "see" him (12:20–22). Jesus responds on a different plane of meaning, revealing how one can truly "see" him. He tells the disciples that he is about to "die" and be "glorified" (12:23–24), adding that if one "follows" him, "where I am, there shall my servant be also" (12:25–26), anticipating his later claim that those who believe will join him in the Father's house, so that where he is they "may also be" (14:2–3). The Gospel leaves another riddle of the departure hiding in plain sight.

As the chapter ends, however, it strikes a pessimistic note, revealing again that the world cannot, and will not, follow Jesus. After answering the disciples and proclaiming the arrival of the "hour," Jesus addresses the Father directly (12:27–28). The Father audibly responds, confirming Jesus's origins and destiny ("I have glorified [the Name], and I will glorify it again"). The surrounding crowd, however, cannot recognize the voice as God's own (12:29), consistent with the principle that only the one who is of God can recognize the words of God—the words Jesus himself speaks (8:47; cf. 12:49–50; cf. 8:47).

The chapter concludes with Jesus's final appeal to the crowds: "the light is with you for a little longer ... while you have the light, believe in the light" (12:35–36). But as the narrator points out, "they could not believe" (12:39; cf. v. 37). The narrative bears this out. According to the text, when Jesus finished these final public teachings, "he departed and hid himself from them"

(12:36). This detail is more than a plot element. It is an unmistakable double entendre, a sign that the time has arrived when the world will "see" Jesus "no more" (14:19).

B. 13:1-35: The Indwelling as "Love"

As chapter 13 begins, Jesus is fully conscious that "his hour had come to depart out of this world to the Father" (13:1), and he prepares his disciples for this reality. Extending the pattern observed in previous chapters, this section of the Gospel begins with an introductory symbolic episode: another nonmiraculous scene supposedly representing an unrecorded incident from Jesus's life. The Synoptics all record that, on the night before his death, Jesus shared a final supper with his disciples (Mark 14:12-31; Matt. 26:17-35; Luke 22:7-38) before going up the nearby Mount of Olives to pray before his arrest (Mark 14:32-42; Matt. 26:36-46; Luke 22:39-46). John sets its scene "during" that supper (13:2). According to the text, "knowing that ... he had come from God and was going to God," Jesus "rose from supper, laid aside his outer garments, and took up a towel ... poured water into a basin, and began to wash the disciples' feet" (13:3-5). Then, Jesus takes up his outer garments again and reclines (13:12). The discourse that follows is the Farewell Discourse, the longest and climactic speech of the Gospel (13:31-17:26).

Various details indicate that the opening scene's meaning is symbolic of Jesus's departure and his dwelling in humans—the salient themes of the Farewell Discourse. First, the narrator stresses that Jesus performs the act of foot washing, conscious of his impending departure (13:3-6).[76] Second, Jesus indicates that the gesture has a meaning that is not immediately evident but that can be appreciated later: "what I am doing you do not know now, but afterward you will understand" (13:7).[77] Additionally, Jesus seems to invest a surprising level of significance to the gesture, saying, "If I do not wash you, you have no part in me" (13:8).

What, then, is the meaning of Jesus's act? Taken in all its facets, the complex gesture symbolizes the final acts of Jesus's "love": the laying down of his life, his departure, and his indwelling of his disciples, which grants them life. The narrator describes Jesus "laying down" (*tithēsin*) his outer garments and ultimately "taking up" (*elaben*) his outer garments with the same verbs as Jesus describes his death and resurrection: "I lay down [*tithēmi*] my life that I may take it up [*labō*] again" (10:17, 13:4, 12).[78] As Jesus says later in the discourse: "greater love has no one than this, that one lay down [*thēi*] their life for their friends" (15:13). No less fitting, when Jesus takes up his outer garment again, the narrator reports that he "reclined again" (13:12), a subtle allusion to the idea that he will return to the Father's bosom, in the "glory" he had there "before the world was made" (1:18, 17:5; cf. 13:25).

The gesture of washing feet represents the Spirit-mediated result of those climactic acts: his coming to believers and indwelling them.[79] First, as we have seen, the Gospel consistently uses water as a symbol for the indwelling Spirit (7:37–39). Second, Jesus's claim "if I do not wash you, you have no part in me" (13:8) anticipates his later claim that one must experience the mutual indwelling: "If one does not dwell in me, that one is cast forth" (15:6). Third, Jesus casts the foot washing as an expression of his love (13:14, 34), just as he casts his secret coming to and indwelling of the disciples as the consummate expression of his love: "My Father will love the one who loves me, and I will love that one and manifest myself to them.... If someone loves me, they will keep my word, and my Father will love that one, and we will come to him and dwell with them" (14:21, 23). And as Mary Coloe suggests, it seems fitting that the author captures these ideas in a scene about foot washing. In ancient Palestine, hosts offered guests foot washing immediately when entering a home. In line with this, Jesus performs the act immediately before a discourse in which he speaks of ushering believers into the "Father's house" through his indwelling.[80]

Following a familiar pattern in the Gospel, however, Peter confuses the external symbol for the spiritual reality, illustrating that he indeed does not "know" or "understand" Jesus's gesture (13:7). Upon hearing Jesus stress the necessity of this washing, Peter begs Jesus to wash "not my feet only but also my hands and my head" (13:9). Jesus cryptically responds, "the one who has bathed does not need to wash; he is clean all over" (13:10).[81] The statement likely means that one who has received the (higher-order, spiritual) bathing represented by the sign—the coming and indwelling of the Spirit—does not need (literal, external) washing.[82] Only that higher-order "bathing" makes one "clean"; as Jesus tells the disciples later, "you have already been cleansed by the word that I have spoken to you" (15:3). (Recall that the "word" of Jesus is "spirit" [6:63].) In removing his garment and washing his disciples' feet, then, Jesus signifies all the acts of his love: he will lay down his life for his own and indwell them through the Spirit.

After performing the act of foot washing, Jesus states, "if I then, your Lord and Teacher, have washed your feet, you also ought to wash one another's feet.... I have given you an example, that you should do" (13:14–15). This instruction anticipates Jesus's "new commandment" to "love one another; even as I have loved you" (13:34).[83] It is, in effect, a call for humans to emulate Jesus and perform all the acts of love he does—that is, to lay down their own lives, impart the Spirit to one another, and indwell one another. In this dialogue, Jesus is emphatic that he has also "sent" believers "into the world" (13:16, 17:18; cf. 3:16) precisely to follow the plan of his departure. They must also perform the "greater works" of imparting the Spirit and eternal life to others through their word (14:12; cf. 5:20–21). They must also attain a mutual indwelling and oneness with one another, as Jesus asks the Father, "may [they] be one even as we are one, I in them and you in me, that they may become perfectly one" (17:22–23).[84] And they must "lay down" their lives in the face of the world's hatred (15:13, 20), as Jesus has, and thereby "glorify" the Father (15:8, 17:1). In short, Jesus's disciples continue not only his mission in the world but also his departure—his gestures of love, symbolized in the acts of chapter 13. In this, we see the full ramifications of Jesus's prediction: "you will follow me afterward" (13:36).

During the scene, however, a different drama plays out in Judas's life. Earlier in the Gospel, Jesus has indicated that some are "of" a different "father": "the devil" (8:44).[85] As such, these individuals are devils themselves; John's Jesus expressly calls Judas "a devil" (6:70–71). These individuals are not "made clean" by receiving Jesus's indwelling "word" (15:3); thus Jesus tells his disciples, "not all of you are clean," alluding to Judas (13:10–11). As a consequence, these persons experience a different sort of indwelling: a negative one. When describing the supper that follows, the narrator records that "Satan entered into [Judas]" (13:27)—an obvious foil to the indwelling disclosed in the Farewell Discourse.[86] No less tellingly, the narrator adds that Judas "immediately went out; and it was night"—language evoking Jesus's later claim that the Father drives out all who do not belong to him (15:2, 6) as well as Jesus's earlier warning that those who do not receive the light "in" themselves are condemned to "darkness" or "night" (12:35, 46, 11:10).

C. 15:1–8: Dwelling in the Vine

Within the Farewell Discourse itself, Jesus captures these dueling destinies in a symbolic figure, one articulated around the image of a vinedresser, vine, and branches.[87] The vinedresser "cleanses/prunes" (*katheirei*) those branches of the vine that bear fruit, precisely so that they may bear more fruit (15:2–5). Conversely, he takes away the branches that do not bear fruit, leaving them to wither and be burned (15:2, 6).

John's Jesus glosses the image as he develops it. He begins by stating, "I am the true vine, and my Father is the vinedresser" (15:1). The branches that bear fruit seem to be those humans in whom the essential "work of God" is manifest—that is, belief (3:21, 6:28–29, 9:3).[88] These individuals are cleaned by their reception of the word/*Logos*, which comes to dwell in them: "you are already clean [*katharoi*] by the word that I have spoken to you" (15:3; cf. v. 7). Those persons "dwell/abide" in the vine (15:4), whose vital force produces "more fruit" in them, up to and including "eternal life" (15:2; cf. "fruit for eternal life" in 4:36).

By contrast, the branches that do not bear fruit seem to represent those humans who fail to manifest belief. The image captures the condemnation of unbelieving humans. The language of the Father "taking" these branches "away" (*airei*; 15:2) recalls Jesus's ordering others to "take away" (*arate*) those things defiling his "Father's house" (2:16). Unbelieving persons do not find a lasting place, a dwelling, in the Father's house (8:35). Their destiny, instead, is death.

D. Historical Issues

The triumphal entry of Jesus into Jerusalem is taken from the Synoptics with few alterations, though John configures this story to fit his narrative more closely. In his account, the crowd greets Jesus precisely because "he called Lazarus out of the tomb and raised him from the dead" (12:17–18). The other elements of the chapter are unique creations of the author, transparently suited to stage and symbolize his distinctive views. The motif of the voice of God—a "voice . . . from heaven"—is a feature of the Synoptic accounts of Jesus's baptism (Mark 1:11; Matt. 3:17; Luke 3:22) and transfiguration (Mark 9:7; Matt. 17:5; Luke 9:35). This is the first and only time the divine voice is heard in John (which, for that matter, does not contain a transfiguration scene). The words spoken by the voice, however, as well as the people's response, echo the author's distinctive views, betraying the scene as yet another invention.

The foot-washing episode—an element in no other gospel—is probably also contrived. We can even identify a compelling inspiration for the scene. According to Luke, Jesus "sat at table" during the last supper (22:14). Several verses later, Luke quotes Jesus saying, "who is greater: the one who sits at table, or the one who serves? Is it not the one who sits at table? But I am among you as one who serves" (22:26-27). Luke, however, never depicts Jesus rising from the table, nor does he clarify how or in what manner Jesus "serves" his disciples. Most likely, he assumes that Jesus's distribution of a cup and bread represents his manner of service (22:17-22). The author of John may well have exploited this loose end to develop another compelling water image able to carry the weight of his distinctive theology. His text depicts Jesus rising from the table to assume a servant posture; as Harold Attridge claims, "the Johannine last supper dramatizes the Lukan saying."[89]

Other features of the story point to a Lukan inspiration. Luke is also the only gospel to depict the practice of washing feet, and tellingly the same gospel casts the gesture as a symbol of "love." In the Lukan story of the woman anointing Jesus, Jesus reprimands his host for not washing his feet when welcoming him into his house for a meal. He also casts the woman who anoints him—who, critically, washes his feet with her tears—as one who "loved" him "much" (7:44-47). The Johannine version of this woman, Mary of Bethany, who also washes Jesus's feet, is one whom Jesus "loves" (11:5). Our author, then, could have identified foot washing as a useful gesture to represent the theme of mutual "love" woven through the Farewell Discourse, especially in a Gospel that regularly uses scenes set in and around water to introduce discourses (chs. 2, 4, 5, 6, 9).[90]

Jesus's longest discourse suits the predilection for farewell speeches in ancient literature.[91] The themes of this discourse may be a dramatic, creative transformation of isolated expressions distributed across the parallel Synoptic passages (that is, the Last Supper, the walk to the Mount of Olives, and the Garden of Gethsemane). Many scholars observe a probable connection between John's "hour" and Jesus's words in the Synoptic Gethsemane scenes: "the hour has come" (Mark 14:41; Matt. 26:45). Tantalizingly, "vine" and "fruit" imagery, like that of 15:1-4, appears in the Last Supper accounts (Mark 14:25-26; Matt. 26:29). Jesus speaks of "going before" his disciples in two accounts (Mark 14:28; Matt 26:32). And Jesus's final instruction to his disciples in the Garden of Gethsemane is that they "stay/remain" with him (*meinate hōde*; Mark 14:34; Matt. 26:38), the same verb underlying the command to "dwell" with him in the Farewell Discourse (*menō*; e.g., John 14:23, 15:4). John takes the few scattered words of Jesus in the parallel Synoptic passages and weaves them into a more complex elaboration of his theology. The book casts earlier Jesus traditions as mere echoes or fragments of a larger discourse only John relates.

VII. Chapters 18 (Continued) through 20

After the Farewell Discourse, the Gospel transitions to an account of Jesus's arrest, interrogations, crucifixion, and resurrection. That account follows the Synoptics to a great extent and hosts some of the most substantial parallels between John and earlier works. Nevertheless, even this section of the Gospel contains new, symbolic scenes.[92]

A. 18:1–19:27: The Disciple Exalted

One example of symbolism occurs during the scenes of Jesus's arrest. Jesus and a disciple—the nameless "disciple whom Jesus loved"—enter the "courtyard" of the house of the high priest (18:15; cf. 20:2). Peter, however, is not given passage through the "gate/door" until the other disciple goes out and asks the "gatekeeper" to admit Peter (18:16). The reader is clearly meant to connect this scene to the Shepherd Discourse; several linguistic parallels bind this passage to 10:1–3. (The term "courtyard" is the same word as for "sheepfold" [*aulē*], and the words "gate/door" and "gatekeeper" also appear in the discourse.) Together, these parallels cast the disciple as one who is being exalted into Jesus's likeness—one who gains the same access to the "fold" as Jesus possesses, and who, like Jesus, can lead others through "the door." In Wendy North's words, the disciple becomes "Jesus's *Doppelgänger* on earth."[93]

A second scene, set at the crucifixion, further illustrates the disciple's exaltation. In his final moments, Jesus sees his disciple standing beside the cross and tells his mother, "Woman, here is your son" (19:26). "From that hour," the narrator says, "the disciple took her into his own home" (19:27). The scene captures the idea that those who follow Jesus become "sons" precisely at this climactic "hour": "In becoming 'son' to the mother of Jesus, the disciple becomes brother/sister to Jesus and child of the one Jesus calls 'Father.' . . . through the gift of the Spirit, discipleship becomes divine filiation in the

Johannine perspective. Following this scene, when the Risen One appears to Mary Magdalene, he tells her, 'Go to my brothers and sisters (*adelphoi*) and say to them, I am ascending to my Father and your Father, to my God and your God' (20:17)."[94]

B. 18:1–19:27: The Spirit within Jesus

A later element of the crucifixion story highlights a different thread of John's thought: the idea that believers have the Spirit within themselves. When Jesus dies, his body remains on the cross until a Roman soldier pierces his side with a spear. At that time, the narrator records, "blood and water" came out of Jesus's body (19:30–34). The narrator then seals this report with an affidavit: "the one who saw this has testified so that you also may believe . . . he knows that he tells the truth" (19:35). These words hint at the symbolic value of the image; like other "signs" in the text, the report is given "so that you may also believe" (19:35; cf. 20:31). The meaning of the image is not difficult to ascertain. In other dialogues, Jesus describes the Spirit as "a spring of water" "in" the human person, "gushing up to eternal life" (4:14, 7:38–39). The narrator's report confirms that Jesus has "life in himself" (5:26) and "gives life to whomever he wishes" (5:21). In this way, John reveals that believers will participate in the same "life."

C. 20:1–21: Making the *Pneumatic* Life Visible

The ultimate and climactic demonstration of Jesus's power to give life—the greatest miraculous "sign" in the text—is his own resurrection (cf. 2:18–19). At the end of the crucifixion account, Joseph of Arimathea and Nicodemus lay Jesus's body in a tomb, completing a full, even excessive embalming ritual for it.[95] In chapter 20, however, Jesus resurrects that body, demonstrating through an empty tomb and lingering wounds that the same person who had died is now alive again (cf. 2:21, 20:20, 27, 29).[96] Like the raising of Lazarus's body, the raising of Jesus's body is a sign of his power to effect spiritual resurrection.

At the same time, Jesus's resurrection externally reveals the nature of that new spiritual existence.[97] In the views of many ancient Christians, Jesus was raised not with a body of flesh but with a body like that of heavenly beings. Recall again that Paul expressly contrasts Jesus's resurrected body to bodies of "flesh," "dust," and other terrestrial elements, insisting that he rose to a "spiritual [*pneumatikos*]" existence as a "spirit [*pneuma*]" (1 Cor. 15:45–48). Building on this premise, he expressly rejects the idea that humans are raised as "flesh and blood" but insists that one must be "changed"—precisely out of the likeness of "the man of dust" and into "the image of" Jesus, "the man of heaven" (1 Cor. 15:48–51). Two texts with Pauline backgrounds share the same idea: Hebrews assumes that "the days of [Jesus's] flesh" is something other than his existence now (5:7), and 1 Peter posits that Jesus was "put to death in the flesh but made alive in the *pneuma*" (3:18).[98]

There are good reasons to suspect that the author of John conceptualized Jesus's post-resurrection body as these authors did—as a body not of flesh but one either already made of spirit/*pneuma* or gradually transforming into spirit/*pneuma*.[99] The Gospel seems to directly echo 1 Corinthians 15 in its insistence that humans, born of "flesh," must become "spirit" to "enter the kingdom" (John 3:5–6)—a kingdom "not of this world" (18:36). It is hard to imagine, then, that the author of John envisioned Jesus ascending out of this world into that kingdom in a body of flesh rather than in a *pneumatic* body. It may also be telling that John speaks of Jesus being "glorified" through his death and resurrection (12:16, 23). For Paul, a human is "glorified" or "raised in glory" by being "raised a spiritual/*pneumatic* body"—a body that bears the "glory" of celestial bodies (Rom. 8:17; 1 Cor. 15:40, 43–44, 48).[100] For that matter, John imagines the body of Jesus engaging with the physical world in a manner like the bodies of these angelic beings; Jesus can touch physical objects, but he can also become visible or invisible to humans at will and penetrate physical barriers (20:11–12; cf. vv. 14, 19, 26).[101]

By the extraordinary, external act of changing his fleshly body into a celestial, *pneumatic* body, then, Jesus boldly demonstrates his power to create a *pneumatic* life within humans. But Jesus cautions his disciples against centering visible realities: "Have you believed because you have seen me? Blessed are those who have not seen and yet have come to believe" (20:29). To the end, the narrative insists that the realities of Jesus's *pneumatic* life and the *pneumatic* life of those "born of spirit" will otherwise remain hidden from view, apprehended only by those who "believe." Thus, believers are meant to recognize that the body Jesus makes visible is the (*pneumatic*) body they already possess within themselves.

In the midst of these revelations, however, the author weaves in additional scenes that extend the symbolism of other chapters. In one, Jesus appears to Mary Magdalene, but she does not recognize him at first, suggesting that his body has undergone some change. When Jesus says her name, however,

Mary instantly recognizes his voice (20:11-16), evoking Jesus's earlier teaching about the Shepherd: "he calls his own sheep by name ... [and] they know his voice" (10:4). At this point, Jesus instructs Mary not to touch him, since his departure is not yet complete: "I am ascending to my God and your God" (20:17). Like the Shepherd, he must "go ahead of" his sheep (10:4; cf. 14:3, 12, 16:28).

The next scenes mark the completion of Jesus's departure and reveal its effects. "On the evening of that day," the narrator writes, "Jesus came and stood among" his disciples (20:19). Jesus then breathes the Spirit to them (20:22), indicating that his departure has been fully realized, consistent with his earlier teaching: "if I do not go away, the Paraclete will not come to you; but if I go, I will send him to you" (cf. 16:7). A week later, Jesus appears to his disciples again, this time in the company of Thomas, who had been absent from Jesus's earlier appearance (20:24-26). When Jesus reveals himself to Thomas, Thomas cries out, "my Lord and my God" (20:28). In the chapter, the disciples call Jesus "Lord" (20:2, 13, 18, 25), and Jesus calls the Father "God" (20:17). The cry "my Lord and my God," then, reveals that Thomas at last perceives the unity and mutual indwelling of the Father and Jesus—the unity he too now shares—consistent with Jesus's promise "you will see me ... in that day, you will know that I am in my Father, and you in me, and I in you" (14:19-20).[102] A gospel that began with the premise that "no one has ever seen God" (1:18) ends with a human seeing God.[103]

D. Historical Issues

The final chapters of the Gospel follow the Synoptics closely in many respects and are rich with historical materials. Their deviations from the Synoptics, however, are most likely the author's own innovations. Note, for example, that each of the symbolic scenes in the crucifixion account revolves around a character unique to and (as we will see) invented for this Gospel: "the disciple whom Jesus loved."

The resurrection appearances seem built upon Synoptic episodes but are shaped around the Gospel's distinctive themes and motifs. For example, Jesus's dialogue with Mary recalls his appearance to women in Matthew 28:8-10. Nevertheless, John's scene is structured by the author's idea of Jesus's departure (20:17) and of the sheep recognizing his "voice" (20:11-16; cf. 10:4). Similarly, Jesus's appearances to his disciples, including Thomas, recall Luke 24:36-51. But John transforms the scene to suggest that Jesus imparted the Spirit to his disciples on the evening after his resurrection rather than at a later point, as Luke narrates (John 20:22; cf. Luke 24:49; Acts 1:5, 8, 2:1–42). The author also orients the scene around his distinctive idea of the indwelling presence of the Father in Jesus (John 20:28).

VIII. Conclusion

Over the past twenty-five years, a vocal contingent of Johannine scholars has argued that the Gospel of John should be reappraised as a valuable source for reconstructing the historical Jesus.[104] These arguments have merit; there are compelling reasons to think that the Gospel depends on some earlier Jesus traditions of historical value, written and oral—at the very least, those found in the Synoptics. And yet, when we appreciate the ideology of John in all its facets, it is still hard to escape the impression that creativity and invention play a significant role in the shape of its narrative materials. Across its many chapters, John portrays scenes in the life of Jesus that often have no parallel in earlier traditions and are conspicuously structured by the text's salient themes. Symbolism is not a detachable element of these scenes; symbolism is, instead, an intrinsic, even determinative feature of each.

In my experience, readers who conceptualize the Gospel as primarily a mosaic of historical traditions are often those least sensitive to the profound literary design of the narrative and those least able to articulate the complex ideology that underpins it. Of course, that design can also easily escape many historical critics whose insistent search for editorial layers precludes their ability to see the unity and consistency of the work. That design can even partly escape literary critics, whose research programs may not always fully incorporate an interest in the theological architecture of the text. John is forged from the fusion of discourse and narrative, idea and story, word and image. It demands that scholars integrate multiple contemporary approaches to the text. Only then can one appreciate the full genius of John's author—a mind that synthesized, recombined, and even invented Jesus traditions to build a compelling new text: a gospel of symbols and signs.

4
An Apocryphal Gospel

The Gospel of John recasts Jesus as the teacher of an intricate system of ideas he never taught: ideas of spiritual birth, celestial access, immortality, and exaltation in this life. It does so by crafting discourses and narratives that communicate these ideas to readers. But why would anyone trust a text introduced nearly a century after Jesus's lifetime as an authority for what he said and did? Why believe a new Gospel—a revisionary account of Jesus's life—when it stands in tension with previous, popular portrayals?

When one examines the Gospel closely, it becomes clear that its author was acutely aware of these potential objections to his work. To meet them, he made several critical moves to bolster his account's perceived reliability and historical accuracy. First, and most consequentially, the author of John falsely positioned his Gospel as an eyewitness account. The text gradually links its contents to the testimony of an invented disciple of Jesus, a nameless "disciple whom Jesus loved," who validates the Gospel's contents for skeptical audiences. As M. David Litwa explains, "introducing an eyewitness was a standard historiographical convention" in antiquity "used to authenticate revisionary works that otherwise might have been questioned for their novelty in form and content."[1]

But the author also pursued other strategies to explain why the material contained in his text appears in no other account of Jesus's life. The Gospel claims it presents unrecorded and private moments in the life of Jesus. It presents its author as a supernaturally gifted writer able to retrieve lost memories of Jesus. And it presents Jesus as a cryptic teacher, poorly understood in his lifetime. The Gospel, in short, positions itself as a text akin to many noncanonical, or so-called apocryphal, gospels—accounts that supposedly restore what was hidden and concealed in earlier narratives of Jesus's life.

I. Revisionary Gospels

For nearly two millennia, Christians have encountered John in the same frame as Matthew, Mark, and Luke. But in many respects, John incorporates features much more comparable to those found in many noncanonical gospels produced in or after the same period as it was written. To appreciate these features—to grasp the subtle ways in which they are deployed and to recognize their significance—it is best to place the Gospel in conversation with these texts.

A. *Gospel of Thomas*

Perhaps the best known of the so-called apocryphal gospels is the Coptic *Gospel of Thomas*, which survives in an intact Coptic translation and several Greek papyrus fragments.[2] Its incipit, or opening line, outlines its central pretense. *Thomas* presents itself as a compilation of the "secret sayings" of Jesus: "These are the hidden sayings that the living Jesus spoke and Didymus Judas Thomas wrote down."[3] What follows this incipit are 114 isolated sayings, or *logia*, of Jesus, which appear without a connecting narrative or apparent ordering principle. Consistent with the document's pretense of presenting "secret," hidden, or previously unpublished sayings of Jesus, most of *Thomas*'s sayings have no parallels in any other gospel. Likewise, some sayings are situated in previously unrecorded moments of the life of Jesus, including at least one private exchange with Thomas.[4]

The incipit also positions the work as an eyewitness account, insisting that a disciple of Jesus, Didymus Judas Thomas, transcribed the sayings. This eyewitness claim does not feature in later sections of the text. Later sections, even those that mention Thomas, are written in a third-person voice.[5] Nevertheless, the Gospel constructs Thomas as an especially insightful disciple of Jesus, one who enjoyed special access to him.[6]

Despite its pretenses, however, *Thomas* is not an eyewitness text and not a reliable source of Jesus's teaching. Although the date of its composition is unknown, recent estimates assign this gospel to the mid-second century CE.[7] More to the point, the text appears to have been written to advance a radical reinterpretation of Jesus's teachings—an intricate system of ideas that finds no trace in earlier traditions of his life and that is implausible for his social and cultural setting. The work teaches that the "kingdom" is not a future reality that comes with external signs; instead, it is a spiritual reality now available to human beings: "what you are looking forward to has come."[8] Through esoteric knowledge of their origins and destiny, humans attain an eternal life now that transcends the moment they will at last cast off their bodies of flesh.[9]

When we understand Thomas as a revisionary text, we can understand why it casts its contents as "hidden" and why it adopts a false eyewitness. These motifs are meant to dispel doubts about the Gospel's unreliable representations of Jesus. The premise that "secret sayings" of Jesus exist explains why certain materials in *Thomas* are not found in earlier gospels. Likewise, the claim that an eyewitness made the compilation bolsters the reliability of these sayings—that they have not been corrupted, distorted, or misrepresented in the text.

The Gospel supports these legitimating strategies with a few others. First, although many of its sayings are invented, *Thomas* also weaves in some sayings that are superficially similar to the sayings of Jesus contained in the Synoptics, sometimes with minor modifications. As Mark Goodacre writes, these more familiar sayings play an essential function. They ensure at least some continuity between the Jesus received from these texts and the Jesus *Thomas* constructs:

> The Synoptic material legitimizes the strange new material, interweaving the familiar with the unique, so providing a new and quite different voice for Jesus that at the same time is plausible enough to sound authentic to Thomas' earliest audiences. The Synoptic sayings are, in other words, the necessary baggage that Thomas chooses to carry to make the voice of his newly constructed "living Jesus" sound sufficiently similar to the known voice of Jesus familiar to his audience. They are there to evoke the authority of Jesus, with one foot in the tradition and one foot in the new Thomasine theology. It is a reinvention of the Synoptic Jesus, a redactional reworking of his distinctive voice.[10]

Interestingly, however, no saying in *Thomas* is identical to its Synoptic counterpart. This too may be by design. In many instances, it is clear *Thomas* has modified a saying to communicate the Gospel's unique theology. Other modifications, however, carry no apparent theological significance.[11] These minor variants may serve to undermine confidence in the tradition or textual transmission of the Synoptics, suggesting that the sayings of Jesus contained in the Synoptics had undergone some degree of distortion, corruption, or misinterpretation and that Thomas's eyewitness-validated record of Jesus is superior to those texts.

Second, *Thomas* gives the sayings of Jesus it presents a cryptic and enigmatic cast. The first *logion* of the text reads, "whoever finds the interpretation of these sayings will not taste death."[12] The idea here is that the sayings elude a straightforward interpretation and require intense study. This establishes a certain continuity with the Synoptics, in which Jesus sometimes hides his teachings in parables so that some hearers "may indeed see but not perceive and may indeed hear but not understand" (Mark 4:11–12; Matt. 13:13; Luke 8:10). But it also enhances the impression that the sayings of Jesus were prone to misinterpretation, confusion, and even distortion through their transmission, underscoring the need to access them through this gospel.

Thomas challenges its readers to recover the hidden meanings of its sayings, and it socializes readers into a reading strategy that can help them unlock those meanings. Specifically, *Thomas* develops ideas through a pattern of restatement and elaboration, through which the author communicates the same ideas multiple times in complementary language and images. Individual *logia* evoke others in the Gospel through a network of shared expressions. By comparing these statements, readers gradually assemble the text's theology; they are to "not cease seeking until they find," reading and rereading the text and combing through its various sections for insights.[13] What is cryptic in one saying is unlocked in the other, and when readers "know what is before" their faces, "what is hidden ... will be disclosed."[14]

B. *Gospel of Mary*

One finds a similar pretense—that a gospel preserves previously unrecorded and private sayings of Jesus, transmitted through an eyewitness—in the *Gospel of Mary*.[15] This early Christian text survives only in a few Coptic fragments. The first and most extensive fragments, which formed part of the papyrus codex *BG* 8502, were discovered in 1896 but not published until 1955. Those fragments consist of four middle folios of the Gospel (pp. 7–10) and the final four folios (15–18). Two more fragments surfaced in the twentieth century: *P. Ryl.* 473 and *P. Oxy.* 3525, whose text overlaps with the above segments.[16] Unlike *Thomas*, no surviving portion of the *Gospel of Mary* makes an eyewitness claim; its extant fragments speak strictly in the third person. Nevertheless, by communicating its theology through the voice of Mary, an in-text character, it implicitly claims an eyewitness source for its teachings.

In its first extant section, the Gospel depicts an otherwise unrecorded and private dialogue between Jesus and his disciples, in which the disciples ask Jesus philosophical questions on the nature and eventual fate of physical matter. Like *Thomas*, *Mary* has Jesus utter phrases drawn from the Synoptics, some subtly reworded or decontextualized to support its distinctive theology.[17] *Mary's* Jesus also directly comments upon and clarifies his language in other Gospels.[18] But *Mary* pairs this material with long, novel dialogues.

After this exchange, Jesus "departs"—ascends—leaving his disciples sad and afraid.[19] What follows is yet another supposedly unrecorded event. When the disciples "discuss the Savior's words," Peter turns to "Mary"— probably Mary Magdalene—and acknowledges her status as a favorite disciple of Jesus, who had special access to him.[20] He then asks her to relate what Jesus had told her in private: "Peter said to Mary, 'Sister, we know that the Savior loved you more than the other women. Tell us the words of the Savior that you remember, which you know and we do not, since we did not hear them.'"[21]

In response to Peter's invitation, Mary proceeds to recount all "that the Savior had spoken with her."[22] At the beginning of this section, Mary describes how she once told Jesus of a special vision she received, a detail that underscores her supernatural insight. She then recounts the private, "hidden" interpretations of that vision Jesus shared with her. Immediately, however, one recognizes that these private teachings—a complex system of cosmological and afterlife speculations—are strikingly different from those attributed to Jesus in earlier gospels. Jesus explains to Mary how the soul ascends to heaven and defeats seven hostile powers on that ascent that would inhibit it from reaching its destination.[23]

When Mary concludes her recollections, Andrew responds with skepticism to her words: "Say what you will about what she has said, but I do not believe that the Savior said these things. For these teachings are strange thoughts indeed."[24] In effect, Andrew speaks for the skeptical reader, who would also be critical of the wide divergences between the teaching of this text and that of the earlier gospels. To meet this skepticism, however, the Gospel doubles down on the idea that the teachings it relates come via the authority of an eyewitness with a unique proximity to Jesus, developing these points over a staged debate between the disciples that concludes the text.[25]

II. How John Writes

In a 1992 essay, Dwight Moody Smith provocatively asks, "Was John the First Apocryphal Gospel?"[26] His essay offers a tentative yes to this question on the grounds that the author of John "is not constrained by Mark or the Synoptics" but breaks free from their narrative structure—a pattern also seen in the later, so-called apocryphal gospels.[27] But there is another comparison to make between these texts. When one explores the Gospel of John, one sees many of the same conventions and motifs taken up by texts such as *Thomas* and *Mary*, such as an eyewitness perspective, the inclusion of supposedly unrecorded and private dialogues between Jesus and others, and an overabundance of cryptic speech.

Recognizing the presence of these strategies helps us do more than merely situate John in its literary context. It also takes us deeper into the inner logic and design of the Gospel, illuminating why it assumes the unique shape it does vis-à-vis the Synoptics. To the extent that form follows function, the form of John speaks to the anxieties of its author pursuing a project like this gospel. The author of John adopts the above strategies because he intends them to serve similar ends. He uses them to validate his own revisionary work, which reimagines the Jesus of the Gospels in a very different form than the Synoptics do.

A. Dubious Eyewitness Claims

First and foremost, John assumes an eyewitness pretense, positioning itself as a text written by one or more individuals who actually saw Jesus. The Gospel does not develop this eyewitness cast all at once, nor does it carry it through every scene. Instead, in a manner reminiscent of *Thomas* (and other works, such as the *Protoevangelium of James*), the Gospel deploys this claim strategically, at specific points. It first lays claim to an eyewitness "we" voice in its prologue, positioning itself as a memoir by those who saw Jesus in his earthly lifetime. Subsequent chapters gradually single out a particular eyewitness—an enigmatic "disciple whom Jesus loved"—as the pen and final guarantor of its contents.

1. Eyewitness Claims in Chapters 1–20

The notion that John is an eyewitness record first surfaces in the Gospel's prologue—a natural site for an author to project his authorial claims. In that passage, one finds a single, brief instance of first-person speech by the narrator: "And the Word became flesh and dwelt among us, and we have seen his glory—glory as of the unique/only son from the Father, full of grace and truth" (1:14). Read in its host sentence, the "we" of 1:14 refers back to those plural individuals "among" whom Jesus lived in the previous clause: "the Word became flesh and dwelt among *us* [*en ēmin*], and *we* have seen [*etheasametha*] his glory" (1.14). By linking the coming of Jesus in the flesh to the narrator's sight of his glory, the syntax implies that the narrator saw Jesus in the flesh. This coheres with later claims that Jesus manifested his glory to others through his miraculous "signs": "Jesus performed this, the first of his signs, at Cana in Galilee, and revealed his glory; and his disciples believed in him" (2:11; cf. 11:40). In the claim "we have seen his glory," then, the text constructs its narrator—and thus the implied author—as an eyewitness to these signs.[28]

At this point, however, the narrative does not clarify the identity of this "we." That "we" could represent (a) the collective voice of a group of people, (b) the voice of an individual author speaking for a group, or (c) the voice of a single individual choosing to speak in a "we" form for stylistic reasons (*nosism*).[29] As the narrative unfolds, however, it guides the reader to link this "we" to a particular in-text figure: a nameless male "disciple whom Jesus loved."[30] The disciple is depicted as a close companion of Jesus during the climactic events of his life. He reclines beside Jesus through the Farewell Discourse (13:23–26); he follows Jesus to his interrogation (18:15; cf. 20:2); he is the only male disciple to stand beside Jesus at the crucifixion (19:26–27; cf. 16:32); and he is the first to believe at the empty tomb (20:1–10).[31] He seems to be one of the Twelve disciples of Jesus, but the text refrains from identifying him with any particular disciple.[32]

Tellingly, when describing the crucifixion, the Gospel casts the disciple as a critical witness for the reports it contains. In chapter 19, the narrator records that, at his death, Jesus was pierced by a spear, releasing not only blood but also (the unexpected, supernatural sign of) water (19:34; cf. 7:38). As if self-conscious about this unusual report, the narrator inserts a parenthetical affidavit, in which an eyewitness validates its historicity: "He who has seen has testified ... so that you may believe" (19:35) This eyewitness is evidently the disciple whom Jesus loved since he is the only male follower of Jesus present at the crucifixion.

But 19:35 implies more; it arguably casts this disciple as a figure involved in the production of the Gospel. If, on the one hand, we interpret the "we" narrator of the text in 1:14 as the collective voice of multiple eyewitnesses to Jesus's life, then the disciple whom Jesus loves naturally belongs to that group. He forms part of this "we." On the other hand, if we identify this "we" with a single author, speaking for a larger group or for himself, it is hard not to identify that "we" with that disciple.[33] Arguably, several features of 19:35 imply that the disciple is a party to the composition. The parenthetical comment "he knows [*oiden*] that he tells the truth" suggests that the disciple is presently alive.[34] And as an affidavit, this statement is more fitting for the figure in question to make about himself—one who can validate his inner mental state.[35] More striking, the same verse claims the disciple's testimony is made precisely to and for the text's readers ("He who saw it has testified ... so that you may believe"), suggesting that this witness is anchored precisely in the production of the Gospel. Finally, the entire comment mirrors the narrator's stated purpose in writing later in the text ("these things are written so that you may believe"; 20:31), consolidating a link between narrator and disciple.[36]

If the disciple whom Jesus loved is involved with the production of the Gospel, is he one member of a group of authors, or is he a single author? Either interpretation is possible. Certainly, ancient readers could have easily read the "we" of 1:14 as a reference to the disciple referred to as a "he" in 19:35. Many ancient historians and biographers—among them Herodotus, Xenophon, Thucydides, Polybius, and Josephus—alternate between first- and third-person self-references in their surviving works.[37] Polybius even explains his pattern of alternation, indicating it was partly motivated by stylistic reasons and partly by a desire for modesty:

> One need not be surprised if we refer to ourselves by proper name and other times by common expressions.... For since we have been much involved in the events to be recorded hereafter, it is necessary to alter our self-designations so that we not ... fall into a boorish rhetorical style without being aware by constantly interjecting "of me" or "on account of me." But by making use of all these and substituting always what is fitting at the time, we should avoid as much as possible the exceeding offensiveness of speaking

about ourselves, since by nature such expression is unacceptable but is often necessary when what is being represented cannot be signified in a different way.[38]

The author of John might also have intended his readers to interpret his narrator's shifting pronouns and designations as those of a single author. Nevertheless, whether intentionally or unintentionally, that author left the relationship of his "we" and "disciple"/"he" ambiguous.

2. Eyewitness Claims in Chapter 21

The idea that an eyewitness "disciple whom Jesus loved" authored the Gospel, either as part of a broader group or individually, was consolidated in the text's later development. As we have seen, chapter 21 is probably not an original segment of John but a later scribe's addition to the text. Sometime after the Gospel was completed, a second hand, probably unconnected to the first, introduced a new chapter to the text, one that expressly affirms the eyewitness authorship of the Gospel up to and (crucially) including the new passage. Not coincidentally, that affirmation combines the language of precisely those verses of chapters 1–20 that articulate the Gospel's eyewitness claim—that is, the statement at 1:14, the affidavit at 19:35, and the text's original conclusion at 20:31. It is intentionally modeled on those verses:

John 21:24–25	John 1:14	John 19:35	John 20:31
This is the disciple who is testifying to these things		cf. "He who saw it has testified"	
And has written these things			cf. "these are written that you may believe"
And we know that his testimony is true	cf. "we"	cf. "his testimony is true, and he knows that he tells the truth"	
But there are also many other things that Jesus did.... were every one of them to be written, I suppose that the world itself could not contain the books that would be written.			cf. "Now Jesus did many other signs in the presence of the disciples, which are not written in this book."

The resulting line, however, is more than the sum of its parts. It resolves some of the ambiguity of the preceding chapters, explicitly asserting that a single male eyewitness, "the disciple whom Jesus loved," has "written these things" (i.e., all its text up to and including the epilogue).[39] That is, the verse selects one of the interpretive options of chapters 1–20 and endorses it.

Even more striking, the author allows the individual "disciple" to inhabit a singular "I" voice for the first time, something the author of chapters 1–20 does not do. Admittedly, the alternation of so many pronouns for a single figure is jarring in such a compressed space, but this speech style is not unprecedented. Earlier in John, Jesus sharply alternates between "I," "we," and third-person self-references: "Amen, amen, I say to you, we speak of what we know and testify to what we have seen, yet you do not receive our testimony. If I have told you about earthly things and you do not believe, how can you believe if I tell you about heavenly things? No one has ascended into heaven except the one who descended from heaven, the Son of Man" (3:11–13). More important, this style is also used by the narrators of other ancient works. For example, in the first book of the *History of the Peloponnesian War*, Thucydides shifts from a third-person reference to himself ("Thucydides, the Athenian, wrote the history of the war between the Peloponnesians and the Athenians") to first-person singular ("I") and plural ("we") self-references.[40] Josephus also alternates between narratorial "we" and "I" in an epilogue: "Here is the end of the history by us, which we promised to convey with total accuracy to those wishing to learn how this war by the Romans against the Jews was waged. How it has been expressed, let it be left to the readers to judge. But concerning the truth, I would not hesitate to say with confidence that I endeavored after this throughout the entire composition."[41] And at a still further extreme, consider the following passage from the writings of Polybius, in which he juxtaposes not three, but five forms in a tightly compressed space: "Polybius," "I," "we," and (in references to himself and Scipio) "the men" and "them." Toward the end of the passage, Polybius even speaks of himself in both the first person and the third person in the same sentence—a confusing formation akin to what one finds in John 21:24–25:

> For *I* promised before to describe in detail why and how the fame of Scipio in Rome advanced so much and burst forth more quickly than was his due and with this how it happened that *Polybius* grew in friendship and intimacy with the aforementioned person to such an extent that, not only did

the report about *them* extend as far as Italy and Greece, but their conduct and companionship also became well-known in more distant regions. *We* have, therefore, indicated in what has been said previously that the beginning of the friendship between *the aforementioned men* came out of a certain loan of books and the conversation about *them*.[42]

The casual drift between "we," "I," and "he/him" language in John 21:24–25 might reflect the redactor's style. Alternatively, the scribe might have compressed all these pronouns into this affidavit to demonstrate his continuity with the Gospel's many ways of referring to the disciple ("we," "disciple," "he/his")—covering all his bases, as it were. His affidavit, after all, is a bricolage of phrases derived from chapters 1–20. Whatever the case, chapter 21 develops the authorial claims of chapters 1–20, affirming that John is the product of an individual disciple of Jesus.[43]

3. A Serious Claim

In its original form and in its later redaction, John makes an eyewitness claim. But was this claim meant to be taken seriously by readers? Admittedly, there are scenarios in which an author may assume a particular persona as a transparent fiction or façade. One thinks, for example, of fictional works or works produced for compositional practice, entertainment, or satire.[44] But in other cases—many cases—ancient authors seem to have wanted their readers to accept such claims at face value. The evidence is found in the strenuous efforts made by authors to assure their readers of their works' authenticity and to provide proof to that effect.[45] It is supported by documents indicating that some ancient persons created forgeries for profit, to defame others, and to amplify ideologies—positive evidence of deceptive intent. It is consistent with accounts of the negative consequences facing those who fabricated texts.[46] And it is confirmed in the simple reality that so many works with these features were received as authentic until recent times.

When we look closely at John, the conclusion seems inescapable: the author hoped to impress his readers with the idea that his account was an eyewitness record. This is especially clear in 19:35, where the author strenuously affirms the reliability of his testimony, pressing his reliability multiple times. In the same verse, he links his reliability to a particular response he hopes for his readers, namely, belief: "He who saw it has borne witness; his testimony is true, and he knows that he tells the truth, so that you may believe."

The seriousness with which the author defends his reliability here is even clearer when we consider these words in their broader rhetorical context, what Andrew Lincoln calls the "lawsuit motif" or "trial motif" in John.[47] It is well known that the Gospel stresses the importance of truthful and reliable "testimony." Words related to "testimony" and "testifying" appear some forty-seven times in the text. The reason, as one author succinctly states the matter, is that "the Fourth Gospel shows a heavy inclination—as the Roman historians do—of associating 'truth' with 'fact/testimony.'"[48] Across its many chapters, then, the Gospel lines up so many witnesses to testify to the claims Jesus makes, and it defends the reliability of their testimony in the same terms as does 19:35.[49] Jesus insists that "the Father who sent me testifies to me" and that the Father's testimony is "true" (8:17–18; cf. 5:32, 37). Jesus also affirms that he testifies to himself, adding, "my testimony is true" (8:14, 18). In later chapters, he claims, "the Spirit of truth . . . will testify to me" (15:26). Elsewhere, he affirms that John the Baptist has "testified to the truth" (5:33).[50] The narrator's affidavit is phrased in the same language as these verses, evidently with a mutually reinforcing effect. A reader is meant to receive the authorial claims of the book in the same receptive posture as they would receive other elements of the book's "testimony."[51]

Likewise, John's Jesus stresses the critical importance of receiving truthful testimony. In chapter 3, as if encapsulating the voice of all these eyewitnesses, Jesus tells Nicodemus, "we speak of what we know, and bear witness to what we have seen; but you do not receive our testimony," linking this stance to the state of being "condemned" (3:11, 18; cf. 3:32). Later he will cast those unwilling to accept his "testimony" as aligned with "the devil" (8:14, 43–44, 47), and lacking eternal life (8:24, 51; 17:3). By contrast, he promises exaltation and oneness with God to those who "believe" the testimony of his disciples—including, undoubtedly, the "disciple whom Jesus loved" (15:27, 17:20–22).

4. Evaluating the Claim

The Gospel of John positions itself as an eyewitness account of the life of Jesus. And yet we have every reason to doubt this claim. The Gospel may preserve some "primitive, undeveloped material" of historical value extracted from a wide range of oral or written sources available to its author.[52] But that material accounts for only a fraction of the Gospel's contents. As we have seen, a far more significant percentage of the text, both discourse material and narrative, is of suspect historicity.[53]

Admittedly, embellishment is not incompatible with eyewitness testimony or with historical writing.[54] But fabrication of the scope and kind seen in John—hundreds of verses of invented discourse amounting to a systemic refiguration of Jesus's teachings—is another matter altogether. This kind of refiguration evokes the *Gospel of Thomas*, a text that also claims an eyewitness but extensively colonizes Jesus's voice to validate its novel theology. It also evokes the *Gospel of Mary*. The fact that John's theology meets our standards of orthodoxy should not obscure its use of the same strategy.

An Integral Claim
Pressed with these problems, it may be tempting to disentangle the Gospel's most problematic materials from its eyewitness claims, treating these as separate issues.[55] And yet we cannot isolate John's eyewitness claims from its extensive fabrications. Those claims are embedded within, intimately connected to the text's invented discourses, using the same language:

Narrator:
And the Word became flesh and dwelled among us, and we have seen his glory. (1:14)

Jesus:
Jesus said to her, "Did I not tell you that if you would believe, you would see the glory of God?" (11:40)

Narrator:
He who has seen has testified; his testimony is true. (19:35)

Jesus:
"There is another who testifies. . . . I know that his testimony to me is true. (5:32)

In short, the same author produced the invented speech of Jesus and the eyewitness claims. Both stem from the same contaminated source, and both rise and fall together. If one is suspect, the other is as well.

Another reason we cannot isolate the text's eyewitness claims from the rest of the text is that the eyewitness pretense of the Gospel is not limited to a few verses. On the contrary, it would seem the text's real author constructed the entire narrative, including so many of its invented or manipulated stories, under the pretense that it relates the experiences and reminisces of an eyewitness. He threaded the text with minor details that regularly suggest its supposed eyewitness character. In fact, as Paul Anderson writes, "John has more archaeological, topographical, sensory-empirical, personal knowledge and first-hand information than all of the other gospels combined."[56]

It is well known that the narrator of John takes pains to incorporate seemingly mundane details in his descriptions, including specific materials, sizes, locations, and positions for objects in his stories.[57] The narrator claims that Jesus performed a miracle on water stored in "six stone jars . . . for the Jewish rites of purification, each holding twenty or thirty gallons" (2:6), and that the bread Jesus multiplied for the crowds was made of "barley" (6:9, 13). He claims that the fire at which Peter denied Jesus was, specifically, "a charcoal fire," lit because the night was cold (18:18; cf. Mark 14:54; Luke 22:55). He states that the tomb in which Joseph deposited the body of Jesus was located "in the place where he was crucified," where "there was a garden" (19:41), and he relates the configuration of Jesus's tomb in detail, claiming that Peter "saw the linen cloths lying, and the napkin, which had been on his head, not lying with the linen cloths but rolled up in a place by itself" (20:6-7). The narrator even positions the two angels within the vacated tomb of Jesus, describing them "sitting where the body of Jesus had lain, one at the head and one at the feet" (20:12).

The narrator of John is also keen to provide specific indications of distance and time. He claims, for example, that Jesus appeared to the disciples on the Sea of Galilee "when they had rowed twenty-five or thirty stadia" (6:19) and that Bethany was "near Jerusalem, about fifteen stadia off" (11:18). He sets the beginning of his narrative in a specific year: forty-six years after Herod ordered work on the Jerusalem temple, or c. 27/28 CE (2:20).[58] The narrator regularly correlates events in his narrative with specific feasts in the Jewish year, often without any apparent motivation (2:23, 6:4, 7:2, 37, 10:22, 11:56, 12:1).[59] And he lists the specific time of events he describes multiple times: "the sixth hour" (4:6, 19:14), the "seventh hour" (4:52-53), the "tenth hour" (1:39).

The narrator of John also clarifies characters and places. He alone claims that the servant who struck Simon Peter's ear was named "Malchus" (18:10). He states two separate times that Judas Iscariot was the son of a man named "Simon" (6:71; 13:2). He indicates that Andrew, Peter, and Philip were from Bethsaida (1:44, 12:20-21) and that Mary, Martha, and Lazarus were from "Bethany" (11:1, 18, 12:1). He attributes words to specific disciples that the Synoptics attribute to the disciples in general.[60] And he expressly names the places where John the Baptist was active as "Bethany beyond the Jordan" (1:28) as "Aenon named Salim" (3:23).

The density of so many references is striking; so too is the impression they give. Together, these imbue the text with the veneer of eyewitness credibility. According to Samuel Byrskog, "seemingly ad hoc pieces of information within passages ... provide, whether historically accurate or not ... a realistic stamp."[61] Building on this idea, Litwa reasons that many of John's details might have been inserted strategically as verisimilitudes, giving "the impression of historical reminisce."[62] Many pseudo-historical narratives from antiquity fold in similar touches at specific points to imbue their narratives with an eyewitness flavor. The same may be true of John. In this case, it would seem the Gospel's eyewitness claims are not merely a function of a few verses; they are, instead, tightly woven into the entire fabric of the narrative.

But where did these excessive details come from? Many might be inventions. This is almost certainly the case for details set in episodes that are mostly or entirely invented or that center on characters that are likely invented (e.g., the calling of Andrew and Peter, the dialogue with Nicodemus, and the raising of Lazarus). Any exercise of fiction can supply details just as concrete and specific. We can also greet with skepticism those details introduced into those episodes that seem built on Synoptic models but which have been altered from those models into forms that contradict the Synoptic accounts, for example, the anointing of Jesus in Bethany (John 12:1–3; cf. Mark 14:3; Luke 7:36–38). We should also recognize that many granular details in the Gospel are unfalsifiable and, for that reason, easily invented. There is no way to judge whether the loaves Jesus fed the crowds were made of barley as opposed to wheat, whether Peter warmed himself before a charcoal fire as opposed to a wood fire, or whether the disciples were, in fact, "twenty-five or thirty stadia" from the shore when Jesus reportedly appeared to them (if we anchor this miracle in historical fact). The text may shift the burden of proof onto us with such details, but we hardly need to play the Gospel's game in the face of its inventions elsewhere.

That being said, some details in the text correspond to known historical markers, and some are at least plausible. Like any historicizing fiction, John would benefit from some share of historical anchors. The Gospel's author might have acquired these details from other, now lost written accounts of Jesus's life or oral traditions, just as he acquired some particulars from the Synoptics. Given the knowledge of Jerusalem's topography, we cannot rule out the possibility that the author lived in or near Palestine (Caesarea Maritima? Damascus?) or at least had personal experiences in the region. Alternatively, he might have known refugees from, or one-time visitors to, the region while living in another region of the empire with a significant Jewish diaspora (Antioch? Alexandria? Asia Minor?). He could have derived some of these details from other literary sources—perhaps historical works, biographies, or travel reports from Palestine. Our author was a wide and eclectic reader, fully capable of synthesizing new products from scattered details in different sources. Recent scholarship on John's use of the Synoptics, which shows how our author could pick and combine information from various sources, gives us some impression of how he could have utilized other (written or oral) sources to sustain a false eyewitness pretense.

A Disguised Work

Of course, if John's eyewitness claims are tightly woven into his text, and if they are false, then we are left with one conclusion: John is a falsely authored work—a text in which an author disguises their identity, indicating to readers that they are someone they are not.[63] This would hardly make John unusual or exceptional. Again, many second-century gospels are falsely authored.

When we set John alongside these other gospels, we can also appreciate how similar its authorial claims are to theirs. It is no coincidence that John claims a disciple as its author; so too does *Thomas* (and *Peter*). For that matter, the significance assigned to the invented disciple of John is also reminiscent of the importance attached to the implied author of *Thomas* and the central character of *Mary*. Each of these gospels leverages the authority of a figure who is singled out as a special intimate of Jesus. In *Thomas*, Thomas receives a unique, ineffable revelation of Jesus surpassing those Jesus gives to other disciples.[64] Likewise, in *Mary*, Levi singles out Mary as a figure who is "worthy" and whom Jesus "loved . . . more than us."[65] Litwa argues that the similarities between John's eyewitness and those found in these gospels "force the critical reader to reflect on why scholars even today argue strongly for the historicity of the Beloved Disciple . . . while easily discounting the historicity of similar eyewitness claims."[66]

Inventing a Disciple

Still, the Gospel of John is distinct from these other gospels in one respect: its author does not assume the guise of a known or otherwise named eyewitness to the life of Jesus. He chooses, instead, to cast his work as one that condenses the testimony of an enigmatic or unknown disciple of Jesus. Indeed, the identity of the "disciple whom Jesus loved" has long drawn readers into what Harold Attridge calls a "restless quest," framed by the fact that "there is simply no sure identification of the figure."[67] All efforts to identify him with a known disciple of Jesus result in "a dead end"; the text "systematically defeats any attempt to identify who that witness was."[68]

The traditional claim—the idea that this disciple is John, the son of Zebedee—is hardly clear or inescapable.[69] The Gospel never attributes a single, distinctive trait of the Synoptic John to this disciple. It never says that the "disciple whom Jesus loved" is from Galilee, and he is never described as a fisherman (Mark 1:16-20). We are never told that he has a brother, and he is never called the "son of Zebedee" or a "son of Thunder" (Mark 1:19, 3:17). For that matter, as Moody Smith observes, "exactly those episodes in which John the son of Zebedee is present in Mark, or the Synoptics generally, from the healing of Peter's mother-in-law to the Garden of Gethsemane, are absent from the Gospel of John (see Mark 1:16-20, 29-31; 3:13-19; 5:35-43; 9:2-8; 10:35-41; 13:3; 14:32-42; also Luke 22:7-13)."[70] It is hard to imagine how an eyewitness record by John would lack every single episode featuring John, including central ones, such as the Transfiguration.[71] It is also hard to understand how the author could have John, the Galilean fisherman, in mind when he casts the "other disciple," later identified as the disciple "whom Jesus loved" (20:2), as one "known to the high priest," as in 18:15-16.[72]

No other proposed candidate is compelling either. The disciple cannot be Lazarus, whom Jesus is also said to have "loved" (11:3). Lazarus is never numbered among "the disciples" (cf. 11:7, 8, 16, 54). The attribute of "being loved" is not exclusive to him; his sisters are also "loved" by Jesus (11:5). More important, Lazarus could not be the disciple the author constructs as having privileged access to the high priest's home on the night of Jesus's death since the text claims that, at the time, the high priest's circle was aggressively seeking to kill Lazarus (12:10-11).[73] The disciple whom Jesus loved is also not Thomas, whose initial skepticism at the idea of Jesus's resurrection starkly contrasts the disciple's trusting belief (20:8, 25).[74] He cannot be one of the female disciples of Jesus, such as Mary, since he is spoken of in masculine verb forms (19:35). Nor is there any evidence definitively linking him to the roughly dozen other proposed candidates.

But perhaps there is no need to identify him with a particular figure. Since the literary turn in Johannine studies (1980s-), several writers have argued that the "disciple whom Jesus loved" may be a mere literary device or invention. Every Synoptic parallel that could corroborate his presence at a given moment in Jesus's life does not—not the Synoptic crucifixion scenes

(Mark 15:40–41; Matt. 27:55–56; cf. John 19:26–27) nor Luke's description of Peter's visit to the tomb (Luke 24:12; cf. John 20.2–10). No less problematically, the eyewitness has a highly artificial texture. "Unlike the other Johannine characters . . . he is the ideal disciple, the paradigm of discipleship," who "has no misunderstandings."[75]

Other falsely authored works invent eyewitness authors or sources. Some name these figures, such as the *Diary of the Trojan War*, written by an invented character named Dictys the Crete, and the *Life of Apollonius*, which claims to be based on the memoirs of a supposed disciple of Apollonius named Damis.[76] Others leave these figures unnamed, among them Philostratus's *Heroicus* and the *Martyrdom of Marian and James*.[77] Anonymity can be helpful to a pseudepigrapher's aims; according to Litwa, it can be a "technique to prevent invalidation" as it leaves the eyewitness' existence "unfalsifiable."[78] Similarly, many works cast their invented eyewitnesses in idealized terms, as John does: "[In the *Life of Apollonius*] Damis, for instance, is Apollonius' closest disciple who sticks by him and even suffers arrest in Rome. . . . A basic similarity can be detected in John. Although Jesus loves all his disciples, the Beloved Disciple is arguably the most intimate. Unlike Jesus' other followers, the Beloved Disciple does not abandon Jesus after he is arrested. Instead, he follows Jesus into the courtyard of his enemy (John 18:15). Presumably it was even more dangerous for the disciple to stand at the foot of the cross (John 19:26)."[79] These invented characters can also mingle with real characters, as in John.[80] Even details like those encountered in John 21:21–22—discussions of the eyewitness's death—appear in other texts as verisimilitudes.[81]

The author of John, of course, had every incentive to invent such an eyewitness. Besides supporting the credibility of his fabrications, the device would have positioned his text more competitively in a crowded field of gospels.[82] Mark and Matthew do not claim to be eyewitness accounts. Luke expressly distinguishes himself from "those who from the beginning were eyewitnesses and servants of the word" (1:2). In this case, it may not be a coincidence that the narrator of John chooses to position himself precisely among the eyewitnesses of "the Word" (John 1:14), who had "been with" Jesus "from the beginning" (15:27) and who had been his "servants" (15:15). The invented disciple may be the author's way of laying claim to the sources behind all other gospels, even precisely to supersede the others.

B. Complementary Devices

The Gospel's eyewitness cast is an important way, an especially foregrounded way, it validates its contents. But the text supplements this cast through other devices that suggest why the text's invented materials might not be represented in other accounts of Jesus's life. Many of these also find cognates in the noncanonical gospels we discussed above.

1. Unrecorded Moments

John knows the Synoptics but shares very little material with them. Like the noncanonical gospels discussed earlier, John focuses instead on previously unrecorded scenes in the life of Jesus. Not surprisingly, those scenes contain most of the Gospel's novel and revisionary materials—its new symbolic episodes and extended dialogues. John presupposes the essential contours of the Synoptic gospels, but it circumvents their contents precisely to work out its revisionary image of Jesus.

Interestingly, the author of chapters 1–20 and the redactor who inserted John 21 were so self-conscious of this circumvention of tradition as to address potential criticisms of it preemptively. Both of the text's received endings, 20:30–31 and 21:25, acknowledge that Jesus did many other things not contained in the book. Statements of this kind—that is, implicit apologies for those items omitted from an account—are found in other Greco-Roman texts as conventional conclusions.[83] In John, as in these other works, these conclusions acknowledge the existence of other, earlier accounts on the same theme; here, the conclusions at 20:30–31 and 21:25 indicate John's familiarity with other, earlier accounts of the life of Jesus—minimally, the Synoptic Gospels. But they also carve out space for John as an entrant in the same tradition.[84] The ending creates space for the composition of John by gesturing toward the limitless possibilities, the unbounded horizon of gospel writing. It insists that there is no limit to what one can write about Jesus, licensing the creation of new compositions like itself, rich with new content.[85]

2. Private Exchanges

John is similar to many so-called apocryphal works in its construction of supposedly lost episodes in the life of Jesus. But it is also similar to many of these works—especially *Mary*, *Judas*, and the *Apocryphon of James*—in its emphasis on private discourses. As Jerome Neyrey observes, unlike the Jesus of the Synoptics, John's Jesus "holds long, extended conversations in private with select persons in which things are said which are not communicated to the crowds," at least at the same length and, often, with the same clarity.[86]

Tellingly, these discourses introduce many of the most critical teachings of the Gospel. In private encounters with Nicodemus and the Samaritan woman, Jesus reveals that humans can be born of *pneuma* and receive eternal life now. Likewise, in a private exchange with Martha, Jesus reveals the spiritual resurrection (11:20–27). In a private conversation with Pilate, Jesus indicates that his kingdom is "not of this world" (18:36). And climactically, chapters 13–17 portray an intimate conversation, evoking Greco-Roman farewell discourses, in which Jesus clarifies his teachings in full detail.[87] In the privacy of a night hour and surrounded by his closest companions, who had followed him "from the beginning" (15:27), Jesus fleshes out the Gospel's complex theology of celestial access and oneness at length. In each of these new, unfamiliar, and intimate scenes, the author entices readers with the notion that they are listening in on teachings of Jesus disclosed only to a select, privileged few, often in private conversations—conversations to which other gospel authors might not have been privy but which an intimate disciple of Jesus might have known.[88]

3. Supernaturally Retrieved Memory

A skeptical reader might wonder why other gospels omit some of these unrecorded or private moments detailed in John. Anticipating this question, the Gospel reinforces the above strategies with yet another; it plants the idea that many materials it contains, both teachings and sayings, were forgotten, at least for a time. After expounding a particular set of teachings with no cognate in the Synoptics—the ideas of celestial access and indwelling—Jesus tells his disciples, "These things I have spoken to you, while I am still with you. But the Paraclete, the Holy Spirit, whom the Father will send in my name, will teach you all things and bring to your remembrance all that I have said to you" (14:25–26). Later in the same discourse, Jesus implies that his disciples will need to recall another teaching he had just uttered (16:4).

The pretense here is that the disciples could not, and did not, hold all that Jesus had taught and did in their memory—including the cryptic and challenging teachings he had just spoken. But John's Jesus implies that those memories, once lost, would be supernaturally retrieved after the coming of the Spirit. In turn, the Gospel positions itself as a text built from those retrieved memories. In it, the narrator registers instances in which the disciples "remembered" a particular saying or gesture of Jesus only at a later time, folding these instances into his text (2:22, 12:16). The author deploys these details strategically to cast his entire work as established on the more complete, retrieved memory of the disciples.[89]

4. Spiritual Insight
Just as Jesus tells his disciples in the Farewell Discourse that the Spirit "will bring to your remembrance all that I have said to you," he claims that the same Spirit "will teach you all things" (14:26). This idea is stressed at other points in the same section, in one instance coupled with the notion that Jesus had more teachings to impart to his disciples: "I still have many things to say to you, but you cannot bear them now. When the Spirit of truth comes, he will guide you into all the truth; for he will not speak on his own authority, but whatever he hears, he will speak, and he will declare to you the things that are to come. He will glorify me, for he will take what is mine and declare it to you" (16:13–14; cf. 15:26). These words suggest that the disciples would eventually receive greater data and insight than Jesus could have possibly communicated to them in his lifetime. This would include, above all, the narrator of the text: the "disciple whom Jesus loved." The very description of the character evokes Jesus's claim that the one whom he "loves" will enjoy the Spirit-mediated indwelling (14:21, 23). The description, in short, implies the disciple is Spirit-filled and endowed with the special gifts of insight the Spirit brings.[90]

This idea—that Jesus provided a revelation more capacious than his earthly teachings but which the narrator can unlock—licenses several moves seen in the Gospel. First, it validates the narrator's ability to relate additional ideas Jesus does not communicate in the Synoptics, such as his prehuman origins as the *Logos* (1:1–18). This is especially true in light of 15:26, in which Jesus claims that the coming Spirit "will testify about me."[91] It also gives the narrator freedom to authoritatively interpret Jesus's teachings at critical junctures (e.g., at 2:21 and 7:39) or to authoritatively interpret scriptures.[92] For that matter, it may also explain how the narrator could know of and portray events he did not directly witness. John, in short, harnesses the divide between memory and forgetting. It offers its readers an eyewitness account of the life of Jesus, but to deflect any skepticism over its novel materials, it also claims a charismatic authority for its eyewitness voice.

5. Cryptic Speech

John presents Jesus as a teacher who discloses all secrets to his disciples: "all that I have heard from my Father I have made known to you" (15:15). Nevertheless, the Gospel indicates that Jesus did not always present this material in a straightforward manner, but sometimes spoke in cryptic forms, figures, or riddles. As Jesus tells his disciples later in the Farewell Discourse, "I have said this to you in figures [*en paroimiais*]; the hour is coming when I shall no longer speak to you in figures [*en paroimiais*] but tell you plainly [*parrēsiai*] of the Father" (16:25).

The idea that Jesus's teachings could be opaque likely reflects Mark's claim that Jesus spoke to those "outside" in parables (4:11).[93] John, however, develops this device further, extending Jesus's speech into a broader range of techniques and contexts. In the end, nearly all of Jesus's speech in the Gospel is written in a cryptic style pervaded by non sequiturs (e.g., 3:2–3), ciphers (e.g., 4:10; cf. 7:38–39; also 6:56, 63), ambiguous statements and double entendres (e.g., 2:19, 3:3, 5), half-truths or progressive revelations (e.g., 7:8–10, 34; cf. 13:33, 36), opaque figures reminiscent of parables (e.g., 10:1–6, 14:1–3, 15:1–7), and what M. W. G Stibbe correctly identifies as an "extravagant use of metaphor" (e.g., light, darkness, day, night, dwell, bread, vine, house).[94] The elusive nature of Jesus's speech tests the patience of the narrative's characters, many of whom respond with dismay (6:41–42, 60, 66), verbalize their confusion (e.g., 7:35–36), ask follow-up questions (e.g., 3:4, 4:11, 13:36), and struggle to understand Jesus's often impenetrable clarifications (e.g., 14:5, 8, 22).

As in *Thomas*, many of Jesus's discourses are structured as stacked statements and restatements of the same puzzling ideas (e.g., 5:21–30, 6:35–59).[95] And also as in *Thomas*, John builds discourses whose meaning is unlocked by a careful reader who engages in comparative reading of these words, coordinating multiple sayings to find their interpretation. This way of framing and reorienting Jesus's language plays an important role in how the Gospel communicates its eschatological ideas.[96] Chapter by chapter, John takes up expressions typical of future-eschatological concepts in the Synoptics, but it gradually assimilates them into its realized-eschatological vision. John's Jesus evokes the Synoptic expectation of his future, visible return, promising that he will "come again" (14:3; cf. Mark 8:38, 14:62). In the lines that follow, however, he gradually clarifies that he is coming in a manner the world at large cannot see (14:18–19). Similarly, Jesus teaches a coming "kingdom" (cf. Mark 1:15), but he incrementally develops the idea, contrary to the Synoptics, that Jesus's "kingdom is not of this world" (John 18:36) and is accessed only by "spirit," not in the "flesh" (3:5). John's Jesus also promises "eternal life" (cf. Mark 10:30; Luke 18:30), but unlike the Synoptics, which situate this life in the future, John recasts this life as one humans can now possess (3:36, 6:47).

Not coincidentally, this strategy works in close conjunction with the eyewitness claims of the Gospel. By falsely claiming to be an eyewitness, the author positions his text as a more complete and accurate transcript of Jesus's teaching than other early Jesus traditions, oral and written. In this way, he also positions his text as the only one that can contextualize Jesus's actual words and clarify his intended meanings (e.g., on the nature of his coming or kingdom)—meanings he bends toward his distinctive ideology.

We can also connect this pattern to the Gospel's pervasive symbolic program, discussed in the previous chapter. In many ways, the actions and gestures of Jesus throughout the Gospel are yet another kind of metaphoric and cryptic communication: performed "figures," which elicit the same sort of confusion or lack of understanding from observers as his verbal "figures" (12:16, 20:9). And as we saw, they too draw readers into the same practice of comparative reading and rereading, pondering and decipherment.

6. Strategic Overlap with the Synoptics

A final technique evident in John and reminiscent of *Thomas* and *Mary* is the strategic use of Synoptic materials. Certain stories in John are direct cognates of Synoptic stories (e.g., 6:1–21), while others are at least reminiscent of them (e.g., 2:13–22, 4:46–54). Additionally, John also adapts some Synoptic sayings, modifying them to bear the weight of the Gospel's distinctive theology as in, for example:

> The one who loves their life loses it, and the one who hates their life in this world will keep it for eternal life. (12:25)

Compare:
For whoever would save his life will lose it, and whoever loses his life for my sake and the gospel's will save it. (Mark 8:35; cf. Matt. 10:39, 16:25; Luke 9:24, 17:33)

> Amen, amen, I say to you, unless one is born of water and the Spirit, he cannot enter the kingdom of God. (3:5)

Compare:
Amen, I say to you, unless you turn and become like children, you will never enter the kingdom of heaven. (Matt. 18:3)

As in *Thomas*, the Synoptic-like character of these sayings gives them, and the materials around them, the impression of continuity with earlier strands of Jesus tradition.[97]

Likewise, even though John does not share many materials with the Synoptics, it uses many expressions uncannily evocative of images or phrases found in the Synoptics. These include "shepherd" and "sheep" (10:11; cf. Mark 6:34, 14:27; Matt. 18:10–14; Luke 15:3–7), "harvest" (4:35–38; cf. Matt. 9:37–38; Luke 10:2), giving "blood" to drink (6:53–56; cf. Mark 14:23–24); "bridegroom" (3:29–30; cf. Mark 2:19), the expression "not taste death" (8:52; cf. Mark 9:1), "the light of the world" (8:12; cf. Matt. 5:14), "knowing" the Father (1:18, 8:19, 10:15, 14:7; cf. Luke 10:22), glorifying or hallowing "the name" (12:28; cf. Matt. 6:9; Luke 11:2), bearing "fruit" (15:8; cf. Mark 4:20; Matt. 7:17–19; 13:23; Luke 3:8–9, 6:43, 13:9), the image of a "vine" (15:1, 5; cf. Mark 14:25), and talk of good or new "wine" (2:10; cf. Mark 2:22). These commonalities suggest an intentional strategy of echoing earlier Synoptic materials even in completely new, invented discourses. Together, these images and turns of phrase give the sayings found in John the feel of verisimilitude.

C. A Competitive Gospel

When we lay out these techniques, we can appreciate the revisionary nature of the Gospel of John. And yet revision can imply different kinds of intertextual relationships. For example, a text might see itself as *displacing* or replacing previous works; that is, it might imply that it alone is worthy of reading and encourage the reader to discard those other works in favor of itself.[98] Alternatively, a text might pretend to *supplement* other texts. It might respect the authority of previous works but imply that those works are incomplete or lacking something vital—something it alone can supply. In a third scenario, a text might merely *complement* earlier works. Here, there is no suggestion that a previous work is wrong or lacking anything, but the new work augments the witness of the earlier works, adding further, if nonessential materials.

John does not cleanly fit these categories. It clearly leans on other gospels. It anticipates that its readers know material from the Synoptics and expects them to fill gaps in its narrative from those other works (e.g., alluding to events it does not narrate [3:24] or expecting its readers to know characters introduced in other gospels [11:1–2]). John also introduces new materials. And yet the Gospel of John pushes against earlier gospels as well. It undermines—even contradicts—those other texts, calling into question their details and claims (cf. John 12:27–28 and Mark 14:35–42; John 1:21 and Matt. 17:11–13), even their chronologies (e.g., 13:1–4; cf. Mark 14:12). We can conceptualize John, then, as occupying a *competitive* posture.[99] It inserts itself into an established tradition, but it subordinates the tradition to itself as if it were a superior account of Jesus's life, one that can augment and correct the works that came before it.[100]

III. Publishing John

To this point, we have established that John was written by an individual who worked clandestinely, disguised his identity, and composed a revisionary, competitive account of the life of Jesus. But how did this author succeed in getting his text read by others? How were falsely authored works like John disseminated in the ancient world? The reality is that few ancient texts illuminate this process. Just as they effaced their names and identities, ancient pseudepigraphers also concealed how they introduced their works. And even where we find these works condemned, we find few, if any, discussions of how they might have initially entered into circulation; in most instances, it is safe to presume that the people encountering and condemning these works did not know where they came from. For this reason, we should assume that these texts were probably not developed in a visible, public manner but surreptitiously.

Nevertheless, it is possible to peer into this darkness to some extent. Scanning the extant body of ancient literature, one finds evidence of different modes by which Greco-Roman writers introduced products of disguised authorship. At least two are potentially relevant for John's origins: (a) distribution through correspondence and (b) tampering with literary collections and libraries. That pseudepigraphers utilized these channels is not particularly striking. These were, in fact, the primary channels by which many ancient books entered circulation.

A. Correspondence

Many scholars uncritically assume that the first readers of the Gospel of John were those in the author's local context—the people he lived beside and, perhaps, with whom he gathered for meals or worship. But this is not necessarily the case; we have ample evidence that ancient authors often shared, exchanged, and circulated works by sending them to peers in other cities as gifts, either with no restrictions on their being copied or even with a cover letter actively encouraging the recipient to circulate these texts. In one letter, for instance, Cicero encourages Atticus that if he should "like the book" Cicero has sent, he should "see that it is made available at Athens and the other Greek towns."[101] As Starr notes, "when strangers could acquire copies of a work, that work can be said to have been made public or to have been released."[102]

This mode of publication was especially well suited for the circulation of falsely authored works. The essential exercise of literary forgery is, after all, the effacement of a real author's context. When one writes from a geographical remove, one can maintain a significant degree of control over what information a potential reader can and cannot access about a text's production. One is in a better position to deny any involvement in the authorship of a work; one can also invent circumstances for how one came across a work—circumstances a person at a geographical remove is not always in a position to validate or invalidate. It is little wonder, then, that ancient sources describe disguised authors circulating their works in this manner. For example, the Greek geographer Pausanias (second century CE) indicates that Anaximenes of Lampsacus imitated the writing style of his rival Theopompus and "inscribed his name upon the book and sent it round to the cities."[103] Our Christian evidence is more lacunose and late, but it demonstrates that Christians had developed multiple channels as well as their own "organized system for publication and distribution of Christian literature."[104] It also indicates that falsely authored Christian texts also moved through these channels.[105]

B. Tampering with Library Collections

Another way to disseminate literary fakes was to introduce them to the shelves of libraries or literary collections or to interpolate them into the manuscripts held by such facilities. Ancient associations and individuals kept collections of books for a variety of reasons, including personal reference, communal reading, and merely to display their wealth and status. Although these libraries were designed to keep texts secure, they were also vulnerable to tampering. Certain works of dubious pedigree are said to have suddenly surfaced in a library or treasury store.[106] And Diogenes Laertius, for example, tells us that the Stoic philosopher Athenodorus Cananites was dismissed from his position as keeper of the library of Pergamum because he had abused his position, altering sections from the texts of Zeno.[107] For a pseudepigrapher, interpolating a library text or planting a document in a library had obvious benefits. A work surreptitiously inserted into an existing collection would have no chain of custody or transmission. Under the right circumstances, it would not be apparent when or how the text was introduced to the collection, making it much harder to demonstrate its recent vintage.

Nearly all Christian communities of the period maintained similar collections, consisting of at least the books read in the group's gatherings and worship. As literate individuals, early Christian forgers would have enjoyed access to these collections, if not custody of them—especially if they were able to copy the manuscripts as they became worn.[108] From these positions of trust, they could introduce falsely authored works by altering existing manuscripts or surreptitiously depositing new ones in the collections. "The six forged letters of the Long Recension of Ignatius were intermingled with the authentic seven, which were themselves interpolated by the forger of the six," Ehrman writes.[109] Similarly, Clare Rothschild speculates that Hebrews first surfaced as a late insertion into a collection of Paul's letters.[110] Longer texts, like the *Gospel of Thomas*, might well have been left on a shelf to be found by inquisitive readers.

IV. How John Emerged

Although we will never know specific details about how the Gospel of John was produced or published, the evidence above offers us tantalizing clues as to what an alternative history of the Gospel—a history of this text as a falsely authored work—could look like. History, of course, is always an exercise in informed, probabilistic imagination. In this final section, I would like to engage in precisely such an act of imagination, assembling a tentative portrait of the origins of John.

A. Planning and Crafting the Gospel

As I argued in the first chapter, the author of John was almost certainly a male, educated Greek speaker living around the turn of the second century who was integrated into Christian networks. The author had been exposed to the earliest narrative accounts of Jesus's life: the Synoptic Gospels of Mark, Matthew, and Luke. Evidently, he found these accounts inadequate. He likely found Mark and Matthew's idea of the kingdom of God/heaven too crudely material and earth-bound, especially given his engagement with Hellenistic philosophical currents. He might also have counted the Markan line "some standing here who will not taste death until they see the kingdom of God come with power" (9:1; cf. 13:30) as evidence against the idea of an earth-bound kingdom. For the author, this saying was impossible to reconcile with the failure of any such kingdom to materialize by his day, a time when virtually all of Jesus's disciples had passed away. No doubt, the author also saw these gospels as missing key ideas and emphases central to his own thinking, from the notion of Jesus's preexistence as the *Logos* to the idea that Jesus came to provide a new, *pneumatic* life and celestial access now to humans.

We have no idea how many others in the author's immediate social circles shared his views.[111] Perhaps our author represents the widely held teachings of one or more local Christian assemblies, groups steeped in a very similar synthesis of Hellenistic Jewish and Pauline thought. Or perhaps our author's views reflect those of a group within a group: a small circle of members in his assembly who prided themselves as being more sophisticated interpreters of Jesus and Paul than their peers. Our author might have developed his views in conversation with other sorts of groups, such as a network of local friends or a philosophical guild. Or perhaps he crystallized his ideas through correspondence with literate, like-minded thinkers in other cities or by reading works with similar views circulating across Christian networks. In this case, he might have been a marginal figure within his local church assembly, friend groups, or family relations—a person whose views were the focus of considerable debate among his peers.[112] We cannot even rule out the possibility that our author was a disaffected member of certain local circles in which he had been formerly engaged and that he was no longer an active participant in local church assemblies.[113] There are many more ways to conceive of the author's relationship with his social contexts than the classical "Johannine Community" hypothesis envisions.[114]

Whatever his social context, our author came to believe that the deficiencies in other gospels called for one solution: the production of a new gospel that would supersede and correct earlier accounts of the life of Jesus. That new gospel would depict Jesus uttering new sayings and carefully hint that earlier accounts of Jesus's life had misrepresented and misunderstood his essential teachings. The author planned entire, novel discourses for Jesus. He also built upon the memory that Jesus sometimes performed symbolic gestures typifying themes in his preaching—a premise reflected in Mark (8:22–30, 11:12–20)—inventing new scenes to align with his newly composed discourses.

We can imagine our author developing his revisionary Gospel over several months or years, working in a nonlinear fashion, composing and revising individual sections of the work before uniting them later. This was typical. James Barker observes that most ancient authors did not sit down and immediately write book-length works on their final surface (the parchment roll/scroll). Rather, they first drafted their works on smaller, cheaper materials, trying out different wordings and different structures through a process of extensive, continuing revision.[115] Although an author could use a parchment notebook or a reused roll for such drafts, the most common writing materials were waxed wooden tablets, many of which were combined into polytychs (multiple tablet "pages" between covers) to accommodate longer compositions.[116] John probably began as scratchings on dozens of wax surfaces, incrementally taking shape through thousands upon thousands of scribbles, erasures, changes, and reversals. The author consulted tablets containing his own ideas and notes as well as others summarizing or excerpting the words of other gospels. He tried his hand at composing some passages. He wrote them and rewrote them. He played with different orderings of material, sometimes physically rearranging his tablets. When at last he was satisfied with his drafts, he gathered them and carefully transferred their text to his larger parchment.[117] At times, he set his project aside—a few days here, perhaps a few months there—only to return to it again.

This extended creative process came with a price. The glaring aporiae in John hint that its author fought editorial fatigue working with such a complex manuscript.[118] It is also possible that these errors slipped through as the author opted to restrict some forms of authorial support that helped other gospel authors develop cleaner manuscripts. Jeremiah Coogan and Candida Moss write that "textual production was far from the tidy, self-contained affair we imagine"; rather, "servile workers were in every stage of writing from taking dictation, editing drafts, collating documents, excerption and supplementing texts."[119] Authors also often relied on the helpful feedback of other literate writers in their social circles, sharing drafts in progress.[120] The problem, however, is that falsely authored texts were widely stigmatized.[121] Writing one, then, invited some measure of secrecy. In that case, we can easily imagine the author of John being more circumspect with his project, involving other laborers or collaborators sparingly and strategically. For example, he might have limited the interventions of such persons to isolated and less incriminating sections of his text and to more mundane processes (e.g., preparing writing materials, reproducing other texts for study and excerption, copying text). Or he might have divided the labor of such persons, albeit in ways that undermined the coherence of his final product.[122] Many times, he might have opted to work alone.[123]

As he developed his text, the author probably anticipated and hoped for "broader dissemination in Christian circles ... from the outset" through "further, secondary distribution."[124] Mark, a template for his project, was already in wide circulation, as were Matthew and Luke. To ensure that these audiences would not reject his invented materials, our author positioned his work as an eyewitness memoir, articulating it around an invented disciple of Jesus. And yet he also opted to keep this latter figure veiled in not only anonymity but also ambiguity. (Is he a single author? Is he one of several authors?) Mining the history of fabrications and hoaxes, the psychologist Peter Hancock concludes that such ambiguities have distinct advantages:

> If the hoax is to raise contention, it must possess characteristics that are open to some degree of interpretation and contention by both sides involved in the associated argument.... components of the actual artifact itself that are not evident giveaways actually serve to foment greater interest, discussion, and debate.... The most effective way of providing such ambiguity is to leave crucial aspects under-specified. That is, do not overelaborate the hoax itself, leave room for the participation and contribution of others. Hoaxes that provide complete, closed-end explanations are not generative and fail to allow involved individuals to actively participate in the discovery, elaboration, and elucidation. Evidence that is discovered by an individual who is not the primary deceiver is particularly persuasive.[125]

The author of John was nothing if not skilled at his craft.

B. Justifying the Product

The scale of the author's inventions and fabrications are dramatic—so much so that they naturally prompt the question: How did the author justify his project? We will never know for sure. We cannot rule out the possibility that the author of John, whoever he was, believed that he possessed the very charismatic gifts Jesus promises his disciples in the text: the ability to retrieve individual events in Jesus's life supernaturally and interpret them with special insight (14:26, 16:12–14).[126] Some authors of modern pseudo-historical gospels similarly claim to have received their accounts through supernatural revelation, perhaps sincerely (*Aquarian Gospel*, *Oahspe*). In this case, our author might have seen the composition of his gospel as a charismatic or spiritual exercise: a Spirit-mediated restoration of the actual actions and teachings of Jesus, which had been lost.[127]

Alternatively, our author might have been perfectly conscious that his work involved historical invention, finding various justifications for the practice—perhaps several fluid ones over the course of his life. To quote the historian David Hackett Fisher, a person who commits a particular act "does it for every reason he can think of, and a few unthinkable reasons as well."[128] Our author might have convinced himself that his invention of an eyewitness narrator was spiritually valid or commendable—an act of modesty, self-effacement, or self-negation. Or he might have insisted to himself that constructing an invented author served the higher cause of securing an audience for his work.[129] (One ancient pseudepigrapher, Salvian, unites the two justifications, implying that he wrote pseudonymously "to avoid the vanity of worldly glory" and "lest the insignificance of his person detract authority from his salutary statements.")[130] Alternatively, the author of John might have reasoned that there was no sin in assuming a description as devoid of specificity as "the disciple whom Jesus loved"—a description that could ostensibly apply to any believer. (Salvian would similarly argue that there no "falsehood" in writing under the pseudonym "Timothy" since the name merely means "honor of God.")[131] Following this line of justification, our author might have insisted that his invented discourses were a reasonable reconstruction of Jesus's actual words—more accurate than those of the real gospels. He might also have seen his invented narratives—the raising of Lazarus, for example—as appropriate as they only enhanced the reputation of Jesus. (One ancient writer caught inventing narratives intended "to add of his own to Paul's reputation" "professed he had done it for love of Paul.")[132]

Our author might even have been cynical about his activity.[133] There are many possibilities to consider, none of which we will ever be able to affirm with confidence.

C. Disseminating the Gospel

While he prepared the final, clean copy of his manuscript, the author probably considered the best way to release it to a general readership. Any distribution channel I discussed in this chapter is plausible, though the first—distribution through remote correspondence—might well have provided him the best cover. Since the author of John was educated and highly literate, he probably had a higher socioeconomic status and connections to similar elites in other cities. His designs may have gradually settled on a specific individual as an initial audience: someone well connected with the resources to validate, copy, and further disseminate the text. Hancock writes that historical fabrications typically involve "an *unsuspecting champion*"—a "target" naturally sympathetic to the recovered object, who can help disseminate it. "If they have the imprimatur of authority, so much the better," he insists, "for their opinions carry all the more weight."[134] We can imagine the author isolating an individual whom he had a positive rapport with, someone already inclined to trust him. It would especially help if that person was in a position of influence, perhaps a wealthy owner of a house church or the leader of a Christ association. It would also help if he knew that person was likely to be receptive to the Gospel, someone who was an avid consumer of the many new "apostolic" texts surfacing in the late first and early second centuries or as a person with theological sympathies similar to his own.

When he was finally pleased with his manuscript, our author would have dispatched it to the target reader(s), probably employing a messenger, either an enslaved person or a hired hand. It is possible he sent the text in conjunction with a covering letter or an oral message offering a false narrative of how the Gospel had come into his possession. Fabrications of all sorts, whether forged texts, invented relics, or artistic frauds, typically emerge under conditions that obscure their provenance "so that the origins themselves cannot be unequivocally fixed."[135] Perhaps the author claimed that he found the text in an old literary collection. Perhaps he wrote that a friend, named or unnamed, passed the work along to him—as a gift, as an inheritance.

AN APOCRYPHAL GOSPEL 135

Whatever the case, he effaced the last of his contributions to his text, vanishing into history.

The author's efforts proved a success. The text's initial reader(s), whoever they might have been, were receptive to the new book. They instructed scribes to copy it, and they circulated it across their social networks. More copies of the Gospel were made, allowing it to penetrate still more geographies and readerships. Although we can imagine that the text met resistance in at least some of these settings, it eventually carved out a dedicated, even enthusiastic audience among early Christians. The positive reception of the Gospel across multiple Christ-believing groups and communities ensured its survival.[136]

It is not difficult to see what drew many readers to the book. Only so much Christian literature existed in this period, sparking at least a baseline interest in any new literary work exploring the life of Jesus—not least one relating supposedly lost episodes of his life.[137] Although some of John's teachings deviate from the Synoptics, many of those teachings were ones acceptable to Christians who revered Paul (preexistence of Jesus, indwelling/participation, etc.). No doubt many readers were awed by the cosmic vision of John, impressively articulated in its opening verses. And, of course, the text's eyewitness claims commanded their attention—claims most audiences were not in a position to either verify or disprove. Many accepted them.

Our author might have hoped that his text would eclipse the earlier gospels of Mark, Matthew, and Luke. He won an adequate consolation prize. Many Christians merely read his Gospel beside these earliest accounts, synthesizing their thought. In this way, however, the new Gospel still achieved some measure of influence, ensuring it would inform, shape, and even direct many of the emerging theological syntheses of the period. Of course, the same process of harmonization obscured some of John's revisionary elements.

The reason why John could be synthesized with other texts—even some with very different perspectives—may reflect a flaw in its design. As we have seen in this chapter, the Gospel tends to press its corrections of other gospels in a subtle manner. In fact, one might argue that it presses its critiques in too subtle a manner, at least to achieve a consistent reception across all audiences. John, for example, does not explicitly polemicize the idea of a fleshly resurrection; instead, it takes up the language of resurrection and only gradually spiritualizes it (5:21–30). Likewise, the Gospel does not directly rule out a future second coming of Jesus; instead, it has Jesus speak of "coming again," all the while subtly reorienting this promise toward Jesus's coming in, through, or as the Spirit (14:3, 18–20). In this way, the author unintentionally invested his text with a level of ambiguity or malleability that gospels such as *Thomas* and *Mary* did not have—a feature that would allow it to be more easily synthesized with the Synoptics. For centuries, readers have read both a literal resurrection and a literal second coming into the above statements.[138]

Nevertheless, some of the ambiguity of the Gospel was probably unintentional, a result of the ambiguity inherent in all human communication. Words and phrases can have different possible meanings, and syntax is often open to multiple analyses. Additionally, when a text leaves the author's hand, the author loses interpretive control over it. In this case, a phrase such as "my kingdom is not of this world" (18:36)—a phrase intended to rule out the idea of a material, earth-bound "kingdom of God"—can be vulnerable to other possible readings. These potential misunderstandings might well have been a net gain for the author, however; many Christians would have rejected the author's undistilled vision had they grasped it more clearly. The (mistaken) perception that John could be reconciled with other gospels ensured the text's survival, popularity, and, in turn, influence. The Gospel became a landmark work of Christian literature.

V. Conclusion

Across its many chapters, in explicit and implicit ways, the Gospel of John positions itself as the written memoir of an invented eyewitness to the life of Jesus. It casts this disciple as a special intimate of Jesus who walked beside him during his public ministry, who had greater access to him than his peers, and who possessed special insight into the meaning of his often cryptic words. It also leverages the disciple's supposed proximity to Jesus and spiritual insights to authenticate its account. This disciple, however, is an invention—as ahistorical as the many details to which he testifies.

The presence of this false implied author casts John, like so many other gospels of the period, as a falsely authored work. In fact, John may be the earliest example of a gospel written by a disguised author. Tellingly, the Synoptics do not claim eyewitnesses for their authors. Mark and Matthew are strictly anonymous; Luke seems to distinguish previous gospel writers from the eyewitnesses to Jesus's life, claiming that "those who have undertaken to compile a narrative about the events" of Jesus's life transmitted what they learned from "those who from the beginning were eyewitnesses" (1:1–2). Additionally, scholars assign the many pseudonymous gospels—works such as the *Gospel of Peter* and *Gospel of Thomas*—to dates later than the presumed date of John. In this case, there is good reason for suspecting that the author of John might have pioneered the practice of writing gospels in the name of close associates of Jesus. At the very least, his work probably accelerated the practice, forcing later entrants in the same genre to escalate their authorial claims to position themselves more competitively in this field of writing. By the same token, by the second century Christians attributed even the anonymous Gospels of Mark, Matthew, and Luke to writers in Jesus's circle or their close associates. John's strategy might have set new expectations of eyewitness lineages and testimony for gospels. In this case, too, we can see the invention of the "disciple whom Jesus loved" as a decisive, watershed event in the history of gospel writing.

Nevertheless, John's influence would be felt well beyond gospel literature. As we have seen, the author of John did not merely invent a gospel; he also invented a new, artificial fold in Christian memory—namely, the supposed existence of a particular "disciple whom Jesus loved," who wrote from his personal experience with Jesus. In time, the eyewitness voice of John would soon be enlisted in new works—works that would find their own lasting place in Christian memory.

PART II
AFTERLIVES

I had much to write to you.

—3 John 13

5
Invented Letters

The author of John falsely positioned his book as an eyewitness work: the memoir of an invented disciple of Jesus. This strategy helped the Gospel secure a broad and positive reception among Christians. By the second century, we find authors of various intellectual persuasions embracing the Gospel's invented disciple as a historical figure. But this strategy also secured a specific reception for the Gospel its author could hardly have envisioned.

Falsely authored works were common in antiquity, not least in Christian circles.[1] Writers seeking to advance their views co-opted the identities of Jesus's earliest followers and composed narratives and letters in their names. As the enigmatic disciple of John was woven into the same collective memory as Peter, Paul, and Jude, his identity became a viable mask for other authors engaged in disguised authorship and pursuing their own agendas. And indeed, not long after John's publication, the invented disciple would speak again. As we have seen, he would speak in interpolations to the Gospel, especially John 21, which was likely added only a few decades after the text entered into circulation. But he would soon also speak in entirely new works: independent letters, narratives, and treatises that co-opted the mysterious "we"/"I" voice of John in the service of new agendas.

In this chapter, I will argue that three other biblical books—the Epistles, or letters, of 1, 2, and 3 John—are falsely authored works of this kind. Today most scholars agree that these works directly imitate the language, ideas, and style of the Gospel. As I will demonstrate, there is a reason for this extensive borrowing. The three letters position themselves as works by the same implied author as John. They are a chain of falsely authored letters. Together, then, the Epistles of John represent one of John's least understood but most profoundly consequential receptions: the creation of fabricated letters in the voice of the invented eyewitness.[2]

The Gospel of John. Hugo Méndez, Oxford University Press. © Oxford University Press 2025.
DOI: 10.1093/9780197686157.003.0005

I. Literary Dependence

The New Testament contains not one but four texts that bear the name "John" in their title. The first and largest, of course, is the Gospel, the focus of our text to this point. But bundled near the end of the Christian Bible are three small epistles titled "1 John," "2 John," and "3 John."[3] The fact that all four texts share the same name suits a particular quality of these texts: they are strikingly similar in language, ideas, and style.

For centuries, many Christians had a ready explanation for these similarities; they believed that the Gospel and Epistles shared so many common features because they shared a common author—an author conflated with a known disciple of Jesus named "John" (ergo, the title applied to each). In the early twentieth century, however, critical scholars began to recognize subtle but meaningful differences in the ideas and language of the Gospel, on the one hand, and the Epistles, on the other—differences pointing to different authors for these texts.[4] To explain how different authors could have produced such similar works, scholars have proposed that these authors might have been linked by social bonds. In this standard reconstruction, the four texts were written by members of the same, closely bound "community" and/or "school."[5]

There is, however, another way to explain these kinds of similarities and convergences: the similarities may be deliberate—the products of direct contact and literary borrowing. Even writers with no connection to one another can produce works with similar features if one author is familiar with the work of another and chooses to incorporate that work's language and ideas into their own. And in fact, most critical scholars today—even those who posit a Johannine "community" or "school"—agree that the parallels between the Gospel and the Epistles of John are too close and too extensive to have emerged independently. As George Parsenios writes, "the vast majority of scholars assume one of the Johannine texts is the model for the others."[6]

A. Verbal Similarities

The most obvious sign of literary borrowing—of the reuse of written materials—is close similarities in language. Tellingly, the Gospel and Epistles are exceptionally close in language, sharing roughly forty characteristic expressions, including twenty-six that appear nowhere else in the New Testament:[7]

1. the light shines	15. the world does not know God
2. the true light	16. abide in Jesus/God
3. walk in the light/darkness	17. Jesus/God abides in a person
4. do truth	18. word of God abides in you
5. know the truth	19. to love Jesus/God is to keep the commandments
6. be of the truth	
7. the Spirit of Truth	20. a new commandment
8. know the true one/the true God	21. lay down one's life for others
9. be of/from [*ek*] God	22. Jesus takes away sin
10. be born of/from God	23. to pass from death to life
11. be of/from the devil	24. water and blood
12. be of/from the world	25. we have known and believed
13. conquer the world	26. joy fulfilled
14. the world hates you	

Even more remarkable than the number of these similarities is their dense concentration in the Epistles. In 1 John—a text with only 105 verses—one finds over seventy points of contact with the language of the Gospel.[8] In turn, 2 and 3 John together—with twenty-eight verses in total—contain fifty-four points of contact with the Gospel and seventy-four with 1 John.[9] (Looking at 2 John alone, 57/151 words [37.7%] parallel those in John and 1 John, with an overlap of 51/70 words [72.9%] in vv. 4–7 [cf. John 10:18; 1 John 2:7, 22, 28, 3:11, 4:1–3, 5:3]). In a discussion of any other ancient texts, such an extensive network of linguistic correspondences would be considered strong evidence of a literary relationship.

Admittedly, a few scholars argue against literary contact, emphasizing the differences between the Gospel and Epistles above their similarities. Raimo Hakola, for one, insists that "clear differences in how common idioms and themes are developed" point away from "direct literary dependence" between the texts.[10] Similarly, Judith Lieu argues that "there is no compelling evidence of a direct literary relationship between 1 John and the Gospel" because "the consistent subtle differences of wording, inference, context, and combination even where close parallels appear suggest that both writings draw independently on earlier formulations."[11]

The problem with these objections is that "the absence of agreement . . . says nothing about the presence of agreement when assessing literary relationships."[12] A literary relationship exists between texts whether one is 5% derivative from the other or 95% derivative. Indeed, "only one direct-connect parallel is required to demonstrate literary dependence between two documents."[13] This is especially true since plagiarists and imitators are known to incorporate language selectively and rework that language at different rates.[14] In short, the only positive evidence one can offer against literary dependence is the absence of similarity, not the presence of differences.[15]

B. Similarities in Form

As extensive and dense as these linguistic parallels are, an even stronger case for literary contact between the Gospel and Epistles of John can be made from their formal similarities, that is, from their shared body features. Taken together or individually, Parsenios writes, "these larger structural bonds ... make it extremely difficult to imagine how a 'Johannine tradition' does not rely on literary dependence in some form."[16]

1. John and 1 John

John and 1 John share two peculiar structural features. The first is the use of a stylistic prologue or proem at the beginning of the text (John 1.1–18; 1 John 1.1–4). The presence of these passages is surprising enough; they are not required by the genre of either text (narrative gospel/*bios* and tractate or epistle). More to the point, these passages "though by no means identical ... stand together against anything else in the NT, sharing a large number of common features in a short space":[17]

   a. They introduce the term "beginning" (*archē*) in their first clauses.
   b. They refer to Jesus as the "word" (*Logos*).
   c. They identify the "word" (*Logos*) with "life" (*zoē*).
   d. They affirm that Jesus was "with the Father" (*pros ton patera*) in the beginning.
   e. They adopt a first-person plural narratorial voice.
   f. They position the narrator among those who "have seen" (*eōrakamen*) Jesus.
   g. They share other key terms (e.g., *martureō*).[18]

With each point of overlap, the possibility of coincidence—even within a shared social milieu—becomes remote.

Second, both texts incorporate statements of purpose, in which the author indicates his rationale for writing. Tellingly, these statements are also very close in language. In both, the narrator links the task of writing to the idea that one may possess "life" by believing in the "name" of the "Son of God":

> But these have been written that you may believe that Jesus is the Christ, the Son of God, and that by believing, you may have life in his name. (John 20:31)

> I write these things to you who believe in the name of the Son of God that you may know that you have eternal life. (1 John 5:13)

Parsenios's analysis of this parallel rings true: "This kind of close association suggests more than a coincidence arising from a common tradition. If the various terms and phrases that the texts share were randomly scattered throughout the works, then their similarities might be merely coincidental. . . . More than a common tradition seems to be at work when two texts not only use the same words but also use them in the same places."[19]

2. John and 3 John

One might not expect points of contact between the Gospel and 3 John since the latter text is small enough to fit on a single papyrus sheet and adheres tightly to a standard epistolary form. And yet one such point of contact exists. Both texts include an affidavit, in which the narrator testifies to a fact and affirms the truth of his testimony. Hans-Joseph Klauck avers that the wording of these two affidavits is so close as to leave "no doubt" of "a relationship between these texts":[20]

> He who has seen has testified—his testimony is true, and he knows that he speaks the truth. (John 19.35; cf. 21.24)

> We also testify, and you know that our testimony is true. (3 John 12)

3. 1 John and 2 John

First John and 2 John share so much material that the two can seem redundant, the latter representing something like an abridgment of the former. And yet the close relationship between these texts is crystallized at an especially striking formal parallel. In both texts, the narrator directly addresses his readers and declares that he is "writing" a "new commandment" while simultaneously insisting that this commandment is, in fact, one they have "heard" "from the beginning":

> Brethren, I am writing you no new commandment but an old commandment you had from the beginning... which you have heard. (1 John 2:7)

> And now I ask you, Lady, not as one writing you a new commandment, but one we have had from the beginning... as you have heard from the beginning. (2 John 5–6)

Since these parallel statements presuppose the act of "writing," their similarities beg for a literary explanation.

4. 2 and 3 John

Finally, no Johannine scholar questions a relationship between 2 and 3 John, the most similar texts in the collection. Both documents explicitly identify themselves as works by the same sender ("the Elder"). They are roughly the same length. Most striking of all, their introductory and concluding materials mirror one another nearly verbatim:

> The elder to the elect lady and her children, whom I love in the truth. (2 John 1)

> The elder to the beloved Gaius, whom I love in the truth. (3 John 1)

> Though I have much to write to you, I would rather not use paper and ink, but I hope to come to see you and talk with you face to face, so that our joy may be complete. (2 John 12–13)

> I had much to write to you, but I would rather not write with pen and ink; I hope to see you soon, and we will talk together face to face. (3 John 13–14)

Either these are works of a common author, or one is modeled on the other.

C. Direction of Influence

If we see signs of direct copying in the four Johannine texts, the next question is: Who copied from whom? What is the line of descent between these texts? Here again, most scholars agree: the Gospel of John was written first and served as a model for the Epistles of John, which imitated its distinctive language.[21]

First, the parallels between John and 1 John make better sense if we assume the priority of the former. Consider the passage I highlighted as the locus of the densest parallels between these works: their opening lines. The Gospel has strong, independent motivations for using the phrase "in the beginning" (*en archē*) in its first clause (John 1:1). The expression is one of several parallels to LXX Gen. 1 in the prologue—a passage Daniel Boyarin characterizes as a midrash on the creation account.[22] The term "beginning" (*archē*) also appears in the first clause of Mark—a generic template for John, with which the text's author was familiar: "the beginning [*archē*] of the gospel of Jesus Christ" (1:1). By contrast, no such motivations exist for the phrase's appearance in 1 John. In this case, 1 John probably takes up the expression in imitation of the Gospel.[23] Certain lines in 1 John are also challenging to interpret without prior knowledge of the Gospel; as François Vouga explains, "only through the structure of JohEv can the associations in the thought process of 1 John be explained."[24] For example, the passing reference to "water and blood" in 1 John 5:6–8 is opaque to readers unfamiliar with the Gospel (John 19:34). So too is the text's confusing characterization of the mandate to love as "no new commandment" and a "new commandment" (1 John 2:7–8; cf. John 13:34).

If the Gospel predates 1 John, it should also predate 2 or 3 John. Given their brevity, it is prima facie unlikely that either was a source for the Johannine tradition. The two, after all, contain only a limited number of expressions found in John or 1 John. More to the point, the two letters surface surprisingly late in the historical record; 2 John is attested no earlier than the late second century, and 3 John is attested no earlier than the third century (and even then, only in fragments preserved in a fourth-century source).[25] For that matter, the earliest texts to mention both letters together indicate that a significant segment of early Christians dismissed them as inauthentic. Assuming that the fourth-century author Eusebius faithfully reproduced his words, the third-century writer Origen of Alexandria observed that although "there may be a second or a third" letter attributed to the author of the Gospel, "not all say they are genuine."[26] Eusebius himself ranked both letters among the texts "disputed" by many Christians.[27] Syriac Bibles excluded both 2 and 3 John into the sixth century. This troubled reception history hardly casts either text as the earliest, core Johannine literature, but it is a history perfectly compatible with the hypothesis that 2 and 3 John are later derivative compositions.

Other evidence confirms the derivative nature of 2 and 3 John. Lieu builds a persuasive case for 2 John's "close literary dependence" on 1 John from its severely abbreviated argumentation—the result of an author trying to compress the contents of 1 John onto a single sheet.[28] Individual arguments in 2 John can be "difficult to understand . . . without reference to the passage in 1 John" to which they correspond, presupposing knowledge of that text.[29] The same compression produces grammatical difficulties, including a perplexing sentence structure at vv. 5–6 and an abrupt shift from plural to singular at v. 7. For that matter, 3 John also contains evidence of its later composition. Toward the end of the epistle, the sender claims to have previously "written something to the church" (v. 9). If, as many scholars believe, that letter corresponds to one of 3 John's extant companions—probably 2 John—it should date to the latest stratum of Johannine texts.[30]

II. A Common Authorial Claim

Most scholars today recognize that the Gospel and Epistles of John form a single literary lineage, linked by bonds of literary contact and dependence. As Wendy Spronston North writes, "by far the most commonly held" view posits that the Epistles knew and imitated the Gospel.[31] But why do the Epistles imitate the Gospel so closely and pervasively? As I will argue here, the letters of 1, 2, and 3 John imitate the Gospel because they participate in the same authorial fiction as the Gospel.[32]

Today nearly all critical scholars have abandoned the traditional view that John and 1 John share a common author. But this tradition has a shade of truth to it; it rests on a valid observation. Even if the Gospel and Epistles do not share a real author, they share a common implied author. Each letter positions itself as a work by the same anonymous eyewitness who wrote the Gospel, a figure recognizable by his distinctive idiolect. The narrator of the Gospel alternates between speaking in the plural "we" and the singular "I" (1:14, 21:24–5). Remarkably, so do the narrators of all three epistles (e.g., 1 John 1:1, 2:1; 2 John 5, 8, 12; 3 John 1, 12–14). No less striking, the narrator of the Gospel claims to be an eyewitness to the life of Jesus who "testifies" to what he has "seen" and who insists that his "testimony is true" (19:35; cf. 1:14, 21:24). So too does the narrator of

1 John, who stresses the fact that he has "seen" Jesus "with his own eyes" and who claims to "testify" concerning what he has seen (1:1-4). And in 3 John, the narrator reminds his audience, "you know my testimony is true" (v. 12). And, of course, the narrators of all four texts speak in a nearly identical idiolect—taking up the same, very distinctive turns of phrase. These correspondences are not coincidences. Instead, they are evidence that the Epistles are falsely authored texts, as indeed some ancient and medieval Christians suspected all three of being.[33]

A. 1 John

Unsurprisingly, 1 John lays its most direct claim to the implied author of the Gospel of John in a passage I have highlighted as a site of deliberate imitation: the epistle's opening lines. Like the Gospel prologue, that passage (a) is written in an exclusive first-person plural ("we") and (b) presents the text's implied author as one who has "seen" Jesus. To complete the effect, the text (c) incorporates language from the narrator's affidavit in 19:35: "That which was from the beginning, which we have heard, which we have seen with our eyes, which we have looked upon, which our hands have touched—concerning the word of life ... we have seen and testify and proclaim to you the eternal life which was with the Father and was made manifest to us. That which we have seen and heard we also proclaim to you, so that you may have fellowship with us. ... And we are writing this that our joy may be complete" (1:1-4).

In later passages, the narrator extends his use of this "we" but juxtaposes it with a second form: a singular "I" ("My little children, I am writing this to you" [2:1]; "Beloved, I am writing you" [2:7; cf. 2:12-14, 21, 26, 5:13]). Like John 1-20, the epistle does not expressly define the relationship between this "we" and "I." Does the narrator speak on behalf of a broader group of eyewitnesses? Is the "we" simply interchangeable with "I?"[34] Whatever the case, the resemblance to the Gospel is unmistakable; the epistle clearly aligns its narrator with the narrator of the Gospel. The text consolidates this link by placing the Gospel's distinctive teachings and speech patterns on its own narrator's lips. The voice of 1 John reminds his readers of the "new commandment" and the "water and blood." He implores his readers to be "born of God" and "abide in him." And near the conclusion of his text, he repeats his now-routine purpose for writing: he writes to assure his readers of "eternal life... in the name of the Son of God." Line by line, the text constructs its implied author as a familiar voice: the voice of the Gospel.[35]

Despite these impressive links, many scholars fail to connect the authorial claims of John and 1 John. They fail to do so because of the scholarly assumptions before them—namely, that the texts have different authors and that a complex community history lies behind their formation.[36] Certain writers, including Brown, even deny that 1 John claims an eyewitness as its author at all, arguing that 1:1–4 implies only the author's "vicarious participation" in the eyewitness experience of others.[37] Bart Ehrman's critique of these views rings true: "When more critical commentators—Brown, Lieu, Schnackenburg, and others—reject the idea that the author is claiming to be an eyewitness to the fleshly reality of Jesus in his public ministry, it is almost always because they are convinced that in fact he was not an eyewitness."[38] Each author "fails to consider the possibility that the author wants to portray himself as an eyewitness in order to validate his claims about the real fleshly existence of Jesus ... following established patterns of forged writing from antiquity."[39]

Nevertheless, even those scholars who recognize the literary deceit at play can find it difficult to disentangle their conclusions from the premise that John and 1 John have different authors. In the same discussion, Ehrman identifies 1 John as an "anonymous" text, which does not construct its implied author as any "specific" persona.[40] In fact, 1 John co-opts a very specific identity: it positions itself as an exhortation penned by the same author who wrote John—an author who, however enigmatic, was accepted as a flesh-and-blood figure by those who embraced the Gospel.

B. 2 John and 3 John

What is true of 1 John is true of the other epistles. Admittedly, 2 John and 3 John present themselves as works by "the Elder." This title, however, is not incompatible with the idea that the letters share the same authorial cast as 1 John. On the contrary, the characterization of the narrator is so consistent across the Epistles that, even today, most critical commentators speculate that a single author penned the three letters.[41]

The evidence is strong that 1 John and 2 John share the same implied author. Tellingly, 2 John presumes the same situation as 1 John, citing the threat of "antichrists" who "have gone out into the world" and who deny "the coming of Jesus Christ in the flesh" (v. 7; cf. 1 John 2:18–19, 4:1–3). It also constructs an implied author with the same ideological position as the implied author of 1 John. And, of course, 2 John's narrator speaks in the same ways as the narrator of 1 John, extensively co-opting his idiolect and reproducing his statements nearly word for word (as in 2 John 5–6; cf. 1 John 2:7). The text invites the reader to identify the narrators of the two texts.

Third John, in turn, continues this program. By presenting itself as a letter from "the Elder" and deploying his familiar formulae and greetings verbatim, the text introduces itself as the work of the same hand as 2 John. But 3 John reaches further back in the Johannine tradition. Near the end of the letter, "the Elder" emulates the affidavit of the Gospel's narrator, positioning himself as the same figure: "We also testify, and you know that our testimony is true" (3 John 12). This statement—the only instance of a first-person plural in the epistle—evokes the narrator speaking in John 19:35 and 1 John 1:1–4.[42] In turn, the claim "you know our testimony is true" may allude to the Gospel on another level, reminding the text's real readers of their existing trust in the author.

Although the title "Elder" appears in no previous Johannine work, it was certainly fitting for the invented disciple who supposedly penned John and its derivative texts. The term is used fluidly in early Christian writings; sometimes it signifies persons of advanced age, but it is also sometimes used for a specific leadership role (firmly or loosely defined). In one or another of these senses, the term came to be applied to the disciples of Jesus in some second-century sources. In the pseudonymous 1 Peter, the voice of "Peter" identifies himself as "a fellow elder [*sumpresbyteros*] and a witness to the sufferings of Christ" (5:1; cf. 1:1).[43] And in the extant fragments of his *Exposition of the Sayings of the Lord*, Papias glosses the words that "the Lord's disciples had said" as the "words of the elders."[44] For that matter, as John Painter writes, "the author's reference to himself as 'the elder' ... draws attention to his position of authority"; that is, through it, "he presents himself as an authoritative teacher" and "an authoritative bearer of tradition."[45]

C. Indirect but Effective Claims

Another reason why some scholars fail to see the connection between these authorial casts is that the Epistles make their authorial claims indirectly. None, for example, has its narrator self-identify as "the disciple whom Jesus

152   THE GOSPEL OF JOHN

loved."[46] There was hardly a need for the authors to make this kind of identification, however. The strategies used by these texts—the indirect ways they co-opt the voice of the Gospel's narrator—convinced many ancient readers of these works that a single pen wrote them. It hardly makes sense to claim, then, that a given author should have employed a particular strategy when the strategies they did employ proved successful.

For that matter, authors were hardly obliged to make their claims explicit. The Book of Wisdom never names its implied author, keeping him veiled in anonymity. Later in the text, however, that implied author tells God, "you have chosen me to be king of your people . . . [and] you have commanded the building of a temple on your holy mountain," and he asks for "wisdom" to be worthy of his "father's throne" (Wisdom 9:7–12). The implication is clear: the author of the text is the biblical king Solomon, who built a temple for God (1 Kings 7–8) and prayed for wisdom to rule the throne of David, his father (1 Kings 3:5–10).[47] Wisdom shies away from an explicit claim but does everything to imply it. We might even see this ambiguity as strategic. Some readers might have been more likely to scrutinize a text claiming to be written by Solomon. The choice to avoid such a name, however, leaves space for receptive and skeptical readers alike to engage the text and defer judgment on authorship, even as the text subtly consolidates its pseudepigraphal claim. Hebrews gestures at Pauline authorship in the same, indirect way in 13:22–25, as well as in its broader features.[48]

Other texts mirror 2 and 3 John by declining to name an author, substituting an unprecedented and ambiguous title instead. For example, the narrator of Ecclesiastes refers to himself as "the Teacher/Qoheleth" (1:1), a title never applied to Solomon in earlier texts. Nevertheless, in the verses that follow, the same narrator intimates that this "Teacher" is none other than Solomon; he describes himself as a "king in Jerusalem" who "acquired great wisdom" and "set in order many proverbs" (Eccl 1:1, 16, 12:9; cf. 1 Kings 4:32). One also finds the use of a vague title in place of a more express identification in pseudonymous Greek letter collections. One example appears in the pseudepigraphal letters of Diogenes, composed by multiple hands between the first century BCE and the first century CE.[49] *Letter* 49, thought to be one of several penned by a single author interpolating the collection, has Diogenes identify himself merely as "the Cynic" in its prescript:[50]

The Cynic to Aroueca. Know yourself (for this you would do well) and,
  if there is any disease afflicting your soul, senselessness for example, get a

doctor for it. And pray the gods that you do not do more harm than good by choosing. One that only seems to be a good physician. Do not thus delay, for wine is being stored up for you, but you will ruin it if you do not filter it. But if you do this, you will be a valuable friend, not only to me but to all the others true. My greeting and salutation has been sent on the condition that you do not disregard what is written.[51]

Finally, it is worth noting that there are other plausible reasons why the authors of the Epistles might have avoided the designation "disciple whom Jesus loved" in their first-person writing. For one, the Gospel's narrator never takes up the title in his first-person speech, merely referring to "the disciple whom Jesus loved" in the third-person narration throughout chapters 1–20. For that matter, even chapter 21—a secondary addition to the text—takes up the expression only in the context of third-person narration, linking this figure to the narrator without breaking third-person speech: "the saying spread abroad among the brethren that this disciple was not to die.... This is the disciple who is bearing witness to these things, and who has written these things" (John 21:23–24). Both the author of chapters 1–20 and the scribe who introduced chapter 21 might have felt that first-person self-references as "the disciple whom Jesus loved" would have undermined narratorial modesty. Whether or not this was the case, there was ample precedent for the authors of 1, 2, and 3 John also to shy away from using the designation "the disciple whom Jesus loved" in their first-person literary products.

D. Falsely Authored Texts

Once we recognize that the Gospel and Epistles share a common implied author, the conclusion is unavoidable: the Epistles are falsely authored works. They are falsely authored because the Gospel and Epistles do not share a common author.[52] But they are also falsely authored because the implied author of the Gospel—the disciple whom Jesus loved—is, as we have seen, a literary fiction, an invention. If the Gospel is a falsely authored work, so are the Epistles.

Other ancient literary corpora grew through similar processes, that is, as later authors added their own falsely authored works to an earlier core. These cores might be pseudonymous. For example, the letter collections of Diogenes, Crates, and Hippocrates are entirely pseudonymous, but they grew through the activity of multiple authors.[53] Similarly, all the supposed works of Peter are pseudonymous, including 1 Peter, 2 Peter, the *Epistula Petri* (embedded in the *Pseudo-Clementine Homilies*), the *Gospel of Peter*, the *Apocalypse of Peter*, the *Coptic Apocalypse of Peter*, and the *Kerygma Petri*. Each, however, was written by a different hand.[54] Other collections grew around authentic cores and involved multiple writers. For example, the canonical collection of the letters of Paul was augmented by at least five different authors: the author of Ephesians, the author of Colossians, the author of 2 Thessalonians, the author(s) of the Pastorals, and, in my view, the author of Hebrews.[55] If we include noncanonical Pauline texts, that number expands further to include such writers as the author of *3 Corinthians*, the author of the *Epistle to the Laodiceans*, the author of the *Letters of Paul and Seneca*, and the author of the *Apocalypse of Paul*.[56]

There is no evidence that the many authors expanding these corpora collaborated with previous authors. On the contrary, coordination between authors would have been flatly impossible in the case of works such as 2 Thessalonians and the (Latin) *Epistle to the Laodiceans*—works that enter the historical record centuries apart. For that matter, authors engaged in expanding these collections worked unaware of the pseudepigraphal nature of (at least some, if not all) earlier works in the same collection or literary tradition.[57] It is plausible, then, that the authors of the Johannine Epistles were also not connected directly but indirectly—that is, as readers of earlier Johannine works, who each chose to co-opt the same authorial persona. Rather than locate the Gospel and the Epistle in the same single "community," as scholars so often do, we should entertain the possibility that these works might have been produced by authors from different (intellectual, social, geographical, and temporal) contexts. As it stands, many of the dissimilarities between these works—their distinct agendas, their different reception histories—suggest more variety than meets the eye. In short, understanding the Gospel and Epistles as a chain of falsely authored works opens new ways of thinking about their provenance.

III. Motivations

If 1, 2, and 3 John are pseudepigraphal texts written in the persona of the eyewitness author of John, then the question naturally arises: Why were these texts produced? What could have motivated multiple authors to co-opt the narrator of the Gospel and compose new works in his voice? To answer these questions, one must understand each text's distinctive interests and emphases.

A. 1 John

As I noted above, there is compelling evidence that 1 John is probably the oldest of the letters and the letter on which 2 and 3 John are based. In this case, 1 John represents a critical node in the Johannine tradition. This text pioneered the practice of writing pseudo-historical letters in the voice of John's nameless eyewitness disciple. In this respect, 1 John fits neatly into a broad and well-documented trend in early Christian writing. By the end of the first century, Christians had begun penning falsely authored letters in the names of Jesus's disciples. As Margaret Mitchell writes, this turn in early Christian memory—this refiguring of the disciples into prolific, engaged letter writers—represents an assimilation of these figures to the earliest known Christian writer, Paul: "Paul's letters are the oldest preserved 'early Christian' texts, and likely were the oldest, since literary legacies of Paul's contemporaries, such as Peter and James, were only written later, and in imitation of Paul, not only in genre and expected content, but in emulation of the precedent he set (as is mimicked also in the Acts of the Apostles, also under Pauline influence) that apostles should have been letter writers in the first place."[58] In 1 John, we see how even an *invented* disciple could be caught up in the same currents of invention and embellishment.

For many Christian writers, the decision to falsely author a text in the name of a disciple served a specific purpose: it allowed them to leverage the authority of that disciple in support of their distinctive agendas or, if the figure had a supposed literary corpus already, to establish interpretive control over previous works written by him. The author of 1 John probably shared the same motivations. Unlike some of the later Johannine epistles, 1 John is almost entirely devoted to defending and elaborating a particular theological idea: that the state of being "born of God" and the divine indwelling, first described in the Gospel, is incompatible with sin.

The Gospel of John never elucidates whether or how sin factors into the experience of someone who has received this new birth. Can someone who has received the Spirit sin? And if so, can such persons be forgiven? The author of 1 John co-opts the voice of the Gospel's eyewitness narrator to fill these gaps, ventriloquizing him to share his perfectionist views. At the outset of the epistle, the voice of the eyewitness claims that he has "heard" from Jesus that "God is light, and in him is no darkness at all" (1:5). In effect, he delivers a new saying of Jesus, omitted from the Gospel. In the chapters that follow, he then works out the implications of this claim. In his view, if no darkness—no sin—can be "in" God, then no one who sins can claim to have ever been "in" God. That is, sin is a sign that one has never truly attained the divine indwelling: "no one who sins has either seen him or known him" (3:6; cf. 3:15). For the author, those who have been genuinely "born of God" and have come to experience the divine indwelling are prevented from sinning. In a startling line, the author insists that "no one born of God commits sin; for God's seed abides in him, and he cannot sin because he is born of God" (3:9). The author repeats this point in the climactic conclusion of this text: "we know that anyone born of God does not sin, but he who was born of God keeps him, and the evil one does not touch him" (5:18).

The author develops this claim by contrasting his hearers with a set of persons he calls "antichrists" (2:18). As the author constructs this group, they are individuals who once moved among believers but abandoned their ranks. For the author, the departure of these persons can only be understood as a sign that they were never actually "of us," that is, "of" God and "in" God: "they went out from us because they were not of us" (2:19; cf. 1:3–4, 4:6).

The Epistle fills in one more lacuna of the Gospel. The Gospel is famously thin on explicit ethical instruction.[59] While tracing out its vision of a sinless life, however, the Epistle fleshes out the obligations incumbent on humans, linking Jesus's command to "love" (1 John 3:23; cf. John 13:34) to the obligation to exercise hospitality and charity (3:17), to avoid murder and "hate" (3:15), and to eschew "the desire of the flesh, the desire of the eyes, the pride of life" (2:16). From this perspective, the author's choice to speak in the voice of Johannine eyewitness seems to be a strategic one, a way of giving the author interpretive control over the Gospel to fill perceived lacunae in the teachings of that text.

We do not know when the epistle was produced, though it appears to have been soon after the Gospel was written.[60] According to the fourth-century writer Eusebius, Papias cited 1 John in his *Exposition of the Sayings of the Lord*, a lost source dated to the first half of the second century.[61] A date for 1 John between 100 and 120 seems reasonable.[62] Whenever it emerged, the text made a decisive impact on how Christians imagined the Johannine eyewitness. Forever after, the figure was remembered as a writer not only of gospels but also of letters—an innovation that inspired new works in his name. In succeeding decades, more letters emerged in the name of this same figure.

B. 2 John

Much of 2 John condenses the contents of 1 John. This sort of imitation is not necessarily unusual for a pseudonymous letter; 2 Peter reproduces many of the contents of Jude, and the pseudonymous letter of Paul to Titus presupposes the same situation as the equally pseudonymous 1 Timothy. But why would someone have written a seemingly redundant letter? To address this question, we might consider what features make 2 John distinct from its predecessor.

The first unique characteristic of 2 John is that it is a proper letter, strictly adhering to Greco-Roman epistolary form. The change might be accidental: the instinct of a writer falling back on ingrained conventions when writing a letter. Alternatively, it might have been a deliberate move, deepening the analogy between the eyewitness disciple and other apostles. Paul utilizes a standard letter form in his epistles.[63] One also finds a standard letter form in the epistles attributed to Peter (1 Peter, 2 Peter). Interestingly, 2 John approximates other features of these works, beginning with the "grace . . . and peace" salutation first seen in the writings of Paul and continued in the Deutero-Pauline and Petrine epistles.[64] In fact, the specific salutation used in 2 John finds a nearly perfect parallel in the salutations of two pseudo-Pauline epistles, 1 and 2 Timothy:

Grace, mercy, and peace from God the Father and Jesus Christ (2 John 3)

Grace, mercy, and peace from God the Father and Christ Jesus our Lord (1 Tim. 1:2; 2 Tim. 1:2)

Second John is also distinct from its predecessor in incorporating a single, new instruction. After condemning those "who will not acknowledge Jesus Christ, coming in the flesh" (1:7), the narrator writes: "If anyone comes to you and does not bring this doctrine, do not receive him into the house or give him any greeting; for the one who greets that person shares his wicked work" (2 John 10–11).[65] Although this instruction is brief, it accounts for some 13% of the (short) epistle—a fact that suggests it may be integral to the purpose of the epistle. Interestingly, other texts of the period, including some falsely authored works, incorporate similar warnings:

> Do not even listen to anyone except the one who speaks truly concerning Jesus Christ. For some are accustomed with evil deceit to carry about the Name [of God], at the same time doing things unworthy of God, whom you must avoid.... There is one physician, both fleshly and spiritual begotten and unbegotten, come in flesh, God, in death, true life, both of Mary and of God, first passible and then impassible. Jesus Christ, our Lord. So let no one deceive you, as indeed you are not deceived. (Ignatius, *Eph.* 6:2–8:1)[66]

> For by his own body Jesus Christ saved all flesh.... They who follow them are not children of righteousness but of wrath, who despise the wisdom of God and in their disbelief assert that heaven and earth and all that is in them are not a work of God. They have the accursed belief of the serpent. Turn away from them and keep aloof from their teaching. (*Acts of Paul*; 3 Cor. 2–21)[67]

In this case, we might conceive of 2 John as a work possibly written to expand the eyewitness's supposed corpus and to press a warning relevant to Christians of the period.[68]

Since the earliest writers to mention 2 John assume its author is the same as that of 1 John, we have every reason to suppose that the author of 2 John also circulated his text under the pretense that it was an authentic letter of the Johannine eyewitness.[69] To give this false authorial claim a veneer of credibility, the author of 2 John was keen to imitate and adapt the language of earlier Johannine texts. He did so in more extensive and mechanical ways than the author of 1 John, however, producing a text whose body can be analyzed as a cento or mosaic of earlier texts. This form of borrowing is atypical of ancient literary fakes but not unprecedented. A helpful comparison for this project can be seen in a Christian text written sometime between the second and fourth centuries: the pseudo-Pauline *Epistle to the Laodiceans*. Written to supply the supposedly lost "letter from Laodicea" mentioned in another Pauline fake (Col. 4:16)—a quasi-biographical aim—some 90% of the letter consists of fragments adapted from earlier works attributed to Paul.[70]

At the same time, the strong links from 2 John to 1 John might have served another purpose; they might have given the author a plausible wedge to insert himself into the Johannine literary tradition. Many modern commentators convinced of the authenticity of 2 John speculate that it might have represented a covering letter for 1 John.[71] Ancient covering letters often provided the personal address and formal greetings missing in the documents appended to them and condensed or abstracted their contents. Of course, 2 John presupposes the same situation, and presumably the epistolary occasion, as 1 John. It may also be significant that several ancient writers conflate 1 and 2 John, perhaps indicating that they interpreted the two letters as parts of a single correspondence.[72] This view, however, is far from certain; 2 John does not mention an appended document as so many ancient covering letters do—at least those we can recognize as covering letters. The sender's claim that he has "much to write" but "would rather not use paper and ink" (v. 12) also seems less compatible with the image of a covering letter.

However he conceptualized his new work, the author probably introduced the letter by appending it to a manuscript containing 1 John. Many pseudonymous letter collections grew precisely by manuscript interpolation.[73] Unfortunately, we have no way of knowing when he did this. There is no question that 2 John is a second-century work since Irenaeus quotes the letter in his *Against the Heresies* (c. 180).[74] But the epistle might have emerged decades after 1 John, not least since so many early Christians questioned its authenticity.

C. 3 John

Since both 2 and 3 John present themselves as works of "the Elder" and are similar in size, many scholars assign them to the same author. Nevertheless, there are compelling reasons to assume that 3 John was written by a different hand. For one, 3 John has a different linguistic profile than the other two letters, folding in certain expressions that appear nowhere else in the Johannine literature.[75] Second, 2 and 3 John differ in style; whereas 2 John addresses its readers—evidently, congregations—in cryptic terms ("the elect lady and her children," "children of your elect sister"), 3 John speaks concretely of "churches" (vv. 6, 9–10) and freely names its intended reader ("Gaius") and other individuals ("Diotrephes," "Demetrius"). Last, 3 John enters the historical record later than its predecessors, and it seems 1 and 2 John circulated without 3 John in at least some regions.[76]

In this case, it seems safest to assign 3 John to another writer—a fifth individual contributing to the same tradition as the author of John 1–20, the scribe who added John 21, the author of 1 John, and the author of 2 John. The participation of so many writers in a single literary tradition is not unusual; as I noted above, scholars reconstruct at least nine authors participating in what we might broadly call the "Pauline" tradition. But when we recognize this author as a distinct figure, we can identify his project as a distinct and independent one.

Unlike the first two epistles, 3 John is surprisingly thin in teaching or exhortation. Its natural comparands, then, would seem to be the hundreds of pseudo-historical letters written in the Second Sophistic period (60–230), many of which were composed primarily for "quasi-biographical" interest.[77] In these letters, as Patricia Rosenmeyer writes, "the principal impulse behind the role-playing of a pseudonymous letter writer may have been precisely a glimpse into the ... past from a more personal angle, and the illumination of a particular historical figure," to "supplement existing information or to replace information that had been lost over the years."[78] Many such letters are brief and focused on merely ordinary, humdrum, and quotidian interactions— "aspects of history that could never have been part of the standard historical record."[79] Consider, for example, the following brief letter composed in the persona of Apollonius of Tyana: "To Ferocianus: I was very pleased by the letter that you sent me, since it showed such friendliness and recollection of our blood tie. I am convinced of your eagerness to see me and be seen by me. I will therefore come in person to you all as soon as possible, especially since God seems so to advise me, so please remain where you are. As I come near, you will meet with me before the rest of my intimates and friends, since that privilege is yours by right."[80] Another classicist, Ronald Syme, agrees that letters such as these might have served only "the satisfying of curiosity about the lives and writings of authors who subsequently achieved the ranks of 'classics.'"[81]

Third John does make sense of a letter of the same type—an ostensibly personal letter of the eyewitness written only to illuminate mundane dimensions of his life and extend his corpus. Although 2 John elaborates the memory of the Johannine eyewitness, it remains a rather two-dimensional portrait, incorporating anonymous characters ("elect lady," "elect sister"). It also mostly reproduces the polemics of 1 John. Not so 3 John. Whoever wrote that letter opted to construct a more realistic and vibrant world around the figure, possibly for biographical interest. Third John is the first and only Johannine epistle to set the Elder in relation to specific, named persons: Gaius, Diotrephes, and Demetrius. More to the point, this letter adds richer texture to the life of the Elder, depicting a personal conflict between him and a named individual (Diotrephes), whom the Elder claims has turned away his emissaries and slandered him personally (vv. 9-10). This letter also portrays the Elder ready to visit the group to reprimand Diotrephes personally: "if I come, I will bring up what he is doing, prating against me with evil words" (v. 10). Evidence of these sorts of conflicts and threats litter Paul's letters (Galatians; 1 Cor. 4:18-21; 2 Cor. 13:1-2, 10). Evidently, the author of 3 John found it useful to infuse the expanding literary corpus of the eyewitness/Elder with the same color.

Of course, even quasi-biographical letters can incorporate at least some instructions, exhortations, or ethical counsel. An author might include them for verisimilitude. (Real personal letters contain these materials, after all.) But these materials may also speak to an author's secondary interests. In the case of 3 John, one finds a call to render hospitality to itinerants (vv. 5-8)—a call one finds even in non-Christian pseudo-historical letters.[82]

We do not know how 3 John surfaced, but like 2 John, it might have also been interpolated into a manuscript already containing 1 and 2 John. One detail in the letter may suggest as much. As I noted earlier, the Elder claims to have "written something to the church" in 3 John 9. This lost letter might be a strictly imaginary document; some ancient pseudo-historical letters situate themselves in invented correspondence. But it is equally likely that the text alludes to one of the other Johannine works. Interestingly, many scholars also compare 3 John to ancient covering letters, including letters of recommendation, and propose links between it and other Johannine works.[83] The author might have intended precisely this sort of reception. In this case, the scholarly suggestion that 1, 2, and 3 John once formed a single "epistolary package" may reflect the design of the author of 3 John.[84]

The dating of 3 John remains a mystery. The earliest mentions of the text appear in fragments from the third-century writings of Origen and Dionysius of Alexandria reproduced in Eusebius's fourth-century *Church History* (assuming Eusebius has not inserted these references).[85] And the earliest manuscripts to contain 3 John are the fourth-century codices Sinaiticus and Vaticanus. All one can say, then, is that 3 John was written sometime in the second century, but perhaps as late as the third century. At so late a date, it may be the latest New Testament text of all.

IV. Conclusion

Within a few years of its publication, the Gospel of John had carved out a dedicated readership beside the earlier gospels of Mark, Matthew, and Luke. Those readers who accepted the text as a reliable account of Jesus's life accepted the historical existence of its enigmatic author—the invented "disciple whom Jesus loved"—as a matter of course. But in a period in which writers were actively producing falsely authored works in the personas of individual disciples of Jesus, that false authorial cast was vulnerable to the activities of new, would-be pseudepigraphers. As I have argued in this chapter, three such authors produced the epistles we now know as 1 John, 2 John, and 3 John, adopting the voice of the eyewitness disciple as their own. These letters are a chain of falsely authored works.

The power of this thesis is its ability to make sense of so many attributes of the Epistles that conventional scholarly models—those that cast these works as first-century products by different authors writing in their own names—have difficulty explaining. It explains why the Epistles would contain such extensive, direct verbal overlap with the Gospel and with one another (something hardly necessary for one text, let alone all three). It also explains why most Christians have historically attributed John, 1 John, 2 John, and 3 John to the same pen. This was not a coincidence, nor was it a careless mistake; rather, it was a directed outcome influenced by the texts themselves. This thesis also makes sense of why the authenticity of several of these texts—especially 2 and 3 John—was so widely questioned in antiquity. These doubts were warranted; all the letters had dubious pedigrees. (First John mostly managed to escape the same scrutiny as 2 and 3 John, just as 1 Peter mostly escaped the scrutiny faced by the equally pseudonymous 2 Peter.)[86]

Even if the Epistles of John shared a common authorial pretense, however, they do not seem to have shared a common motivation. Whereas 1 John has a clear theological agenda, 3 John may reflect a quasi-biographical interest. These authors also did not produce the same sort of work. Whereas 1 John is a paranetic, or exhortative, text, 2 and 3 John are modeled after personal letters. In these three epistles, probably produced across the second century, one sees the rich and complex flowering of a surprising literary tradition. Above all, one also sees the full development of a single literary character: the invented disciple of Jesus, a figure who, in the end, would indeed "have much to write" to his many, many readers (2 John 12; 3 John 13).

6
Becoming John

The Gospel of John triggered the production of other works co-opting the voice of its invented eyewitness narrator. I have identified 1, 2, and 3 John, three anonymous letters penned in and around the second century, as works in this tradition, but there were others. Around the same time the Epistles were written, other texts surfaced with similar claims—works such as the *Secret Book* (or *Apocryphon*) *of John* and the *Epistula Apostolorum*. Unlike the Epistles, however, these texts are not anonymous; instead, their narrators freely take up the name later Christians assigned to the author of the Gospel: John.

Contemporary scholars generally refer only to the Gospel and Epistles as "Johannine literature" proper, relegating these other works to the category of Christian apocrypha.[1] This distinction, however, is shot through with canonical bias. If the Gospel and Letters of John are a lineage of falsely authored works whose authors had no particular connection to one another, then we have no historical basis on which to privilege them above other such texts. All of the above works, including the *Secret Book of John* and the *Epistula Apostolorum*, participate in the same tradition of disguised authorship; all are equally "Johannine." In this case, we can begin conceptualizing the "Johannine literature" as an expansive and open catalogue filled with a richer and more diverse library of texts.

In this chapter, I will explore how the identification of the disciple whom Jesus loved with John, the son of Zebedee, emerged. I will also explore some of those entrants in the Johannine tradition that bear the name of John, recognizing their full and equal place among the imagined literary corpus of the disciple. In these works, we see a broader field of responses, reuses, and reimagining of the Gospel of John, shaped by the anxieties of second-century Christians. They are other imagined memoirs of the disciple whom Jesus loved, other works that capture the disciple's voice, elaborate his story, and extend his unique witness to later generations.

I. Early Traditions of John

As we have seen, the Gospel of John never names its invented eyewitness narrator, leaving him anonymous and enigmatic. This is hardly unusual for the period and genre; earlier gospels—Mark, Matthew, and Luke—also fail to name their narrators. Nevertheless, some early Christians found this anonymity intolerable. As early as the second century, one finds evidence that readers of these texts were actively speculating who wrote each of them and in what circumstances. Early church traditions assigned Matthew to a disciple of Jesus, Mark to a close associate of Peter, and Luke to a companion of Paul. The Gospel of John was subject to the same intense speculation. What emerged in the wake of that speculation and conjecture was a consensus among many Christian groups that the enigmatic eyewitness author of the Gospel corresponded to a specific, named figure from the Synoptic Gospels: John, the son of Zebedee, one of the three inner disciples of Jesus.

A. John, the Son of Zebedee

We know little about the historical John.[2] The Synoptic Gospels indicate that he lived by the Sea of Galilee and worked as a fisherman alongside his father, Zebedee, and his brother, James. According to the Synoptics, when Jesus encountered John and his brother fishing and called them to "follow" him, they immediately left their father and fishing nets behind (Mark 1:19–20). Evidently, John quickly gained a high status among Jesus's earliest followers. All the Synoptics list him in the exclusive circle of twelve disciples (e.g., Mark 3:17). The Synoptics also depict Jesus folding John into his innermost circle alongside his brother, James, and Peter (Mark 5:37; 9:2, 14:33; cf. 13:3).

John preserved some of this clout after Jesus's death. Paul lists him among three Christian leaders he met at Jerusalem who were "reputed to be pillars" of the church (Gal. 2:1, 9). Acts affords him a similar profile, positioning him as a leader in the Jerusalem church beside Peter (8:14). The same text also incorporates John into three narratives on the early experiences and exploits of the apostles (1:13, 3:1–4:31; 8:14–24).

As a rural, Aramaic-speaking fisherman, it is improbable that John had access to the formal education and literacy necessary to produce major literary works in Greek. Acts calls both him and Peter "uneducated" or "unlettered" (*agrammatoi*; 4:13).³ This, however, did not prevent the emergence of pseudepigraphal works in his name any more than Peter's stated illiteracy in Acts prevented the emergence of pseudepigraphal works in his name (i.e., 1 Peter, 2 Peter, the *Apocalypse of Peter*, and the *Gospel of Peter*). The Johannine Gospel and Epistles would be attributed to John in time, but perhaps the earliest work explicitly attributed to John was an apocalypse, now included in the New Testament canon: Revelation.

1. Revelation

Revelation, also known as the Apocalypse of John, positions itself as a "prophecy" communicated by God, through an angel, to "his slave John" (1:1, 3). The text that follows is written by John in his "I" voice. John addresses seven churches located in the Roman province of Asia in his name, beginning with the church of Ephesus (1:4, 9; cf. v. 11). Beyond that name and the simple, passing note that the author is writing from the Aegean island of Patmos, however, the text offers no other biographical data on the author (1:9).

Despite the opaque nature of the text's authorial cast, the earliest writers to discuss Revelation assume that its "John" is none other than the apostle John, the son of Zebedee. Already in the mid-second century CE, for example, Justin Martyr credits the work to "John, one of the apostles of Christ" in his *Dialogue with Trypho*.⁴ Tertullian concurs.⁵ This opinion was not shared by all Christians, however. The third-century writer Dionysius of Alexandria indicates that many Christians "rejected and altogether impugned the book, examining it chapter by chapter and declaring ... its title false. For they say it is not John's ... and that the author of this book was not only not one of the apostles, nor even one of the saints."⁶ Dionysius himself staked an intermediate position in this debate; in the surviving fragments of his work, he defends the view that the author was indeed "named John" (i.e., the work is not pseudonymous) but that this John was not "the apostle, the son of Zebedee, the brother of James" but another figure by the same name.⁷ Over the next several centuries, however, Revelation would gain gradual acceptance by Christians of all regions.

Faced with the memory of these arly debates, many contemporary scholars remain agnostic on the identity of the John mentioned in Revelation. It is common to see scholars reconstruct this figure as an unknown early Christian prophet by the same name.⁸ I, however, see every reason to conclude that the John who supposedly writes the text is none other than John, the son of

Zebedee, albeit as a pseudonym.[9] The fact that Revelation carried a dubious canonical status for centuries, coupled with evidence of its later date, makes it unlikely to have come from the hand of one of the most recognized early disciples of Jesus.

It is true that the attribution of the text to "[God's] slave John" is ambiguous and open to multiple candidates, known and potentially unknown. Of course, it is no less, but also no more, ambiguous than the attribution of the epistle of James to "James, a slave of God, and of the Lord Jesus Christ" (1:1). The name "James" was also common in antiquity and borne by several early Christians (e.g., James, the brother of the Lord; James, the son of Zebedee; and James, the son of Alphaeus [Mark 3:17–18; 6:3]). Nevertheless, most critical scholars today are convinced that the Epistle of James is a pseudepigraphal work inhabiting the voice of the most visible and influential James of the first-century church: James the brother of the Lord.[10] As Bart Ehrman notes, the simplicity with which the author identifies himself as James means "that he can assume—at least he thinks he can assume—that his readers will know 'which' James he is," even in a letter ostensibly distributed across the Mediterranean.[11] Paul lists James beside Cephas and John, all of whom resided in Jerusalem, as one of the "reputed pillars" of the early Jesus movement (Gal. 2:9). For that matter, the sustained polemic against Paul in the epistle of James suits the fact that Paul indicates he had tensions with James's circle (Gal. 2:12).[12] It would make sense for a pseudepigrapher wishing to attack Paul to do so in the name of perhaps the most prominent Christian leader to come into conflict with him.

If we apply the same standards to Revelation, we have no reason to think that the John in question is anyone other than the disciple of Jesus. He certainly had the necessary prominence to speak as one well-known to his readers; again, Paul lists John beside James as one of the "pillars" of the early Jesus movement (Gal. 2:9). John was also well-known to early Christians as a member of the innermost circle of Jesus's disciples (Mark 5:37, 9:2, 13:3, 14:33). The text also implies that its author is ethnically Jewish, as John was.[13]

Attributing Revelation to John, the son of Zebedee, would also make sense of one of its most interesting features: its apparent tensions with the Pauline tradition. Revelation's condemnation of those who eat meat sacrificed to idols runs counter to Paul's more nuanced teachings on the matter (Rev. 2:2, 14, 20; cf. 1 Cor. 8:4–13). Some scholars even detect in the text a broader polemic against Paul and/or his later followers.[14] Whether Revelation is merely pushing back against Paul or outright rejecting him, it would make sense for a pseudepigrapher to do so in the voice of someone of comparable or greater heft: an apostle in his own right and a leading light of the Jerusalem church. (As I noted, other texts problematizing the Pauline legacy often do so in the voices of figures such as James and Jude.)[15] More to the point, several aspects of John's authorial cast position him as an apostle in his own right, one who could counter, balance, rival, or even displace Paul. Paul claimed to be an apostle on the basis of his supernatural visions of Jesus, through which he was caught up into heaven (Gal. 1:11-16; 1 Cor. 15:8-9; 2 Cor. 12:1-7), and Paul exercised his authority as an apostle by sending epistles. Similarly, Revelation's John also experiences a supernatural vision of Jesus in which he is caught up into heaven, albeit a vision that undermines the teachings of Paul. He also condenses these teachings in a divinely sanctioned apocalypse-epistle (Rev. 1:2-5, 9).[16] These molds suit John, the son of Zebedee.

The arguments marshaled against John, the son of Zebedee, are unpersuasive. For example, the fact that the author does not expressly identify himself in the apocalypse as an apostle is not a problem since John's self-presentation as a "slave" of Jesus (1:1) mirrors the prescripts of such pseudo-apostolic letters as Titus and 2 Peter (each of whose senders claims to be an apostle; Titus 1:1; 2 Peter 1:1) as well as James and Jude (whose senders do not apply the term to themselves, as Revelation does not). As John Christian Eurell writes, "John's presentation as 'slave of Christ' (1:1) ... is thus entirely fitting for a pseudepigraphon ascribed to John the Apostle."[17] The fact that the apocalypse also fails to give additional biographical background for John and fails to appeal to other Johannine works is also not a problem.[18] Dale Allison has noted that "pseudepigrapha, including pseudepigraphical epistles, do not always parade the credentials of their purported authors if those authors are sufficiently well known. Simple names, for example, suffice."[19] For that matter, one cannot ignore the fact that Revelation was successful in convincing many Christians it was written by John, the son of Zebedee, without any of these features. If those features were not needed to achieve this outcome, then we can hardly fault the text for not including them. Last, one should not rule out John, the son of Zebedee on the grounds that the text mentions "the apostles" in 18:20 and 21:14 without identifying the narrator as part of that group. The voice of Peter also mentions the apostles without explicitly situating himself among them in one of the pseudonymous letters written in his name: "you should remember the words spoken in the past by the holy prophets and the commandment of the Lord and Savior spoken through your apostles" (2 Peter 3:2).[20] The sense that the narrator of

Revelation is speaking of the apostles as a group that existed in the past may say more about the book's pseudonymous and late character than about its implied authorship.

Revelation, then, would seem to be a pseudonymous apocalypse written in the name of John, the son of Zebedee, as indeed many Christians suspected it of being in antiquity.[21] At the very least, the text was accepted by some second-century Christians as a work by John. From this position, it would inform early Christian memories of this disciple as well as speculations about the origins of the Gospel and Letters of John.

2. The Gospel and Letters

From a very early period, Christians began considering not only Revelation but also the Gospel and Epistles of John as works penned by John, the son of Zebedee. Our earliest evidence of this view dates to the late second century. It would flourish in succeeding centuries, however, taking various forms.

John as Author

The earliest source to directly mention the Gospel of John is also the first to identify its author. In the first book of *Against the Heresies*, Irenaeus states that "John the disciple of the Lord" wrote the Gospel.[22] In the same passage, he also quotes the Valentinian teacher Ptolemy making the same claim, indicating that this view was already widespread in his day: "Further, [the Valentinians] teach that John, the disciple of the Lord, indicated the first Ogdoad, expressing themselves in these words: 'John, the disciple of the Lord, wishing to set forth the origin of all things, so as to explain how the Father produced the whole, lays down a certain principle' [*Latin:* 'So says Ptolemæus']."[23] Likewise, when Irenaeus cites passages from John, 1 John, and 2 John, he cites them as passages from "his"—that is, John's—"epistle."[24] (Irenaeus, again, shows no knowledge of 3 John.) Like some other second-century Christians, however, Irenaeus also believed that the same John wrote Revelation. He introduces a quote from Revelation 1:12 with the words "John also, the disciple of the Lord, when beholding the priestly and glorious advent of His kingdom, says in the Apocalypse."[25]

Admittedly, neither Ptolemy nor Irenaeus uses the more unambiguous formula "John, the son of Zebedee" when indicating the authors of these texts. (In fact, Irenaeus does not use that epithet anywhere in his writings, preferring "John the disciple of the Lord" or "John.") Nevertheless, both refer to precisely this John.[26] The very fact that Irenaeus also uses the formula "John, the disciple of the Lord" or merely "John" so consistently in his writings shows that he saw nothing ambiguous or imprecise in the formula but used it as a designation for a single, specific person whom his readers would instantly recognize. More to the point, Irenaeus refers to "John, the disciple of the Lord" (or simply "John") in other passages as "the apostle" or one of "the apostles."[27] Elsewhere in his writings, Irenaeus reserves the term "apostle" for the twelve disciples of Jesus.[28] (Note that Irenaeus also applies the language of both "apostle" and "disciple" to another member of the twelve: Peter).[29] Last, Papias, one of Irenaeus's most important sources, lists John (the son of Zebedee) among the "disciples of the Lord," anchoring Irenaeus's use of the same expression for John.[30] Ptolemy also applies the title "apostle" to the author of the Gospel.[31]

John Writing John

Irenaeus is not only the first writer to identify John as the author of the Gospel; he is also the first extant writer to relate a particular tradition regarding the origins of the Gospel of John—that is, the circumstances under which it was written and the place where it was written. He affirms that John wrote his Gospel after the Synoptics had been completed: "afterwards, John, the disciple of the Lord, who also had leaned upon His breast, published a Gospel while residing at Ephesus in Asia."[32] In another passage, Irenaeus clarifies the chronology of John's residency in Ephesus, indicating that John remained among the presbyters "until the times of Trajan [i.e., 98 to 117]."[33]

Similar traditions feature in the writings of later Christian authors. For example, Eusebius preserves a fragment of Clement of Alexandria's now lost *Hypotyposes* that reaffirms that "John, last of all, conscious that the outward facts had been set forth in the Gospels, was urged on by his disciples, and, divinely moved by the Spirit, composed a spiritual Gospel."[34] In a similar passage, preserved by Eusebius, Origen concurs that John wrote "after them all."[35]

Eusebius, in turn, offers his own developed portrait, which he credits to an unnamed source. His account also affirms that John wrote in response to the requests of those around him precisely to supply what was absent in earlier gospels:

> John, it is said, used all the time a message which was not written down, and at last took to writing for the following cause. The three gospels which had been written down before were distributed to all including himself; it is said

that he welcomed them and testified to their truth but said that there was only lacking to the narrative the account of what was done by Christ at first and at the beginning of the preaching. The story is surely true. It is at least possible to see that the three evangelists related only what the Saviour did during one year after John the Baptist had been put in prison and that they stated this at the beginning of their narrative.... Thus John in the course of his gospel relates what Christ did before the Baptist had been thrown into prison, but the other three evangelists narrate the events after the imprisonment of the Baptist.... John passed over the genealogy of our Saviour according to the flesh, because it had been already written out by Matthew and Luke, and began with the description of his divinity since this had been reserved for him by the Divine Spirit as for one greater than they.[36]

A still more embellished tradition appears in the Muratorian Fragment.[37] Most significant, that source indicates that the friends who entreated John to write included "his fellow disciples" among the Twelve—a move that gives a further apostolic imprimatur to the Gospel: "The fourth of the gospels by John, one of the disciples: At the urging of his co-disciples and bishops, he said, 'Fast with me today for three days, and whatever has been revealed to each, let us narrate [it] one to another.' On the same night, it was revealed to Andrew, one of the apostles, that, by the acknowledgment of everyone, John would write down everything in his own name."[38] Finally, the *Acts of Timothy* casts John as not only the author of the Fourth Gospel but the one who named, edited, and compiled the earlier gospels of Mark, Matthew, and Luke as well, producing the fourfold canonical set.[39]

B. Between Memory and History

These various sources sketch out the contours of a common, flowering array of traditions that linked the Fourth Gospel to John, the son of Zebedee, and to Ephesus as a city. But how should we evaluate these traditions? Some scholars, including most conservative-leaning scholars, argue that those traditions linking the Gospel to John, the son of Zebedee, are plausible.[40] Others entertain the possibility that these traditions may preserve at least some kernel of historical fact, distorted through centuries but recoverable through careful historical reconstruction.[41] For example, some argue from these "early Christian memories" that the Fourth Gospel was indeed written by a "John," albeit a different John: the "John the Elder" known to Papias, whom they place at Ephesus.[42] Many more scholars shy away from identifying the Gospel's author(s); nevertheless, some speculate from patristic traditions that the Gospel, the Letters, and the hypothetical Johannine Community hail from Ephesus.[43]

It is understandable why certain scholars want to take this stream of early Christian memory seriously. The internal evidence of the Johannine texts offers us no meaningful alternatives to these traditions, no rival candidates to be the author of John. These traditions also date to an early period and seem to have been widely held. It seems presumptuous, if not arrogant, to dismiss them out of hand. Nevertheless, there are sound reasons to be skeptical of historical reconstructions articulated around "early Christian memory."

1. The Problem with "Memory"
First, any appeal to "early Christian memory" collectively must also contend with the obvious tensions, if not disagreements, in the sources in question. Irenaeus claims that Mark wrote his Gospel after Peter's death ("departure"); Clement, by contrast, claims that Peter was made aware of Mark's composition in his lifetime.[44] Similarly, whereas Irenaeus assumes 1 and 2 John shared a single author, Eusebius proposes the two might have been written by writers "of the same name."[45] And although Justin, Irenaeus, and Tertullian claim John the Apostle wrote Revelation, Dionysius of Alexandria denied that claim based on internal evidence. These are not firm memories and should not be treated as such; in several instances, they look more like competing readings and inferences comparable to those scholars make today.

Second, the results of modern biblical scholarship have demonstrated time and time again that patristic traditions are flatly unreliable on the origins of the gospels. Stunningly, every claim Irenaeus and Clement make that can be empirically verified has been falsified. For example, following Papias, Irenaeus identifies the gospel we now know as Matthew as a text originally written in Hebrew.[46] Contemporary biblical scholars, however, find no evidence of a Hebrew substrate in the text.[47] Likewise, Irenaeus and Clement claim that Matthew wrote his Gospel first, before Mark wrote his own. Today, however, scholars are virtually unanimous in affirming that Mark must have been written before Matthew and Luke and that it was a critical source for both works (Markan Priority). For that matter, none of these early traditions acknowledge literary dependence as the source of material in the Synoptics despite overwhelming and convincing evidence of such literary relationships; the above writers invoke recollection and oral preaching alone as the source of individual gospels. Last, this study has already compiled evidence against Irenaeus's and Clement's essential claims about the Johannine literature—namely, that the Gospel is an eyewitness record of Jesus's life and teachings and that the same hand that composed the Gospel also composed 1 John, 2 John, and Revelation.[48]

Of course, many scholars are aware of these problems and assume that although some of these traditions are clearly mistaken, others are not (conveniently, those that cannot be falsified). Nothing in the above track record should inspire our confidence in these traditions, however. On the contrary, the fact that certain traditions are flatly false requires us to assume, as a starting point, that their other traditions are at least dubious. And if they are dubious, then they are hardly appropriate materials for historical reconstruction.

More problematic still, scholars who insist on the possible value of patristic memories tend to work with this evidence in selective, arbitrary ways. They do not take patristic traditions at face value; rather, they handle them unevenly, assembling bricolage reconstructions that no ancient witness would recognize. For example, Martin Hengel cites patristic data to propose that Papias's enigmatic John the Elder is responsible for the Gospel of John (assuming that this figure existed, which is not clear).[49] And yet no ancient writer associates the Gospel with John the Elder. Eusebius is the only writer to expressly propose that John the Elder might have been a Johannine author, but he speculates that John the Elder authored Revelation.[50] He leaves no doubt that John, the son of Zebedee, authored the Gospel. Hengel's reconstruction is an artificial mosaic of evidence that no patristic writer could have endorsed. Similarly, Paul Anderson claims that the core of the Gospel of John was the work of one author but that the epistle of 1 John was the work of a different writer: once again, John the Elder.[51] And yet not a single patristic voice would speak in his favor. Every ancient writer to comment on the authorship of John and 1 John attributed both texts to the same hand. The very scholars who claim to take "early Christian memories" seriously often, in practice, do not.

2. Textual Inferences

Given these problems, I would argue that we should consider other ways of explaining how these sprawling and contradictory traditions emerged in the first place. As it turns out, the basic contours of these early Christian "memories" are relatively simple to extract from the Johannine works themselves. We have no reason to presuppose a lost historical core or external lineage for these traditions; we can build these traditions just as easily from the ground up.

John as Author

In all likelihood, the association of "John the Apostle" with the Gospel of John began as a simple authorial inference. As we have seen, the Gospel of John invents a "disciple whom Jesus loved" as an eyewitness narrator—a figure it positions as one of Jesus's most intimate disciples, if not his closest associate. At the last supper, that disciple occupies the most privileged position at the table—closer even than Peter, who must have his questions to Jesus relayed through this disciple (13:23–25). Of course, any reader of the Synoptic Gospels would know that Jesus had three inner disciples: Peter, James, and John. For such a reader, the identification of John as the disciple amounts to arithmetic. The disciple could not have been Peter since Peter appears beside the disciple in certain scenes (13:23–24, 20:2–3). He was also unlikely to be James since, according to Acts, James was killed not long after Jesus (Acts 12:1–2). That leaves John.[52] This deduction could have succeeded due to (a) its simplicity, (b) its popularization by early, prominent writers, and (c) the absence of a serious alternative.

Links to Revelation

Of course, once the Gospel was identified as John's, it was only natural to assume that it was written by the same author as Revelation, a figure who expressly calls himself "John." This link was not unproblematic; the Gospel and Revelation are very different in ideology, style, and language—a point writers like Dionysius and Eusebius seized upon as evidence that the two works had different authors. And yet we know that many second-century readers uncritically made the connection. Irenaeus, the earliest writer to identify John as the author of the Gospel, also identifies him as the author of Revelation.

Links to Ephesus

The idea that John wrote the Gospel at Ephesus also requires no line of oral tradition; it too is a detail that can be inferred from those texts associated with the memory of John. In Revelation, John addresses seven churches in the Roman province of Asia in his name, beginning with the church of Ephesus (1:4, 9; cf. v. 11). The apocalypse does not indicate why he specifically addresses these churches. It is possible the author of Revelation knew that the historical John resided in Asia for a time. But it is equally likely that the author of Revelation invented a connection between John and Asia because of the significance he attached to the region personally or prophetically.[53] Early Christian works situate John in Palestine, with no indication that he later left the region (e.g., Gal. 2:1, 9; Acts 8:14). From there, a trusting reader of Revelation could easily have inferred John's connections to Ephesus. Paul wrote to communities he was personally connected to—both those he had visited (Corinth, Thessalonica, Galatia, Philippa) and those he planned to visit (Rome). In this case, a reader could have assumed similar connections between John and the city of Ephesus, among others.

Whether by memory or invention, then, a second-century tradition linked the John of Revelation to Asia and Ephesus in particular. It hardly seems to be a coincidence, then, that writers would infer that the Gospel was written in the same region. What so many scholars miss is that the earliest writers to identify the Gospel with Asia and Ephesus are precisely those who also identify the Gospel and Revelation as works of the same pen (Irenaeus, Clement). These traditions are completely entangled from the very first mention of them for a reason: they go hand in hand.[54] It makes little sense for scholars to cherry-pick from this coherent body of tradition, discarding one claim (joint authorship for the Gospel and Revelation) but preserving another (Ephesus as the place of writing).[55]

John as the Last Gospel

Perhaps the only tradition that might have a kernel of historical memory is the tradition that the Gospel was written after Luke (so Irenaeus) or "last of all" (so Clement and Origen). As we have seen, scholars today find compelling evidence for John's dependence on Mark, Matthew, and Luke.[56] The tradition that John was written last, then, may reflect a lingering memory that John entered into circulation later than the other three.

Purposes in Writing

Ancient writers offer competing interpretations of the reasons why John wrote his gospel. None is based on anything more than close readings and textual inferences. For example, Clement's claim that John, "seeing that what was corporeal was set forth in the Gospels . . . composed a spiritual Gospel," makes sense in a passage in which he seems concerned with the presence of "genealogies" in certain gospels. His point seems to be that while Matthew and Luke provide human genealogies for Jesus ("what was corporeal"), John explores Jesus's celestial origins in his prologue (his "spiritual" descent). Likewise, Eusebius's claim that John wrote to describe "the period which had been omitted by the earlier evangelists" is a textual inference of its own—an attempt to grapple with chronological issues in John (e.g., why Jesus cleanses the Temple so early in his narrative) and why he incorporates events that occur over multiple Passovers before the one in which he met his death (John 2:13, 2:23, 6:4). Seizing on a passing chronological note in John 3:24, "John had not yet been put in prison," Eusebius claims that John meant to highlight a forgotten period in Jesus's life: the period before John was put into prison. In short, neither author provides information that could not be gleaned from the text itself.

Communal Composition

Clement depicts groups of people begging Mark and John to compose their texts. This motif does not require a historical anchor; instead, it makes perfect sense as an invention and apologetic device—a way of closing off the inference that later Gospel writers wrote because they saw earlier gospels as defective. The motif frames the Gospel writers as reluctant pens who did not initially even see a need to write further gospels given the existence of other solid accounts of Jesus's life.

Interestingly, the Muratorian Fragment takes this motif further, expressly naming the disciples who entreated John and involving them in all aspects of the Gospel. Andrew receives a divine vision indicating that John should write a gospel; later, the disciples "review" John's completed manuscript. These details are obvious embellishments in the tradition meant both to give John an apostolic imprimatur and to soften the apparent tensions between John and the other Gospels; the passage underscores this very point: "and for that reason, although various origins may be taught in the individual books of the Gospels, nevertheless, the faith of believers differs in no respect."[57] Still, one can find possible textual bases for these traditions. The Muratorian Fragment's claim that John composed his Gospel with the consent of and in concert with other eyewitnesses to the life of Jesus may be a way of explaining why John takes up a narratorial "we" voice in his Gospel. In turn, the singling out of Andrew as a catalyst for the creation of John suits a gospel in which Andrew is the first disciple named in the text (1:40).[58]

3. Responses to Pseudepigraphy

In the end, there is no evidence the earliest Christian writers had any valuable, external information that could illuminate the origins of the Gospel and Epistles of John. This is understandable; the texts in question were written under false authorial personas. In this case, they probably surfaced under conditions that occluded their true origins. No useful information about their origins was on hand. To assign any of these texts to a particular author, geography, or situation, ancient Christians had to rely on the internal data of these texts, just as contemporary scholars must do today. The difference, of course, is that these persons generally handled the evidence of the text less carefully and critically than contemporary scholars do. They adopted several claims of the text uncritically (e.g., its eyewitness origins), and to fill in gaps in their knowledge, they coordinated ideas from other texts (e.g., the Synoptic Gospels, Revelation). What emerged from these efforts was an increasingly elaborate mythology centered on the figure of John, the son of Zebedee—a mythology we can safely retire.

II. Other Second-Century Johannine Texts

The image of John as the author of the Fourth Gospel does not meet the high standards of twenty-first-century scholarship. Nevertheless, it was a widespread view shared by many Christian movements in the mid-second century. We have seen this view taken up by figures associated with the development of Valentinian Christianity (Ptolemy) and Proto-Catholic Christianity (Irenaeus, Clement, Eusebius). The same ideas also seem to have found a place in so-called Sethian Gnostic and Montanist circles, among others.

Once this identification was in place, however, a person seeking to co-opt the voice of the invented disciple could have invoked him under the name he had now become so closely associated with in various Christian circles: John. Not all did, of course. The authors of 1 John, 2 John, and 3 John did not. Avoiding the name, of course, had certain advantages. For one, it ensured consistency with the Gospel of John, which refuses to name its enigmatic author—a move that might have been attractive to a pseudepigrapher seeking to avoid detection. In the third century, Dionysius of Alexandria would argue against the common authorship of John, 1 John, and Revelation by noting that whereas the first two are anonymous, the last one names its author.[59]

Nevertheless, some authors opted to take up the name "John," perhaps to press their authorial pretense as explicitly as possible. Among the many Christian pseudo-historical works composed in the second and third centuries, one finds several texts that expressly echo the authorial claims of the Gospel but whose narrators freely self-identify as John, the disciple of Jesus, the son of Zebedee. These texts do not necessarily represent a later phase of Johannine authorship than the Epistles; at least one text in the tradition, the *Secret Book of John*, may well predate 3 John. We should think of these works as forming a separate branch in the Johannine tree, growing and flowering in parallel to the Epistles. Texts in that branch share a single innovation, a single shared mutation: the use of a pseudonym. In them, we see other possibilities for Johannine pseudepigraphy and other entrants in this expansive literary tradition.[60]

A. *Secret Book (Apocryphon) of John*

The *Secret Book of John* is a classic example—in fact, the type specimen—of Gnostic thought in the so-called Sethian tradition. The *Secret Book* was originally written in Greek but survives in two recensions across four Coptic manuscripts—three third-century manuscripts from Nag Hammadi and one version in the fifth-century *Berolinensis Gnosticus*.[61] It is unclear when the original text was written, though scholars confidently place its composition in the second century.

As its name implies, the *Secret Book of John* is pseudepigraphal, inhabiting the voice of John, the son of Zebedee.[62] As in other such texts, however, the authorial claims are developed fluidly. Both recensions of the text begin with a scene written in the third person, which describes a time after Jesus's ascension into heaven when "John, the brother of James, the son of Zebedee," goes to the Temple Mount. There, John encounters a Pharisee named Arimanios, who asks, "Where is your teacher, the one whom you used to follow?" John answers in terms evocative of the Gospel of John, demonstrating the *Secret Book*'s dependence on that text: "He returned to the place from which he came" (cf. John 12:28). In reply, Armanios ridicules John, exposing the latter's insecurities about all he does not understand about Jesus's teachings. At the end of this scene, the text abruptly switches to a first-person narration in the voice of John himself, who relates the many anxieties and questions flooding his mind at that moment: "When I heard these words, I turned away from the temple towards the barren mountain, and I was very distressed, saying, 'How indeed was the savior chosen? And why was he sent into the world by his parent who sent him? And who is his parent who [sent him]? And what is that realm like, to which we shall go? For what . . . he told us that this realm . . . has been stamped in the mold of that incorruptible realm, and did not tell us what that other one is like.'"[63] John's questions are occasioned by the Gospel, which claims that the Father "sent" Jesus into the world (3:17) and in which Jesus promises his disciples that they will be with him where he is after his departure (14:1–3).

At this critical moment, however, John sees the polymorphic Jesus, who says he has come to instruct John, addressing his questions at the beginning of the text.[64] In the dialogue that follows, Jesus communicates a Sethian Gnostic cosmogony and myth to John, describing the origins of the many aeons of heaven, the creation of the material world, and the path by which human beings may be restored to the *pleroma*.[65] At the end of the dialogue, the narrative restores its original, third-person perspective: "And he came to his fellow disciples and informed them of what the savior had told him."[66]

Set against the work's many allusions to the Gospel of John, the choice of John, the son of Zebedee, as a narrator for the text seems strategic. The *Secret Book* assumes the name "John" to position itself as a successor work to the Gospel, penned by the same hand—what scholars have called "a kind of continuation to John's gospel" and "a concluding sequel to the Fourth Gospel."[67] It portrays a later episode—a final, climactic discourse scene—outside the scope of the Gospel's narrative, which offers readers "in the form of a narrative . . . an interpretive key for the enigmatic content of the Fourth Gospel . . . to make up for it[s] communicative weakness and polemical shortcomings."[68] Karen King elaborates this concept:

> The fact that the entire Secret Revelation of John is framed as the return of Christ to complete his revelation and show the way back to the Divine Realm makes it possible to read it as the completion of Christ's revelation in the Gospel of John, the fulfillment of his promise to return and show them the way back to the Father. The Secret Revelation of John is filling the gaps in Christ's revelation in the Gospel of John, offering a fuller narrative of the Divine Realm, the creation of the world and humanity, the condition of humanity in the world, and salvation. The ascription of the work to John

overtly places the Secret Revelation of John in the tradition of Johannine Christianity and it has the effect of asking readers to interpret the Gospel of John within the framework of Christ's revelation.[69]

The text, in short, commandeers the voice of the Johannine eyewitness, here expressly identified as John, to orient the Gospel toward a Sethian Gnostic worldview.

In a novel move, however, the text positions itself as a specific kind of entrant in the Johannine canon: a "secret" or esoteric one. At the end of his teachings, Jesus instructs John to compose the *Secret Book*, but precisely as a record to be shared secretly: "I have told you all things, so that you might write them down and transmit them secretly to those who are like you in spirit."[70] As we saw, the Gospel uses a motif of private or secret speech to explain why certain teachings of Jesus might have been missing from earlier sources. The idea of a secret book takes this idea further; it intimates that its readers have never heard the *Secret Book*'s unusual teachings before because Jesus never meant to disseminate those teachings publicly. Not surprisingly, the motif appears in other revisionist works of the period, including the *Gospel of Thomas* and the *Book of Thomas the Contender*, the latter of which also takes the form of a post-resurrection dialogue.[71]

B. *Epistula Apostolorum*

We have already explored some ways Proto-Catholic Christians were intervening in the nascent Johannine tradition in the second century. Another product of this activity is the *Epistula Apostolorum* (that is, the *Epistle of the Apostles*). Although the work was probably composed in Greek, it survives in Coptic, Latin, and Ethiopic (Ge'ez) versions. Internal indications suggest the work was written in the late second century, especially since it locates Jesus's coming within a century and a half of his resurrection and presupposes the devastation of the "Antonine Plague."[72]

As its name indicates, the *Epistula Apostolorum* was written pseudonymously in the name of the apostles of Jesus. In its preface, a narratorial "we" voice casts the work as a record of "what Jesus Christ revealed to his disciples," that is, "what we heard and remembered."[73] The text then continues with a standard epistolary prescript, in which the senders of the letters identify themselves by name: "John and Thomas and Peter and Andrew and

James and Philip and Bartholomew and Matthew and Nathanael and Judas the Zealot and Cephas to the churches of the east and the west, to those in the north and the south: proclaiming and declaring to you our Lord Jesus Christ, as we heard so have we written; and we touched him after he rose from the dead when he revealed to us what is great and wonderful and true."[74] What scholars fail to realize, however, is that this false authorial pretense is, in fact, a "Johannine" one. As we saw, John and 1 John position themselves as works by a plural "we." This pronoun is ambiguous, but it can be understood as a reference to the collective body of eyewitnesses to the life of Jesus, if not the disciples in particular (especially at John 1:14). The *Epistula* selects this interpretive option, explicitly identifying those eyewitnesses with the eleven disciples of Jesus, sans Judas Iscariot. Of course, John and 1 John also single out a single eyewitness, a single voice, among the eyewitnesses: an individual later conflated with the biblical John. So too does the *Epistula*, albeit in a new way. Tellingly, the *Epistula* lists John first among the disciples, a position he occupies in no earlier list of Jesus's disciples. The move is significant; it casts John as the ultimate or primary author of the work. (Other texts written in the voices of multiple authors list their primary author first.)[75] In effect, then, the *Epistula* lays claim to the same implied author(s) of the Gospel, albeit in a manner refracted through later Christian speculations of who that author is. It too is a work of the beloved disciple John, who speaks in unison with the collective "we" voice of all Jesus's disciples. The epistle works from a slightly different interpretation of the Gospel's "we"/"I" language than the *Secret Book of John*, but it co-opts it for the same ends as that other source.

The suspicion that the *Epistula* means to inhabit a specifically Johannine voice deepens in the lines that follow, lines that reveal the text's dependence on the Gospel of John.[76] In an obvious evocation of 1 John 1:1–4, the "we" stress their eyewitness access to Jesus, asserting as a group that they have "heard" and "touched" the risen Jesus.[77] Another unmistakable allusion to the prescript of 1 John appears in an initial confession of faith that follows, in which the "we" "confess the Word who became flesh."[78] The same line also borrows unabashedly from the Gospel's prologue, affirming Jesus was born "not by the desire of the flesh but by the will of God."[79] Later passages have the disciples confess an episode appearing only in John: the wedding at Cana.[80] The implicit point is the same: in the *Epistula*, one hears another testimony of the same figures who produced other Johannine works. In the *Epistula*, however, the figures are explicitly named to leave no ambiguity as to their identities and to leverage their authority more dramatically.

Within the *Epistula*, the disciples "confess" a single episode that does not appear in the Gospel: an extended dialogue between Jesus and his disciples on the day of his resurrection (chs. 11–51). In John's Farewell Discourse, Jesus tells his disciples, "I have yet many things to say to you, but you cannot bear them now" (16:12). He also predicts a coming time when he will "tell" his disciples the mysteries of God "plainly" (14:25). The *Epistula* presents itself as a record of what Jesus taught his disciples on the day they were finally able to "bear" what Jesus could not tell them at the Farewell Discourse: "I know indeed that you will bear it and that your heart is pleased to hear me. So ask about what you wish, and I will gladly speak with you."[81] Seeing the risen Jesus before them, the disciples now receive the clear, direct teachings they did not previously have—teachings that ostensibly clarify what has been ambiguous to them in other sections of John.

What Jesus relates to his disciples is a robust defense of Proto-Catholic beliefs regarding the goodness of human life in the material flesh. When he first encounters his disciples, Jesus offers proof that his own resurrected body is flesh, inviting his disciples to touch him and to see that his feet touch the ground.[82] As the dialogue continues, Jesus affirms in the most express terms possible, "I have put on your flesh, in which I was born and in which I was crucified and raised," and he affirms that he came in flesh precisely "so that you who were born in flesh might be raised in your flesh."[83] (When his disciples ask whether it is "possible for what is dissolved and destroyed to be saved"—a reference to corruptible, material flesh—Jesus insists that even "what is weak will recover."[84] Jesus also teaches that "those who are lost will be lost eternally and tormented alive and punished in their flesh and their soul."[85] Finally, toward the end of the text, Jesus predicts the rise of persons introducing "strange teaching and strife"—evidently, those who will deny these ideas—insisting that "they will be eternally punished."[86]

The fact that the *Secret Book of John* and the *Epistula Apostolorum* imagine the same situation—a post-resurrection dialogue between Jesus and his disciples—has not escaped scholars. Ehrman observes that the *Epistula*'s author "took up the weapon of his enemies to fight against them."[87] Nevertheless, the two texts imagine very different circulations for themselves. Whereas the *Secret Book*'s John envisions his new book as an esoteric one that will be disseminated "in secret," the *Epistula*'s John says with the other disciples that what they "have heard and remembered" they have also "written for the whole world."[88]

C. Revelation

As we have traced out other branches of the Johannine family tree, we have not yet considered a text traditionally assigned to the same family: Revelation. As we saw, many ancient Christians attributed the work to the same author as that of the Gospel and Epistles. And yet contemporary scholars tend to reserve the label "Johannine literature" for the Gospel and Epistles of John alone. Should Revelation be considered a Johannine text? I believe so, though the case is more complex.

1. The Date of Revelation

To connect the Gospel of John and Revelation, one must first determine when the latter text was written. The problem is that scholarly estimates for the date of Revelation vary widely. Nevertheless, Kelhoffer observes that "the consensus dating for Revelation" presently extends "to ca. 90–110 C.E. and, possibly, even later"—a span encompassing the latter part of the reign of Domitian (81–96) as well as the reigns of Nerva (96–98), and Trajan (98–117), if not also Hadrian (117–138).[89] Tellingly, most years in this series fit scenarios in which John could have been written first and Revelation written in its wake.[90]

2. John and Revelation

Once we establish that Revelation might have been written after the Gospel, the next question is whether there is evidence of a literary relationship between the texts. Here again, the data is less clear. Although many scholars have noted parallel features in the two works, none necessarily requires direct contact.[91] For example, both John and Revelation contain the language of one "testifying ... to all that he saw" (Rev. 1:2; John 3:11), but this sort of language appears in other early Christian writings (e.g., Acts 26:16). Both call Jesus the "Word of God," but Revelation does not do so with the philosophical overtones of John (Rev. 19:13; cf. John 1:1).[92] Both call Jesus "the Lamb," but they do so using different Greek terms (Rev. 5:6–10; cf. John 1:29). Both associate Jesus with the gift of the "water of life/living water" (Rev. 7:17, 21:6, 22:1, 17), but Revelation does not identify this "water" as Spirit, as John does (cf. John 4:14, 7:37–39). Both also cast Jesus as the "shepherd" (Rev. 7:17; cf. John 10), but so do the Synoptics (Mark 14:27), Hebrews (13:20), and 1 Peter (2:25, 5:4). Both also stress the importance of keeping the commandments, though with different priorities (John 14:15, 21, 15:10; Rev. 12:17, 14:12).

In each case, the evidence of a firm relationship is inconclusive. This does not rule out a relationship between the texts, but it makes it difficult to speak of a link with confidence. The coincidence of so many parallels is tantalizing, however—so much so that some scholars feel free to entertain a relationship between the texts. Jörg Frey, for one, proposes that Revelation may be something like a Johannine pseudepigraphon, taking up a common implied author with at least some other Johannine works.[93] Although I disagree with the particulars of Frey's proposal, I agree with its basic insight: Revelation belongs in the same family of texts as John.[94]

It is striking that Revelation introduces John as "the one who testifies to the Word/word of God and the testimony of Jesus Christ, even to all that he saw" (1:2; cf. 1:9). This language strongly evokes John and perhaps also 1 John, each of which casts their common implied author as one who has "seen" Jesus (John 1:14; 1 John 1:1–3), who "testifies" to the "Word" (John 19:35, 21:24; 1 John 1:2), and who relates what Jesus himself "testified" while on earth (John 3:11, 32; 1 John 1:5).[95] An author familiar with the Gospel and wishing to lay claim to its author would hardly have needed even these many connections to link his "John" character to the narrator of these texts, who was known as "John" from an early date.[96] As we saw above, the *Secret Book of John* lays claim to the author of the Gospel by doing little more than naming him "John."

Of course, very little else of Revelation mirrors John. The apocalypse takes up a starkly different set of interests, ideas, and critical terms than the Gospel—a set so different that the two texts hardly seem related at all. Then again, Dale Allison observes that many pseudepigraphers, once they have established false authorial personas, often feel no need to demonstrate further continuity with their models: "after naming their writer in the title or first sentence or two, they go on to other things."[97] Derivative pseudepigrapha can differ significantly from their models in language. (Compare 2 Peter to 1 Peter, to which it expressly alludes [2 Pet. 3:1].) They can also differ wildly from their model texts in ideology. (Compare the *Secret Book of John* to the Gospel of John.)[98] In this case, it is interesting to observe, with Frey, that "some 'Johannine' elements in Revelation occur most frequently in the framing chapters (Rev 1–3 and 21–22)."[99] These are, of course, the very sections where the text deploys its authorial claim. We might infer that the author's investment in the Gospel was most acute when he was most conscious of his authorial impersonation. Otherwise, it was unimportant to him.

In the case of Revelation, it also makes sense why an author would be disinclined to follow the Gospel closely in language or ideology in most chapters. Whoever wrote Revelation was writing an apocalypse, a genre different from that of the Gospel the Epistles, and one that answers to different models (e.g., Daniel and the Enochian literature). The author of Revelation also set out to articulate different ideas.[100] The apocalypse seems to challenge Paul's stance on the consumption of food offered to idols. It purports to give its readers access to divine secrets concerning the world's end, engaging in antichrist speculation and gematria. And it encourages Christians facing persecution with a future-eschatological hope of Jesus's return. These interests set Revelation on a very different trajectory from the Gospel. They would also make it a unique branch on the Johannine tree—perhaps the most elusive and compelling Johannine pseudepigraphon of them all.[101]

3. An Early Identification

If Revelation is among the earliest Johannine pseudepigrapha, then it stands to reason that at least some Christians were identifying the narrator of the Gospel with John, the son of Zebedee, from a remarkably early date, even within a decade or two after the publication of the Gospel. This is not hard to imagine; again, the deduction that John is the anonymous author of the Gospel takes mere seconds to make. But this insight is critical nonetheless. It helps us appreciate how central the "restless quest" for the identity of John's anonymous author has been throughout the entire history of readerly engagements with the Gospel.[102] As long as people have read John, they have tried to extract the identity of its enigmatic narrator.

The same idea also enriches our study of all the other Johannine works. It suggests that the *Secret Book* and the *Epistula Apostolorum* stand within an even older tradition of attributing the Gospel to John, the son of Zebedee. It also suggests that anonymity was not the only possibility for the author of 1 John. That author chose to keep his eyewitness veiled in anonymity to mimic the Gospel, but he might well have already identified that eyewitness with John, even at so early a date.

III. Conclusion

By the mid-second century, readers had conflated the invented disciple—the supposed author of the Fourth Gospel—with one of Jesus's closest disciples: John, the son of Zebedee. All the while, Christians did not stop expanding the literary corpus of that disciple, sometimes anonymously (1 John), sometimes under the cryptic title "Elder" (2 and 3 John), and often, as it turns out, under the name by which readers had come to know him: John (*Secret Book of John, Epistula Apostolorum*, and likely *Revelation*). In these other texts—arguably the truest "Johannine" texts, since their implied authors actually assume the name "John"—we see still other imagined afterlives of the disciple. And in each, we see an old project continued: the project of defining or redefining the eyewitness disciple's outlook in relation to the critical issues debated by Christians of the day.

The works surveyed in this chapter are hardly the only ones that speak in the name of the Gospel's author, however. The Johannine literary tradition would fan out in later centuries, assuming other, equally intriguing forms. John speaks as the one who leaned on Jesus's breast and as one whom Jesus loved in the so-called Gospel of the *Acts of John*.[103] John also narrates the *1 Apocryphal Apocalypse of John*, the *Mysteries of John*, the *Dormition of the Virgin by the Apostle John*, and the *Questions of John* (*Interrogatio Iohannis*).[104] The fourth-century *Apostolic Constitutions* incorporates a constitution supposedly written by John, who freely states, "I who am loved by the Lord."[105] John also writes a chapter of the seventh-century *Gospel of the Twelve Apostles* (ch. 7).[106] And of course, the voice of this disciple would long be heard in quotations found in a wide range of works. These include titles such as the *3 Apocryphal Apocalypse of John*, the *Dialogue of the Revealer and John*, *John and the Robber*, the (Latin) *Revelation of John about Antichrist*, and the *Questions of James to John*.[107] They also include so many apocryphal acts describing the disciple's life, such as the *Acts of John in Rome* and the *Acts of John of Prochorus*.[108] The last text even embeds supposed letters from John—distant kin to the Johannine Epistles. And of course, all these works represent but a small sliver of a much broader field of reuses and receptions of John through the centuries.[109]

The eyewitness disciple, then, first heard in a single work—a revisionary Gospel—would continue writing, continue teaching. With perhaps no small touch of irony, he has truly become a "we" voice, embodying so many individual authors. He has certainly proven to be "beloved," amassing billions of readers. He has indeed filled the world with his many, many books. And in all these works, written across the centuries, he has proven himself to be no less than the disciple who does "not die." Across two millennia, in memory and devotion, literature and song, and in the branching, flowering tree of texts bearing his name, he lives on.

Notes

Introduction

1. My construction of a single "author" for John acknowledges that ancient processes of textual production generally involved other (often enslaved) literary experts in various roles and at various stages—laborers commonly excluded from ancient conceptions of "authorship" (see discussions in Richards, *Secretary*; Fitzgerald, *Slavery*; Fitzgerald, "Slave"; Moss, "Between the Lines"; Moss, "Secretary"; Moss, "Fashioning Mark"; Moss, *God's Ghostwriters*; Coogan and Moss, "Textual Demiurge"; and essays in Coogan, Moss, and Howley, *Writing*). It is reasonable to infer that the author of John relied on such labor, though we do not know the extent of that collaboration, especially in the context of disguised authorship (see chapter 4). My use of the term "author" also respects scholarship complicating the stability and coherence of the "author" as a construct (Foucault, "Author"; Griffith, "Anonymity"), including studies focused on the ancient Mediterranean (e.g., King, "Author"; Wyrick, *Ascension*; Moss, Coogan, and Howley, "Socioeconomics"; Coogan and Moss, "Textual Demiurge").
2. Because of this, I avoid using the thought of the Epistles to supplement or clarify the thought of the Gospel, as most studies of the Gospel's theology do.
3. The term "implied author" was popularized by Booth, *Rhetoric*. For the reception of this category and competing views, see Kindt and Müller, *Implied Author*.
4. "If recent research on [disguised authorship] has made anything at all clear, it is the fact of the variety and complexity of the phenomenon" (Aune, "Reconceptualizing," 794).
5. Fischer, *Historians' Fallacies*, 214–15.
6. Ehrman centers polemic as a catalyst for Christian disguised authorship in *Forgery*.
7. Ehrman, *Forgery*, 97–98.
8. Rosenmeyer, *Ancient Epistolary Fictions*; Peirano Garrison, *Roman Fake*.
9. Stang, *Apophasis*; Najman, *Seconding Sinai*; Najman, *Past Renewals*.
10. Coogan and Moss, "Textual Demiurge."
11. Peirano Garrison, *Roman Fake*, 3.
12. Najman and Peirano Garrison, "Pseudepigraphy," 332.
13. Some scholars see little to no relation between ancient pseudepigraphy and modern literary forgery (e.g., Piovanelli, "Pseudepigraphy"). Against this view, see Ehrman, *Forgery*, 11–148. As I see it, it is problematic to suggest an exceptional quality or status for ancient falsely authored works vis-à-vis their later cognates. There are also ethical problems with this move, especially in an age of widespread misinformation and disinformation (on this issue, see Klawans, "Deceptive Intentions").
14. Ehrman, *Forgery*; Speyer, *Fälschung*.
15. Metzger, "Literary Forgeries," 4; cf. Speyer, *Fälschung*, 94; Ehrman, *Forgery*, 30. That is, the term "forgery" denotes a text that deliberately projects a false author, named or unnamed, to misdirect or deceive unknowing readers. Although "forgery" can carry negative connotations, religious studies scholars theorizing the term have either described the practice in neutral language (Speyer, *Fälschung*) or they have pointed out that the literary practices in question were viewed in a negative light by many ancient groups (Ehrman, *Forgery*).
16. Studies calling for or modeling more nuanced explorations of pseudepigraphy include Merz, *Fiktive Selbstauslegung*; Najman, *Seconding Sinai*; Najman, *Past Renewals*; Najman and Reinhardt, "Exemplarity"; Najman and Peirano, "Pseudepigraphy"; Stang, *Apophasis*; Reed, "Pseudepigraphy"; Reed, "Construction"; Mroczek, *Literary Imagination*; Krueger, *Writing*; Uusimäki, *Lived Wisdom*; Rothschild, *Hebrews*. See also essays in Frey et al., *Pseudepigraphie*.
17. In my usage, the "Johannine Community" does not refer to any and every conceivable social context for John's author. Instead—and in line with how most scholars use the expression—the phrase refers to a specific context reconstructed for the Gospel and Epistles of John with specific characteristics. To be precise, scholars conceptualize the Johannine Community as

(a) a single, definable network (b) of ancient churches (c) that shared a common, distinctive theological outlook, (d) that produced not only the Gospel of John but also most or all of the Epistles of John, and (e) whose history is represented in the Epistles. Landmark works developing this view include Martyn, *History and Theology*; Meeks, "Man from Heaven"; Brown, *Community*; Brown, *Gospel*; and Brown, *Epistles*. Recent defenses of this model include de Boer, "Story" and de Boer, "Community." A related view would analyze the Gospel and Letters of John as products of a Johannine "school" parallel to ancient philosophical schools (classically articulated in Culpepper, *Johannine School*). Against these views, see the distinct critiques of Bauckham, *Gospels*; Reinhartz, "Toothpicks"; Reinhartz, "Women"; Reinhartz, *Covenant*; Stowers, "Community"; Méndez, "Johannine Community"; Méndez, "Historical Criticism"; and Méndez, *Epistles*. My view is that the Gospel and Letters of John were written by four authors who were not socially or institutionally connected to one another but who hailed from different social (ideological/social/geographical) matrices. What binds these authors is that they adopted the same authorial persona within a single tradition of disguised authorship—a persona they bent to their particular agendas. In turn, the image of a network of churches projected by the Epistles is a literary invention.

18. This view is defended in Brown, *Epistles*, 14–115; Hakola, *Reconsidering*, 67–95.
19. Méndez, "Johannine Community"; Méndez, "Historical Criticism"; and most comprehensively, Méndez, *Epistles*.

Chapter 1

1. On anonymity in early Christian writings, see Wolter, "Anonymen Schriften"; Baum, "Anonymity"; Coogan, "Imagining"; Ullucci, "Anonymity." On anonymity in the broader Roman world, see Geue, *Author Unknown*.
2. In defense of this, the majority view, see Petersen, "Evangelienüberschriften"; Ullucci, "Anonymity" (*pace* studies critiquing initial anonymity such as Hengel, *Johannine Question*, 74; Hengel, *Four Gospels*, 50; Gathercole, "Anonymity"). Among other lines of evidence, the term "gospel"—not least in the specialized sense given it in the title—is foreign to the Gospel of John (Schnelle, *Evangelium*, 321). The title "Gospel according to John" is also not of a standard form for an author to have applied to his own text but one that suits the bibliographic efforts of a scribe cataloguing multiple similar works. Last, there are reasons to question the attribution to "John" (see chapters 4, 6).
3. On my use of the term "author" in light of the complex ancient realities of book production, see the introduction, note 1. As I use the term, the author directs all the synchronic labor that produces a text (a reality perhaps better captured by the expression "primary author").
4. For a compelling case that the gospels originated as written products rather than oral/performed texts, see Barker, *Writing*, 27–31.
5. On John's use of the Synoptics, see Attridge, "Other Gospels"; Barker, *John's Use*; essays in Denaux, *John;* and essays in Becker, Bond, and Williams, *John's Transformation*.
6. De Boer, "Story," 73. Works propagating the idea include Boismard and Lamouille, *Jean*; Brown, *John*, xxxiv–xxxix; Brown, *Introduction*, 62–69, 75–89; Lindars, *Behind*; von Wahlde, *John*.
7. The most prominent hypothesis was the idea of John's dependence on a "Signs Source," popularized by Rudolf Bultmann (*Johannes*) and taken up in Fortna, *Gospel of Signs*; Nicol, *Semeia*; and Siegert and Bergler, *Synopse*. A convincing critique of this project appears in Van Belle, *Signs Source*.
8. Frey, "Johannine Theology," 354.
9. De Boer, "Attack," 219n41.
10. Larsen, "Accidental Publication"; Larsen, *Gospels*, 11–36.
11. Friedman, *Bible*, 27.
12. Friedman, *Bible*, 28 (also Baden, *Composition*, 31–32).
13. As I will show in chapter 3, it is possible to explain 6:1 on the basis of John's use of the Synoptics.
14. On the unity of these chapters, see Kellum, *Unity*.
15. On the "synchronic turn" in Johannine studies, which has resulted in widespread confidence in the literary unity of the Gospel (or at least of chapters 1–20), see Labahn, "Literary Sources." This turn is often traced to the publication of Culpepper, *Anatomy*. Critical commentaries assuming John's unity in the wake of Culpepper's work include Moloney, *John*; Thyen, *Johannesevangelium*; Thompson, *John*.
16. This is also evidence that the Gospel's prologue should also be considered an original composition of the author (see also Engberg-Pederson, *Philosophy*, 37).

17. Culpepper, *Anatomy*, ix.
18. Attridge, "Other Gospels," 47.
19. Koester, *Word*, 3.
20. De Boer, "Story," 73.
21. The line also appears to be a bricolage of narrator comments from other parts of the Gospel, melding elements from 1:14, 19:35, and 20:31. See analysis in chapter 4.
22. On this passage and its complex reception history, see Knust and Wasserman, *Cast*; Keith, *Pericope Adulterae*, 119–140.
23. Beyond these additions, John would also experience a host of textual changes as part of the continuing, ordinary processes of maintaining, correcting, and curating manuscripts (described in Nonbgri, "Maintaining"; Kearing, "Editing"; Schultz, "Collection"). These include the numerous changes described in Ehrman, *Orthodox Corruption*.
24. A comprehensive survey of the manuscript evidence for the episode appears in Petersen, *Text-Critical Studies*, 303–12.
25. Becker, *Ehebrecherin*, 68–74.
26. The best recent defense of chapter 21 as a secondary addition to the Gospel appears in Baum, "Original Epilogue." Today, however, this still widespread view has lost ground to a spate of studies defending the literary unity of John 1–21 (e.g., Ruckstuhl, "Aussage"; Carson, *John*, 684; Breck, "John 21"; Ellis, "John 21"; Busse, "Hellenen"; Gaventa, "Archive"; Schlatter, *Johannes*, 363–64, 375–77; Reim, "Johannes 21"; Hasitschka, "Zeichen"; Spencer, "Narrative Echoes"; Jackson, "Self-Referential Conventions," 17–24; Minear, "John 21"; 85–98; Thyen, "Entwicklungen"; Thyen, *Johannesevangelium*, 794–95; Keener, *John*, 2.124; Bauckham, "153 Fish"; Porter, "Ending"). Some such studies defend the unity of chapters 1–20 and chapter 21 on the basis of stylistic similarities as well as narrative and thematic connections between these chapters. These similarities are not probative, however, since a redactor composing chapter 21 could have easily imitated the style, themes, and narrative features of chapters 1–20. Other studies defend this idea on the basis of purported structural/chiastic parallels linking these chapters. These appeals are also unpersuasive, however, since the evidence for these structures is often weak or subjective (e.g., supposed chiasms) and since a later editor could also produce these sorts of parallels.
27. Schenke, "Erscheinen" has proposed the existence of one such manuscript, but see Chris Keith's response in *Gospel*, 133n7.
28. *Pace* scholars who argue that 20:30–31 is the conclusion only of chapter 20 (e.g., Vorster, "John 21"). See arguments in Baum, "Original Epilogue," 234–38.
29. *Test. Sol.* 26:8 (OTP 1.987).
30. Lucian, *Dem.* 67 (LCL 14.172–73). Other examples of apologies for the premature ending of a work include Aphthonius, *Progymnasmata* 83 (*Rhetores Graeci* 10, 24.20–21).
31. Joseph. *Ap.* 2.287–99 (LCL 186.406–11).
32. This is all the more unusual since "Jesus' disciples have not been portrayed as fishermen in John, nor has their future mission been described in those terms [as in Mark 1:16–20; Luke 5:1–11]" (Thompson, *John*, 431).
33. Brown, *John*, 1067, concurring with Loisy, *Quatrième Evangile*, 515.
34. Baum, "Original Epilogue," 246, 267.
35. Although certain scholars attempted to ground this secondary status in other linguistic considerations, including apparent distinctions in the grammar and vocabulary of the passage (Bultmann, *John*, 700; Barrett, *John*, 576–77; Lightfoot, *Biblical Essays*, 194–95), Brown rightly notes that these features represent an "uncertain criterion" on which to base its secondary status (*John*, 1080). See arguments in Porter, "Ending," 227–32.
36. This approach characterizes, among others, Minear, "John 21"; Porter, "Ending."
37. There is no evidence of major editorial interventions by this scribe across other chapters of John. On the contrary, "In light of the highly unified content and style of the Fourth Gospel, any hypotheses that go beyond what can be deduced from the epilogues remain highly speculative" (Baum, "Original Epilogue," 267–68).
38. *Pace* Baum ("Original Epilogue," 267), one does not need to posit a social or institutional link between the author and redactor to explain the similarities binding chapters 1–20 and 21. A skilled interpolator can easily imitate the style of an existing work.
39. Quote from Keith, *Gospel as Manuscript*, 133n7, who credits James Barker for this observation. This suggests that chapter 21 might have been added at a time when John had not yet circulated

too widely (Elder, *Gospel Media*, 268), though this would not necessarily require that the scribe who produced it was an associate of the initial author (*pace* Knust and Wasserman, *Cast*, 71–72).
40. A Galilean appearance of Jesus is predicted in Mark 16:7. On the especially tantalizing parallels between John 21 and *GPet* 14.58–60, see Watson, *Gospel Writing*, 401–5.
41. Note that there was no compelling need to resolve Peter's storyline; Mark does not.
42. Dunderberg plausibly reads 21:23 as a response to the delay of the Parousia, evoking and undercutting Mark 9:1 ("Beloved Disciple," 248–51).
43. Watson, *Gospel Writing*, 403.
44. So, e.g., de Boer, "Story," 72–73.
45. On the broader problems of the Markan Community as a construct, see Bird, "Markan Community"; Peterson, *Origins*. One could hypothetically analyze Matthew as an attempt to revise Mark (so, e.g., Larsen, *Gospels*, 99–120), and yet scholars recognize these authors as hailing from distinct segments of the early Jesus movement. Likewise, a later hand added the *Pericope Adulterae*, but no one counts that hand as part of the Johannine Community.
46. Note, however, that these interventions were not necessarily problematic or illicit since manuscripts often demanded maintenance, copying, and—for many scribes—corrections (Coogan and Moss, "Textual Demiurge," n36). On these processes, see Nongbri, "Maintenance"; Keary, "Editing"; Schultz, "Collection"; Coogan, Moss, and Howley, "Socioeconomics of Fabrication").
47. It is certainly the default assumption of other fields such as classics and Near Eastern studies: "in all other areas that study ancient Mediterranean and West Asian literature, a writing is studied as the product of an individual writer working in a particular social and historical context, not as the product of a community" (Stowers, "Community," 247).
48. Another reason why scholars claim that the Gospel is the product of a "community" is that other texts exist with very similar features as the Gospel—especially the letters of 1 John, 2 John, and 3 John. As we will see in chapter 5, however, these texts are later pseudepigrapha derived from the Gospel.
49. That is, unless the implied readers of a text are invented, as in many pseudepigrapha.
50. Goodacre builds this into a compelling case for John's knowledge of the Synoptics in *Fourth Synoptic Gospel*, 73–92. See also Bauckham, "Readers" (and North's rejoinder ["Readers"]).
51. Bauckham, "Readers," 153.
52. The author cites or alludes to biblical literature in John 1:23, 1:45, 2:17, 3:14, 5:46, 6:31, 45, 7:38, 42, 8:17, 10:34, 12:13, 14–16, 38, 40–41, 13:18, 15:25, 17:12, 19:24, 28, 36, 37, 20:9. Some authors read this evidence as an indication that the author presupposed ethnic Jewish readers for his text (e.g., Edwards, *Discovering John*, 46–49), but many non-Jews, including gentile converts to the early Jesus movement, had the same literacy (Reinhartz, *Covenant*, 143–45). Paul's letter to the Galatians is addressed to an ethnically non-Jewish audience (see, e.g., 2:7, 4:8), but it is no less steeped in references to Jewish scripture and a sophisticated engagement with first-century Jewish thought.
53. Attempts to conceptualize the implied and/or real readers of Mark include Collins, *Mark*, 96–102; Marcus, *Mark 1–8*, 25–29; Rhoads, Dewey, and Michie, *Mark as Story*, 2, 137–51; Beavis, *Mark's Audience;* Henderson, "Double Audience."
54. Marcus, *Mark 1–8*, 35–36. A discussion of Jewish washing practices illuminating and complicating Mark's report appears in Collins, *Mark*, 344–49.
55. Barus, "John 2:12–25," 126.
56. Note, however, that the parenthetical statement on Jewish-Samaritan relations does not appear in all early witnesses. According to Metzger, "the omission, if not accidental, may reflect the scribal opinion that the statement is not literally exact" since many Jews do have dealings with Samaritans, and that the statement "therefore should be deleted" (*Textual Commentary*, 177).
57. The latter is cited in Reinhartz, *Covenant*, 134 as evidence that the Gospel has a gentile audience. Reinhartz also draws attention to the fact that the narrator glosses the Hebrew *rabbouni* as "teacher" (20:16) (*Covenant*, 134).
58. Reinhartz, *Covenant*, 133–34. No less striking is the construction of Jesus as someone who distances himself from the Torah. In two verses, he speaks of the Torah to Jewish audiences as "your law" (Reinhartz, *Covenant*, 134).
59. Stowers, "Community," 257. This idea is elaborated in Walsh, *Origin*.
60. On these formations, see Walsh, *Origin*, 105–33.
61. Becker, Bond, and Williams, "Introduction," 1. This view was popularized by Gardner-Smith, *Saint John*; Dodd, *Interpretation*. Studies tracing the history of scholarship on this question

include Smith, *John among the Gospels*; Neirynck, "John and the Synoptics"; Attridge, "Other Gospels."

62. Unfortunately, we have no data to illuminate this broader field of sources. As Robyn Walsh observes, oral sources are "irretrievable to us" (*Origins*, 156). Furthermore, scholars have found no conclusive evidence indicating that John relied on the extant noncanonical gospels, most of which date to later periods. Although some have proposed *PEgerton* 2 as a candidate (e.g., Koester, *Gospels*, 205–6; Watson, *Gospel Writing*, 286–340), Attridge is correct that the source's claim "that [Jesus's] opponents do not know where Jesus is from (*P. Eger.* Fr. 1 verso, ll.16–17 // John 9:29) reflects not simply a floating tradition, but a theme that structures a major portion of the Fourth Gospel. This strongly suggests that the papyrus depends on the Gospel" ("Other Gospels," 56).

63. In short, earlier scholars set the evidentiary bar too high by insisting that John could not have known the Synoptics if there were no signs of verbatim overlap between these gospels. This is the fallacy of the inverse (P → Q ∴ ¬ P → ¬ Q): "If the Synoptics and John share extensive overlap, then they are dependent." "The Synoptics and John do not share extensive overlap." "Therefore, they are not dependent."

64. Persuasive arguments in favor of *Thomas*'s knowledge of the Synoptics include Goodacre, *Thomas*; Gathercole, *Composition*; Gathercole, *Thomas*, 176–84. See also recent responses by Kloppenborg ("New Synoptic Problem") and Patterson ("Twice More"), as well as rejoinders by Gathercole ("Thomas Revisited") and Goodacre ("Response"). On *Mary*'s relationship to the canonical gospels, see Tuckett, *Mary*, 55–74.

65. In French and German scholarship, the thesis of John's knowledge of one or more Synoptics was advanced by the Louvain School (exemplified by essays in Denaux, *John and the Synoptics* and Neirynck, *Jean et les Synoptiques*). It has also found support among such prominent German-language scholars as Thyen ("Synoptiker" and *Johannesevangelium*), Schnelle ("Synoptiker"), and Frey ("Hintergrund"). (Theobald prefers independence [*Evangelium*, 76–81].) Twenty-first-century English-language studies defending this increasingly popular view include Mackay, *Relationship*; Viviano, "John's Use"; Allison, "Reflections"; Bauckham, "Readers"; Barker, *John's Use*; Attridge, "Other Gospels"; the collected essays in Becker, Bond, and Williams, *John's Transformation*; North, *What John Knew*; and Corsar, "John's Use of Mark." As Frey ("Johannine Theology," 355) observes, the surge in support for this hypothesis can be correlated with the decline of the "Signs Source" hypothesis.

66. Goodacre, "Parallel Traditions," 84 (also Brodie, *Quest*, 51; Bauckham, "Readers," 151; Lincoln, *John*, 27). These sorts of parallels are probably not ones we can trace to oral tradition, since we have no evidence for an oral canon or cycle of Jesus stories observing precisely the pattern of the written gospels extant to us (in effect, a lost oral gospel). For that matter, when the gospels mention oral traditions, they give the distinct impression of disaggregated streams of transmission (Matt. 28:15; John 21:25).

67. Frey, "Johannine Theology," 355. See discussion in Frey, "Hintergrund," 93–100.

68. Elder, *Gospel Media*, 263.

69. Adapted from Goodacre, "Parallel Traditions," 83.

70. Streeter's analysis is especially incisive: "in John the phrase occurs in the story of the lame man at Bethesda, in Mark in that of the paralytic borne of four. But Christ did not speak in Greek; the identity, therefore, of the Greek phrase seems most naturally explained if the vocabulary of Mark was familiar to John. Analogous instances of this trick of memory by which a phrase used in one incident by Mark is transferred to another are specially frequent in Matthew" (*Four Gospels*, 398).

71. Streeter, *Four Gospels*, 398.

72. Frey, "Hintergrund," 86–93.

73. "The fact is that there crops up repeatedly in John evidence that suggests that the evangelist knew a body of traditional material that either was Mark, or something much like Mark; and anyone who after an interval of nineteen centuries feels himself in a position to distinguish nicely between 'Mark' and 'something much like Mark,' is at liberty to do so. The simpler hypothesis, which does not involve the postulation of otherwise unknown entities, is not without attractiveness" (Barrett, "Synoptic Gospels," 232). Frey formulates the argument in related terms: "it would be an unnecessarily complicated hypothesis if one were to assign such knowledge only to the level of the tradition or redaction and did not also let it apply to the evangelist" ("Johannine Theology," 355; see arguments in Frey, "Hintergrund").

192   NOTES

74. This methodology was popularized by Koester (*Synoptische Überlieferung* and "Written Gospel") and is applied to Matthew and John in Barker, *John's Use*, 16–36; Goodacre, *First Synoptic Gospel*, 46–56.
75. Allison, "Reflections," 55–57.
76. An extended defense of the view that John's account depends upon Matthew appears in Barker, *John's Use*, 63–93 (*pace* the skepticism of, e.g., Menken, "Quotations from Zech 9,9").
77. See discussion in Allison, "Reflections," 55. These are also the only works to identify Peter's father (John 1:42; Matt. 16:17) and to name Caiaphas as the high priest at the time of Jesus's arrest (John 11:49, 51, 18:13, 24, Matt. 26:3, 57).
78. Allison, "Reflections," 49–50.
79. Allison, "Reflections," 47–49. As Allison astutely notes, this problem is especially acute for advocates of the Two-Source Hypothesis who assume that Matthew's version is a redaction of a lost Q source. In this case, we would have another clear instance of Mark picking up Matthean redaction ("Reflections," 48–49).
80. On the many textual forms of Matthew in antiquity, including the source later labeled *The Gospel According to the Hebrews*, see Coogan, "Ways."
81. So Allison, who links this to Matthew's Moses typology ("Reflections," 57).
82. A compelling demonstration of Luke's relationship to John appears in Goodacre, *First Synoptic Gospel*, with arguments from Luke's redaction of Mark on 56–72.
83. Citing instances in which manuscripts confuse the names Martha and Mary, Elizabeth Schrader speculates that John originally lacked Martha as a character ("Mary of Bethany"). This is an overdetermined explanation for what more likely began as a scribal misspelling (the two names are a single letter apart: iota/theta). It is also difficult to reconstruct a coherent original version of John 11 lacking Martha without exceeding the manuscript evidence and treading into extreme speculation.
84. Wolter, *Luke*, 2.442. One could add Luke 24:12, assuming it is not a later corruption (but see Ehrman, *Orthodox Corruption*, 212–17).
85. These and other parallels in the Passion narratives are listed in Wolter, *Luke*, 2.441–43. Other details bind the Passion narratives of the two gospels together—among them, that Peter ran to the tomb of Jesus on the morning of the resurrection to inspect it himself (Luke 24:12; John 20:3–10), that Jesus saluted his disciples with the words "Peace be with you" (Luke 24:36; John 20:19), and that Jesus offered his resurrected body for his disciples to inspect (Luke 24:39; John 20:27). These, however, are among the "Western non-interpolations" of Luke—passages Ehrman argues are likely later, non-Western, "orthodox corruptions" of Luke (*Orthodox Corruption*, 212–21).
86. Streeter, *Four Gospels*, 405.
87. "The assumption cannot be avoided that the author of the present version of the Gospel of John knew the Gospel of Luke" (Wolter, *Luke*, 2.444).
88. *Pace* Matson, *Dialogue*; Shellard, "Luke and John." The most visible defender of John's use of Luke has been Frans Neirynck (e.g., "John and the Synoptics"). On this debate, see Gregory, "John and Luke" and *Luke and Acts*, 56–69.
89. Goodacre, "Parallel Traditions," 83–84.
90. Those sources are Mark and either Matthew (under the Farrer Hypothesis) or Q (under the Two-Source Hypothesis) An introduction to these theories appears in Goodacre, *Synoptic Problem*.
91. Studies discussing the use of waxed tablets in gospel composition include Poirier, "Wax Tablet"; Goodacre, *Thomas*, 150–52; Barker, *Writing*, 34–38. Note that the author might have enlisted enslaved scribal labor to perform this act and others envisioned here.
92. Allison, "Reflections," 60.
93. Frey, "Johannine Theology," 355.
94. Attridge, "Other Gospels," 48.
95. Major studies exploring the development of the Pauline letter collection include Trobisch, *Letter Collection*; Laird, *Pauline Corpus*. On the history of scholarship on this question, see Porter, "Pauline Canon."
96. See, for example, the many works discussed in Ehrman, *Forgery*, 155–90, 239–322. Many New Testament texts engage Paul's thought, usually also showing knowledge of the Pauline Epistles we still possess today. This is true of the six Deutero-Pauline Epistles, the Petrine Epistles, James, Hebrews, Jude, and (likely) Revelation (see Ehrman, *Forgery*, 155–90, 239–322; Rothschild, *Hebrews*; Frankfurter, "Fiction"). Paul is a central figure in Acts. Some

scholars also see evidence of Pauline influence in gospels such as Mark and Matthew (e.g., Becker, Engberg-Pedersen and Mueller, *Mark and Paul*; Ferguson, "Paul's Possible Influence"; Marcus, "Interpreter of Paul"; Sim, *Matthew*; Wischmeyer and Sim, *Paul and Mark*).

97. As Frey remarks, the current trend away from positing a relationship between the Pauline letters and John is surprising given that scholars often place the hypothetical Johannine Community in Ephesus—a community associated with Paul's ministry in Acts 18–20 and the Epistle to the Ephesians ("Johannine Theology," 356). One study proposing such a relationship is Engberg-Pedersen's *Philosophy*.

98. Jülicher, "Religion Jesu," 96. Theobald proposes "common tradition-historical roots" instead (*Evangelium*, 75–76). This hypothesis allows for some of the comparative reading I engage in, but it too quickly dismisses other ways Pauline influence could have shaped an author writing decades later.

99. This verse is sometimes conceptualized as belonging to a pre-Pauline hymn, but see Edsall and Strawbridge, "Songs."

100. On Hebrews as a pseudo-Pauline text, see Rothschild, *Hebrews*.

101. David Sim argues in "Family," 97 that "Mark betrays his impeccable Pauline credentials" through the same strategy.

102. The Synoptics depict Jesus calling Peter to be his disciple (Mark 1:16–18; Matt. 4:18), consistently name Peter first in lists of the disciples (Mark 5:37, 9:2, 13:3, 14:33; Matt. 10:2, 17:1; Luke 6:14, 8:51, 9:28), and single Peter out as the first disciple to appreciate Jesus's messianic identity (Mark 8:27–30; Matt. 16:13–20). In John, by contrast, Andrew brings Peter to Jesus, and Andrew—not Peter—is the first to recognize Jesus as "the Messiah (that is, the Christ)" (1:40–42). John also privileges another disciple over Peter, the enigmatic "disciple whom Jesus loved," whom it depicts as a closer and more ideal follower of Jesus (13:23–26; implicitly 20:6–8). This literary motif is probably meant to construct the superiority of the Gospel's eyewitness (chapter 4). It presses this evidence too far to use it to link this motif to an otherwise unattested rivalry between Johannine and Petrine Christianities (as in Brown, *John*, 2.1082).

103. So Stowers, "Dilemma," 180; Engberg-Pedersen, *Paul*. Engberg-Pedersen interprets Paul's thought as Stoic (*Cosmology*). Stowers, however, finds that Paul's vision is not entirely consistent with or comprehensible through classical Stoicism ("Dilemma," 159–80). Meanwhile, arguments for Paul's appropriation of Platonic thought appear in Stowers, *Rereading*; multiple essays in Stowers, *Christian Beginnings*; Wasserman, *Death of the Soul*; Wasserman, "Paul"; van Kooten, *Paul's Anthropology*; Litwa, *Transformed*.

104. For possible evidence of Stoic ideas in John, see Engberg-Pedersen, *Philosophy* and Buch-Hansen, *Spirit*. John's possible connections with Wisdom literature are explored across Coloe, *John*.

105. On the life and thought of Philo, see Niehoff, *Philo*. Studies comparing John and Philo include Dodd, *Interpretation*, 54–73; Borgen, *Gospel of John*, 43–66; Runia, *Philo*, 78–83; Buch-Hansen, *Spirit*, 59–60; Attridge, "Two Riffs"; Holladay, "Philo"; Puskas and Robbins, *Conceptual Worlds*, 56–68.

106. Runia, *Philo*, 83.

107. Paul's own thought is contrasted with that of Philo in Stowers, "Dilemma," 170–76.

108. Runia, *Philo*, 78, 85. On these parallels, see also Sanders, *Paul*, 75–87.

109. Attridge, *Hebrews*, 5n44. Authors proposing an Alexandrian setting for Hebrews include Spicq, *Hébreux*, 1.209; Michel, *Hebräer*, 40; Runia, *Philo*, 78.

110. Jewish Wisdom literature, including the Book of Wisdom, is also perceived to be an intersecting stream of influence. John applies the term *monogenēs* (unique/only son) to the *Logos*, a term found in Wisdom 7:22. The motifs of Wisdom's preexistence (Prov. 8:22–31), association with light (Wisdom 7:26, 29–30) also evokes threads in John's teaching on the *Logos*. For a commentary drawing out centering these connections, see Coloe, *John*.

111. Harris, *Ancient Literacy*. But see recent attempts to highlight the invisible or suppressed role of women in textual production in King, "Author"; Ahuvia, "Reimagining"; Coogan and Moss, "Textual Demiurge."

112. Theobald, *Evangelium*, 96.

113. As I will argue in chapter 6, early Christian traditions placing the author at Ephesus are unreliable. We also cannot reconstruct the early circulation of the Gospel from our limited manuscript evidence.

114. On the possible Levantine origins of John, see Wengst, *Bedrängte Gemeinde*, 77–93; Theobald, *Evangelium*, 94–98.

115. Kloppenborg, "Luke's Geography."
116. Sheila Gyllenberg reads John's references to sites not attested in the Synoptics as evidence of its "good knowledge of locations from an independent, probably first-hand, source" ("Geography," 125).
117. J. Louis Martyn famously argued that this otherizing rhetoric and predictions that believers would be expelled from synagogues in the Gospel (16:2; cf. 9:22, 12:42) indicate that the author of John was situated in a local community of ethnically Jewish believers in Jesus that had been expelled (*History*) from synagogues for their belief. As I see it, however, we cannot confidently use this data to reconstruct a local situation. Even if the author knew of (sporadic) synagogue expulsions affecting Christians, there is no way of knowing how widely, how often, or even where such expulsions occurred. They could have occurred 5 kilometers or 500 kilometers away. Predictions of synagogue expulsion could also have been constructed from traditions reporting that Jesus was expelled from a synagogue (Luke 4:28–29) and that Paul had sought out Christians in synagogues (Acts 9:2).
118. A positive reference to Jews in the text (4:22) is compatible with Pauline thinking about the place of Jews in salvation history (cf. Rom. 9:4–5).
119. The manuscript tradition offers us no data to clarify this date further. Attempts to use P52 to narrow the date of John are now rightly dismissed as too problematic (see Nongbri, "Use"). On the general problems of paleographic dating—the primary method used to date the early manuscripts of John—see Nongbri, *God's Library*, 47–82.
120. Frey, "Johannine Theology," 353; cf. Theobald, *Evangelium*, 93. John also alludes to another event from the second half of the first century: the death of Peter (13:36–38; more explicitly in 21:18) (Frey, "Johannine Theology," 353). Some scholars read 5:2 ("there is a pool, called in Hebrew Bethzatha, which has five porticoes") as definitive evidence that John was written before 70 CE, reasoning that the porticoes in question were probably destroyed in the First Jewish-Roman War since they seem to have no longer been standing by the fourth century (Wallace, "John 5,2"; Bernier, *Rethinking*, 97–102). There are several problems with this view, however. First, the use of the pool as a healing site and the architectural features of the nearby colonnades seem to suit a post-70 CE context (Magness, "Sweet Memory"; Duprez, *Guérisseurs*, 37–38; *pace* von Wahlde, "Pool(s) of Bethesda"). Second, even if the colonnades antedate 70 CE, there is no direct evidence that these structures were destroyed during the First Jewish-Roman War; they might have been destroyed in the Third Jewish-Roman War. Last, 5:2 is not a certain guide to the dating of the text since the claim "there is a pool ... which has five porticoes" could also be a chronological fiction complementing the text's pseudepigraphal character, implying that the Gospel was composed prior to 70 CE, when it was not.
121. Surveys of the second-century reception of John appear in Nagel, *Rezeption*; Hill, *Johannine Corpus*; Rasimus, *Legacy*; Barker, "Acts of John." (Note, however, that certain suggested allusions and the dating of individual sources are subject to debate.)
122. Attridge, "Johannine Christianity," 126. If, however, Steve Mason is correct that the author of Luke drew information from Josephus's *Antiquities* (c. 94 CE), it may be safest to narrow those dates still further to c. 100–110 CE. (See Mason, "Author," developing a thesis initially laid out in Mason, *Josephus*, 251–96.)

Chapter 2

1. Lincoln, "Testimony," 187.
2. See Fredriksen, "Mandatory Retirement"; Fredriksen, "Early High Christology"; Fredriksen, "Philo." For current debates, including opposing views, see essays in Stuckenbruck and North, *Monotheism*. As Brakke succinctly puts it, "No ancient person (even one who was a Jew or Christian) was a monotheist in our sense" (*Gnostics*, 61).
3. Fredriksen, "Early High Christology," 297.
4. Philo, *Somn.* 1.229 (LCL 275.418–19). On Philo's conception of God in relation to his conception of the *Logos*, see Niehoff, *Philo*, 209–24.
5. Forger, "Divine Embodiment," 224.
6. Forger, "Divine Embodiment," 225.
7. Philo, *Spec.* 1.81 (LCL 275.146–47); *Somn.* 1.241 (LCL 261.424–25); *QG* 2.62 (Eng. tr., LCL 380:150).
8. *Somn.* 1.228–29 (LCL 275.418–19).
9. *Conf.* 146 (LCL 261.88–89).

NOTES   195

10. See discussions in Martin, *Corinthian Body*, 104–38; Engberg-Pedersen, *Cosmology*, 8–74; Thiessen, *Paul and the Gentile Problem*, 142–47; Litwa, *Transformed*, 119–51; Stowers, "Dilemma." Many Jewish and Christian sources associate stars with angelic beings (e.g., Dan. 8:10; 1QHa 9.11b–14a; *Joseph and Asenath*, 14.1–4; Philo, *QG* 4.87; Rev. 1:20, 3:1, 8:10–11, 9:1, 12:4), and many consistently conceptualize angelic beings as spirits (e.g., LXX Ps. 103:4; 1 Enoch 15:4, 6; *Jub.* 2:2; 1QM 13:10–12; Philo, *Abr.* 113; *Test. Ab.* (B) 13.7; Heb. 1:7, 14; Rev. 1:4, 3:1, 8:2). Echoing LXX Psalm 103:4, Hebrews 1:7 expressly claims that God "makes his angels *pneumata*." See also Tatian, who says that "none of the demons possess a particle of flesh; their constitution is *pneumatic*, like fire and air" (*orat.* 15.3 [PG 6.839–40; Eng. tr. mine]).
11. On the ambiguities of John 1:1, intersecting scholarly discussions of Colwell's Rule, see Wallace, *Greek Grammar*, 256–70.
12. For example, Attridge, "Philo and John"; Holladay, "Philo," 160–74; Schenck, *Philo*, 86–91.
13. John 17:3; cf. Philo, *Somn.* 1.229 (LCL 275.418–19). In John, Jesus says "the Father is greater than I" (14:28).
14. John 1:1; cf. *Somn.* 1.228–29 (LCL LCL 275.418–19). I use the lowercase "god" to capture the difference between arthrous and anarthrous *theos* in 1:1. The same patern may also hold in John 20:28, where "*o theos mou*" likely refers to the Father (see discussion in chapter 3).
15. Runia, *Philo*, 83 (see also Holladay, "Philo," 162).
16. Philo applies the language of "first-begotten son" (*prōtogonon huion*) to the Word (*Agr.* 51 [LCL 247.134–35; cf. *Conf.* 146–47 [LCL 261.88–89]). John, by contrast, acknowledges the *Logos* as "son" (1:18, 34) but uses "unique/only son" (*monogenēs*; 1:14, 3:16, 18). Wisdom 7:22 applies the same term to personified Wisdom.
17. In John 17:11, Jesus claims that he has been given "the Name" of God: "Holy Father, keep them in your name, which you have given me" (cf. 5:43). In the words of James McGrath, "What is distinctive in John among the New Testament literature is the conviction that Jesus bore that name not as a result of his exaltation . . . but even during his earthly life" (*Apologetic Christology*, 65). But Jesus may also be understood as the incarnation of that Name. Just as the voice of God states, "I have glorified [my Name], and I will glorify it again" (12:28–29), Jesus later prays, "glorify me in your own presence with the glory that I had with you before the world was made" (17:5; cf. 17:1, 12:23). Along these lines, the Valentinian *Gospel of Truth* states, "the Name of the Father is the Son. . . . He gave to him a name that was his" (38.6–12 [ValC 148–49]).
18. John 1:1–18; cf. Philo, *Opif.* 24, 26 (LCL 226.20–21). Philo expressly calls the *Logos* "the beginning" (*Conf.* 146 [LCL 261.88–89]).
19. John 1:4; cf. Philo, *Somn.* 1.75; (LCL 275.336–37); Philo, *Opif.* 29–35 (LCL 226.22–27); *Conf.* 60–63 (LCL 261.42–45) (Holladay, "Philo," 163–64).
20. John 1:3b–5, 6–9, 14; cf. *Fug.* 77–78, 97 (LCL 275.52–53, 62–63).
21. Philo, *Mos.* 2.134 (LCL 289.214–15), where the advocate is there to "plead . . . that sins may be remembered no more and good gifts showered in rich abundance." Jesus's identity as the Paraclete is implicit in John 14:16.
22. Attridge, "Two Riffs," 58.
23. John 1:51, 14:10; cf. *Migr.* 6 (LCL 261.134–35).
24. John 2:1–11; cf. Philo, *Leg.* 3.82 (226.354–55); *Somn.* 2.249 (LCL 275.554–55).
25. John 4:10, 13–14, 7:37–39; cf. *Fug.* 97 (LCL 275.62–63); *Spec.* 1.303 (LCL 320.274–77); *Somn.* 2.241–45 (LCL 275.550–53). The last of these texts also presents the *Logos* as drink for a feast (*Somn.* 2.248–49 [275.554–55]; cf. John 2:1–11).
26. John 10:1–30; cf. *Agr.* 51–54 (LCL 247.134–37).
27. John 6:31–59; cf. *Her.* 79, 190–91 (LCL 261.320–21, 378–79).
28. Philo, *Spec.* 1.81 (LCL 275.146–47) and *Opif.* 24 (LCL 226.20–21).
29. On the descent of the *Logos* as the central metastory of John, see Reinhartz, *Word*.
30. These assertions stand in clear tension with earlier biblical and Jewish traditions that relate visions of God by figures such as Moses (Ex. 33:23) or translations into heaven by figures such as Enoch (Gen. 5:24) and Elijah (2 Kings 2:11) (Hakola, *Identity Matters*, 215–21; Loader, "Law"; DeConick, *Seek*, 72–73; Litwa, *Found Christianities*, 35). Although John resources these biblical books, it seems to do so selectively, as if it considers those biblical books imperfect accounts— narratives that transmit some valid prophecies (e.g., 5:39, 8:56, 12:38–41) but that may not be entirely reliable sources. Similar ambivalences toward the Old Testament can be found in other second-century Christian currents, such as Sethian Gnosticism, a movement that also saw the Old Testament as a useful but mixed record subordinate to the revelations or visions described

in its core, pseudepigraphic texts, such as the *Secret Book of John* (see discussion in Brakke, *Gnostics*, 70–71).
31. Jesus claims that "the ruler of the world is coming" (14:30) as Judas approaches him—a figure possessed by "Satan" in the preceding chapter (13:27).
32. Culpepper, *Anatomy*, 88.
33. These probably allude to instances in which biblical traditions claim a prophet saw a divine figure (e.g., Isa. 6:1) or in which "the Word of the Lord came to" a certain prophet (e.g., Isa. 38:4; Jer. 1:2; Ezek. 1:3; Hos. 1:1; Joel 1:1; Mic. 1:1).
34. For example, Engberg-Pedersen (*Philosophy*) and Buch-Hansen (*Spirit*) look particularly to Stoic conceptions of *pneuma* to understand this event. Adele Reinhartz recommends Aristotle's theory of the *Epigenesis* as a possible background ("Children").
35. Most scholars assume that the *Logos* became incarnate through the conception and birth of Jesus. Studies linking the coming of the *Logos* to his baptism (alluded to in 1:31–32) include Loisy, *Quatrième Évangile*, 228–32; Fuller, "Christmas"; Hartin, "Community," 45; Watson, "John's Christology"; McGrath, "Johannine Christianity," 4–7; McGrath, *Apologetic Christology*, 140n37; Kinlaw, *Christ*, 109–71; Talbert, *Development*, 131–41; Buch-Hansen, *Spirit*, 159–216; Engberg-Pedersen, *Philosophy*, 65–73, 110.
36. "The most widely accepted background to the 'I am' sayings . . . lies in the use of ἐγώ εἰμι in Deuteronomy 32:39 and its repetition in Isaiah 43:10 and 46:4" (Macaskill, *Union*, 258). In two verses of John, Jesus's use of the phrase has an especially dramatic effect on his hearers, suggesting its unique weight. In one, those who hear Jesus use the phrase try to stone him for blasphemy (8:58–59); in another, the phrase strikes his hearers down to the ground (18:6–8). On the biblical backgrounds of *egō eimi* and on the expression as a sign of Jesus's divinity in John, see Ball, "I Am"; Williams, *I Am*, 255–99.
37. This form is probably a form as spirit, following the logic of Phil. 3:21; 1 Cor. 15:43.
38. Although the meaning of the term "Paraclete" is ambiguous, many scholars situate the functions of the Spirit in John within the Gospel's legal/forensic metaphorical system and recommend the translation "advocate" (Williams, "Faith," 356–59; Shelfer, "Legal Precision"; Lincoln, *Truth on Trial*, 110–23).
39. One critical question is Jesus's relationship to the Spirit. A survey of recent scholarship on the Spirit in John appears in Orr, *Exalted*, 54–61.
40. Other significant elements include the idea that the *Logos* came to "cast out" and "judge" "the ruler of this world" (12:31, 16:11) and possible traces of a sacrificial/atonement theology (e.g., 1:29), threads that also connect the Gospel to Pauline thought. These threads appear in far fewer verses of the Gospel, however, and they are subordinate to the vision of human transformation and exaltation. For example, Jesus breaks the power and influence of "the ruler of this world" precisely to elevate humans to the new existence in which they are "kept . . . from the evil one" (17:15).
41. Overviews of Jewish and Christian views appear in Collins, "Afterlife," 119–38; Nickelsburg, *Resurrection*; Lehtipuu, *Resurrection*, 109–57; Elledge, *Resurrection*, 19–43.
42. Scott, *Life of the Stars*, 55.
43. See, for example, Dan. 8:10; 1QHa 9.11b–14a; *Joseph and Aseneth*, 14.1–4; Philo, *QG* 4.87 (LCL 380.364–65); Rev. 1:20, 3:1, 8:10–11, 9:1, 12:4.
44. On this passage, see Collins, "Apocalyptic Eschatology," 33–37.
45. OTP 1:85.
46. OTP 1:638.
47. OTP 1:195.
48. This view is implicit in Daniel 8:10, which associates angels with stars (see Hasslberger, *Hoffnung*, 190–91; Goldingay, *Daniel*, 283). The Enochian literature presents Enoch as a figure who acquires a celestial, angelic, and divine nature (1 Enoch 71:14–17; 2 Enoch 22:10; 3 Enoch 15). On these texts, see Orlov, *Enoch-Metatron Tradition*; Alexander, "Son of Adam." Vocabularies of angelification are also found in Qumranic sources, such as 1QS XI.7–8; Songs of the Sage (4Q511 f35:2–4); and the Self-Glorification Hymn (4Q491^c, frag. 20–22; 4Q471b, frag. 1–2; 4Q427 (4QHa), frag. 7 col. I and frag. 12; 1QHa XXVI). On these and other sources, see Gieschen, *Angelomorphic Christology*, 173–75, 180–81; Fletcher-Louis, *Luke-Acts*, 184–98; Fletcher-Louis, *Glory of Adam*, 174–76, 199–216; Sullivan, *Wrestling with Angels*, 145–78; Dimant, "Men as Angels," 93–103; Wassen, "Angels," 499–523; Alexander, *Mystical Texts*; Schäfer, *Jewish Mysticism*, 146–51; Collins, "Self-Glorification Hymn," 25–40; Walsh, *Angels*.

Philo also presents Moses as a being who was angelified (Litwa, *Posthuman Transformation*, 74–93).
49. OTP 1.638.
50. OTP 2.170. See discussion in Himmelfarb, *Ascent*, 55–58.
51. On the term *isangeloi* and its later Christian reception, see Litwa, "Equal." Traces of the same concept also appear in Acts 6:15, in which—perhaps gesturing back to the above thread in Luke—Stephen's face becomes "like the face of an angel" immediately before his death (Litwa, "Equal," 606).
52. The contrast between *psychic* and *pneumatic* also distinguishes persons in this life—the former who do not possess the Spirit and the others who do (1 Cor. 2:14–16). Paul arguably uses *psychic* interchangeably with *sarkic* ("fleshly") (1 Cor. 3:1–3).
53. Litwa, *Transformed*, 130–31; Stowers, "Dilemma," 164–65.
54. "The *pneuma* given now is a guarantee of the full pneumatic existence" (Stowers, "Dilemma," 167).
55. Competing interpretations of Paul's anthropology appear in Engberg-Pedersen, *Cosmology*; Wasserman, *Death*; Stowers, "Dilemma."
56. For Paul, Christians are fully adopted as sons at the resurrection: "we ourselves, who have the first fruits of the Spirit, groan inwardly as we wait for adoption as sons, the redemption of our bodies" (Rom. 8:23). This is different from John, which anchors sonship more thoroughly in the present.
57. Thompson connects these verses in *John*, 82.
58. Since John never attributes *pneuma* to unbelievers, Jaime Clark-Soles reasons that in John "*pneuma* is not a natural, normal part of a person's constitution" but "a gift bestowed by God and available only to those who believe" (*Death*, 118–19). Alternatively, John might have assumed that "there were various kinds and qualities of *pneuma* in the workings of the world" as Paul possibly assumes in 1 Corinthians 2:11–12 (Stowers, "Pauline Participation," 192). In this scenario, there is both a divine *pneuma* and other forms of "*pneuma* related to ordinary consciousness and cognition that all human beings possess" (Stowers, "Dilemma," 163).
59. Engberg-Pedersen, *Philosophy*, 96. "From above" remains the primary sense of *anōthen*, as seen in 3:12–13, 31, but not to the exclusion of a double entendre with "again" in 3:3–4.
60. Some interpreters see the phrase "water and spirit" as evidence that the Spirit is received through water baptism (e.g., Brown, *John*, 1.144; Koester, *Symbolism*, 163–67; Engberg-Pedersen, *Philosophy*, 130). Several early Christian texts link the Spirit to baptism (e.g., 1 Cor. 6:11; Titus 3:5; Acts 19:5–6 as a separate step). Alternatively, the phrase "water and spirit" may only be a hendiadys, with "water" being a metaphor for "spirit" (Dodd, *Interpretation*, 314n2; Dunn, *Baptism*, 191–92; Kruse, *John*, 107). The Gospel uses "water" to symbolize the Spirit elsewhere (7:37–39). It also deploys "water" imagery elsewhere in ways that do not map onto ritual baptism but seem to be strictly metaphorical (e.g., the Spirit as water within, or in the heart, of persons in 4:14, 7:38). Third, the narrative does not link the disciples' reception of the Spirit to ritual baptism (20:22). Last, John contrasts his baptism "of water" to that of Jesus, which is "of Spirit" (1:31, 33). (The same verses raise important questions about how the author evaluated the importance and meaning of water baptism. A minority of second-century Christians rejected the practice [Iren. *haer.* 1.21.4 [SC 262.304–5]; Tert. *Bapt.* [CCSL 1.275–96].) Less persuasive are attempts to connect the phrase "water and spirit" to ancient conceptions of semen (Reinhartz, "Begotten," 96; Buch-Hansen, *Spirit*, 302–4) or studies that read "water" as a reference to natural birth (e.g., Thyen, *Johannesevangelium*, 190–91).
61. This verse is one of several that knit the Spirit and Jesus together. Elsewhere in John, Jesus also claims that his hearers "do not know where I come from or where I am going" (8:14). A second double entendre—the ambiguity of "sound"/"voice" (*phōnēn*)—also evokes references to Jesus's "voice" elsewhere in the Gospel (3:29, 5:28, 10:3, 27, 18:37).
62. The life as spirit is the "good wine" kept until "now"—the realized-eschatological "now" of the Gospel (2:10; cf. 12:31).
63. Himmelfarb, *Ascent to Heaven*, 47–71.
64. This discourse is also significant as a private conversation between Jesus and his disciples—precisely the context in which we would expect Jesus to disclose privileged information (Neyrey, "Secrecy," 275). By its position, it also represents the climactic discourse of Jesus in the text, providing his definitive body of teaching.
65. The discussion that follows agrees with Martinus de Boer that although "Jesus' promise to 'come again' in 14,3 seems at first glance to be a reference to the Parousia (cf. 21,22), or perhaps to his

resurrection appearances (he 'comes' to the disciples in 21,19,24) ... within the context of ch. 14 the promise is probably a reference to his 'coming' to believers (14,18.23.28) as 'the Paraclete, the holy Spirit' (14,25; cf. 14,16–17), whereby he shall take believers 'to himself,' and thus into heavenly and familial fellowship with himself and the Father (cf. 14,6b)" ("Jesus' Departure," 14; so also Becker, "Abschiedsreden"; Stimpfle, *Blinde Sehen*, 147–216; Kammler, "Jesus Christus," 104n68; Coloe, *God Dwells*, 157–78; Buch-Hansen, *Spirit*, 394; Thyen, *Johannesevangelium*, 618–20). Other interpreters see an "intended double meaning" in the saying (e.g., Gundry, "Father's House," 72; Meeks, "Man from Heaven," 65) or see the saying as holding different conceptions in a process of supplantation, reinterpretation, or correction (so Brown, *John*, 646n3; Dietzfelbinger, *Abschied des Kommenden*, 99; Theobald, *Herrenworte*, 518).

66. The paradoxical idea that Jesus will go to the Father but is also "in the Father" (10:38) is brought out even in the first departure prediction. There, Jesus describes the place to which he will go as the place "where I am" (7:34).

67. Frey (*Eschatologie*, 3:134–78) claims that the chapter merely pairs complementary understandings of Jesus's "coming," so that 14:18–21 represents a distinct conception of Jesus's "coming" from 14:2–3. This view fails to appreciate the chapter's early moves to deconstruct literal interpretations of verses 2–3 (as in vv. 4–11). Instead, for John, "Jesus' appearance after the resurrection and his bestowal of the Holy Spirit constitute the second coming" (Clark-Soles, *Death*, 129–30).

68. A rich literature explores Paul's theology of "participation" (e.g., Deissmann, *St. Paul*, 133–47; Schweitzer, *Mysticism of Paul*; Dunn, *Theology*, 390–412; Litwa, *Transformed*; van Kooten, *Paul's Anthropology*; Campbell, *Paul*; Morgan, *Being "in Christ"*; Eastman, *Oneself*; Stowers, "Pauline Participation").

69. On the non-Pauline authorship of Ephesians, see arguments and bibliography in Ehrman, *Forgery*, 182–88.

70. "The locative sense of this expression is being used here (believers are found in Christ—located in his body)" (MacDonald and Harrington, *Colossians and Ephesians*, 232). This would cohere with the Gospel's equation of the Father's house (14:2–3) with the body of Jesus (2:21).

71. John does not detail the destiny of nonbelievers beyond the vocabularies of perishing and condemnation. Then again, neither does the *Gospel of Thomas*. In both, the fate of nonbelievers is a secondary concern. Nevertheless, a single verse in John (15:6) may be evidence that the author assumed such persons would finally be "burned," perhaps in the sort of cosmological fire (*ekpyrōsis*) assumed in many ancient systems of thought, some Christian (cf. 1 Cor. 3:12–15; 2 Peter 3:7, 10; perhaps *GThom*. 10–11, 57 [AG 312–13, 322–25]; Iren. *Adv. Haer.* 1.7.1 [SC 264.102–3]).

72. The saying evokes Paul's seed metaphor for resurrection in 1 Corinthians 15:37–38, 42–44, but modifies it through engagement with the vine metaphor developed in John 15:1–11 (especially at v. 2).

73. In John, "following" Jesus is connected to the concepts of death (13:36–37; cf. 21:18–19) and celestial access (14:3) since the two are entangled.

74. See also Jesus's promise to Martha: "the one who believes in me, even they should die, will live" (11:25).

75. These lines imbue the "hour" of Jesus's departure with an unambiguous eschatological color. Thus, although that "hour" is likely rooted in the "hour" mentioned in Mark 14:41 (so Frey, "Hintergrund," 266–68), it has been transformed, perhaps against the eschatological "hour" of Daniel 12 (as argued in Ferraro, *"L'Ora,"* 69–81; Mihalios, *Danielic Eschatological Hour*).

76. Although many interpreters assume this verse refers to a future, physical resurrection, the verse is best understood as a reference to the Spirit-realized resurrection (Kammler, *Christologie*; Méndez, "Mixed Metaphors").

77. Clark-Soles, *Death*, 129–30.

78. Buch-Hansen, *Spirit*, 385–87.

79. See extended discussion in Méndez, "Last Day."

80. On the symbolism of these scenes, see chapter 3.

81. Collins, "Afterlife," 124.

82. 1 Enoch 103:3–4 (OTP 83–84). Most scholars identify a similar concept in *Jubilees* 23:31: "and their bones will rest on earth, and their spirits will increase joy" (OTP 2.102).

83. 2 Clement 9:1 (LCL 24.178–79); 3 Clement 24 (LCL 24.178–79; ANT 381).

84. Hipp. *Refutatio*, 10.13.3 (Litwa, *Refutatio*, 716–17). Traces of this theology may appear in the *Treatise on the Resurrection* (ValC 155–63).

NOTES   199

85. *GThom.* 113 (AG 334–35); cf. 3 (AG 310–11).
86. *GThom.* 21, 37 (AG 314–17, 318–19). In *Thomas*, "the terms spirit and soul do not seem clearly distinguished, nor do body and flesh" (Gathercole, *Thomas*, 150).
87. *GThom.* 111 (AG 335); cf. 1, 51, 58, 113 (AG 320–21, 322–25, 334–35).
88. Paul's soteriology is often described as a "deification," though Paul shies from this vocabulary. For a survey of this scholarship, see Reardon, "Becoming God." Studies advancing this view include Finlan, "Theosis"; Blackwell, *Christosis*; Litwa, "2 Corinthians 3:18"; Litwa, *Transformed*; Gorman, *Participating*.
89. In a parallel vein, Paul anticipates a future in which Christians assume a likeness to Jesus. He claims that those who believe will receive a full "adoption as sons," precisely through "the redemption of our bodies" (Rom. 8:23). Through this change, humans will become fully "conformed to the image of [God's] Son," who is from then on "the firstborn among many brothers" (Rom. 8:29; cf. Phil 3:20–21).
90. Three recent studies also detect a notion of "deification" in John: Byers, *Ecclesiology*; Gorman, *Abide*; Humphrey, "Synoptics." The fact that these proposals use the same language, however, does not necessarily mean that they are interchangeable with one another or with my proposal. As Grant Macaskill writes, the term "deification" "is under-determined in the sense that the terminology of theosis can be applied to a broad range of theological accounts that vary in significant ways. . . . It is over-determined in the sense that the modern doctrine, with all its varieties, has come to operate within a certain conceptual framework that may not be directly mapped onto that of the New Testament writers" (*Union*, 75). I apply the term "deification" to the process suggested in the Fourth Gospel whereby humans are elevated to a divinity like that of the *Logos* by their participation in and assimilation by the *Logos*. This vision does not map onto formulations of *theosis* in later Christian traditions, Catholic and Orthodox, which have different parameters (e.g., an affirmation of the consubstantiality of Father and Son, a distinction between divine essence/energies, and a distinction between the deity of Jesus and of deified humans). Hence I avoid using the language of *theosis* familiar from my Eastern Christian practice. This vision also differs from the view of Gorman, who, taking cues from Catholic and Orthodox theology, undercuts the likeness of Jesus and deified humans (*Abide*, 18).
91. On the text-critical issues concerning this verse, see Peppard, "Sons," 104–5.
92. Peppard, "Sons," 108. "The υἱός is different from the τέκνα in gender and number, not nature" (Peppard, "Sons," 108–9).
93. Extracting language from Peppard, "Sons," 109. Although the term *monogenēs* is often used to indicate an "only child," it can also be used for children who are deemed, in one way or another, "unique" among their siblings, for example, Isaac (Heb. 11:17; Joseph. *A.J.* 1.222 [LCL 242.208–9]), as well as "unique nonhuman things" (Peppard, "Sons," 106–9). According to David Meconi, Augustine distinguished between the one supreme God and all other gods in a similar way, contrasting "(1) the only true God who alone can deify, and (2) those who are called gods because they have been made so through grace and adoption" (*One Christ*, 95).
94. On these, see Litwa, "Deification," 17–20.
95. Stowers, "Dilemma," 168–69.
96. This can be true even though the Gospel mostly lacks "noetic" language (Clark-Soles, *Death*, 122; but see John 12:40). It also strongly evokes Paul's "remarkable combination of Stoic materialism and Platonic mentalism, with the latter seemingly rendered material" (Stowers, "Dilemma," 169).
97. Here again, I use the lowercase "god" to capture the difference between arthrous and anarthrous *theos* in 1:1.
98. Byers, *Ecclesiology*, 197. In a similar move, Humphrey correctly reasons that "in the fourth gospel . . . the name 'child' is not simply honorary, but implies participation in divinity" ("Synoptics," 85).
99. For a defense of this view, over and against the idea that the text might envision other beings such as angels, see Neyrey, "You Are Gods"; Byers, *Ecclesiology*, 186–98.
100. Litwa, *Desiring Divinity*, 86.
101. *Pace* McGrath, who anchors the verse in traditions about God's revelation at Sinai by emphasizing rabbinical interpretations of Psalm 82 (*Apologetic Christology*, 122–23).
102. This view finds support in other passages. For example, John's prologue describes those who believe as ones "born . . . of God" (1:13), and elsewhere in John that which is born of a thing is that thing by nature: "that which is born of the flesh is flesh, and that which is born of the Spirit is spirit" (3:6). Accordingly, to be born of God is, by the same reasoning, to be (a) god.

103. *Thomas* has its characters shy away from directly articulating its most radical (and not dissimilar) views (e.g., *GThom.* 13 [AG 312–13]).
104. On a historical level, that penchant for silence and subtlety might well have ensured the Gospel's survival relative to other apocryphal gospels with not dissimilar visions.
105. On Acts 6:15, see Litwa, "Equal," 606. This idea may also be reflected in another episode in Acts. In 12:15, Peter's former companions, assuming he is dead, mistake him for his own "angel," a term David Daube believes refers to Peter's postmortem exalted form ("Acts 23," 495–97). Other writers contend that there is not enough evidence to support this interpretation (Parker, "Angel," 351; Litwa, "Equal," 606–7).
106. Tert. *Cult. fem.* 1.2.5 (CCSL 1.54); *Res.* 36.5 (CCSL 2.969); *Marc.* 3.9.7 (SC 399.106–7).
107. *Mart. Poly.* 2.3 (AM 4–5).
108. *Comm. Matt.* 17.30 (GCS 40.671; Eng. tr. mine).
109. Or. *Hom. Luc.* 39.2 (PG 13.1898; Eng. tr. Halton, *Homilies*, 159).
110. Brown, *John*, 88.
111. In Matthew and Luke, the heavens "open" when the Spirit descends to indwell Jesus (Matt. 3:16; Luke 3:21; cf. Mark 1:10), but Jesus makes this statement later than that event in John, and the Gospel never depicts another opening of the heavens.
112. In this respect, I agree with Buch-Hansen that this text is trained on realities materializing around the ascension of Jesus (*Spirit*, 273).
113. For example, one does not claim that the exalted humans are literally "sheep," despite the use of that image to describe them (10:1–30).
114. Forger, "God's Word(s)," 280.
115. Works exploring the idea of a *logos prophorikos* (uttered *Logos*) across Stoic and Philonic uses to illuminate John include Dodd, *Interpretation*, 263–86; Engberg-Pedersen, *Philosophy*, 82–112; Forger, "God's Word(s)."
116. Forger, "Divine Embodiment," 245.
117. Forger, "Divine Embodiment," 244.
118. Buch-Hansen, *Spirit*, 312.
119. Likewise, in the Farewell Discourse, Jesus claims that the words he utters are not his own speech but reflect the indwelling of the Father (14:10) (Buch-Hansen, *Spirit*, 312).
120. Philo, *Her.* 234 (LCL 261.400–401); Philo, *Fug. 10* (LCL 275.14–15).
121. Philo, *Fug.* 133 (LCL 275.80–81; Eng. tr. mine).
122. Philo, *Opif.* 8 (LCL 226.10–11).
123. Philo, *Spec.* 1.66 (LCL 320.136–39). As he says elsewhere, angels are "wholly mind, wholly incorporeal" (Philo, *QE* 2.13 [LCL 401.48–49]).
124. Philo, *QG* 2.8 (LCL 380.80–81). Philo also calls the angels "holy and divine beings" in *Abr.* 115 (LCL 289.60–61); *Conf.* 133 (LCL 261.80–83). In *QG* 4.188, Philo applies this language to "the divine beings [*daimones*], which the sacred word of Moses is wont to call 'angels' [*angelous*], and the 'stars' [*asteres*]" (LCL 380.471–72; cf. *Somn.* 1.141 [275.372–73]).
125. Philo, *Somn.* 1.115 (LCL 275.358–59; Eng. tr. mine).
126. Litwa, *Posthuman Transformation*, 91.
127. Philo, *QE* 2.29 (LCL 401.70).
128. Philo, *Virt.* 76 (LCL 341.208–9).
129. Philo, *Sacr.* 8–9 (LCL 227.98–101).
130. Philo, *Mos.* 2.288–91 (LCL 289.592–95, capitalization modified).
131. Philo, *Somn.* 75 (LCL 5.336–37).
132. Philo, *QE* 2.29, 40 (LCL 401.70, 82).
133. See, e.g., Philo, *Det.* 161 (LCL 227.308–9); *Legat.* 118 (LCL 379.58–59). Thus, as Litwa writes, "depending on what passage one highlights, Philo seems to both clearly assert and strongly deny Moses's deification" ("Deification," 1).
134. Litwa, "Deification," 27. Likewise, Litwa notes that "Philo describes angels in a way similar to his description of the transformed Moses," so that "Moses 'angelified' is also Moses deified'" (Litwa, "Deification," 25n100). Tellingly, although Philo conceives of the *Logos* as "god," he also identifies the *Logos* as the one "who holds the eldership among his angels" and is "an angel" and "archangel" (*Conf.* 146 [LCL 261.88–89]; *Mut.* 87 [LCL 275.184–85]; *Her.* 205 [LCL 261.384–85]; Eng. tr. mine).
135. Philo, *Sacr.* 9 (LCL 227.100–101).
136. Philo, *Sacr.* 9–10 (LCL 227.100–101).
137. Philo, *Sacr.* 9 (LCL 227.100–101).

138. Philo, *Sacr.* 8 (LCL 227.98–99).
139. Philo, *QG* 1.86 (LCL 380.286–87); *Sacr.* 8 (LCL 227.98–99).
140. Philo, *Mos.* 2.291 (LCL 289.594–95).
141. Philo, *QE* 2.40 (LCL 401.82–83).
142. Philo, *Migr.* 48–49 (LCL 4.158–59).
143. Lori Baron argues that "according to John, Jesus does not violate the unity of God as it is proclaimed in the Shema. Rather, Jesus resides within that unity (10:30)" (*Shema*, v).
144. One word Philo uses for Moses's translation (*anabasis*) is a word John uses to describe Jesus's ascent to heaven (20:17)—the ascent his followers also undertake (14:2-3).
145. On John's prologue as an interpretive key, see Painter, "Prologue."
146. The nearest parallel, Matthew 10:28, reflects a different system of thought (immortality of the "soul").
147. Culpepper, *Anatomy*, 40.

Chapter 3

1. In fact, certain episodes—for instance, Jesus's stay in Sychar (4:1–42)—meld features of discourse/dialogue and symbolic narrative.
2. Koester, *Symbolism*, 79.
3. Koester, *Symbolism*, 79.
4. On the literary techniques of Mark, see Rhoads, Dewey, and Michie, *Mark*.
5. Mark contains at least two symbolic episodes. In one, Mark 8:22–26, Jesus makes two attempts to heal a visually impaired person, mirroring his frustrated attempts to help his disciples perceive his identity. In another, Mark 11:12–21, Jesus curses a tree on the way to the Jewish Temple, foreshadowing the fate of the Temple (cf. Mark 13:2).
6. Schneiders, "History," 376.
7. The terminology used to describe these scenes varies by interpreter. Koester analyzes a range of episodes as "symbolic actions" (*Symbolism*, 79–140). Lee in *Symbolic Narratives* identifies a narrower set of six episodes (3:1–36, 4:1–42, 5:1–47, 6:1–71, 9:1–41, 11:1–12:11), all of which contain such elements as misunderstandings, confessions of faith, and statements of rejection, as "symbolic narratives." Painter applies the term "narrative symbol" to John 9:1–41 ("John 9," 42). Some studies describe only the Gospel's miracles as symbolic, preferring to analyze them under the text's internal language of "signs" (e.g., Salier, *Rhetorical Impact*; Welck, *Erzählte Zeichen*). Olsson, by contrast, uses the term "symbolic-narrative texts" to describe "a narrative which seeks to convey a message apart from the actual texts described" (*Structure*, 95).
8. As we will see, some episodes veer toward the quasi-allegorical. Most, however, remain at the level of the merely evocative, consistent with Attridge's description of John's imagery as "cubist": "the complex image refracts attention and establishes connections with several other important images and themes within the Gospel" ("Cubist Principle," 49).
9. The method of detecting Johannine symbolism here rests on a linguistic criterion—detecting key terms—that helps resolve scholarly anxieties about the potential of John to host an "endless" range of possible meanings (Zumstein, "Bildersprache," 139). The closed nature of the set of Johannine key terms limits the specific themes to which each episode alludes.
10. I have divided this survey into arbitrary units for convenience, bundling individual chapters together. This survey is also not comprehensive.
11. Dodd, *Interpretation*, 383.
12. I teach my students that this symbolism is evident only to the reader who "reads John backwards"—that is, who first fully internalizes the teachings of the text's Farewell Discourse (chs. 13–17), among other discourses, before reengaging its narratives.
13. To the extent that these symbols take quasi-allegorical forms, the author also might have drawn inspiration from allegorical or symbolic modes of exegeting scriptures such as Genesis (as in Philo). Perhaps not coincidentally, the author cloaks the opening words of his Gospel in the language of Genesis (cf. John 1:1; Gen. 1:1).
14. Coloe, *Dwelling*, 72, 173.
15. Given the connection to the Jacob story and the emphasis on "seeing" throughout the passage, it seems relevant that a folk etymologization interpreted the term "Israel" as meaning "one who sees God" (Smith, "Prayer," 265–68; Waetjen, *Gospel*, 32, 313, 316). This verse may also demonstrate that the author conceived of "Israel" as an ethnonym for the celestial humans—an idea in continuity with ideas in early Christian works that all believers are incorporated into a glorified or spiritualized Israel.

16. Nathanael also confesses that he is the "Son of God" (1:49), again underscoring the fact that the sheep too "know" Jesus.
17. Coloe recognizes the story as seeding the idea of Jesus as "the house of God" but does not recognize the image of "angels ascending and descending" as referring to humans (*God Dwells*, 73, 215).
18. The use of the term "signs" is widely understood as a Johannine hint of the symbolic meaning of these miracles. In 12:33, the verb *sēmainō* is applied to a thing that foreshadows or signifies another reality (though that verse does not concern the Johannine miracles).
19. On the symbolism of this pattern and its connection to the departure of Jesus, see Méndez, "Secret Journey." (In that essay I use "Secret Reversal" rather than "Secret Action.")
20. Various commentators connect these verses but do not foreground that connection in their interpretations of the story (e.g., Lincoln, *John*, 129; Michaels, *John*, 151n39).
21. On the symbolism of water in John, see Jones, *Water*; Lee, *Flesh*, 65–87.
22. On the meaning of this motif, see Méndez, "Secret Journey."
23. Engberg-Pedersen characterizes this as "probably a hint of the eschatological 'now'" (*Philosophy*, 121). The contrast the steward draws between "inferior wine" and "good wine" is probably also symbolic of ideas in the discourse that follows. It may allude to either the contrast of "flesh" and "spirit" in the dialogue with Nicodemus or the inferiority of John the Baptist and his baptism (cf. John 3:22–36).
24. Frey, "Sēmeia Narratives," 221.
25. Coloe correctly identifies this scene as another nonmiraculous "narrative symbol" (*God Dwells*, 79–84).
26. The mention of "three days" binds this story to the preceding one, which is set "on the third day" (2:1), indicating that the two gesture toward the same realities.
27. Engberg-Pedersen, *Philosophy*, 121–23, 420; Buch-Hansen, *Spirit*, 420. The idea of Jesus's body as a spiritual temple is threaded through other verses of John, including 4:21–23 (see Kerr, *Temple*; Macaskill, *Union*, 171–78).
28. Not coincidentally, the narrator claims that the disciples "believed" this word only after the resurrection, revealing that these words are fulfilled in that event (2:22).
29. Jesus articulates the same idea later, under a household metaphor: "The slave does not have a permanent place in the household; the son has a place there forever" (8:35).
30. Some scholars also find symbolic resonances in the dialogue scenes themselves (e.g., Lee, *Symbolic Narratives*, 36–97; Koester, *Symbolism*, 45–52) or the characters they employ (Hylen, *Imperfect Believers*, 23–40; Koester, "Theological Complexity," 165–81).
31. The scene's mentions of Jacob (4:6, 12) also link the scene to 1:51.
32. The water is clearly not physical water since it becomes a spring gushing up within the human person (4:14).
33. In Matthew, Jesus renames Simon "Peter" after his confession (Matt. 16:18). John places that event here.
34. These lines are problematic for the thesis, articulated by Blomberg, that the Synoptics make better sense if Jesus had met the disciples earlier (*Historical Reliability*, 80). If the disciples recognized Jesus as the Messiah so early, why would they have left him?
35. Due to its enumeration of the "signs" of Jesus, the passage was classically assigned to a "Signs Source." For arguments against the existence of such a source, see Van Belle, *Signs Source*.
36. Coloe, *God Dwells*, 84. Similarly, Schnelle argues that the episode anticipates the entire purpose of Jesus's mission (*Evangelium*, 66).
37. McGrath speculates that John 2:19 may be "the most likely original form of the saying, at least as plausibly as the versions found in other written sources" ("Destroy," 41). Alternatively, John may simply be constructing a new saying from Mark 15:29 (cf. Matt. 27:40) to advance a theological agenda.
38. Miller, "Woman."
39. Afterward, Luke notes that Jesus moved on to "another village" (9:56), without clarifying whether that village was Samaritan. At a still later point in the text, Luke places Jesus on the periphery of Samaria but not within it (17:11).
40. Thompson, *John*, 113.
41. The phrase "the hour is coming and is now" in 5:25, like the similar expression in 16:32, indicates that an action is imminent (*pace* Frey, *Eschatologie*, 2.145, which unpersuasively tries to distinguish the expressions in the two verses).

42. I am inclined to read "eating" in a metaphorical, noetic sense—that is, as a cipher for believing in and receiving the indwelling presence of *pneumatized* Jesus (Méndez, "Mixed Metaphors," 722). Others associate this "eating" with the literal consumption of the Eucharist (e.g., Engberg-Pedersen, *Philosophy*, 153–169; Buch-Hansen, *Spirit*, 389–91; Schenke, "Johannine Schism," 214–15). This is possible if the author of the Gospel has been influenced by Paul's characterization of the Eucharist as a "spiritual food and spiritual drink" that configures Christians into the *pneumatized* "body of Christ" and makes them into "one body" (1 Cor. 10:3–4, 16–17). Nevertheless, the absence of a Last Supper scene in the Gospel raises questions about whether the Eucharist formed a meaningful part of the author's theological vision. We know some second-century Christians critiqued the Eucharistic practices and teachings of other Christians (as attested by Ign. *Smyr.* 7.1 [Schoedel, *Ignatius*, 238 with discussion on 240–42] and as illustrated by the *Gospel of Judas* 33–36 [GS 67–68; see discussion in Brakke, *Judas*, 51–58]). On the contested meaning of John 6, see discussion and bibliography in Menken, "John 6," 183–204.
43. The crumbs are gathered in "twelve" baskets (6:13), one for each disciple sent out (cf. the chapter's multiple references to the "twelve" disciples in 6:67, 70, 71).
44. Buch-Hansen recognizes the idea of "Jesus' coming 'through the darkness' [cf. 20:19] as God's Spirit to the frightened disciples" on the day of the resurrection in this scene, but she settles on a metaphorical goal: they "immediately reach the goal for which they had been striving, namely earthly and eternal life" (*Spirit*, 455). The symbol is better connected to the idea of celestial access and arriving at the Father's House from chapter 14.
45. The transformation of the "slave" into a "son," for one, secures an additional linguistic link to the discourse that follows; in chapter 5, Jesus refers to himself exclusively—no less than ten times—as "the Son."
46. Judge, "Royal Official," 92.
47. It is harder to find a mechanism and rationale for a hypothetical transposition of chapters 5 and 6.
48. Von Wahlde creates a false dichotomy when he insists that the "remarkably detailed distinction of the place" excludes the possibility that "the name is symbolic rather than actual" ("Archeology," 559–60). An author can provide detailed information of the site and still utilize it as a symbolic or figurative setting.
49. Magness, "Sweet Memory," 327–28. On the archaeology of the Sheep Pool, see Gibson, "Pool."
50. The author also does not narrate the uniquely Matthean description of Peter attempting to walk on water as well (Matt. 14:28–31).
51. Lincoln, *John*, 243. Attridge notes that "most commentators prefer to treat 7:1–13 as simply introductory material setting the external stage for the dialogues to follow" ("Thematic Development," 107). On the symbolism of this scene, see Méndez, "Secret Journey."
52. Ancient interpreters connecting this language include Ephrem (*Comm. Dia.* 14.28; Epiphanius, *Pan.* 51.25.4–6). Among modern interpreters, see Hoskyns, *Fourth Gospel*, 312–13; Brown, *John*, 1.308; Smith, "Deception," 177–86; Thyen, *Johannesevangelium*, 387–88.
53. Interpreters analyze this about-face as evidence that 7:8 was a blatant lie (so Reinhartz, "Lyin' King"). Others distance Jesus from the specter of lying by framing his response as a morally permissible response to duress (Wengst, *Johannesevangelium*, 1.285–86), a cryptic statement meant to be understood on a different plane (e.g., Brown, *John*, 1:308; Smith, "Deception") or one that did not mean to exclude a later journey to Jerusalem (e.g., Barrett, *John*, 311; Blank, *Evangelium*, 1b:83–84; Theobald, *Evangelium*, 511–12). I have argued that the statement is better understood as a "half truth" (Méndez, "Secret Journey").
54. Painter, *Quest*, 248.
55. Buch-Hansen, *Spirit*, 420–21.
56. See discussions in Byers, *Ecclesiology and Theosis*, 206–13, especially 207; Parsons, "John 9:9," 175–79. On *egō eimi* language as a sign of Jesus's divinity in John, see Ball, "I Am"; Williams, *I Am*, 255–99.
57. Byers applies this phrase to the entire Gospel (*Ecclesiology and Theosis*, 200).
58. On the backgrounds and use of the term *paroimia* in John, see Zimmermann, "Imagery," 9–15; Tops, *Paroimia*. Comparable speech forms appear in 3:3, 5, 29, 8:35, 11:11–16, 12:35, 15:1–6, 16:21–23. A possible "hidden" or implicit parable appears in 5:19–30 (so Dodd, "Hidden Parable"). On the identification of "parables" or vestiges of "parables" in John, see Dodd, "Hidden Parable"; Lindars, "Two Parables"; Schweizer, "Parables"; Zimmermann, "Imagery," 23–24.
59. Becker, "Herde" connects these passages directly.

60. Dodd, *Historical Tradition*, 383. Similar claims that the passage unites two parables appear in Robinson, "The Parable," 233–40; Brown, *John*, 1.392–93. Dewey sees a third parable at 10:11b–13 as well as other "midrashic expansions" ("Paroimiai," 88). Works defending the unity of the figure include Lewis, *Rereading*; Painter, *Quest*, 346–49.

61. Jesus's claim that he has "other sheep that are not from this sheepfold" whom he intends to "bring" "so that there will be one flock" (10:16), may be a reference to gentiles (Schnackenburg, *John*, 2.299; Beasley-Murray, *John*, 171; Moloney, *John*, 137–38).

62. The "hired hand" who runs at the first sign of threat may symbolize those who fall away or fail to stand with Jesus (6:66), perhaps some of the believing Jewish authorities (12:42–43). The disciples are the sheep who are "scattered" (10:12; cf. 16:32).

63. Jesus speaks of the gift of "living water"—that is, the Spirit (7:37–39). He also reiterates that he has come to bring "light" and "life" to those who "follow" him (8:12).

64. On these options, see von Wahlde, "Pool," 155–73; Magness, "Sweet Memory," 328–34.

65. Dodd (*Interpretation*, 289) popularized the convention of dividing John into halves at 13:1, divisions now better known by the designations Raymond Brown attached to them: the "Book of Signs" and the "Book of Glory" (*John*, cxxxviii–cxxxix). But as D. A. Carson remarks, this "basic structure seems fairly simple until one starts to think about it," and the nomenclature is also problematic since "20:30–31 makes it clear that from the Evangelist's perspective the entire Gospel is a book of signs" (*John*, 103). The choice to begin this chapter with John 11–12 respects the position of these units of John as a kind of "bridge-section" in the narrative (Mlakuzhyil, *Literary-Dramatic Structure*, 202).

66. Clark-Soles, *Death*, 129.

67. *Pace* Carson, who correlates "resurrection" with the content of v. 25b and future eschatology, and the promise of "life" with the content of v. 26a with realized eschatology (*John*, 413). Nothing in the text supports the correlation of "resurrection" with future eschatology alone and "life" with realized eschatology alone. On the contrary, the text reinterprets the concept of a resurrection along realized-eschatological lines in 5:19–30. Second, Carson recognizes that the language of 11:26a finds a parallel in 5:25, a verse that clearly articulates a realized eschatology.

68. Frey differs, arguing that the addition of "even if they should die" changes "the context" of 11:25, so that "what is meant is a life in the event of a possibly future bodily death, that is, a future state of life" (*Eschatologie*, 3:451n170). I disagree. There is no reason to suppose that 11:25 differs significantly in focus or meaning from the realized-eschatological statements given their strong linguistic similarities. The additional clause "even if one dies" merely tailors that statement to the central question in the narrative—namely, is the promise of "eternal life" negated by bodily death?

69. Stibbe arrives at the same interpretation by positing a chiasm: "He who believes in me will live (spiritually), even though he dies (physically); and whoever lives (physically) and believes in me will never die (spiritually)" ("Tomb," 51).

70. On 5:25, 28–29 as references to spiritual resurrection, see Kammler, *Christologie*; Méndez, "Mixed Metaphors."

71. To see Lazarus's rising out of the tomb as the fulfillment of 11:25–26 is to confuse Jesus's signs with his reality, as so many characters in the Gospel do (e.g., 6:26–32).

72. Thompson, *John*, 261.

73. Mary's anointing of the feet of Jesus evokes Jesus's washing his disciples' feet in chapter 13 (Koester, *Symbolism*, 127). In this case, we can also conceptualize this anointing as an example of Mary "serving" Jesus.

74. Goodacre, "Parallel Traditions," 83–84.

75. Bauckham's defense of the historicity of this episode relies on the premise of a pre-Markan Passion source and a wholly unconvincing hypothesis of "protective anonymity" ("Bethany Family," critiqued in Hakola, *Reconsidering*, 17–19). The idea that John manipulates Synoptic tradition is a far more satisfying explanation.

76. Schneiders writes that "the introduction, therefore, makes it clear that what follows is not simply a good example in humility but a prophetic action" ("Foot Washing," 81).

77. Not coincidentally, similar statements in the Farewell Discourse have the coming of the Spirit as their target time (13:36, 14:26).

78. Koester, *Symbolism*, 116; Coloe, "Foot Washing," 407. Culpepper argues that "the foot washing scene, therefore, functions metaphorically and proleptically in relation to Jesus' death" ("Johannine *Hypodeigma*," 139). Not coincidentally, the next time the narrative shows

Jesus's outer garment removed is at the cross, further demonstrating that his death is what is symbolized by the act (Koester, *Symbolism*, 132).
79. Jesus stresses in several places that his death is necessary to accomplish the indwelling (e.g., 14:3, 16:7).
80. Coloe, "Foot Washing," 415. Alternatively, consider how Philo frames the foot washing of Temple priests as a symbol of a celestial journey: "by the washing of feet is meant that his steps should be no longer on earth but tread on the upper air" (*Spec.* 1.207 [LCL 320.216–17]).
81. This *brevior* reading (lacking "—except for his feet—") is found in Codex Sinaiticus, some Old Latin and Vulgate texts, as well as Origen and Tertullian, and is favored by Bultmann, *John*, 469; Schnackenburg, *John*, 3.20–22; Brown, *John*, 567–68; Lindars, *John*, 451; Barrett, *John*, 441–42; Moloney, *John*, 15n44; Beasley-Murray, *John*, 229. Thompson, by contrast, defends the longer reading on the grounds that the *brevior* reading "does not explain what Jesus is actually doing: washing the disciples' feet. He is not 'bathing' the disciples" (*John*, 288). This argument overlooks Jesus's pattern of replying to queries in cryptic terms on a high-order, symbolic plane (e.g., 2:4, 19). The bathing Jesus refers to is clearly the higher-order "cleansing" by Jesus's "word" (15:3).
82. Some scholars limit the scope of each verb in 13:10, arguing that "bathing" refers to a cleansing of the whole body and "washing" to a cleansing of parts of the body (so, e.g., Thompson, *John*, 288). Nevertheless, Barrett is correct that "while the two verbs used are not identical in meaning ... John's fondness for pairs of words (e.g. εἰδέναι, γινώσκειν) makes it impossible to feel certain that he distinguished clearly between them" (*John*, 441). Additionally, the "bathing" of 13:10 may not be external baptism since Jesus expressly says later in the discourse that it is the "word" that "cleanses" (15:3).
83. Coloe, "Sources," 79.
84. The call may also be understood as a command to emulate Jesus in all things, including the willingness to "lay down" one's own life (15:12–13) as a command to avoid "falling away" into apostasy, that is, into "the world" (16:1). The world, after all, persistently "hates" believers (15:18–19), even to the point of persecution (15:20, 16:2–3).
85. A syntactic ambiguity in the Greek suggests an alternative reading, in which these humans share the same "father" as the devil (DeConick, "Hiding"; Litwa, *Evil Creator*, 40–54).
86. Thompson, *John*, 294.
87. The image is akin to the Shepherd figure of chapter 10 and evokes the grain figure nestled in 12:24.
88. In the Gospel, belief is produced by the "labor" of the Father and the Son (4:38; cf. 6:44).
89. Attridge, "Other Gospels," 50.
90. Clark-Soles, "Footwashing," argues for the plausibility of certain scene elements without considering these intertextual connections.
91. Parsenios, *Departure*; Kennedy, *New Testament*, 76–77.
92. I do not address these scenes comprehensively.
93. North, *What John Knew*, 24.
94. Coloe, *Dwelling*, 75.
95. In Mark and Luke, Jesus's body is entombed before it is fully embalmed, so that a group of women must go to the tomb two days later to complete the embalming (Mark 16:1; Luke 23:55–24:1). Not so in John, where Nicodemus brings an excess of spices on the day of Jesus's death, ensuring that the "body" of Jesus is fully anointed and prepared "in linen cloths and with spices, as is the burial custom of the Jews" (20:39–41). For this reason, John does not have a group of women run to the tomb with spices, though one woman, Mary Magdalene, does go to the tomb on the day of the resurrection, presumably to mourn Jesus (20:1). Wayne Meeks correctly observes that Nicodemus's "ludicrous 'one hundred pounds' of embalming spices indicate clearly enough that he has not understood the 'lifting up' of the Son of Man" ("Man from Heaven," 55).
96. The proofs Jesus provides Thomas in John are oriented not toward proving his physicality (as in Luke 24:37–43) but toward establishing his identity, demonstrating that the same man who was crucified is now risen (John 20:24–29).
97. So Haenchen, *John*, 2.210. Certain commentators plausibly claim that in John, Jesus's body is already undergoing a transformation before his resurrection, merely from his earlier contact with the Spirit (1:32). Although mortal and prone to weariness (4:6), he does not seem to need drink (4:7–10), he refuses food offered him (4:31–34), and he berates those seeking "the food that perishes" (6:27). Buch-Hansen compares these changes to Philo's vision of Moses's translation into a noetic form (*Spirit*, 379–89).

98. On Hebrews as Pauline in inspiration, see Rothschild, *Hebrews*. On 1 Peter's indebtedness to the Pauline letters, see Ehrman, *Forgery*, 239–59.
99. Other scholars affirming this idea include Schenke, "Johannine Schism," 214, 215n21; Engberg-Pedersen, *Philosophy*, 109; Buch-Hansen, *Spirit*, 347–404.
100. It is also telling that, in the Farewell Discourse, Jesus indicates that he will be present to the disciples after his death through the Spirit/*Pneuma* (14:16–23). Buch-Hansen finds evidence in John 6 that Jesus's flesh and blood are converted into *pneuma* (*Spirit*, 389–91). Luke famously deviates from the views of Paul and other writers by depicting Jesus insisting that he is still "flesh and bones" and "not a spirit" and proving his fleshy nature by consuming "broiled fish" (24:39–43). And yet Luke's view is internally tensive since he ascribes some supernatural abilities to Jesus's risen body (Riley, *Resurrection*, 50–58; and from a different perspective, Prince, "Ghost"). "For Luke," then, "Jesus's resurrected body may undergo some change" (Wilson, *Embodied God*, 224). For example, Luke may imagine Jesus's body as being in an intermediate stage on its way to a new, *pneumatic* form. In this case, it seems telling that John intensifies these spiritual characteristics of Jesus's body, especially in its claim that Jesus could materialize through locked doors (20:19).
101. The fact that Thomas can touch Jesus does not necessarily demonstrate that he has "flesh." On the contrary, ancient texts envision angelic beings coming into tactile contact with humans (1 Kings 19:5; Acts 12:7) or objects (Rev. 10:10). The angels in John can be seated on the slab inside the tomb (20:12). In turn, the fact that Jesus has marks where he was pierced in the flesh is not an indication that Jesus inhabits a flesh-and-blood body since, as Candida Moss notes, many ancient sources depict non-enfleshed entitles (e.g., shades and souls) preserving "not only that person's disabilities and—to ancient eyes—deformities, but also the wounds that caused his or her death" (*Divine Bodies*, 31–40), and Christian sources such as Mark 9:47-48 assume that disfigurements could appear even on glorified bodies (*Divine Bodies*, 41–65).
102. In my reading, Thomas's cry also affirms Jesus's divinity, but precisely insofar as Jesus's divinity is implicit in his oneness with the Father.
103. In light of 14:19–20, this act of seeing also marks Thomas's own reception of the Spirit.
104. This effort is most closely linked to the *John, Jesus, and History* seminar (essays in Anderson, Just, and Thatcher, *John*), but it also encompasses conservative treatments of the Gospel such as Blomberg, *Historical Reliability*.

Chapter 4

1. Litwa, *Gospels*, 203. On eyewitness testimony as an authenticating strategy in John (albeit with different assumptions than this study), see Luther, "Authentication of the Past," 74–76.
2. Coptic text, Greek fragments, and English translation, with introduction, in AG 303–49.
3. *GThom.* incipit (AG 310–11).
4. *GThom.* 13 (AG 312–13).
5. The text's sole mention of Thomas appears in *GThom.* 13 (AG 312–13).
6. *GThom.* 13 (AG 312–13).
7. Persuasive arguments for a date after 135 appear in Gathercole, *Thomas*, 112–24; Goodacre, *Thomas*, 180. A table of other opinions on the date of *Thomas* appears in Gathercole, *Thomas*, 125–27.
8. *GThom.* 51 (AG 322–23).
9. This transition, communicated through a metaphor of undressing, appears in *GThom.* 37 (AG 322–23).
10. Goodacre, *Thomas*, 180.
11. *GThom.* 26; cf. Matt. 7:3–5; Luke 6:41–42.
12. *GThom.* 1 (AG 310–11).
13. *GThom.* 2 (AG 310–11).
14. *GThom.* 5 (AG 310–11).
15. Coptic text, Greek fragments, and English translation, with introduction, in AG 587–605. Major studies include Tuckett, *Gospel of Mary*; King, *Gospel of Mary*.
16. On the manuscripts of *GMary*, see Tuckett, *Gospel of Mary*, 3–10.
17. For example, *GMary* 7 (cf. Mark 4:9; Matt. 11:15 [AG 592–93]) and *GMary* 8 (cf. Luke 24:36; John 20:19–20; Luke 17:21; Matt. 7:7–8; Luke 11:9–10; Matt. 28:19–20 [AG 592–93]).
18. For example, *GMary* 7 (cf. John 1:29 [AG 592–93]); *GMary* 8 (cf. John 14:27 [AG 592–93]).
19. *GMary* 9 (AG 592–93).
20. On the identity of this Mary, see Tuckett, *Gospel of Mary*, 14–18.

21. *GMary* 10 (AG 594–95). On the identity of this Mary, see discussion in Tuckett, *Gospel of Mary*, 14–18.
22. *GMary* 10 (AG 594–95).
23. *GMary* 10–17 (AG 594–97).
24. *GMary* 17 (AG 596–97).
25. *GMary* 17–18 (AG 596–99).
26. Smith, "Problem of John."
27. Smith, "Problem of John," 161.
28. Theobald (*Evangelium*, 130–31) persuasively demonstrates that this statement is exclusive; that is, it does not include later readers with spiritual experiences of Jesus, as in Schnelle, *Evangelium*, 41.
29. Von Harnack, "'Wir,'" 96–113; Jackson, "Self-Referential Conventions," 12.
30. Note the masculine forms in 19:26–27, 35.
31. Later references to the disciple appear at 21:7–25.
32. The Gospel does not clearly identify this disciple as one of "the Twelve," though there are good reasons for thinking that he is, especially (a) his prominence, (b) his close association with Peter, (c) the fact that by the end the text seems to speak of "the Twelve" and the "disciples" interchangeably (20:24; cf. 6:66–67), and (d) the fact that Jesus expressly claims to have "chosen" those at the Farewell Discourse, including the "disciple whom Jesus loved" (John 15:16, 19), just as he claims to have "chosen" the Twelve in 6:70 (see Goodacre, *First Synoptic Gospel*, 108–10). Certainly, all other figures named at the Farewell Discourse are also numbered among the Twelve in other gospels, specifically Peter, Philip, and Thomas.
33. If we were to distinguish the "we" from the disciple, we would have to explain why an eyewitness narrator would have to rely on the testimony of another eyewitness in 19:35. We would also wonder why the narrator would invest another character with special authority he did not have.
34. For *oida*, the perfect functions as a present tense, and the pluperfect as the imperfect.
35. The choice to do so in the third person would suit other conventions described in Jackson, "Self-Referential Conventions."
36. Lincoln, *John*, 480; Attridge, "Restless Quest," 72. Against the idea that the witness here is the centurion, see Lincoln, "Beloved Disciple," 13. The third person can be used to imbue a text with an atmosphere of objectivity (e.g., Grant, *Ancient Historians*, 116).
37. An excellent survey of these patterns appears in Campbell, "Narrator," 27–47. Scholars link the use of the third person to the desire to imbue the text with an atmosphere of objectivity (e.g., Norden, *Agnostos Theos*, 317; Grant, *Ancient Historians*, 116).
38. Polyb. *Hist.* 36.12.1–4 (LCL 161.416–18; Eng. tr. Campbell, "Narrator," 35–36).
39. This interpretation holds whether the text imagines the author holding a pen or merely dictating the text (Bauckham, *Eyewitnesses*, 358–63). Ancient "writing," in any case, was frequently done by dictating to scribes. On writing and dictation, see Elder, *Gospel Media*, 125–71.
40. See examples in Campbell, "Narrator," 28–31.
41. Joseph., *War* 7.454–55. Since epilogues often sat at the boundary of narrative and authorial comment, juxtapositions of this sort were natural in those passages. On similar alternations elsewhere in Josephus's works, see Campbell, "Narrator," 37–42.
42. Polybius, *Hist.*, 3.23.2–4 (LCL 161.228; Eng. tr. Campbell, "Narrator," 37, emphasis mine).
43. Citing the shift from first to third person in 21:24 ("we know that his testimony is true"), some argue that the Gospel constructs the author not as an eyewitness but as one who "bases his material directly on an identifiable eyewitness" (Brown, *Introduction*, 192–96; so also Becker, *Evangelium*, 651; Schnelle, *Evangelium*, 320–21; Wengst, *Johannesevangelium*, 2.326; Ehrman, *Forgery*, 270–71). This view is compatible with the thesis of this chapter as the "we" could also be a false authorial construct. It would be a mistake to insist on this thesis, however, since other interpretations of the "we" and "I" are possible. The two may be interchangeable, perhaps in an attempt to reconcile the "we" of 1:14 and the "he" of 19:35. Alternatively, the "we" may be associative ("you and I"). The "we" could also refer to a larger group for whom the single disciple-narrator speaks.
44. For a survey of this literature, see Rosenmeyer, *Ancient Epistolary Fictions*. On these motivations, see Ehrman, *Forgery*, 11–14, 97–121.
45. Ehrman, *Forgery*, 121–28.
46. Ehrman, *Forgery*, 14–27.
47. Lincoln elaborates on this motif in *Truth on Trial*.
48. Van de Weghe, "Beloved Eyewitness," 355 (with sources in n20).

49. Bauckham connects the two in *Eyewitnesses*, 386–89.
50. Even inanimate objects testify to Jesus, including the "scriptures" (5:39) and the "works" Jesus performs (10:25; cf. 5:36).
51. The ethics of this practice are another issue altogether. We might analyze the text as engaged in an unethical practice. Alternatively, Karen King recognizes the possibility of ethical forms of pseudepigraphy as a "strategic response to exclusionary practices" in the production and dissemination of literature ("Author," 39).
52. Anderson, "Aspects of Historicity," 382.
53. Additionally, "the dependence of the Fourth Gospel upon Mark and Luke is a fact which militates against the acceptance of Apostolic authorship for the Gospel" (Streeter, *Four Gospels*, 394).
54. On eyewitness testimony and embellishment, see Hengel and Schwemer, *Jesus*, 490–91. It is also true that "fictionalization is a constitutive element in historiographical narratives" and "fiction is used for filling out narrative gaps or inconsistencies" (Becker, *Birth*, 90). But John does more than merely fill gaps with its invented elements; the work centers its fabrications, and it has a fundamentally revisionist character. We must grapple with this reality. We also cannot merely suspend a careful evaluation of the historicity of John's narratives, a move seen in Luther, "Authentication of the Narrative"; Luther "Authentication of the Past."
55. Even in the twenty-first century, a minority of scholars would assign these eyewitness claims to a different editorial layer (e.g., von Wahlde, *Gospel and Letters*).
56. Anderson, *Quest*, 4–5 (cf. Streeter, *Four Gospels*, 405, who noted "an enhanced definiteness and vividness"). Anderson, of course, uses this argument to ground the Gospel's historicity. Nevertheless, a fiction can be just as detailed.
57. Often this material supplements what the Synoptics describe in parallel stories (Streeter, *Four Gospels*, 402–3). On John's penchant for mundane detail, also see Litwa, *Gospels*, 203–4.
58. Lincoln, *John*, 140; McGrath, "Destroy," 40.
59. Scholars have attempted to find symbolism in these festal choices (e.g., Yee, *Jewish Feasts*; Wheaton, *Jewish Feasts*), but these links are open to question or, in some cases, strained.
60. Barker, *Writing*, 102–3, citing as examples (a) Mark 6:35–36; Matt. 14:15; Luke 9:12; John 6:5; (b) Mark 6:37 and John 6:7; (c) Mark 6:38; Matt. 14:17; Luke 9:13; John 6:8–9; and (d) Matt. 26:8 (cf. Mark 14:4) and John 12:4–5.
61. Byrskog, "History," 263. On the challenges of using this material to confirm an eyewitness perspective, see Sturch, "Eyewitness Material."
62. Litwa, *Gospels*, 203.
63. On the idea that the disciple may represent a literary fiction, see Charlesworth, *Beloved Disciple*, 134–41. Studies suggesting the disciple may be a literary fiction to at leasr some degree include Lindars, *John*, 33–34; Kügler, *Jünger*, 429–38; Dunderberg, *Beloved Disciple*; Schenke, "Function and Background"; Attridge, "Restless Quest"; Litwa, *Gospels*, 194–208.
64. *GThom.* 8 (AG 312–13).
65. *GMary* 18 (AG 598–99).
66. Litwa, *Gospels*, 207.
67. Attridge, "Restless Quest," 27.
68. Attridge, "Restless Quest," 27.
69. Attridge, "Restless Quest," 26; *pace* Goodacre, *First Synoptic Gospel*, 107–33 (which otherwise correctly sees pseudepigraphy at play).
70. Smith, *John*, 26. Blomberg's counterargument—that John might have had "good theological and/or literary reasons for omitting much of what he knew and for including what he did" (*Historical Reliability*, 26)—understates the extent of John's complete absence from the Gospel and fails to grapple with how far the Gospel rewrites some episodes featuring John in the Synoptics (e.g., the call of the disciples and the events in Gethsemane).
71. Theobald is likely correct that, in 21:2, the sons of Zebedee are distinguished from two unnamed disciples, one of whom may be the disciple whom Jesus loved ("Jünger," 524n156).
72. Besides the evidence of 20:2, this "other disciple" also behaves like the "disciple whom Jesus loved," staying with Jesus as all others gradually abandon him. See also the case against John made in Myles and Kok, "Implausibility."
73. For that matter, Lazarus may well be an invented character since he never appears in Lukan passages describing Mary and Martha (so, e.g., Lindars, *John*, 384–86; Brodie, *John*, 86–88; against this view, see Bauckham, "Bethany Family").
74. *Pace* Charlesworth, *Beloved Disciple*. See arguments in Attridge, "Restless Quest," 24.
75. Culpepper, *Anatomy*, 121.

NOTES   209

76. On the ahistoricity and false authorship of the *Diary of the Trojan War*, see Merkle, "True Story." Greek text and English translation of the *Life of Apollonius*, with introduction, appear in LCL 16, 17, 458. On the ahistoricity of Damis and other elements of Apollonius's account, see Meyer, "Apollonios"; Bowie, "Apollonius"; Bowie, "Philostratus"; Dzielska, *Apollonius*, 19–49; Edwards, "Damis." On both works within broader discussions of pseudo-historical sources, see Mheallaigh, "Pseudo-Documentarianism"; Litwa, *Gospels*, 194–208.
77. *Pace* Brown, who claims that while "it is true that such an attribution may have been added to the Gospel [of John] as an attempt to clothe an anonymous work with the mantle of apostolic authority . . . an attribution without a personal name does not seem specific enough" to sustain a false authorial pretense (*John*, 1.xciii; echoed in Jackson, "Self-Referential Conventions"; Bauckham, *Eyewitnesses*, 409). Philostratus's *Heroicus* places eyewitness accounts of the Trojan War by one Protesilaos on the lips of an invented character known only as "the Vinedresser" (introduction and text in LCL 521.3–330). The *Martyrdom of Marian and James* relates the death of two Christian martyrs through the eyes of an anonymous, invented eyewitness (introduction and text in AM xxxiii–xxxiv, 194–213). Another example may be Acts, whose anonymous "we" narrator may be a false authorial construct (so Ehrman, *Forgery*, 263–82). Anonymous texts that construct their unnamed narrators as visionaries or eyewitnesses may fit into this category as well (see, e.g., the implied author of Sethian Gnostic *Reality of the Rulers* [introduction and text in GS 93–107]).
78. Litwa, *Gospels*, 206.
79. Litwa, *Gospels*, 204–5.
80. *Pace* Theobald, *Evangelium*, 92.
81. So, for example, the death of Damis in the *Life of Apollonius* (Litwa, *Gospels*, 206; *pace* Blomberg, *Historical Reliability*, 84; Theobald, *Evangelium*, 91). Note, however, that scholarly readings of John 21:23 regularly move beyond a careful reading of the text. The verse presupposes the spread of a rumor among the disciples ("the brothers"; cf. 20:17) in the aftermath of Jesus' statement. It does not (or does not necessarily) envision a longer tradition as the NRSV suggests (fancifully translating *adelphoi* as "community"). Likewise, the verse also does not indicate that the disciple has died by the time the Gospel was written (an idea difficult to square with 19:35 and 21:24), though it does suggest his future death.
82. "If" the author of John "knew the Synoptic Gospels (as seems likely to many scholars), he may have used the eyewitness authenticating device to outperform his perceived competitors" (Litwa, *Gospels*, 203).
83. Baum cites several examples in "Original Epilogue," 236.
84. Keith, *Gospel*, 131–54.
85. Cf. Kreps, *Crucified Book*, 17. This ending also validates John's choice to focus on only select events. John includes those signs that can lead persons to "believe" and receive "life."
86. Neyrey, *Rhetorical Perspective*, 252. At one point, Jesus claims, "I have said nothing in secret" and "I have spoken openly to the world" (18:20). By this, Jesus means that he has communicated the content of even his private discourses in public settings (albeit in a concealed, coded manner).
87. On the Greco-Roman backgrounds for the Farewell Discourse, see Parsenios, *Departure*.
88. The *Life of Apollonius* claims that Apollonius disclosed events to Damis that Damis was not present for, making it possible for him to document them (e.g., at 3.27.1 [LCL 16.278–79], noted in Litwa, *Gospels*, 204). The Gospel of John does not claim that Jesus disclosed his private conversations to the disciple he loved. Still, by constructing a close intimacy between Jesus and the disciple, it leaves this possibility to the reader's intuition.
89. Maurice Casey writes that the author of John takes this idea "almost to the point of a theory of authorship" (*John's Gospel*, 152).
90. That the Spirit can bring extraordinary insight also appears in Jewish writings, including those of Philo (Levinson, *Spirit*, 167–216).
91. Casey, *John's Gospel*, 152–53.
92. On the disciple as a supernaturally gifted interpreter of scripture, see Lindenlaub, *Beloved Disciple*.
93. On the connections between Mark and John on this point, see Poplutz, "Paroimia." Mark's emphasis on secrecy fits into that gospel's theological program and sits beside the related "Messianic Secret" motif.
94. Stibbe, "Elusive Christ," 26.
95. On this practice, see essays in Van Belle, Labahn, and Maritz, *Repetitions*.
96. On this strategy in John, see Stimpfle, *Blinde Sehen*; Méndez, "Mixed Metaphors."

97. John also alludes to Synoptic sayings (e.g., 4:44; cf. Mark 6:4).
98. In Johannine studies, this view is typified by Windisch, *Johannes*.
99. The term "competitive" is productively applied to John in Keith, "Competitive Textualization."
100. In this respect, it positions itself almost as an interpretive key for all other works.
101. Cic. *Att.*, 21 (II.1) (LCL 7.126–27).
102. Starr, "Circulation," 215.
103. Paus. *Graec. desc.* 6.18.5 (LCL 272.108–9).
104. Kruger, "Manuscripts," 35. On these channels, see discussion in Gamble, *Books*, 82–143; Thompson, "Holy Internet"; Alexander, "Book Production."
105. We know of a literary fake that followed this channel of distribution: Salvian's *Ad Ecclesiam*. For text and commentary, see Haefner, "Unique Source"; also see discussion in Ehrman, *Forgery*, 94–96.
106. So, for example, the discovery of Deuteronomy, described in 2 Kings 22:8; 2 Chron. 34:15. The planting of forgeries in libraries and collections is attested throughout history (for an example from recent centuries, see Booth, "Dr. Drewe").
107. Diog. Laert., *Vit.*, 7.1.34 (LCL 185.144–45). See also Galen's speculations about the origin of falsely attributed works in libraries (Baum, "Authorship," 29–30).
108. As Gamble notes, citing the *Gesta apud Znophilium*, lectors were often "the custodians of the books and could be expected to have some of them in their homes" (*Books*, 147).
109. Ehrman, *Forgery*, 128.
110. "Unlike all other authentic and inauthentic Pauline letters, Hebrews does not identify an author or recipients, and the standard Pauline greeting and thanksgiving sections are omitted. Given these highly non-Pauline traits, it would seem Hebrews had to be closely associated with other Pauline letters from the outset to be understood as Pauline so securely for so many years. The best explanation of the most data is that Hebrews never circulated independently, but was written into an early corpus Paulinum—published as such and never circulating apart from this context" (Rothschild, *Hebrews*, 147).
111. In the Johannine Community hypothesis, scholars often assume a tight correspondence between the author's views and those of a single, geographically anchored network of early house church(es) or associations. In fact, we know less than we would like about the shape, gathering patterns, and intellectual diversity of early "churches" or "Christ groups." (A survey of scholarship appears in Ascough, "Christ Groups.") We also know next to nothing about the extent of our author's attachment to any such assembly, even if we can safely presuppose at least some past or present involvement with at least one such group. We do not know, for example, if our author was connected to only one such association or if he drifted among several competing Christian associations in the same area so that his views combine multiple influences. We do not know whether our author was geographically stationary or mobile, living in different places and picking up different ideas in each. (Bauckham, "For Whom," 33–34 calls attention to the mobile life of some Christians.) For that matter, we do not know if our author still consistently attended gatherings of any community or maintained strong social relationships with their participants, even if he had in the past.
112. At least some notions appearing in John are condemned in other works produced in the same period, indicating their controversial character, among them notions of a spiritualized resurrection (2 Tim. 2:17–18).
113. Christians participated in communal gatherings to different extents. Hebrews 10:25 warns its readers against "neglecting to meet together, as is the habit of some," suggesting at least some attended such gatherings irregularly. Would this warning have applied to the author of John?
114. Stowers challenges scholars to imagine the social matrix of the Gospel beyond the narrow and unsubstantitated frame of a "community" ("Community," 249–50).
115. Barker, *Writing*, 38–39.
116. Barker, *Writing*, 34–35.
117. On whether John was written on a roll or codex, see Elder, *Gospel Media*, 268–71. On these technologies, see Nongbri, *God's Library*, 21–46; Barker, *Writing*, 38–41.
118. Analogous problems appear in the Synoptics, often in adapting earlier sources. See, for example, the forms of "muddle" detected by Michael Goulder and critically evaluated by Mark Goodacre (*Goulder*, especially at 230–37) as well as Goodacre's own observations of "editorial fatigue" in the Synoptics ("Fatigue"). Redaction may be a factor in John's aporiae. Goodacre has observed in multiple settings that many of John's aporiae appear precisely where John seems to be adapting Synoptic materials (e.g., John 6:1, 14:31).

NOTES   211

119. Coogan and Moss, "Textual Demiurge." On the use of enslaved labor, see Fitzgerald, *Slavery*; Fitzgerald, "Slave"; Richards, *Secretary*; Moss, "Between the Lines"; Moss "Secretary"; Moss, "Fashioning Mark"; Moss, *God's Ghostwriters*; Coogan and Moss, "Textual Demiurge"; Coogan, Moss, and Howley, *Writing*.
120. On collaboration between literate writers, see Walsh, *Origins*, 105–33.
121. Ehrman, *Forgery*, 81–85.
122. One must not insist too strongly on this possibility, however, since aporiae such as those visible in John were hardly a characteristic or inevitable feature of falsely authored works. For that matter, it is also conceivable that some enslaved laborers could be fully privy to the dubious aspects of a project and still cooperate with the text's production and release. Enslaved persons, after all, could not refuse work; they generally lacked the social standing and credibility to challenge a falsely authored work once in circulation; and they could be harshly disciplined for failure to guard their enslaver's secret. If an author was reluctant to involve enslaved Christ believers in his activities, they could purchase or borrow these services (Coogan and Moss, "Textual Demiurge").
123. "Scribes could work alone when they copied texts, as the early Christian visionary Hermas described himself doing (Herm. Vis. 2.4)" (Barker, *Writing*, 42).
124. Gamble, *Books*, 101, 106–7.
125. Hancock, *Hoax*, 181 (note too: "it is apathy and neglect, not criticism, that kills a viable hoax" [182]). Attridge, then, is likely correct when he speculates that the elusiveness of John's eyewitness construct "performs primarily a literary role, re-engaging the reader, drawing her back time and again" ("Restless Quest," 29).
126. In this vein, B. H. Streeter speculates that the author believed "the discourses came to him 'in the Spirit'" (*Four Gospels*, 401). Streeter further speculates that this sort of supernatural mechanism could have led the author to have "genuine sayings" "amplified and re-orientated by the subconscious workings of the prophet's mind," and that this mechanism "would give an added meaning to the reiterated emphasis in the Gospel on the work of the Spirit as illuminating and interpreting at some later time the actual teaching of the historic Christ," citing John 16:12–14 (*Four Gospels*, 401).
127. The parallel of John 1:1 and Genesis 1:1 may also indicate that the author imagined his work as a new scripture. In this case, we can consider John in conversation with other works asserting their divine origins and authority (e.g., the *Gospel of Truth* as discussed in Kreps, *Crucified Book*).
128. Fischer, *Historians' Fallacies*, 214.
129. Some writers cast disguised authorship as a possible response to their social marginalization (King, "Author," 39; Moss, "Secretary," 46n100; Coogan and Moss, "Textual Demiurge").
130. Salvian, *ep.* 9 (O'Sullivan, *Writings of Salvian*, 260–61).
131. Salvian, *ep.* 9 (O'Sullivan, *Writings of Salvian*, 261–62).
132. Tert. *Bapt.* 17.5 (CCSL 1.291–92; Eng. tr. Evans, *Homily on Baptism*, 36–37).
133. If we grant some of the possibilities listed here, we also cannot rule out the potential influence of psychological factors.
134. Hancock, *Hoax*, 181.
135. Hancock, *Hoax*, 180. On discovery narratives in literary forgeries, see Speyer, *Bücherfunde*; Ehrman, *Forgery*, 123–26.
136. It is therefore unnecessary to believe that a definable "Johannine Community" was necessary to preserve the Gospel.
137. Although an audience may have "its supporters and its detractors... often the supporters who assert the positive case have the easier task... [because] the general public already wants to believe" (Hancock, *Hoax*, 182).
138. These assumptions are even reproduced in contemporary scholarship on these passages (e.g., see discussion and critique of future-eschatological readings of 5:21–30 in Méndez, "Mixed Metaphors").

Chapter 5

1. Speyer, *Fälschung*, 79–82.
2. This chapter condenses the more detailed arguments of Méndez, *Epistles*.
3. First John is technically not a letter since it lacks standard letter conventions (see Brown, *Epistles*, 86–92; Klauck, *Johannesbriefe*, 68–74).
4. On these differences, see Brown, *Epistles*, 19–30; Hakola, *Reconsidering*, 67–95.

5. De Boer, *Story*, 63–64. See, for example, extended argumentation in Klauck, *Johannesbriefe*, 89–126.
6. Parsenios, *First, Second, and Third John*, 13.
7. So Hakola, *Reconsidering*, 69–71, which organizes the more exhaustive catalogue in Brown, *Epistles*, 755–59.
8. Based on the table provided in Hakola, *Reconsidering*, 69–71.
9. Marty, "Contribution," 202–3.
10. Hakola, *Reconsidering*, 90.
11. Lieu, *I, II, and III John*, 17; see also Schnelle, "Reihenfolge," 102.
12. Goodacre, *Thomas*, 36.
13. Zamfir and Verheyden, "Allusions," 260.
14. Goodacre, *Thomas*, 54–56 calls this "the plagiarist's charter."
15. Confusion over this point has also negatively impacted other areas of Johannine research. For example, Brown, *John*, 1.xlv cites dissimilarities between John and the Synoptics to argue for their independence. Keith, "If John" is also correct that differences can evince use, albeit in a critical posture.
16. Parsenios, *First, Second, and Third John*, 12.
17. Painter, *1, 2, and 3 John*, 69.
18. If we expand the scope of the relevant text, we could also include *phaneroō* (John 1:31).
19. Parsenios, *First, Second, and Third John*, 12–13.
20. Klauck, *Zweite und dritten Johannesbrief*, 19.
21. The scholars who deviate from this view do so on problematic grounds. The most prominent proposal, by Udo Schnelle, dates the Epistles against what he surmises to be the most plausible, linear evolution of Johannine thought within "the Johannine school." He insists that 2 and 3 John must be the earliest Johannine texts, citing "the comprehensive reduction of every form of theology (especially Christology)" in these letters ("Reihenfolge," 113). Nothing, however, demands that the theology of the "Johannine school" would have developed in a linear fashion (if such a school even existed). For that matter, it is unusual that Schnelle would count the "reduced" theology of 2 and 3 John as a criterion for dating them given their extreme brevity and the personal/pastoral character of at least 3 John. Last, Schnelle's claim that 2 and 3 John are the earliest Johannine texts is also implausible given that these texts entered the historical record at a late date and had their authenticity questioned for centuries. These traits are inconsistent with the idea that 2 and 3 John are the core texts of the Johannine tradition.
22. Boyarin, "Logos," 546–49.
23. Parsenios, *First, Second, and Third John*, 13.
24. "Nur durch den Aufbau des JohEv können die Associationem im Gedankegang des 1Joh erklärt werden" (Vouga, *Johannesbriefe*, 11). This relationship was initially demonstrated in Holtzman, "Problem."
25. On the reception of 2 and 3 John, see Lieu, *Second and Third John*, 5–36; Barker, "Acts of John."
26. Eus. *h.e.* 6.25.10 (LCL 265.76–77). Barker, however, argues that this line may be a Eusebian interpolation ("Acts of John," 346–48).
27. Eus. *h.e.* 3.25.1–5 (LCL 153.256–57).
28. Lieu, *I, II, and III John*, 239.
29. Lieu, *I, II, and III John*, 252.
30. On the letter as 2 John, see Strecker, *Johannine Letters*, 263; Schnelle, "Reihenfolge," 97; Painter, *1, 2, and 3 John*, 374–77.
31. North, *Lazarus Story*, 11.
32. At present, the only letter widely suspected of being a derivative, pseudepigraphal work is 2 John (Bultmann, *Epistles*, 1; Heise, *Bleiben*, 164–70; Schunack, *Briefe*, 108–9; Lieu, *I, II, and III John*, 7, 18, 239–65; Edwards, *Johannine Epistles*, 32). Hirsch considered not only 2 John but all three epistles pseudo-historical (*Studien*, 170–79), a view I too have defended (Méndez, "Johannine Community") and, more recently, Corsar, "Legacy."
33. On ancient doubts about all three Epistles, see Lieu, *Second and Third John*, 5–36.
34. This ambiguity supports the idea that the pronouns of 1:1–4 are not determined by an external reality but are modeled after the Gospel's language.
35. Corsar highlights particular points of continuity in "Legacy," 165–68.
36. Exceptions include scholars who cite the same data to posit a common author for John and 1 John (e.g., Marshall, Hengel, Köstenberger). These scholars reach the wrong conclusion by

NOTES 213

weighing the similarities between the texts against their differences. One should synthesize the two. The similarities construct a common authorial claim; the differences falsify it.

37. Brown, *Epistles*, 136.
38. Ehrman, *Forgery*, 423.
39. Ehrman, *Forgery*, 422n32, 423.
40. Ehrman, *Forgery*, 419, 425.
41. For example, Brown, Bauckham, Klauck, Painter, Schnackenburg, von Wahlde.
42. Since the narrator addresses a member of the community in Gaius, this "we" is probably not a community voice (so Brown, *Epistles*, 724), though the author could have mistaken 1 John's "we" as such.
43. Like 2 John, 1 Peter also personifies churches as women: "she ... who is likewise chosen sends you greetings" (5:13).
44. Quoted in Eus. *h.e.* 3.39.4 (LCL 153.292–93; Eng. tr. mine). On this passage, see Carlson, *Papias*.
45. Painter, "Johannine Literature," 583.
46. This assumes that the authors of the Epistles recognized the "disciple" within or as the "we" voice, which is extremely likely.
47. "Without mentioning Solomon by name, in accordance with a stylistic feature of certain genres of Hellenistic literature ... he nevertheless now clearly identifies himself with that illustrious king" (Winston, *Wisdom*, 5). On these Hellenistic backgrounds, see 139–140.
48. See arguments in Rothschild, *Hebrews*.
49. Malherbe, *Cynic Epistles*, 17. Malherbe outlines various hypotheses regarding the authorship of the letters (14–18).
50. It is possible that other pseudepigraphal letters used epithets, but that those epithets—and any other elements of the letters' prescripts—were removed by scribes. Here, we are fortunate to possess a letter with an intact prescript. Note also the brevity of the text at seventy-one words in Greek. Brevity, of course, is perhaps the most striking feature of 2 and 3 John.
51. Malherbe, *Cynic Epistles*, 180–81.
52. This is true even if one believes that the hand that wrote 1 John also edited the Gospel (so, e.g., Raymond Brown and Paul Anderson).
53. On the inauthenticity and multiple authorship of the letters of Diogenes, see Malherbe, *Cynic Epistles*, 14–18. On the inauthenticity of the Socratic letters, see 27–29. On the inauthenticity of the letters of Crates, see 10–13. On the Hippocratic letters, see Smith, *Hippocrates*, 18–34. The Socratic letters—thirty-five in number—are also overwhelmingly pseudonymous, with the possible exception of *ep.* 28 (so Bickermann and Sykutris, *Speusipps Brief*). (As Malherbe notes, *Ep.* 35 is misattributed and "really belongs to the Pythagorean literature" [*Cynic Epistles*, 27].)
54. Second Peter seems to construct a Petrine letter collection since it references 1 Peter (2 Peter 3:1). For evidence of the pseudonymity and distinct authorship of these letters, see discussion and sources cited in Ehrman, *Forgery*, 239–59 (1 Peter), 222–29, 259–63 (2 Peter), 305–8 (*Epistula Petri*), 445–51 (*Apocalypse of Peter*), and 401–4 (*Coptic Apocalypse of Peter*).
55. For evidence of the pseudonymity and distinct authorship of these works, see discussion and sources cited in Ehrman, *Forgery*, 156–171 (2 Thessalonians), 171–182 (Colossians), 182–192 (Ephesians), and 192–217 (the Pastorals, which Ehrman attributes to a single author). On the pseudonymity of Hebrews, see Rothschild, *Hebrews*.
56. On the pseudepigraphal character of these texts, see discussion and sources cited in Ehrman, *Forgery*, 425–32 (3 Corinthians), 439–45 (*Laodiceans*), 520–28 (*Letters of Paul and Seneca*), and 451–54 (*Apocalypse of Paul*). This, of course, excludes the author of other pseudo-Pauline works, such as the *Apocalypse of Paul*. The Ignatian epistles represent a similar tradition, assuming they contain an authentic core; those epistles grew to a collection of fourteen epistles of mixed pedigree in multiple recensions (Schoedel, *Ignatius*, 3–7). On the debate over the authenticity of the letters of Ignatius, see Lookadoo, "Ignatian Letters," 88–114.
57. In many cases, these derivative works imitate earlier pseudepigrapha, suggesting they saw earlier texts as authentic. See, for example, Ephesians' dependence on the pseudonymous Colossians (Ehrman, *Forgery*, 182–88).
58. Mitchell, *Christian Textuality*, xiii.
59. "We look in vain for equivalents to Jesus' teaching on divorce, oaths and vows, almsgiving, prayer, fasting, or the multitude of other specific moral directives strewn across the pages of Matthew's Gospel. Everything comes down to imitating Jesus' love for his disciples; what concrete and specific actions should flow from this love are largely left unspoken" (Meier, "Love,"

47–48). Attempts to recover a robust, if often implicit ethic from the text appear in Brown and Skinner, *Ethics*; van der Watt, *Grammar*.
60. We also do not know how the text first surfaced, though there is no evidence it ever circulated with the Gospel.
61. Körtner notes that "the majority of scholarship points to the date of writing as 125/130," though he argues for a date closer to 110 (*Papias*, 88–94, 236).
62. No feature of the epistle—even its use of an "I" voice—requires knowledge of John 21.
63. It is helpful to compare 2 John to Philemon, the only extant personal letter from Paul's pen and his shortest extant letter (303 words). Both Philemon and 2 John open with a conventional prescript identifying sender and addressee ("A to B"; e.g., Phlm. 1–2; 2 John 1–2), salutations (Phlm. 3; 2 John 3), and opening thanksgivings based on positive reports (Phlm. 4–7; 2 John 4). Both conclude with promises to visit (e.g., Phlm. 22; 2 John 12) and parting greetings (e.g., Phlm. 23–24; 2 John 13).
64. On the dependence of the Petrine letters on Paul, see arguments and works cited in Ehrman, *Forgery*, 239–63.
65. First John indicates the doctrines that should be used to "test" "false prophets" (4:1–6), but it does not indicate what actions should be taken against a figure exposed as "false."
66. Schoedel, *Ignatius*, 59 (capitalization altered). Similar warnings appear in Ign. *Smyrn.* 2:1–4:2; cf. 7:1 [Schoedel, *Ignatius*, 225, 230, 238].
67. ANT 380–81.
68. Lieu, who also holds that 2 John was a later literary fake, agrees: "although heavily dependent on 1 John, [2 John's] function was to give directions on wandering teachers who do not follow the Johannine norms as conceived by the Elder" (*Second and Third Epistles*, 164).
69. Irenaeus and Clement of Alexandria accepted it as a work of the same author as 1 John (e.g., Iren. *haer.* 1.16.3 [SC 264.262]; 3.16.8 [SC 211.318–21]; Clem. *Strom.* 2.15.66 [SC 38.87]), while others questioned its authenticity (Origen, fragment cited in Eus. *h.e.* 6.25.10 [LCL 265.76–77]).
70. On this source, see Ehrman, *Forgery*, 439–45; Walsh, "Laodiceans."
71. Perkins, *Johannine Epistles*, 76; Painter, *1, 2, and 3 John*, 42–43, 57, 126, 336; Thompson, *1–3 John*, 21, 150; Johnson, *Writings*, 497; Puskas, *General Letters*, 6.
72. For example, in a section in which Irenaeus quotes multiple times from 1 John, he introduces a line from 2 John as "words of the aforementioned epistle," immediately before providing a quote from 1 John, which he credits "again" to "the epistle" (*haer.* 3.16.8). Commenting on this fact, Painter reasons that "the form in which Irenaeus knew 1 and 2 John did not distinguish the two Epistles," perhaps because "2 John was originally the covering letter for 1 John and it was in that combined form that 1 and 2 John were known to Irenaeus in Asia Minor" (*1, 2, and 3 John*, 42). Also interesting is the convergence of Clement of Alexandria's claim that 2 John was written "to the virgins" (surviving in Lt. as *ad virgines*, but reconstructed as Gk. *pros parthenous*; Clem. *Ad. II Io.* [GCS 17.215]) with the claim of Augustine and other Latin writers that 1 John was written *ad Parthos* ("to the Parthians" (Aug. *Tract.* 10 [PL 35.1977–78])—possibly a mistranslation or corruption of *parthenous*. The application of the same title to both 1 and 2 John—albeit in a corrupted form—may reflect a tradition linking the texts to the same recipients.
73. This is true of the letters of Plato and Ignatius, for example (Ehrman, *Forgery*, 128). We have also seen it in the case of the letters of Diogenes (Malherbe, *Cynic Epistles*, 14–18).
74. Iren. *haer.* 1.16.3 (SC 264.262), 3.16.8 (SC 211.318–21).
75. Lieu, *I, II and III John*, 277. These include, but are not limited to, "church" (vv. 6, 9–10) and "fellow workers" (v. 8), "for the sake of the Name" (v. 7), and a wish that the "soul" of its recipient may "prosper" (v. 2). The concentration of linguistic peculiarities is especially striking given the text's brevity.
76. On the reception history of 3 John, see Barker's survey of the patristic and manuscript evidence for each of the epistles in "Acts of John," 342–52, 355–57. For evidence that 1 and 2 John circulated in some regions without 3 John, see Lieu, *Second and Third John*, 18–30.
77. I first linked 2 and 3 John to practices of literary *ēthopoiia* in a 2021 workshop at Durham, UK, and in a 2023 Society of Biblical Literature presentation. Elizabeth Corsar has subsequently developed this idea, providing an excellent defense of it in Corsar, "Legacy."
78. Rosenmeyer, *Ancient Epistolary Fictions*, 197.
79. Rosenmeyer, *Ancient Epistolary Fictions*, 203.
80. (Ps.-)Apollonius, *ep.* 49 (LCL 458.42–45).
81. Syme, "Fraud and Imposture," 9.
82. For example, (Ps.-)Philostratus, *ep.* 71 (LCL 234.538–41).

NOTES 215

83. Thompson, *1–3 John*, 21; Painter, "1, 2, and 3 John," 1512; Johnson, *Writings*, 497; Puskas, *General Letters*, 6.
84. Johnson, *Writings*, 497; Heil, *1–3 John*, 1.
85. Eus. *h.e.* 6.25.10; 7.25.11 (LCL 265.76–77; 265.200–201). See Barker, "Acts of John," 346–49 for an argument that these mentions of 3 John are Eusebius's own interpolations.
86. Most likely, 1 John escaped that scrutiny due to its early introduction and its strictly anonymous cast (like the Gospel's own and unlike 2 and 3 John's use of "the Elder"). On the pseudonymity of both Petrine letters, despite their different reception histories, see Ehrman, *Forgery*, 239–59 (1 Peter), 222–29, 259–63 (2 Peter).

Chapter 6

1. This comes with no small irony since the texts we exclude from the category of "Johannine" are the only ones that use the name "John."
2. Studies exploring the origin and development of traditions surrounding John, albeit guided by different assumptions than appear in this book, include Culpepper, *John*; Kok, *Beloved Apostle*; Furlong, *Identity*. For traditions surrounding the "John" of Revelation, see Boxall, *Patmos*.
3. On the apostles as illiterate in Christian memory, with an emphasis on Acts 4, see Hilton, *Illiterate Apostles*.
4. Just. *dial*. 81 (Marcovich, *Dialogus*, 211; Eng. tr. mine).
5. Tert. *Marc*. 3.14 (SC 399.132–33).
6. Quoted in Eus. *h.e.* 7.25.1–2 (LCL 265.196–97).
7. Quoted in Eus. *h.e.* 7.25.7 (LCL 265.198–99).
8. Some attribute Revelation to an unknown early Christian prophet (Collins, *Crisis*, 27–44; Culpepper, *John*, 96; Koester, *Revelation*, 68–69).
9. Studies claiming that Revelation is pseudonymously written in the name of John include Strecker, "Chiliasm," 49; Witulski, *Johannesoffenbarung*, 344–45; Vanni, *Apocalisse*, 76, 117; Eurell, "John." Frey sees Revelation as a work pseudonymously attributed to John the Elder by his disciples ("Erwägungen," 425–27; "Apokalypse des Johannes"; "God's Dwelling," 84–85). This hypothesis does not exclude the more nuanced and insightful analysis of the text's "author function" in King, "Author," especially 26–31.
10. There is a continuous tradition of readers assigning the letter to James, the brother of the Lord, dating to the time of Origen (*Comm. Rom.* 4.8 [PG 14.989]). (Note that this identification is still likely even if the author conflated this James with other figures bearing the same name.) Focused discussions of the authorship of the epistle appear in Dibelius, *James*, 11–22; Johnson, *James*, 92–106; Ehrman, *Forgery*, 283–97; Allison, *James*, 3–32.
11. Ehrman, *Forgery*, 284 (also Dibelius, *James*, 11–12).
12. On the anti-Pauline agenda of James, see Allison, *James*, 32–50; Ehrman, *Forgery*, 283–97. This identification is likely even if the author conflated this James with other figures bearing the same name.
13. The author "embraces the label *Ioudaios* and resents that certain others take it illegitimately [2:9; 3:9]. Furthermore, he composes a book based on Jewish traditions of apocalyptic mediation that is steeped in Jewish scripture and that promotes his self-definition as an Israelite tribe member, a suffering Jewish prophet, and an angel/priest of the heavenly cult, while also laying out a perspective fixed on Jerusalem. For such reasons, most commentators have viewed John of Patmos as being an ethnic Jew himself" (Frankfurter, "Jews," 410).
14. This view, first proposed by the Tübingen school, has been recently elaborated by Frankfurter, "Jews"; Frankfurter, "Fiction"; Tomson, *If This Be*, 374–75; Pagels, *Revelations*, 44–64; Trebilco, "John's Apocalypse."
15. Ehrman, *Forgery*, 288–322.
16. The work also embeds seven divine epistles, as if seeking to exceed apostolic authority (Frankfurter, "Seven Letters").
17. Eurell, "John," 514.
18. So, for example, Collins, *Crisis*, 28; Koester, *Revelation*, 67–68.
19. Allison, *James*, 8. (Allison defends this point by citing *1 Enoch*, the *Epistle of Jeremiah*, *3 Baruch Greek*, the *Apocalypse of Peter*, the *Apocalypse of James*, *PBodmer* 5, *Protoevangelium Jacobi*, the *Vision of Ezra*, the *Letters of Paul and Seneca*, the *Apocalypse of Thomas*, *Ep. Peter to James*, and the *Epistles of Socrates*. Many more examples could be added.)
20. Second Peter definitively claims the persona of the apostle Peter (1:1, 16–18, 3:1).
21. On early Christian debates over Revelation, see Nicklas, "Revelation."

22. Iren. *haer.* 1.8.5 (SC 264.128–29). Irenaeus repeats this claim in 2.2.5, 2.22.3, 5, 3.1.1, 3.3.4, 3.11.1–3, 3.16.8, 3.22.2, 4.20.11, 4.30.4, 5.18.2, 5.26.1, 5.33.3, 5.35.2 (SC 294.40–41, 218–19, 224–25, 211.24–25, 40–41, 138–49, 318–19, 436–37, 100.662–63, 786–87, 153.240–41, 324–25, 414–15, 448–49).
23. Iren. *haer.* 1.8.5 (SC 264.128–37).
24. Iren. *haer.* 3.16.5, 8 (SC 211.308–9, 318–21). On the problem of Irenaeus's conflation of 1 and 2 John, see Painter, "Johannine Epistles," 243.
25. Iren. *haer.* 4.20.11 (SC 100.662–63). Also 4.30.4, 5.26.1 (SC 63.786–87, 153.324–25).
26. Exploiting this ambiguity, some scholars speculate that another figure named "John" might be the text's author—perhaps the enigmatic "John the Elder" mentioned by Papias (Hengel, *Johannine Question*; Bauckham, *Testimony*, 33–72; Bauckham, *Eyewitnesses*, 412–71). Nevertheless, as Lorne Zelyck has convincingly shown, the thesis that Irenaeus indicates John the Elder by the epithet "John, the disciple of the Lord" has no positive arguments in its favor and creates several problems ("Irenaeus," 239–58). Irenaeus expressly distinguishes "John, the disciple of the Lord," from "the elders," and he expressly identifies the "elders" Papias cites as "the disciples of the apostles" (*haer.* 5.5.1, 5.36.2 [SC 153.64–65, 458–59]). It is difficult, then, to imagine that Irenaeus could have referred to Papias's John the Elder as an apostle and thus as the Gospel writer. Later authors are also explicit in identifying the Johannine literature with John, the son of Zebedee. On the problems surrounding Irenaeus's claim to personal connections with John via Polycarp, see Hartog, *Polycarp's*, 11–16.
27. For example, Iren. *haer.* 1.9.2–3, 2.22.5, 3.3.4, 5.35.2 (SC 264.138–45, 194.224–25, 211.38–45, 153.448–49).
28. Iren. *haer.* 1.3.2. 3.12.1 (SC 264.52–53, 211.176–77). See arguments in Zelyck, "Irenaeus," 244–52.
29. For example, Iren, *haer.* 1.25.2, 3.12.4–5 (SC 264.334–35, 211.124–25). Calling John "the disciple of the Lord" would also fit the Gospel's use of the epithet "disciple whom Jesus loved" for its narrator.
30. Quoted in Eus. *h.e.* 3.39.4 (LCL 153.292–93).
31. *Letter to Flora*, 3.6 (in ValC 18–19).
32. Iren. *haer.* 3.1.1 (SC 211.24–25; Eng. tr. mine).
33. Iren. *haer.* 2.22.5 (SC 194.224–25; Eng. tr. mine).
34. Quoted in Eus. *h.e.* 6.14.5–7 (LCL 265.46–49).
35. Eus. *h.e.* 6.25.6 (LCL 265.74–75). Farmer, "Patristic Evidence," 9–14, argues that the order of these gospels is not chronological but theological. But Carlson counters that this claim is "undermined by the explicit chronological indicators in the texts and uncorroborated by contemporary evidence of that theological order and its dominance" ("Clement," 119n6).
36. Eus. *h.e.* 3.24.7–14 (LCL 153.250–55).
37. Building on the views of Sundberg ("Canon Muratori") and Hahneman ("Muratorian Fragment"), Clare Rothschild has assembled evidence in favor of the fragment's pseudepigraphic nature and fourth-century date in "Roman Fake" and *Muratorian Fragment*, 309–44. Her views withstand the arguments of Ferguson, "Canon Muratori" and the criticisms of Guignard, "Muratorian Fragment."
38. *Mur. Frag.*, li. 9–16 (Rothschild, *Muratorian Fragment*, 33, 38, capitalization altered).
39. *Acts of Timothy* 9 (MNTA 1.403).
40. For example, Morris, *Studies*, 139–292; Morris, *John*, 4–25; Robinson, *Priority*, 92–122; Carson, *John*, 68–81; Köstenberger, *Theology*, 72–79; Blomberg, *Historical Reliability*, 22–41; Keener, *John*, 1:81–139. In a notable exception, Witherington, "Name" attributes the Gospel to Lazarus.
41. A middle position would have the Gospel written by pupils of John, the son of Zebedee, only to be later (mis)attributed to their teacher (e.g., Barrett, *John*, 132–34).
42. The Papian fragment is quoted in Eus. *h.e.* 3.39.4 (LCL 153.292–93). Studies entertaining this identification include Hengel, *Johannine Question*; Bauckham, *Testimony*, 33–72; Bauckham, *Eyewitnesses*, 412–71. Thompson suggests the same possibility (*John*, 17–18).
43. For example, Brown, *Introduction*, 189–204; Beasley-Murray, *John*, lxvi–lxxv, lxxx–lxxxi; Wengst, *Brief*, 30; Moloney, *John*, 5–9, 561–62; Schnelle, *Johannes*, 1–3, 6–7.
44. Compare Iren. *haer.* 3.1.1 (SC 211.22–25) with the quotation of Clement in Eus. *h.e.* 6.14.6–7 (LCL 265.48–49).
45. Compare Iren. *haer.* 3.16.5, 8 (SC 211.308–9, 318–21) with Eus. *h.e.* 3.25.2–4 (LCL 153.256–57).
46. Iren. *haer.* 3.1.1 (SC 211.22–23), echoing Papias as quoted in Eus. *h.e.* 3.39.16 (LCL 153.296–97).

47. "[T]he reasons for believing that Matthew was composed in Greek are so compelling that the quest for a Hebrew original is best regarded as a dead end, no matter how romantic its pursuit might seem" (Gregory, "Jewish-Christian Gospels," 55).
48. Irenaeus claims a personal connection to John via Polycarp (*haer.* 3.3.4 [211.38-45]), but his misunderstanding of John's authorial contributions to the Gospel and Revelation call any such link—or at least the usefulness of such a link—into question.
49. Hengel, *Johannine Question*. Given how little we possess of Papias's work, and given our knowledge of Papias's unreliability, we should also be cautious handling his appeals to eyewitnesses. For example, we have no way of knowing whether Papias invented the otherwise unattested eyewitnesses he supposedly relies on, as other authors did. (For example, Philostratus seems to have invented Damis as a source for the *Life of Apollonius of Tyana* [Litwa, *Gospels*, 200-203].) There are sound reasons to suspect that Papias might have invented John the Elder. For one, "the few surviving traditions from this John do not appear to be plausible. This means that the unique Jesus traditions conveyed by Papias do not commend themselves as particularly reliable for someone situated in the early second century and perhaps only two steps away from Jesus himself" (Carlson, "Papias," 333). This, of course, assumes we should understand John the Elder as a distinct figure from John, the son of Zebedee (as most recently argued in Carlson, "Papias").
50. Eus. *h.e.* 3.39.6 (LCL 153.292-93). Eubseius may also have identified the Elder with 2 and 3 John (3.25.3 [LCL 153.256-57]).
51. Anderson, "Seamless Robes." Following Brown, Anderson envisions a second edition of the Gospel that was completed by the author of the Epistle—another point not indicated in the patristic tradition (200). A no less selective reading comes from Ben Witherington, "Name," who attributes the core material of John to Lazarus and the final compilation of the Gospel to John of Patmos, whom he insists was not the son of Zebedee.
52. Casey uses this inference to explain why someone would think John wrote the Gospel (*John's Gospel*, 164-70).
53. The text's identification of Pergamum as the site of "Satan's throne" (2:12-13) suggests it might have seen the region as playing a dramatic role in final events (cf. 13:2, 16:10). Alternatively, Will Robinson and Stephen Llewelyn speculate that 1 Peter might have been addressed to churches in Asia Minor "because the work was presented elsewhere (e.g. Rome) thus avoiding the question as to why it had never previously been known"—an analysis that could also hold for Revelation ("Fictitious Audience," 945).
54. Culpepper, *John*, 102. Lincoln correctly observes that "there is nothing in [the Gospel and Letters] themselves to support this claim" of an Ephesus provenance (*John*, 58).
55. Invariably, this sort of cherry-picking leads to contorted models. Consider, for example, Hengel's proposal in *Johannine Question* that the Gospel was written at Ephesus but by Papias's "John the Elder." Hengel presumes John the Elder was at Ephesus, but Papias does not tell us this. Eusebius tells us that John the Elder lived at Ephesus, but he infers John's presence there from secondhand information that two tombs bearing the name "John" exist in the city—precisely to support his opinion that the author of Revelation might be a different "John" than composed the Gospel (*h.e.* 3.39.5-6 [LCL 143.292-93]). Jerome, however, reports, "some think that the two monuments are of the same John, the Evangelist" (*De Vir. Illustr.* 9 [PL 23.623-26; Eng. tr. mine]). Most likely, these tombs were rival sites.
56. On John's dependence upon Matthew, see Barker, *John's Use*. On its dependence on both Matthew and Luke, see Goodacre, "Parallel Traditions"; Attridge, "Other Gospels."
57. *Mur. Frag.* li. 16-18 (Rothschild, *Muratorian Fragment*, 33, 38).
58. Compare the position of Andrew after Peter in the call accounts of Matthew 4:18; Mark 1:16; Luke 6:14.
59. Quoted in Eus. *h.e.* 7.25.6-17 (LCL 265.198-203).
60. Some scholars imagine institutional links between the hypothetical Johannine Community and later Gnostic communities (most famously Brown in *Community*, 93-144 and *Epistles*, 69-115). A better model would see the Gospel as one that circulated among a wide range of groups and which provoked many literary receptions or responses (Méndez, "Historical Criticism," 143-45).
61. Synopsis of Coptic texts in Waldstein and Wisse, *Apocryphon of John*. Introduction and English translation used here in GS 25-61.
62. A more nuanced and complex analysis of the "author function" of the *Secret Book of John*, compatible with the basic insight that the text is pseudepigraphal, appears in King, "What Is an Author?," especially 20-26.

63. *Apoc. John* 1 (Eng. tr. adapted from GS 32).
64. *Apoc. John* 2 (Eng. tr. GS 32).
65. This cosmology integrates and dramatically embellishes individual threads in the Gospel of John (preexistent *Logos*; divine "fullness").
66. *Apoc. John* 32 (Eng. tr. adapted from GS 61).
67. Litwa, *Evil Creator*, 52. See also Turner, "Johannine Legacy," 105, which notes that the text is not compatible with 1 and 2 John. Other studies connecting the Gospel and the *Secret Book* include Logan, "John"; Nagel, *Rezeption*, 393–98; Pleše, *Poetics*, 10, 23–24; King, *Secret Revelation*, 235–38.
68. Pleše, *Poetics*, 23–24, n22.
69. King, *Secret Revelation*, 237–38.
70. *Apoc. John* 31 (Eng. tr. GS 61).
71. See *GThom.* 1 (AG 310–11); *Book of Thomas the Contender* 138.1 (GS 92).
72. See arguments in Watson, *Apostolic Gospel*, 8–11. Other studies select a mid- to late second-century date (Hills, *Epistle*, 3; Koester, *Ancient Christian Gospels*, 312) or one in the first half of the second century (Hornschuh, *Studien*, 116–19; Hill, "Epistula Apostolorum"; Hill, *Johannine Corpus*, 366–67; Hannah, "Four-Gospel 'Canon,'" 598). The provenance of the text is unknown.
73. *Ep. Ap.* 1.1, 4 (Watson, *Apostolic Gospel*, 44).
74. *Ep. Ap.* 2.1–3 (Watson, *Apostolic Gospel*, 44).
75. See, for example, the position of Paul's name above that of his co-authors/scribes in 1 Thess. 1:1; 1 Cor. 1:1; 2 Cor. 1:1; Phil. 1:1; Phlm. 1:1.
76. On the dependence of *Ep. Ap.* on John, see Hornschuh, *Studien*, 9; Nagel, *Rezeption*, 120–56; Hill, *Johannine Corpus*, 367–69; Hartenstein, *Lehre*, 122–23; Watson, "Eleven," 201–15.
77. *Ep. Ap.* 2.3; cf. 2.12 (Watson, *Apostolic Gospel*, 44–45).
78. *Ep. Ap.* 3.13 (Watson, *Apostolic Gospel*, 45).
79. *Ep. Ap.* 3.14 (Watson, *Apostolic Gospel*, 45); cf. John 1:13.
80. *Ep. Ap.* 5.1 (Watson, *Apostolic Gospel*, 46).
81. *Ep. Ap.* 20:3–4 (Watson, *Apostolic Gospel*, 57).
82. *Ep. Ap.* 11:7–12:1 (Watson, *Apostolic Gospel*, 50).
83. *Ep. Ap.* 19.18, 21.3 (Watson, *Apostolic Gospel*, 56, 57).
84. *Ep. Ap.* 25.8 (Watson, *Apostolic Gospel*, 59).
85. *Ep. Ap.* 39.12 (Watson, *Apostolic Gospel*, 70).
86. *Ep. Ap.* 50.8, 11 (Watson, *Apostolic Gospel*, 77).
87. Ehrman, *Forgery*, 437.
88. *Ep. Ap.* 1.4 (Watson, *Apostolic Gospel*, 44).
89. Kelhoffer, *Conceptions*, 244. A critical datum is Irenaeus's claim that the "apocalyptic vision" contained in Revelation was not "seen a long time ago, but almost in our age, near the end of Domitian's reign" (Iren. *haer.* 5.30.3 [SC 153.384–85]), a statement "most early witnesses seem to have understood . . . as dating the book itself to the 90s," as "remains the consensus among scholars today" (Boxall, *Revelation*, 8). Although we cannot trust this report out of hand, the existence of an early rumor, report, or inference that the vision contained in John was "seen . . . near the end of Domitian's reign" makes little sense if Revelation was in wide circulation before the time of Domitian—certainly not for the many decades required by the earliest datings of the book (60s CE). This should at least dissuade us from dating Revelation any earlier than the 90s. A late date also suits the text's reference to Rome as Babylon, its use or adaptation of the *Nero redivivus* myth, and its polemic against the imperial cult (Collins, *Crisis*, 57–58; Friesen, *Imperial Cults*, 136–40). From this starting point, most scholars adopt a date under the reign of Domitian. Scholars arguing for a date during the reign of Trajan include Becker, "Erwägungen," 99–102; Downing, "Pliny's Prosecution"; de Jonge, "Function"; de Jonge, "Apocalypse," 128; Aune, *Revelation*, 1.lviii; Reichert, "Durchdachte Konfusion"; Witetschek, "Zeitfenster"; Kelhoffer, *Conceptions*, 243–44. The most robust defense of a Hadrianic date appears in Witulski, *Johannesoffenbarung*. Conversely, a *terminus ante quem* in the mid-second century is appropriate given Justin's knowledge of Revelation (*dial.* 80–81 [Marcovich, *Dialogus*, 210–12]) and the possibility that Papias also knew the book (suggested by Eus. *h.e.* 3.39.12 [LCL 153.294–97]).
90. A date during Trajan's reign or later suits the idea that Revelation 4:11 reflects an anti-Domitianic polemic arising after Domitian's death (Kelhoffer, *Conceptions*, 243). Scholars also lack reliable evidence indicating that Christians were persecuted under Domitian (Jones, *Domitian*, 114–17; Wilson, "Domitianic Date"; Erlemann, "Datierung"), but they do possess

NOTES 219

evidence of anti-Christian persecution during the reign of Trajan in Pliny, *Ep.* 10.96–97 (though see caveats in Corke-Webster, "Trouble").

91. A comprehensive discussion of these similarities appears in Frey, "Erwägungen." For a different view than Frey, see Fiorenza, "Quest."
92. Both do identify Jesus as preexistent (John 1:1; Rev. 1:8, 21:6, 22:13). Ford, however, argues that Revelation 19:13 is more likely inspired by the image of the "Word of God" as a "stern warrior" in Wisdom 18:15–16 (*Revelation*, 81).
93. Frey, "God's Dwelling," 84. See also Frey, "Erwägungen"; Eurell, "John," 518. Similarly, Paul Trebilco finds it "unlikely that John the author of Revelation was totally unaware of John's Gospel," though he cautions against assuming a "direct or special relationship between the Gospel and 1-2-3 John on the one hand, and Revelation on the other" ("John's Apocalypse," 190–91).
94. Frey's model relies on the problematic assumptions that the Gospel and Epistles of John hail from Ephesus, that they were composed within a Johannine "school," and that the authorial pretense of Revelation is specifically Papias's "John the Elder."
95. Juxtaposed references to the "word" and "testimony" also appear in John 1:2, 9, 6:9, 20:4 (cf. 12:17, 14:12). The "testimony of Jesus" in question may well include the earlier teachings of Jesus, since the author says he came to Patmos because of the testimony of Jesus (1:9; Koester, *Revelation*, 213).
96. A model of weak literary dependence between texts is preferable to those that require positing hypothetical/unattested entities and streams of transmission, such as a pre-Johannine oral tradition (e.g., Frey, "Erwägungen").
97. Allison, *James*, 8. Allison defends this point, citing, among other texts, *1 Enoch*, *Epistle of Jeremiah*, *Apocalypse of Peter*, and the *Protoevangelium Jacobi*.
98. It is, of course, precisely these differences that allow scholars to recognize these works as being from different authors. The existence of at least ideological differences makes sense since the goal of many pseudepigrapha is precisely to dramatically revise existing traditions or chart entirely new paths for them. Linguistic differences may reflect the interest and ability of the writer to imitate the style of previous texts.
99. Frey, "God's Dwelling," 84. Frey uses this point to infer a possible redactional history to Revelation. I, however, am convinced of the unity of Revelation, following Koester, *Revelation*, 69–71.
100. There is no need to insist that John and Revelation should have strong ideological overlap (an assumption informed by the Johannine Community hypothesis challenged throughout this book).
101. Alternatively, if John and Revelation have no such relationship, they might represent a convergence of early Christian literary traditions, one in which two texts were (mis)attributed to the same figure. (We could roughly compare the relationship between John and Revelation to the one linking Peter to 1 Peter and the one probably (mis)judging him as the primary source of Mark's material.) After that convergence, John and Revelation would jointly inform an increasingly complex legendarium of John's life.
102. This expression is taken from Attridge, "Restless Quest."
103. Vienna hist. gr. 63, fol. 51v–55v. The *Gospel of the Acts of John* is an independent text currently reconstructed as chapters 87–105 of the earlier *Acts of John* (CCSA 1.188–217; Spittler, "Vienna"). Lalleman places the *Acts of John* in the first half of the second century (*Acts of John*, 208–12, 268–70); Hill adopts a date at midcentury (*Johannine Corpus*, 259); Junod and Kaestli place the text in the second half of the second century but no later because it influenced other apocryphal acts (CCSA 2:694–700). On *Vienna hist. gr. 63, fol. 51v–55v* (1319 CE) as a likely fragment of the *Acts of John*, see Lalleman, *Acts of John*, 25–30. Schäferdiek, "Acts of John," 164, argues that the text is original to the *Acts of John*, whereas Lalleman, "Acts of John," 48–54, credits it to the final editor of the text. Discussions of the text's parallels with the Gospel appear in Lalleman, *Acts of John*, 110–23; Czachesz, "Gospel"; Attridge, "Acts of John." Barker argues "for the inclusion of the Acts of John within" what scholars would call "the Johannine corpus" ("Acts of John," 340).
104. *1 Apocryphal Apocalypse of John* (MNTA 2.378–98), the *Dormition of the Virgin by the Apostle John* (ANT 701–8), the *Mysteries of John* (MNTA 2.481–98), and the *Questions of John* (*Interrogatio Iohannis*) (MNTA 3.565–83).
105. *Apostolic Constitutions* 8.16.1 (SC 336.216–17).
106. *Gospel of the Twelve Apostles* (MNTA 3.12–35).

107. *3 Apocalypse of John* (MNTA 2.423–60), the *Dialogue of the Revealer and John* (MNTA 2.355–77), the *Gospel of the Twelve Apostles* (MNTA 3.12–35), *John and the Robber* (MNTA 1.362–70), the Latin *Revelation of John about Antichrist* (MNTA 1.483–91), and the *Questions of James to John* (MNTA 2.461–80). The *2 Apocryphal Apocalypse of John* (MNTA 1.423–60) is also likely Johannine despite a later (mis)attribution to John Chrysostom.

108. *Acts of John in Rome* (MNTA 3.241–61); *Acts of John of Prochorus* (MNTA 3.262–361). Interestingly, the *Acts of John of Prochorus* claims the supposed scribe of the Gospel, Prochrous, as its author, situating it even more obviously as a branch of the "Johannine" tree. (The text constructs a relationship between John and Prochorus mirroring that of Peter and Mark, in which the former figures are the sources of Jesus memory, and the latter are formally the Gospel writers.) Like 1 John and the *Secret Book*, then, the text positions itself as a work by the same hand that produced the Gospel of John, but it reassigns that hand to a different person.

109. On the popularity and many uses of John in the second century alone, see Hill, *Johannine Corpus*; Rasimus, *Legacy of John*.

Bibliography

Ahuvia, Mika. "Reimagining the Gender and Class Dynamics of Premodern Composition." *Journal of Ancient Judaism* 14, no. 3 (2023): 321–54.
Alexander, Loveday. "Ancient Book Production and the Circulation of the Gospels." In *The Gospels for All Christians: Rethinking the Gospel Audiences*, edited by Richard Bauckham, 71–111. Edinburgh: T&T Clark, 1998.
Alexander, Philip S. "From Son of Adam to Second God: Transformations of the Biblical Enoch." In *Biblical Figures outside the Bible*, edited by Michael E. Stone and Theodore A. Bergren, 87–122. Harrisburg, PA: Trinity Press International, 1998.
Alexander, Philip S. *Mystical Texts*. Companion to the Qumran Scrolls, no. 7. London: T&T Clark, 2006.
Allison, Dale C., Jr. *A Critical and Exegetical Commentary on the Epistle of James*. ICC. New York: Bloomsbury, 2013.
Allison, Dale C., Jr. "Reflections on Matthew, John, and Jesus." In *Jesus Research: The Gospel of John in Historical Inquiry*, edited by James H. Charlesworth and Jolyon G. R. Pruszinski, 47–70. New York: Bloomsbury, 2019.
Anderson, Paul N. "Aspects of Historicity in the Fourth Gospel: Consensus and Convergences." In *John, Jesus, and History*, vol. 2: *Aspects of Historicity in the Fourth Gospel*, edited by Paul N. Anderson, Felix Just, and Tom Thatcher, 379–86. SBLECL, no. 2. Atlanta, GA: SBL, 2009.
Anderson, Paul N. "On 'Seamless Robes' and 'Leftover Fragments'—A Theory of Johannine Composition." In *The Origins of John's Gospel*, edited by Stanley E. Porter and Hughson T. Ong, 169–218. Johannine Studies, no. 2. Leiden: Brill, 2016.
Anderson, Paul N., Felix Just, and Tom Thatcher. *John, Jesus, and History*. 3 vols. Early Christianity and Its Literature. Atlanta, GA: SBL Press, 2007–16.
Ascough, Richard S. "What Are They Now Saying about Christ Groups and Associations?" *CBR* 13, no. 2 (2015): 207–44.
Ashton, John. *Studying John: Approaches to the Fourth Gospel*. Oxford: Clarendon Press, 1998.
Attridge, Harold W. "The Acts of John and the Fourth Gospel." In *From Judaism to Christianity: Tradition and Transition, a Festschrift for Thomas H. Tobin, S.J., on the Occasion of His Sixty-Fifth Birthday*, edited by Patricia Walters, 255–65. NTSupp 136. Leiden: Brill, 2010.
Attridge, Harold W. "The Cubist Principle in Johannine Imagery: John and the Reading of Images in Contemporary Platonism." In *Essays on John and Hebrews*, 79–91. WUNT, no. 264. Tübingen: Mohr Siebeck, 2010.
Attridge, Harold W. *The Epistle to the Hebrews: A Commentary on the Epistle to the Hebrews*. Hermeneia. Philadelphia: Fortress, 1989.
Attridge, Harold W. "John and Other Gospels." In *The Oxford Handbook of Johannine Studies*, edited by Judith M. Lieu and Martinus C. de Boer, 44–62. Oxford Handbooks. Oxford: Oxford University Press, 2018.
Attridge, Harold W. "Philo and John: Two Riffs on One Logos." In *Essays on John and Hebrews*, 46–59. WUNT, no. 264. Tübingen: Mohr Siebeck, 2010.
Attridge, Harold W. "The Restless Quest for the Beloved Disciple." In *Essays on John and Hebrews*, 20–29. WUNT, no. 264. Tübingen: Mohr Siebeck, 2010.
Attridge, Harold W. "Thematic Development and Source Elaboration in John 7:1–36." In *Essays on John and Hebrews*, 105–14. WUNT, no. 264. Tübingen: Mohr Siebeck, 2010.

Aune, David E. "Reconceptualizing the Phenomenon of Ancient Pseudepigraphy." In *Pseudepigraphie und Verfasserfiktion in frühchristlichen Briefen*, edited by Jörg Frey, Jens Herzer, Martina Janßen, and Clare K. Rothschild, 789–824. WUNT, no. 246. Tübingen: Mohr Siebeck, 2009.

Aune, David E. *Revelation*. 3 vols. Word Biblical Commentary, no. 52A–C. Dallas, TX: Word, 1997–98.

Ball, David Mark. *"I Am" in John's Gospel: Literary Function, Background and Theological Implications*. Vol. 124. JSNTSupp. Sheffield: Sheffield Academy Press, 1996.

Barker, James W. "The Acts of John within the Johannine Corpus." In *Studies on the Intersection of Text, Paratext, and Reception: A Festschrift in Honor of Charles E. Hill*, edited by Gregory R. Lanier and J. Nicholas Reid, 340–80. TENT, no. 15. Leiden: Brill, 2021.

Barker, James W. *John's Use of Matthew*. Minneapolis, MN: Fortress, 2015.

Barker, James W. *Writing and Rewriting the Gospels: John and the Synoptics*. Grand Rapids, MI: Eerdmans, 2024.

Baron, Lori A. *The Shema in John's Gospel*. WUNT/2, no. 574. Tübingen: Mohr Siebeck, 2022.

Barrett, C. K. *The Gospel According to St. John: An Introduction with Commentary and Notes on the Greek Text*. 2nd edition. Philadelphia: Westminster, 1978.

Barrett, C. K. "John and the Synoptic Gospels." *Expository Times* 85, no. 8 (1974): 228–33.

Barus, Armand. "John. 2:12–25: A Narrative Reading." In *New Currents through John: A Global Perspective*, edited by Francisco Lozada and Tom Thatcher, 123–40. SBLRBS, no. 54. Atlanta, GA: SBL, 2006.

Bauckham, Richard. "The Bethany Family in John 11–12: History or Fiction?" In *John, Jesus, and History*, vol. 2: *Aspects of Historicity in the Fourth Gospel*, edited by Paul N. Anderson, Felix Just, and Tom Thatcher, 185–201. SBLECL, no. 2. Atlanta, GA: SBL, 2009.

Bauckham, Richard. "For Whom Were Gospels Written?" In *The Gospels for All Christians: Rethinking the Gospel Audience*, edited by Richard Bauckham, 9–48. Edinburgh: T&T Clark, 1998.

Bauckham, Richard. *Jesus and the Eyewitnesses: The Gospels as Eyewitness Testimony*, 2nd edition. Grand Rapids, MI: Eerdmans, 2017.

Bauckham, Richard. "John for Readers of Mark." In *The Gospels for All Christians: Rethinking the Gospel Audience*, edited by Richard Bauckham, 147–71. Edinburgh: T&T Clark, 1998.

Bauckham, Richard. "The 153 Fish and the Unity of the Fourth Gospel." *Neot* 36, nos. 1–2 (2002): 77–88.

Bauckham, Richard. *The Testimony of the Beloved Disciple: Narrative, History, and Theology in the Gospel of John*. Grand Rapids, MI: Baker Academic, 2007.

Baum, Armin D. "The Anonymity of the New Testament History Books: A Stylistic Device in the Context of Greco-Roman and Ancient Near Eastern Literature." *NovT* 50, no. 2 (2008): 120–42.

Baum, Armin D. "Authorship and Pseudepigraphy in Early Christian Literature: A Translation of the Most Important Source Texts and an Annotated Bibliography." In *Paul and Pseudepigraphy*, edited by Stanley E. Porter, 11–63. Pauline Studies 8. Leiden: Brill, 2013.

Baum, Armin D. "The Original Epilogue (John 20:30–31), the Secondary Appendix (21:1–23) and the Editorial Epilogues (21:24–25) of John's Gospel." In *Earliest Christian History: History, Literature, and Theology; Essays from the Tyndale Fellowship in Honor of Martin Hengel*, edited by Michael Bird and Jason Matson, 227–72. WUNT/2 320. Tübingen: Mohr Siebeck, 2012.

Beasley-Murray, George R. *John*. 2nd edition. Word Biblical Commentary. Nashville, TN: Thomas Nelson, 1999.

Beavis, Mary Ann. *Mark's Audience: The Literary and Social Setting of Mark 4.11–12*. London: Bloomsbury Academic, 2015.

Becker, Eve-Marie. *The Birth of Christian History. Memory and Time from Mark to Luke-Acts*. New Haven, CT: Yale University Press, 2017.

Becker, Eve-Marie, Helen K. Bond, and Catrin H. Williams, eds. *John's Transformation of Mark*. London: T&T Clark, 2021.

Becker, Eve-Marie, Helen K. Bond, and Catrin H. Williams. "John's Transformation of Mark: Introduction." In *John's Transformation of Mark*, edited by Eve-Marie Becker, Helen K. Bond, and Catrin H. Williams, 1–8. London: T&T Clark, 2021.

Becker, Eve-Marie, Troels Engberg-Pedersen, and Mogens Mueller, eds. *Mark and Paul: Comparative Essays. Part II. For and against Pauline Influence on Mark*. BZNW, no. 199. Berlin: De Gruyter, 2014.

Becker, Joachim. "Erwägungen zu Fragen der neutestamentlichen Exegese." *Biblische Zeitschrift* 13, nos. 3–4 (1969): 99–102.

Becker, Jürgen. "Die Abschiedsreden Jesu im Johannesevangelium." *ZNW* 61 (1970): 215–46.

Becker, Jürgen. "Die Herde des Hirten und die Reben am Weinstock: Ein Versuch zu Joh 10,1–18 und 15,1–17." In *Die Gleichnisreden Jesu 1899–1999: Beiträge zum Dialog mit Adolf Jülicher*, edited by Ulrich Mell, 149–78. BZNW 103. Berlin: De Gruyter, 1999.

Becker, Ulrich. *Jesus Und Die Ehebrecherin: Untersuchungen Zur Text- Und Überlieferungsgeschichte von Johannes 7,53–8,11*. Berlin: De Gruyter, 1959.

Bernier, Jonathan. *Rethinking the Dates of the New Testament: The Evidence for Early Composition*. Grand Rapids, MI: Baker Academic, 2022.

Bickermann, E., and J. Sykutris, "Speusipps Brief an König Philipp: Text, Übersetzung, Untersuchungen." In *Berichte über die Verhandlungen der Sächsischen Akademie der Wissenschaften zu Leipzig*, 1–86. Philologisch-historische Klasse 80, no. 3. Leipzig: Teubner, 1928.

Bird, Michael F. "The Markan Community, Myth or Maze? Bauckham's 'The Gospel for All Christians' Revisited." *JTS* 57, no. 2 (2006): 474–86.

Blackwell, Ben C. *Christosis: Engaging Paul's Soteriology with His Patristic Interpreters*. Grand Rapids, MI: Eerdmans, 2016.

Blank, Josef. *Das Evangelium nach Johannes*. 3 vols. Geistliche Schriftlesung. Düsseldorf: Patmos, 1981.

Blomberg, Craig L. *The Historical Reliability of the Gospels*. 2nd edition. Downers Grove, IL: IVP Academic, 2007.

Boismard, M.-É., and A. Lamouille, eds. *L'Évangile de Jean*. Synopse des quatre évangiles en français, no. 3. Paris: Cerf, 1977.

Booth, Jennifer. "Dr. Drewe—A Cautionary Tale." *Art Libraries Journal* 28, no. 2 (2003): 14–17.

Booth, Wayne C. *The Rhetoric of Fiction*. 2nd edition. Chicago: University of Chicago Press, 1983.

Borgen, Peder. *The Gospel of John: More Light from Philo, Paul and Archaeology: The Scriptures, Tradition, Exposition, Settings, Meaning*. Leiden: Brill, 2014.

Bowie, E. L. "Apollonius of Tyana: Tradition and Reality." *Aufstieg und Niedergang der römischen Welt*, part 2, 16, no. 2 (1978): 1652–99.

Bowie, E. L. "Philostratus: Writer of Fiction." In *Greek Fiction: The Greek Novel in Context*, edited by J. R. Morgan and R. Stoneman, 181–99. London: Routledge, 1994.

Boxall, Ian. *Patmos in the Reception History of the Apocalypse*. Oxford Theology and Religion Monographs. Oxford: Oxford University Press, 2013.

Boxall, Ian. *Revelation: Vision and Insight. An Introduction to the Apocalypse*. London: SPCK, 2002.

Boyarin, Daniel. "Logos, a Jewish Word: John's Prologue as Midrash." In *The Jewish Annotated New Testament*, edited by Amy-Jill Levine and Marc Zvi Brettler, 546–49. New York: Oxford University Press, 2011.

Brakke, David. *The Gnostics: Myth, Ritual, and Diversity in Early Christianity*. Cambridge, MA: Harvard University Press, 2010.

Brakke, David. *The Gospel of Judas: A New Translation with Introduction and Commentary*. New Haven, CT: Yale University Press, 2022.

Breck, John. "John 21: Appendix, Epilogue or Conclusion?" *SVTQ* 36, nos. 1–2 (1992): 27–49.

Brodie, Thomas L. *The Gospel According to John: A Literary and Theological Commentary*. New York: Oxford University Press, 1997.
Brodie, Thomas L. *The Quest for the Origin of John's Gospel: A Source-Critical Approach*. New York: Oxford University Press, 1993.
Brown, Raymond E. *The Community of the Beloved Disciple*. New York: Paulist Press, 1979.
Brown, Raymond E. *The Epistles of John*. AB, no. 30. Garden City, NY: Doubleday, 1982.
Brown, Raymond E. *The Gospel of John I–XII*. AB 29–29A. Garden City, NY: Doubleday, 1966–70.
Brown, Raymond E. *An Introduction to the Gospel of John*. Edited by Francis J. Moloney. ABRL. New York: Doubleday, 2003.
Brown, Sherri, and Christopher W. Skinner, eds. *Johannine Ethics: The Moral World of the Gospel and Epistles of John*. Minneapolis, MN: Fortress, 2017.
Buch-Hansen, Gitte. *"It Is the Spirit That Gives Life": A Stoic Understanding of Pneuma in John's Gospel*. BZNW, no. 173. Berlin: De Gruyter, 2010.
Bultmann, Rudolf K. *The Gospel of John: A Commentary*. Translated by G. R. Beasley-Murray, R. W. N. Hoare, and J. K. Riches. Philadelphia: Westminster Press, 1971.
Busse, Ulrich. "Die 'Hellenen' Joh 12,20ff. und der sogenannte 'Anhang' Joh 21. Eine Skizze." In *The Four Gospels 1992: Festschrift Frans Neirynck*, vol. 3, edited by Frans Van Segbroeck and Frans Neirynck, 1799–814. BETL 100. Leuven: University Press, 1992.
Busse, Ulrich. "Die Tempelmetaphorik als ein Beispiel von implizitem Rekurs auf die biblische Tradition im Johannesevangelium." In *Jesus im Gespräch: Zur Bildrede in den Evangelien und der Apostelgeschichte*, edited by Ulrich Busse, 213–45. Stuttgarter biblische Aufsatzbände, no. 43: Neues Testament. Stuttgart: Verlag Katholisches Bibelwerk, 2009.
Busse, Ulrich. "Metaphorik und Rhetorik im Johannesevangelium: Das Bildfeld vom König." In *Imagery in the Gospel of John: Terms, Forms, Themes, and Theology of Johannine Figurative Language*, edited by Jörg Frey and Gabi Kern, 279–317. WUNT, no. 200. Tübingen: Mohr Siebeck, 2006.
Byers, Andrew J. *Ecclesiology and Theosis in the Gospel of John*. SNTSMS 166. Cambridge: Cambridge University Press, 2017.
Byrskog, Samuel. "History or Story in Acts—a Middle Way? The 'We' Passages, Historical Intertexture, and Oral History." In *Contextualizing Acts: Lukan Narrative and Greco-Roman Discourse*, edited by Todd C. Penner and Caroline Vander Stichele, 257–83. SBL Symposium Series, no. 20. Atlanta, GA: SBL, 2003.
Campbell, Constantine R. *Paul and Union with Christ: An Exegetical and Theological Study*. Grand Rapids, MI: Zondervan, 2012.
Campbell, William S. "The Narrator as 'He,' 'Me,' and 'We': Grammatical Person in Ancient Histories and in the Acts of the Apostles." *JBL* 129, no. 2 (2010): 385–407.
Campbell, William S. *The "We" Passages in the Acts of the Apostles: The Narrator as Narrative Character*. SBL Studies in Biblical Literature, no. 14. Atlanta, GA: SBL, 2007.
Carlson, Stephen C. "Clement of Alexandria on the 'Order' of the Gospels." *NTS* 47, no. 1 (2001): 118–25.
Carlson, Stephen C. "Papias, John, and Jesus." In *John, Jesus, and History*, vol. 4: *Jesus Remembered in the Johannine Situation*, edited by Paul N. Anderson, Felix Just, and Tom Thatcher, 83–92. SBLECL, no. 34. Atlanta, GA: SBL, 2024.
Carlson, Stephen C., ed. *Papias of Hierapolis Exposition of Dominical Oracles: The Fragments, Testimonia, and Reception of a Second-Century Commentator*. OECT. Oxford: Oxford University Press, 2021.
Carson, D. A. *The Gospel According to John*. Grand Rapids, MI: Eerdmans, 1990.
Casey, Maurice. *Is John's Gospel True?* London: Routledge, 1996.
Charlesworth, James H. *The Beloved Disciple: Whose Witness Validates the Gospel of John?* Valley Forge, PA: Trinity Press International, 1995.
Clark-Soles, Jaime. *Death and the Afterlife in the New Testament*. New York: T&T Clark, 2006.

Clark-Soles, Jaime. "Of Footwashing and History." In *John, Jesus, and History*, vol. 2: *Aspects of Historicity in the Fourth Gospel*, edited by Paul N. Anderson, Felix Just, and Tom Thatcher, 255–70. SBLECL, no. 2. Atlanta, GA: SBL, 2009.

Collins, Adela Yarbro. *Crisis and Catharsis: The Power of the Apocalypse*. Philadelphia: Westminster Press, 1984.

Collins, Adela Yarbro. *Mark: A Commentary*. Hermeneia. Minneapolis, MN: Fortress, 2007.

Collins, John J. "The Afterlife in Apocalyptic Literature." In *Judaism in Late Antiquity*, part 4: *Death, Life-after-Death, Resurrection and the World-to-Come in the Judaisms of Antiquity*, edited by Alan J. Avery-Peck and Jacob Neusner, 119–39. Handbuch der Orientalistik, I, 49,4. Leiden: Brill, 2000.

Collins, John J. "Apocalyptic Eschatology as the Transcendence of Death." In *Seers, Sybils and Sages in Hellenistic Roman Judaism*, edited by John J. Collins, 75–97. JSJSupp 54. Leiden: Brill, 1997.

Collins, John J. "The Self-Glorification Hymn from Qumran." In *Crossing Boundaries in Early Judaism and Christianity: Ambiguities, Complexities, and Half-Forgotten Adversaries*, edited by Andrea Lieber and Kimberly B. Sratton, 25–40. JSJSupp, no. 177. Leiden: Brill, 2016.

Coloe, Mary L. *Dwelling in the Household of God: Johannine Ecclesiology and Spirituality*. Collegeville, MN: Liturgical Press, 2007.

Coloe, Mary L. *God Dwells with Us: Temple Symbolism in the Fourth Gospel*. Collegeville, MN: Liturgical Press, 2001.

Coloe, Mary L. *John*. 2 vols. Wisdom Commentary 44A–44B. Collegeville, MN: Liturgical Press, 2021.

Coloe, Mary L. "Sources in the Shadows: John 13 and the Johannine Community." In *New Currents through John: A Global Perspective*, edited by Francisco Lozada, 69–82. SBLRBS 54. Atlanta, GA: SBL, 2006.

Coloe, Mary L. "Welcome into the Household of God: The Foot Washing in John 13." *CBQ* 66, no. 3 (2004): 400–415.

Coogan, Jeremiah. "Imagining Gospel Authorship: Anonymity, Collaboration, and Monography in a Pluriform Corpus." In *Authorial Fictions and Attributions in the Ancient Mediterranean*, edited by Chance Bonar and Julia Lindenlaub, 203–23. WUNT/2, no. 609. Tübingen: Mohr Siebeck.

Coogan, Jeremiah. "The Ways That Parted in the Library: The Gospels According to Matthew and According to the Hebrews in Late Ancient Heresiology." *Journal of Ecclesiastical History* 74, no. 3 (2023): 473–90.

Coogan, Jeremiah, and Candida R. Moss. "The Textual Demiurge: Social Status and the Academic Discourse of Early Christian Forgery." *NTS* 70, no. 3 (2024): 307–23.

Coogan, Jeremiah, Candida R. Moss, and Joseph A. Howley, eds. *Writing, Enslavement, and Power in the Roman Mediterranean, 100 bce–300 ce*. New York: Oxford University Press, 2024.

Corke-Webster, James. "Trouble in Pontus: The Pliny-Trajan Correspondence on the Christians Reconsidered." *TAPA* 147, no. 2 (2017): 371–411.

Corsar, Elizabeth J. B. "John's Use of Mark: A Study in Light of Ancient Compositional Practices." PhD diss., University of Edinburgh, 2019.

Corsar, Elizabeth J. B. "The Legacy of the Beloved Disciple: The Johannine Letters as Epistolary Fiction." In *The Johannine Community in Contemporary Debate*, edited by Christopher Seglenieks and Christopher W. Skinner, 157–71. Lexington, KY: Fortress Academic, 2024.

Culpepper, R. Alan. *Anatomy of the Fourth Gospel: A Study in Literary Design*. Foundations and Facets: New Testament. Philadelphia: Fortress, 1983.

Culpepper, R. Alan. "The Johannine Hypodeigma: A Reading of John 13." *Semeia* 53 (1991): 133–52.

Culpepper, R. Alan. *The Johannine School*. SBL Dissertation Series, no. 26. Missoula, MT: Scholars Press, 1975.

Culpepper, R. Alan. *John, the Son of Zebedee: The Life of a Legend.* Studies on Personalities of the New Testament. Columbia: University of South Carolina Press, 1994.

Culpepper, R. Alan. "The Relationship between the Gospel and 1 John." In *Communities in Dispute: Current Scholarship on the Johannine Epistles,* edited by R. Alan Culpepper and Paul N. Anderson, 95–122. SBLECL, no. 13. Atlanta, GA: SBL, 2014.

Czachesz, István. "The Gospel of the Acts of John: Its Relation to the Fourth Gospel." In *The Legacy of John,* edited by Rasimus Tuomus, 49–72. NovTSup 132. Leiden: Brill, 2009.

Daube, David. "On Acts 23: Sadducees and Angels." *JBL* 109, no. 3 (1990): 493–97.

de Boer, Martinus C. "Jesus' Departure to the Father in John: Death or Resurrection?" In *Theology and Christology in the Fourth Gospel: Essays by the Members of the SNTS Johannine Writings Seminar,* edited by Gilbert van Belle, Jan G. van der Watt, and Petrus Maritz, 1–19. BETL 184. Leuven: Peeters, 2005.

de Boer, Martinus C. "The Johannine Community under Attack in Recent Scholarship." In *The Ways That Often Parted: Essays in Honor of Joel Marcus,* edited by Lori A. Baron, Jill Hicks-Keeton, and Matthew Thiessen, 211–42. SBLECL, no. 24. Atlanta, GA: SBL, 2018.

de Boer, Martinus C. "The Story of the Johannine Community and Its Literature." In *Oxford Handbook of Johannine Studies,* edited by Judith Lieu and Martinus C. de Boer, 63–82. Oxford Handbooks. Oxford: Oxford University Press, 2018.

DeConick, April D. *Seek to See Him: Ascent and Vision Mysticism in the Gospel of Thomas.* Library of Early Christology. Waco, TX: Baylor University Press, 2017.

DeConick, April D. "Who Is Hiding in the Gospel of John? Reconceptualizing Johannine Theology and the Roots of Gnosticism." In *Histories of the Hidden God: Concealment and Revelation in Western Gnostic, Esoteric, and Mystical Traditions,* edited by April D. DeConick, 13–29. Gnostica. Durham, NC: Acumen, 2013.

Deissmann, Adolf. *St. Paul: A Study in Social and Religious History.* 2nd edition. Translated by W. E. Wilson. New York: Hodder and Stoughton, 1926.

de Jonge, Henk Jan. "The Apocalypse of John and the Imperial Cult." In *Kykeon: Studies in Honour of H. S. Versnel,* edited by H. F. J. Horstmanshoff, H. W. Singor, F. T. van Straten, and J. H. M. Strubbe, 127–42. Religions in the Graeco-Roman World, no. 142. Leiden: Brill, 2002.

de Jonge, Henk Jan. "The Function of Religious Polemics: The Case of the Revelation of John versus the Imperial Cult." In *Religious Polemics in Context: Papers Presented to the Second International Conference of the Leiden Institute for the Study of Religions (Lisor) Held at Leiden, 27–28 April, 2000,* edited by Theo L. Hettema and Aari van der Kooij, 276–90. Studies in Theology and Religion 11. Assen: Van Gorcum, 2004.

Denaux, Adelbert, ed. *John and the Synoptics.* BETL, no. 101. Leuven: Peeters, 1992.

Dewey, Kim E. "Paroimiai in the Gospel of John." *Semeia* 17 (1980): 81–99.

Dibelius, Martin, and Heinrich Greeven. *James: A Commentary on the Epistle of James.* Hermeneia. Philadelphia: Fortress, 1976.

Dietzfelbinger, Christian. *Der Abschied des Kommenden: Eine Auslegung der Johanneischen Abschiedsreden.* WUNT, no. 95. Tübingen: Mohr, 1997.

Dimant, Devorah. "Men as Angels: The Self-Image of the Qumran Community." In *History, Ideology and Bible Interpretation in the Dead Sea Scrolls: Collected Studies,* edited by Divorah Dimant, 465–72. Forschungen zum Alten Testament 90. Tübingen: Mohr Siebeck, 2014.

DiTommaso, Lorenzo, and Lucian Turcescu, eds. *The Reception and Interpretation of the Bible in Late Antiquity: Proceedings of the Montréal Colloquium in Honour of Charles Kannengiesser, 11–13 October 2006.* Leiden: Brill, 2008.

Dodd, Charles H. "The First Epistle of John and the Fourth Gospel." *Bulletin of the John Rylands Library* 21, no. 1 (1937): 129–56.

Dodd, Charles H. "A Hidden Parable in the Fourth Gospel." In *More New Testament Studies,* 30–40. Manchester: Manchester University Press, 1968.

Dodd, Charles H. *Historical Tradition in the Fourth Gospel.* Cambridge: Cambridge University Press, 1976.

Dodd, Charles H. *The Interpretation of the Fourth Gospel*. Cambridge: Cambridge University Press, 1968.

Downing, F. Gerald. "Pliny's Prosecutions of Christians: Revelation and 1 Peter." *JSNT* 11, no. 34 (1988): 105–23.

Dunderberg, Ismo. *The Beloved Disciple in Conflict? Revisiting the Gospels of John and Thomas*. New York: Oxford University Press, 2006.

Dunn, James D. G. *Baptism in the Holy Spirit: A Re-examination of the New Testament Teaching on the Gift of the Spirit in Relation to Pentecostalism Today*. Philadelphia: Westminster Press, 1977.

Dunn, James D. G. *The Theology of Paul the Apostle*. Grand Rapids, MI: Eerdmanns, 2008.

Duprez, Antoine. *Jésus et les Dieux Guerisseurs: A Propos de Jean, V*. Cahiers de la Revue Biblique, no. 12. Pans: Gabalda, 1970.

Dzielska, M. *Apollonius of Tyana in Legend and History*. Rome: L'Erma, 1986.

Eastman, Susan Grove. *Oneself in Another: Participation and Personhood in Pauline Theology*. Cascade Library of Pauline Studies. Eugene, OR: Cascade, 2023.

Edsall, Benjamin A., and Jennifer R. Strawbridge. "The Songs We Used to Sing? Hymn 'Traditions' and Reception in Pauline Letters." *JSNT* 37, no. 3 (2015): 290–311.

Edwards, M. J. "Damis the Epicurean." *Classical Quarterly* 41, no. 2 (1991): 563–66.

Edwards, Ruth B. *Discovering John: Content, Interpretation, Reception*. Grand Rapids, MI: Eerdmans, 2015.

Ehrman, Bart D. *Forgery and Counterforgery: The Use of Literary Deceit in Early Christian Polemics*. New York: Oxford University Press, 2013.

Ehrman, Bart D. *The Orthodox Corruption of Scripture: The Effect of Early Christological Controversies on the Text of the New Testament*. New York: Oxford University Press, 1996.

Elder, Nicholas A. *Gospel Media: Reading, Writing, and Circulating Jesus Traditions*. Grand Rapids, MI: Eerdmans, 2024.

Elledge, C. D. *Resurrection of the Dead in Early Judaism, 200 BCE–CE 200*. Oxford: Oxford University Press, 2017.

Ellis, Peter F. "The Authenticity of John 21." *SVTQ* 36, nos. 1–2 (1992): 17–25.

Engberg-Pedersen, Troels. *Cosmology and Self in the Apostle Paul: The Material Spirit*. Oxford: Oxford University Press, 2010.

Engberg-Pedersen, Troels. *John and Philosophy: A New Reading of the Fourth Gospel*. Oxford: Oxford University Press, 2017.

Engberg-Pedersen, Troels. *Paul and the Stoics*. Edinburgh: T&T Clark, 2000.

Erlemann, Kurt. "Die Datierung des ersten Klemensbriefes—Anfragen an eine Communis Opiniokurt Erlemann." *NTS* 44, no. 4 (1998): 591–607.

Eurell, John-Christian. "Reconsidering the John of Revelation." *NovT* 63, no. 4 (2021): 505–18.

Evans, Ernest, ed. and trans. *Tertullian's Homily on Baptism*. London: SPCK, 1964.

Farmer, William R. "The Patristic Evidence Reexamined: A Response to George Kennedy." In *New Synoptic Studies: The Cambridge Gospel Conference and Beyond*, edited by William R. Farmer, 1–15. Macon, GA: Mercer University Press, 1983.

Ferguson, Cameron Evan. "Paul's Possible Influence on the Synoptics." In *The Oxford Handbook of the Synoptic Gospels*, edited by Stephen P. Ahearne-Kroll, 81–99. Oxford: Oxford University Press, 2023.

Ferguson, E. "Canon Muratori: Date and Provenance." In *Studia Patristica: Eighth International Congress on Patristic Studies, Oxford, Sept. 3–8, 1979*, edited by Elizabeth A. Livingstone, 677–83. Oxford: Pergamon, 1982.

Ferraro, Giuseppe. *Lo Spirito e l' "ora" Di Cristo: L'esegesi Di San Tommaso d'Aquino Sul Quarto Vangelo*. Città del Vaticano: Libreria Editrice Vaticana, 1996.

Finlan, Stephen. "Can We Speak of 'Theosis' in Paul?" In *Partakers of the Divine Nature: The History and Development of Deification in the Christian Traditions*, edited by Michael J. Christensen and Jeffery A. Wittung, 68–80. Grand Rapids, MI: Baker Academic, 2008.

BIBLIOGRAPHY

Fischer, David Hackett. *Historians' Fallacies: Toward a Logic of Historical Thought.* London: Routledge, 1971.

Fitzgerald, William. "The Slave, between Absence and Presence." In *Unspoken Rome: Absence in Latin Literature and Its Reception*, edited by Tom Geue and Elena Giusti, 239–49. Cambridge: Cambridge University Press, 2021.

Fitzgerald, William. *Slavery and the Roman Literary Imagination.* Cambridge: Cambridge University Press, 2000.

Fletcher-Louis, Crispin H. T. *All the Glory of Adam: Liturgical Anthropology in the Dead Sea Scrolls.* Studies on the Texts of the Desert of Judah, no. 42. Leiden: Brill, 2002.

Fletcher-Louis, Crispin H. T. *Luke-Acts: Angels, Christology, and Soteriology.* WUNT, no. 94. Tübingen: Mohr Siebeck, 1997.

Ford, Josephine Massyngberde. *Revelation.* AB, no. 38. Garden City, NY: Doubleday, 1985.

Forger, Deborah L. "Divine Embodiment in Jewish Antiquity: Rediscovering the Jewishness of John's Incarnate Christ." PhD diss., University of Michigan, 2017.

Forger, Deborah L. "Jesus as God's Word(s): Aurality, Epistemology and Embodiment in the Gospel of John." *JSNT* 42, no. 3 (2020): 274–302.

Fortna, Robert T. *The Gospel of Signs: A Reconstruction of the Narrative Source Underlying the Fourth Gospel.* SNTSMS, no. 11. London: Cambridge University Press, 1970.

Foucault, Michel. "What Is an Author?" («Qu'est-ce qu'un auteur?»). In *Textual Strategies: Perspectives in Post-structuralist Criticism*, edited by Josue V. Harari, 141–60. Ithaca, NY: Cornell University Press, 1979.

Frankfurter, David. "The Fiction of the Seven Letters in the Apocalypse: Representing Heavenly Authority in the Shadow of Paul." *HTR* 117, no. 1 (2024): 79–98.

Frankfurter, David. "Jews or Not? Reconstructing the 'Other' in Rev 2:9 and 3:9." *HTR* 94, no. 4 (2001): 403–25.

Fredriksen, Paula. "How High Can Early High Christology Be?" In *Monotheism and Christology in Greco-Roman Antiquity*, edited by Matthew V. Novensen, 293–320. NovTSupp, no. 180. Leiden: Brill, 2020.

Fredriksen, Paula. "Mandatory Retirement: Ideas in the Study of Christian Origins Whose Time Has Come to Go." *Studies in Religion/Sciences Religieuses* 35, no. 2 (2006): 231–46.

Fredriksen, Paula. "Philo, Herod, Paul, and the Many Gods of Ancient Jewish 'Monotheism.'" *HTR* 115, no. 1 (2022): 23–45.

Frey, Jörg. "Das Corpus Johanneum und die Apokalypse des Johannes: Die Johanneslegende, die Probleme der johanneischen Verfasserschaft und die Frage der Pseudonymität der Apokalypse." In *Poetik und Intertextualität der Johannesapokalypse*, edited by Stefan Alkier, Thomas Hieke, and Tobias Nicklas, 71–133. WUNT, no. 346. Tübingen: Mohr Siebeck, 2015.

Frey, Jörg. "Das vierte Evangelium auf dem Hintergrund der älteren Evangelientradition. Zum Problem: Johannes und die Synoptiker." In *Die Herrlichkeit des Gekreuzigten*, 239–96. Tübingen: Mohr Siebeck, 2013.

Frey, Jörg. *Die johanneische Eschatologie.* 3 vols. WUNT, no. 96, 110, 117. Tübingen: Mohr Siebeck, 1997–2000.

Frey, Jörg. "Erwägungen zum Verhältnis der Johannesapokalypse zu den übrigen: Schriften im Corpus Johanneum." In Martin Hengel, *Die johanneische Frage: Ein Lösungsversuch. Mit einem Beitrag zur Apokalypse von J. Frey*, 326–429. WUNT, no. 67. Tübingen: Mohr Siebeck, 1993.

Frey, Jörg. "From the Sēmeia Narratives to the Gospel as a Significant Narrative: On Genre-Bending in the Johannine Miracle Stories." In *The Gospel of John as Genre Mosaic*, edited by Kasper Bro Larsen, 209–32. Studia Aarhusiana Neotestamentica, no. 3. Göttingen: Vandenhoeck & Ruprecht, 2015.

Frey, Jörg. "God's Dwelling on Earth: 'Shekhina-Theology' in Revelation 21 and in the Gospel of John." In *John's Gospel and Intimations of Apocalyptic*, edited by Catrin H. Williams and Christopher Rowlands, 79–103. London: Bloomsbury, 2013.

Frey, Jörg. "Johannine Theology as the Climax of New Testament Theology." In *The Glory of the Crucified One: Theology and Christology in the Fourth Gospel*, translated by Wayne Coppins and Christoph Heilig, 347–76. BMSEC. Waco, TX: Baylor University Press, 2018.

Frey, Jörg, Jens Herzer, Martina Janßen, and Clare K. Rothschild. *Pseudepigraphie und Verfasserfiktion in frühchristlichen Briefen*. WUNT, no. 246. Tübingen: Mohr Siebeck, 2009.

Friedman, Richard Elliott, ed. *The Bible with Sources Revealed: A New View into the Five Books of Moses*. San Francisco: HarperSanFrancisco, 2003.

Friesen, Steven J. *Imperial Cults and the Apocalypse of John: Reading Revelation in the Ruins*. New York: Oxford University Press, 2001.

Fuller, Reginald H. "Christmas, Epiphany, and the Johannine Prologue." In *Spirit and Light: Essays in Historical Theology*, edited by M. L. Engle and W. B. Green, 63–73. New York: Seabury Press, 1976.

Furlong, Dean. *The Identity of John the Evangelist: Revision and Reinterpretation in Early Christian Sources*. Lanham, MD: Lexington Books/Fortress Academic, 2020.

Gamble, Harold Y. *Books and Readers in the Early Church: A History of Early Christian Texts*. New Haven, CT: Yale University Press, 1995.

Gardner-Smith, P. *Saint John and the Synoptic Gospels*. Cambridge: Cambridge University Press, 1938.

Gathercole, Simon J. "The Alleged Anonymity of the Canonical Gospels." *JTS* 69, no. 2 (2018): 447–76.

Gathercole, Simon J. *The Composition of the Gospel of Thomas: Original Language and Influences*. SNTSMS 151. Cambridge: Cambridge University Press, 2012.

Gathercole, Simon J. *The Gospel of Thomas: Introduction and Commentary*. TENT, no. 11. Leiden: Brill, 2014.

Gathercole, Simon J. "Thomas Revisited: A Rejoinder to Denzey Lewis, Kloppenborg and Patterson." *JSNT* 36, no. 3 (2014): 262–81.

Gaventa, Beverly Roberts. "The Archive of Excess: John 21 and the Problem of Narrative Closure." In *Exploring the Gospel of John: In Honor of D. Moody Smith*, edited by R. Alan Culpepper and C. Clifton Black, 240–52. Louisville, KY: Westminster John Knox, 1996.

Geue, Tom. *Author Unknown: The Power of Anonymity in Ancient Rome*. Cambridge, MA: Harvard University Press, 2019.

Gibson, Sheila. "The Pool of Bethesda in Jerusalem and Jewish Purification Practices of the Second Temple Period." *Proche-Orient Chrétien* 55, nos. 3–4 (2005): 270–93.

Gieschen, Charles A. *Angelomorphic Christology: Antecedents and Early Evidence*. Leiden: Brill, 1998.

Goldingay, John. *Daniel*. Revised edition. Word Biblical Commentary 30. Grand Rapids, MI: Zondervan Academic, 2019.

Goodacre, Mark S. "The Beloved Disciple for Readers of the Synoptics." Conference presentation at SBL Annual Meeting, Denver, CO, November 20, 2022.

Goodacre, Mark S. "Did Thomas Know the Synoptic Gospels? A Response to Denzey Lewis, Kloppenborg and Patterson." *JSNT* 36, no. 3 (2014): 282–93.

Goodacre, Mark S. "Fatigue in the Synoptics." *NTS* 44, no. 1 (1998): 45–58.

Goodacre, Mark S. *Goulder and the Gospels: An Examination of a New Paradigm*. JSNT 133. Sheffield: Sheffield Academic Press, 1996.

Goodacre, Mark S. "Parallel Traditions or Parallel Gospels? John's Gospel as a Re-imagining of Mark." In *John's Transformation of Mark*, edited by Eve-Marie Becker, Helen K. Bond, and Catrin H. Williams, 77–90. New York: T&T Clark, 2021.

Goodacre, Mark S. *The Fourth Synoptic Gospel: John's Knowledge of Matthew, Mark, and Luke*. Grand Rapids, MI: Eerdmans, 2025.

Goodacre, Mark S. *The Synoptic Problem: A Way through the Maze*. London: T&T Clark, 2001.

Goodacre, Mark S. *Thomas and the Gospels: The Case for Thomas's Familiarity with the Synoptics*. Grand Rapids, MI: Eerdmans, 2012.

Gorman, Michael J. *Abide and Go: Missional Theosis in the Gospel of John*. Didsbury Lectures 2016. Eugene, OR: Cascade Books, 2018.

Gorman, Michael J. *Participating in Christ: Explorations in Paul's Theology and Spirituality*. Grand Rapids, MI: Baker Academic, 2019.

Grant, Michael. *The Ancient Historians*. New York: Barnes & Noble, 1994.

Gregory, Andrew F. "Jewish-Christian Gospels." *Expository Times* 118, no. 11 (2007): 521–29.

Gregory, Andrew F. *The Reception of Luke and Acts in the Period before Irenaeus: Looking for Luke in the Second Century*. WUNT, no. 169. Tübingen: Mohr Siebeck, 2003.

Gregory, Andrew F. "The Third Gospel? The Relationship of John and Luke Reconsidered." In *Challenging Perspectives on the Gospel of John*, edited by John Lierman, 109–34. WUNT/2 219. Tübingen: Mohr Siebeck, 2006.

Griffin, Robert J. "Anonymity and Authorship." *New Literary History* 30, no. 4 (1999): 877–95.

Guignard, Christophe. "The Muratorian Fragment as a Late Antique Fake?" *Revue des Sciences Religieuses* 93, nos. 1–2 (2019): 73–90.

Gundry, Robert H. "'In My Father's House Are Many Μοναί' (John 14 2)." *ZNW* 58, nos. 1–2 (1967): 68–72.

Gyllenberg, Sheila. "Geography in the Gospels: A Comparative Approach." In *A Handbook on the Jewish Roots of the Gospels*, edited by Craig A. Evans and David Mishkin, 115–26. Peabody, MA: Hendrickson, 2021.

Haefner, Alfred E. "A Unique Source for the Study of Ancient Pseudonymity." *Anglican Theological Review* 16 (1934): 8–15.

Haenchen, Ernst. *The Gospel of John: A Commentary on the Gospel of John*. 2 vols. Translated by Robert W. Funk. Hermeneia. Philadelphia: Fortress, 1984.

Hahneman, Geoffrey Mark. *The Muratorian Fragment and the Development of the Canon*. Oxford Theological Monographs. Oxford: Clarendon Press; 1992.

Hakola, Raimo. *Identity Matters: John, the Jews, and Jewishness*. NovTSupp, no. 118. Leiden: Brill, 2005.

Hakola, Raimo. *Reconsidering Johannine Christianity: A Social Identity Approach*. New York: Routledge, 2015.

Hamid-Khani, Saeed. *Revelation and Concealment of Christ*. Eugene, OR: Wipf & Stock, 2021.

Hancock, Peter. *Hoax Springs Eternal: The Psychology of Cognitive Deception*. New York: Cambridge University Press, 2015.

Hannah, Darrell D. "The Four-Gospel 'Canon' in the Epistula Apostolorum." *JTS* 59, no. 2 (2008): 598–633.

Harris, William V. *Ancient Literacy*. Cambridge, MA: Harvard University Press, 1991.

Hartenstein, Judith. *Die Zweite Lehre: Erscheinungen des Auferstandenen als Rahmenerzählungen frühchristlicher Dialoge*. Berlin: De Gruyter, 2015.

Hartin, P. J. "A Community in Crisis. The Christology of the Johannine Community as the Point at Issue." *Neot* 19, no. 1 (1985): 37–49.

Hartog, Paul, ed. *Polycarp's* Epistle to the Philippians *and the* Martyrdom of Polycarp: *Introduction, Text, and Commentary*. Oxford Apostolic Fathers. Oxford: Oxford University Press, 2013.

Hasitschka, Martin. "Die beiden 'Zeichen' am See von Tiberias: Interpretation von Joh 6 in Verbindung mit Joh 21,1–14." *Studien zum Neuen Testament und seiner Umwelt*, series A, no. 24 (1999): 85–102.

Hasslberger, Bernhard. *Hoffnung in der Bedrängnis: Eine formkritische Untersuchung zu Dan 8 u. 10-12*. Arbeiten zu Text und Sprache im Alten Testament, no. 4. St. Ottilien: EOS-Verlag, 1977.

Heil, John Paul. *1–3 John: Worship by Loving God and One Another to Live Eternally*. Cambridge, UK: James Clarke, 2015.

Heise, Jürgen. *Bleiben: Menein in den johanneischen Schriften*. Hermeneutische Untersuchungen zur Theologie, no. 8. Tübingen: Mohr Siebeck, 1967.

Henderson, Ian H. "Reconstructing Mark's Double Audience." In *Between Author and Audience in Mark: Narration, Characterization, Interpretation*, edited by Elizabeth Struthers Malbon, 6–28. New Testament Monographs 23. Sheffield: Sheffield Phoenix Press, 2009.

Hengel, Martin. *The Four Gospels and the One Gospel of Jesus Christ: An Investigation of the Collection and Origin of the Canonical Gospels*. London: SCM Press, 2000.

Hengel, Martin. *The Johannine Question*, translated by John Bowden. London: SCM Press, 1989.

Hengel, Martin, and Anna Maria Schwemer. *Jesus und das Judentum*. Geschichte des Frühen Christentums, no. 1. Tübingen: Mohr Siebeck, 2007.

Hill, Charles E. "The Epistula Apostolorum: An Asian Tract from the Time of Polycarp." *Journal of Early Christian Studies* 7, no. 1 (1999): 1–53.

Hill, Charles E. *The Johannine Corpus in the Early Church*. Oxford: Oxford University Press, 2004.

Hills, Julian Victor. *The Epistle of the Apostles*. Early Christian Apocrypha, no. 2. Santa Rosa, CA: Polebridge Press, 2009.

Hilton, Allen R. *Illiterate Apostles: Uneducated Early Christians and the Literates Who Loved Them*. LNTS, no. 541. London: Bloomsbury T&T Clark, 2018.

Himmelfarb, Martha. *Ascent to Heaven in Jewish and Christian Apocalypses*. New York: Oxford University Press, 1993.

Hirsch, Emanuel. *Studien zum vierten Evangelium*. Beiträge zur Historischen Theologie, no. 11. Tübingen: Mohr Siebeck, 1936.

Holladay, Carl R. "Philo and the New Testament: Including Passages from Philo as Marginal References in Editions of the Greek New Testament." *SPhilo* 32 (2020): 157–81.

Holtzmann, H. J. "Das Problem des ersten johanneischen Briefes in seinem Verhältnis zum Evangelium." *Jahrbücher für protestantische Theologie*, no. 8 (1882): 128–52.

Hornschuh, Manfred. *Studien zur Epistula Apostolorum*. Berlin: De Gruyter, 1965.

Hoskyns, Edwyn Clement. *The Fourth Gospel*. Edited by Francis Noel Davey. 2nd edition. London: Faber and Faber, 1947.

Humphrey, Edith M. "The Synoptics and the Johannine Literature." In *The Oxford Handbook of Deification*, edited by Paul L. Gavrilyuk, Andrew Hofer, and Matthew Levering, 76–94. Oxford: Oxford University Press, 2024.

Hylen, Susan. *Imperfect Believers: Ambiguous Characters in the Gospel of John*. Louisville, KY: Westminster John Knox, 2009.

Jackson, Howard M. "Ancient Self-Referential Conventions and Their Implications for the Authorship and Integrity of the Gospel of John." *JTS* 50, no. 1 (1999): 1–34.

Johnson, Luke Timothy. *The Letter of James: A New Translation with Introduction and Commentary*. AB, no. 37A. New York: Doubleday, 1995.

Johnson, Luke Timothy. *The Writings of the New Testament: An Interpretation*. 3rd edition. Minneapolis, MN: Fortress, 2010.

Jones, Brian W. *The Emperor Domitian*. London: Routledge, 1992.

Jones, Larry Paul. *The Symbol of Water in the Gospel of John*. JSNT 145. Sheffield: Sheffield Academic Press, 1997.

Judge, Peter. "The Royal Official and the Historical Jesus." In *John, Jesus, and History*, vol. 2: *Aspects of Historicity in the Fourth Gospel*, edited by Paul N. Anderson, Felix Just, and Tom Thatcher, 83–92. SBLECL, no. 2. Atlanta, GA: SBL, 2009.

Jülicher, Adolf. "Die Religion Jesu und die Anfänge des Christentums bis zum Nicaenum (325)." In *Die christliche Religion mit Einschluss der Israelitisch-Jüdischen Religion (=Die Kultur der Gegenwart* I/4), edited by Paul Hinnenberg, 41–128. Berlin: B. G. Teubner, 1906.

Junod, Eric, and Jean-Daniel Kaestli. *Acta Iohannis. 1: Praefatio, textus*. Corpus Christianorum 1. Turnhout: Brepols, 1983.

Kammler, Hans-Christian. *Christologie und Eschatologie: Joh 5, 17–30 Als Schlüsseltext Johanneischer Theologie*. WUNT, no. 126. Tübingen: Mohr Siebeck, 2000.

Kammler, Hans-Christian. "Jesus Christus und der Geistparaklet: Eine Studie zur johanneischen Verhältnisbestimmung von Pneumatologie und Christologie." In *Johannesstudien: Untersuchungen zur Theologie des vierten Evangeliums*, edited by Otfried Hofius and Hans-Christian Kammler, 87–190. WUNT, no. 88. Tübingen: Mohr, 1996.

Keary, T. "Editing." In *Writing, Enslavement, and Power in the Roman Mediterranean, 100 BCE–300 CE*, edited by Jeremiah Coogan, Joseph A. Howley, and Candida R. Moss. New York: Oxford University Press, 2025.

Keener, Craig S. *The Gospel of John.* 2 vols. Grand Rapids, MI: Baker Academic, 2010.

Keith, Chris. *The Gospel as Manuscript An Early History of the Jesus Tradition as Material Artifact*. New York: Oxford University Press, 2020.

Keith, Chris. "If John Knew Mark: Critical Inheritance and Johannine Disagreements." In *John's Transformation of Mark*, edited by Eve-Marie Becker, Helen K. Bond, and Catrin H. Williams, 31–49. New York: T&T Clark, 2021.

Keith, Chris. *The Pericope Adulterae, the Gospel of John, and the Literacy of Jesus*. New Testament Tools, Studies, and Documents, no. 38. Leiden: Brill, 2009.

Kelhoffer, James A. *Conceptions of "Gospel" and Legitimacy in Early Christianity*. WUNT, no. 324. Tübingen: Mohr Siebeck, 2014.

Kellum, L. Scott. *The Unity of the Farewell Discourse: The Literary Integrity of John 13:31–16:33*. JSNTSupp, no. 256. London: T&T Clark, 2004.

Kennedy, George A. *New Testament Interpretation through Rhetorical Criticism*. Studies in Religion. Chapel Hill: University of North Carolina Press, 1984.

Kerr, Alan R. *The Temple of Jesus' Body: The Temple Theme in the Gospel of John*. JSNTSupp, no. 220. London: Sheffield Academic Press, 2002.

Kindt, Tom, and Hans-Harald Müller. *Implied Author: Concept and Controversy*. Narratologia, no. 9. Berlin: De Gruyter, 2006.

King, Karen L. *The Gospel of Mary of Magdala: Jesus and the First Woman Apostle*. Santa Rosa, CA: Polebridge, 2003.

King, Karen L. *The Secret Revelation of John*. Cambridge, MA: Harvard University Press, 2006.

King, Karen L. "'What Is an Author?' Ancient Author-Function in the *Apocryphon of John* and the *Apocalypse of John*." In *Scribal Practices and Social Structures among Jesus Adherents: Essays in Honour of John S. Kloppenborg*, edited by William E. Arnal, Richard S. Ascough, Robert A. Derrenbacker Jr., and Philip A. Harland, 15–42. BETL, no. 285. Leuven: Peeters, 2016.

Kinlaw, Pamela E. *The Christ Is Jesus: Metamorphosis, Possession, and Johannine Christology*. Academia Biblica, no. 18. Leiden: Brill, 2005.

Klauck, Hans-Josef. *Der zweite und dritte Johannesbrief*. EKK, no. 23/2. Zürich: Benziger, 1992.

Klawans, Jonathan. "Deceptive Intentions: Forgeries, Falsehoods and the Study of Ancient Judaism." *Jewish Quarterly Review* 108, no. 4 (2018): 489–501.

Kloppenborg, John S. "Luke's Geography: Knowledge, Ignorance, Sources, and Spatial Conception." In *Luke on Jesus, Paul, and Earliest Christianity: What Did He Really Know?*, edited by Joseph Verheyden and John S. Kloppenborg, 101–43. Biblical Tools and Studies, no. 29. Leuven: Peeters, 2017.

Kloppenborg, John S. "A New Synoptic Problem: Mark Goodacre and Simon Gathercole on Thomas." *JSNT* 36, no. 3 (2014): 199–239.

Knust, Jennifer Wright, and Tommy Wasserman. *To Cast the First Stone: The Transmission of a Gospel Story*. Princeton, NJ: Princeton University Press, 2019.

Koester, Craig R., ed. *Revelation: A New Translation with Introduction and Commentary*. AB, no. 38A. New Haven, CT: Yale University Press, 2014.

Koester, Craig R. *Symbolism in the Fourth Gospel: Meaning, Mystery, Community*. 2nd edition. Minneapolis, MN: Fortress, 2003.

Koester, Craig R. "Theological Complexity and the Characterization of Nicodemus in John's Gospel." In *Characters and Characterization in the Gospel of John*, edited by Christopher W. Skinner, 165–81. LNTS 461. London: Bloomsbury T&T Clark, 2013.

Koester, Helmut. *Ancient Christian Gospels: Their History and Development*. London: SCM Press, 1990.

Koester, Helmut. *Synoptische Überlieferung bei den apostolischen Väter*. Texte und Untersuchungen zur Geschichte der altchristlichen Literatur 65. Berlin: Akademie-Verlag, 1957.

Koester, Helmut. "Written Gospel or Oral Tradition?" *JBL* 113, no. 2 (1994): 293–97.

Kok, Michael J. *The Beloved Apostle? The Transformation of the Apostle John into the Fourth Evangelist*. Eugene, OR: Cascade, 2017.

Körtner, Ulrich H. J. *Papias von Hierapolis: Ein Beitrag zur Geschichte des frühen Christentums*. Forschungen zur Religion und Literatur des Alten und Neuen Testaments, no. 133. Göttingen: Vandenhoeck & Ruprecht, 1983.

Köstenberger, Andreas J. *John*. Baker Exegetical Commentary on the New Testament. Grand Rapids, MI: Baker Academic, 2004.

Köstenberger, Andreas J. *A Theology of John's Gospel and Letters*. Biblical Theology of the New Testament. Grand Rapids, MI: Zondervan, 2009.

Kreps, Anne Starr. *The Crucified Book: Sacred Writing in the Age of Valentinus*. Divinations. Philadelphia: University of Pennsylvania Press, 2022.

Krueger, Derek. *Writing and Holiness: The Practice of Authorship in the Early Christian East*. Philadelphia: University of Pennsylvania Press, 2011.

Kruse, Colin G. *John*. Tyndale New Testament Commentaries. Downers Grove, IL: IVP Academic, 2008.

Kügler, Joachim. *Der Jünger, den Jesus liebte: Literarische, theologische und historische Untersuchungen zu einer Schlüsselgestalt johanneischer Theologie und Geschichte: Mit einem Exkurs über die Brotrede in Joh 6*. Stuttgarter biblische Beiträge 16. Stuttgart: Katholisches Bibelwerk, 1988.

Labahn, Michael. "Literary Sources of the Gospel and Letters of John." In *The Oxford Handbook of Johannine Studies*, edited by Judith Lieu and Martinus C. de Boer, 23–43. Oxford Handbooks. Oxford: Oxford University Press, 2018.

Laird, Benjamin. "Early Titles of the Pauline Letters and the Formation of the Pauline Corpus." *Biblische Notizen* 175 (2017): 55–81.

Lalleman, Pieter J. *The Acts of John: A Two-Stage Initiation into Johannine Gnosticism*. Studies on the Apocryphal Acts of the Apostles 4. Leuven: Peeters, 1998.

Larsen, Matthew D. C. "Accidental Publication, Unfinished Texts and the Traditional Goals of New Testament Textual Criticism." *JSNT* 39, no. 4 (2017): 362–87.

Larsen, Matthew D. C. *Gospels before the Book*. New York: Oxford University Press, 2018.

Lee, Dorothy A. *Flesh and Glory, Symbol, Gender, and Theology in the Gospel of John*. New York: Crossroad, 2002.

Lee, Dorothy A. "Paschal Imagery in the Gospel of John: A Narrative and Symbolic Reading." *Pacifica* 24, no. 1 (2011): 13–28.

Lee, Dorothy A. *The Symbolic Narratives of the Fourth Gospel: The Interplay of Form and Meaning*. Sheffield: JSOT Press, 1994.

Lehtipuu, Outi. *Debates over the Resurrection of the Dead: Constructing Early Christian Identity*. OECS. Oxford: Oxford University Press, 2015.

Leon-Dufour, Xavier. "Towards a Symbolic Reading of the Fourth Gospel." *NTS* 27, no. 4 (1981): 439–56.

Levinson, John R. *The Spirit in First-Century Judaism*. Leiden: Brill, 1997.

Lewis, Karoline M. *Rereading the Shepherd Discourse: Restoring the Integrity of John 9:39–10:21*. Studies in Biblical Literature, no. 113. New York: Peter Lang, 2008.

Lieu, Judith M. *I, II, and III John*. NTL. Louisville, KY: Westminster John Knox, 2012.

Lieu, Judith M. *The Second and Third Epistles of John: History and Background*. Studies of the New Testament and Its World. Edinburgh: T&T Clark, 1986.
Lightfoot, Joseph Barber. *Biblical Essays*. Reprint. Peabody, MA: Hendrickson, 1994.
Lincoln, Andrew T. "The Beloved Disciple as Eyewitness and the Fourth Gospel as Witness." *JSNT* 24, no. 3 (2002): 3–26.
Lincoln, Andrew T. *The Gospel According to Saint John*. Black's New Testament Commentaries, no. 4. London: Continuum, 2005.
Lincoln, Andrew T. *Truth on Trial: The Lawsuit Motif in the Fourth Gospel*. Grand Rapids, MI: Baker Academic, 2000.
Lincoln, Andrew T. "'We Know That His Testimony Is True': Johannine Truth Claims and Historicity." In *John, Jesus, and History*, vol. 1: *Critical Appraisals of Critical Views*, edited by Paul N. Anderson, Felix Just, and Tom Thatcher, 179–97. SBLSymS 44. Leiden: Brill, 2007.
Lindars, Barnabas. *Behind the Fourth Gospel*. London: SPCK, 1971.
Lindars, Barnabas. *The Gospel of John*. New Century Bible Commentary. London: Oliphants, 1972.
Lindars, Barnabas. "Two Parables in John." *NTS* 16, no. 4 (1970): 318–29.
Lindenlaub, Julia D. *The Beloved Disciple as Interpreter and Author of Scripture in the Gospel of John*. WUNT/2, no. 611. Tübingen: Mohr Siebeck, 2024.Litwa, M. David. "The Deification of Moses in Philo of Alexandria." *SPhilo* 26 (2014): 1–27.
Litwa, M. David. *Desiring Divinity: Self-Deification in Early Jewish and Christian Mythmaking*. New York: Oxford University Press, 2016.
Litwa, M. David. "Equal to Angels: The Early Reception History of the Lukan Ἰσάγγελοι (Luke 20:36)." *JBL* 140, no. 3 (2021): 601–22.
Litwa, M. David. *The Evil Creator: Origins of an Early Christian Idea*. New York: Oxford University Press, 2021.
Litwa, M. David. *Found Christianities: Remaking the World of the Second Century* CE. London: T&T Clark, 2022.
Litwa, M. David. *How the Gospels Became History: Jesus and Mediterranean Myths*. Synkrisis. New Haven, CT: Yale University Press, 2019.
Litwa, M. David. *Posthuman Transformation in Ancient Mediterranean Thought: Becoming Angels and Demons*. Cambridge: Cambridge University Press, 2021.
Litwa, M. David., ed. *Refutation of All Heresies*. Writings from the Greco-Roman World 40. Atlanta, GA: SBL, 2016.
Litwa, M. David. "2 Corinthians 3:18 and Its Implications for 'Theosis.'" *Journal of Theological Interpretation* 2, no. 1 (2008): 117–33.
Litwa, M. David. *We Are Being Transformed: Deification in Paul's Soteriology*. BZNW, no. 187. Berlin: De Gruyter, 2012.
Loader, William R. G. "Jesus and the Law in John." In *Theology and Christology in the Fourth Gospel: Essays by the Members of the SNTS Johannine Writings Seminar*, edited by G. van Belle, J. G. van der Watt, and P. Maritz, 135–54. BETL 184. Leuven: Peeters, 2005.
Logan, Alastair H. B. "The Johannine Literature and the Gnostics." In *The Oxford Handbook of Johannine Studies*, edited by Judith Lieu and Martinus C. de Boer, 171–85. Oxford Handbooks. Oxford: Oxford University Press, 2018.
Logan, Alastair H. B. "John and the Gnostics: The Significance of the Apocryphon of John for the Debate about the Origins of the Johannine Literature." *JSNT* 14, no. 43 (1991): 41–69.
Loisy, Alfred. *Le quatrième évangile*. Paris: A. Picard et fils, 1903.
Lookadoo, J. "The Date and Authenticity of the Ignatian Letters: An Outline of Recent Discussions." *CBR* 19, no. 1 (2020): 88–114.
Luther, Susanne. "The Authentication of the Past: Narrative Representations of History in the Gospel of John." *JSNT* 43, no. 1 (2020): 67–84.
Luther, Susanne. "The Authentication of the Narrative: The Function of Scripture Quotations in John 19." In *Biblical Interpretation in Early Christian Gospels*, vol 4. *The Gospel of John*, ed. Thomas R. Hatina 155–66. LNTS, no. 613. London: Bloomsbury T&T Clark, 2020.

MacDonald, Margaret Y., and Daniel J. Harrington. *Colossians and Ephesians.* SP, no. 17. Collegeville, MN: Liturgical Press, 2000.

Mackay, Ian D. *John's Relationship with Mark: An Analysis of John 6 in the Light of Mark 6-8.* WUNT, no. 2, no. 182. Tübingen: Mohr Siebeck, 2004.

Magness, Jodi. "Sweet Memory: Archaeological Evidence of Jesus in Jerusalem." In *Memory in Ancient Rome and Early Christianity*, edited by Karl Galinsky, 324-43. Oxford: Oxford University Press, 2018.

Malherbe, Abraham J., ed. *The Cynic Epistles: A Study Edition.* Sources for Biblical Study, no. 12. Missoula, MT: Scholars Press, 1977.

Marcovich, Miroslav, ed. *Iustini Martyris: Dialogus cum Tryphone.* Patristische Texte und Studien, no. 47. Berlin: De Gruyter, 1997.

Marcus, Joel. "Mark—Interpreter of Paul." *NTS* 46, no. 4 (2000): 473-87.

Marcus, Joel. *Mark 1-8: A New Translation with Introduction and Commentary.* AB, no. 27. New York: Doubleday, 2005.

Martin, Dale B. *The Corinthian Body.* New Haven, CT: Yale University Press, 1999.

Marty, Jacques. "Contribution à l'étude des problèmes johanniques: Les petites épîtres 'II et III Jean.'" *Revue de l'histoire des religions*, Bis 1909: Annales du Musée Guimet, 91 (1925): 200-211.

Martyn, J. Louis. *History and Theology of the Fourth Gospel.* New York: Harper and Row, 1968.

Mason, Steve. "Did the Author of Luke-Acts Know the Works of Josephus?" In *Jews and Christians in the Roman World: From Historical Method to Cases*, 445-88. Arbeiten zur Geschichte des Antiken Judentums und des Urchristentums, no. 116. Leiden: Brill, 2023.

Mason, Steve. *Josephus and the New Testament.* 2nd reprint. Grand Rapids, MI: Baker Academic, 2013.

Matson, Mark A. *In Dialogue with Another Gospel? The Influence of the Fourth Gospel on the Passion Narrative of the Gospel of Luke.* SBL Dissertation Series, no. 178. Atlanta, GA: SBL, 2001.

McGrath, James F. "'Destroy This Temple': Issues of History in John 2:13-22." In *John, Jesus, and History*, vol. 2: *Aspects of Historicity in the Fourth Gospel*, edited by Paul N. Anderson, Felix Just, and Tom Thatcher, 35-43. SBLECL, no. 2. Leiden: Brill, 2009.

McGrath, James F. "Johannine Christianity: Jewish Christianity?" *Koinonia* 8, no. 1 (1996): 1-20.

McGrath, James F. *John's Apologetic Christology: Legitimation and Development in Johannine Christology.* SNTSMS, no. 111. Cambridge: Cambridge University Press, 2001.

Meconi, David Vincent. *The One Christ: St. Augustine's Theology of Deification.* Washington, DC: Catholic University of America Press, 2013.

Meeks, Wayne A. "The Man from Heaven in Johannine Sectarianism." *JBL* 91, no. 1 (1972): 44-72.

Meier, John P. "Love in Q and John: Love of Enemies, Love of One Another." *Mid-Stream* 40 (2001): 42-50.

Méndez, Hugo. "Did the Johannine Community Exist?" *JSNT* 42, no. 3 (2020): 350-74.

Méndez, Hugo. *The Epistles of John: Origins, Authorship, Purpose.* Cambridge: Cambridge University Press, forthcoming.

Méndez, Hugo. "Jesus's Secret Journey in John 7: A Symbol of the Ascension." *HTR* 117, no. 1 (2024): 58-78.

Méndez, Hugo. "The 'Last Day' in John: Future or Realized?" *JTS*, forthcoming.

Méndez, Hugo. "Mixed Metaphors: Resolving the 'Eschatological Headache' of John 5." *JBL* 137, no. 3 (2018): 711-32.

Méndez, Hugo. "Renewing Johannine Historical Criticism: A Proposal." In *The Johannine Community in Contemporary Debate*, edited by Christopher Seglenieks and Christopher W. Skinner, 139-56. Lexington, KY: Fortress Academic, 2024.

Menken, Maarten J. J. "The Quotations from Zech 9,9 in Mt 21,5 and in Jn 12,15." In *John and the Synoptics*, edited by Adelbert Denaux, 571–78. BETL 101. Leuven: Leuven University Press, 1992.

Merz, Annette. *Die Fiktive Selbstauslegung des Paulus: Intertextuelle Studien zur Intention und Rezeption der Pastoralbriefe*. NovT et Orbis Antiquus, no. 52. Göttingen: Vandenhoeck & Ruprecht, 2004.

Metzger, Bruce M. "Literary Forgeries and Canonical Pseudepigrapha." *JBL* 91, no. 1 (1972): 3–24.

Metzger, Bruce M. *A Textual Commentary on the Greek New Testament*. 2nd edition. London: United Bible Societies, 1994.

Meyer, E. "Apollonios von Tyana und die Biographie des Philostratos." *Hermes* 52 (1917): 371–424.

Mheallaigh, Karen Ní. "Pseudo-documentarianism and the Limits of Ancient Fiction." *American Journal of Philology* 129, no. 3 (2008): 403–31.

Michaels, J. Ramsey. *The Gospel of John*. NICNT. Grand Rapids, MI: Eerdmans, 2010.

Michel, Otto. *Der Brief an die Hebräer*. 12th edition. Kritisch-exegetischer Kommentar über das Neue Testament, no. 13. Göttingen: Vandenhoeck & Ruprecht, 1966.

Mihalios, Stefanos. *The Danielic Eschatological Hour in the Johannine Literature*. LNTS, no. 436. London: Bloomsbury T&T Clark, 2012.

Miller, Susan. "'The Woman at the Well': John's Portrayal of the Samaritan Woman." In *John, Jesus, and History*, vol. 2: *Aspects of Historicity in the Fourth Gospel*, edited by Paul N. Anderson, Felix Just, and Tom Thatcher, 71–81. SBLECL, no. 2. Leiden: Brill, 2009.

Minear, Paul Sevier. "The Original Functions of John 21." *JBL* 102, no. 1 (1983): 85–98.

Mitchell, Margaret M. *Collected Essays*. WUNT, no. 393. Tübingen: Mohr Siebeck, 2017.

Mlakuzhyil, George. *The Christocentric Literary-Dramatic Structure of John's Gospel*. 2nd edition. Analecta Biblica, no. 117. Rome: Gregorian & Biblical Press, 2011.

Moberly, Robert B. "When Was Revelation Conceived?" *Biblica* 73, no. 3 (1992): 376–93.

Moloney, Francis J. *The Gospel of John*. SP, no. 4. Collegeville, MN: Liturgical Press, 1998.

Morgan, Teresa. *Being "in Christ" in the Letters of Paul: Saved through Christ and in His Hands*. WUNT, no. 449. Tübingen: Mohr Siebeck, 2020.

Morris, Leon. *The Gospel According to John*. Revised edition. NICNT. Grand Rapids, MI: Eerdmans, 2008.

Morris, Leon. *Studies in the Fourth Gospel*. Devon: Paternoster, 1969.

Moss, Candida R. "Between the Lines: Looking for the Contributions of Enslaved Literate Laborers in a Second-Century Text (P. Berol. 11632)." *Studies in Late Antiquity* 5, no. 3 (2021): 432–52.

Moss, Candida R. *Divine Bodies: Resurrecting Perfection in the New Testament and Early Christianity*. New Haven, CT: Yale University Press, 2019.

Moss, Candida R. "Fashioning Mark: Early Christian Discussions about the Scribe and Status of the Second Gospel." *NTS* 67, no. 2 (2021): 181–204.

Moss, Candida R. *God's Ghostwriters: Enslaved Christians and the Making of the Bible*. New York: Little, Brown, 2024.

Moss, Candida R. "The Secretary: Enslaved Workers, Stenography, and the Production of Early Christian Literature." *JTS* 74, no. 1 (2023): 20–56.

Moss, Candida R., Jeremiah Coogan, and Joseph A. Howley. "The Socioeconomics of Fabrication: Textuality, Authenticity, and Class in the Roman Mediterranean." *Arethusa* 57, no. 2 (2024): 227–53.

Mroczek, Eva. *The Literary Imagination in Jewish Antiquity*. New York: Oxford University Press, 2016.

Myles, Robert J., and Michael Kok. "On the Implausibility of Identifying the Disciple in John 18:15–16 as a Galilean Fisherman." *Novum Testamentum* 61, no. 4 (2019): 367–85.

Nagel, Titus. *Die Rezeption des Johannesevangeliums im 2. Jahrhundert: Studien zur vorirenäischen Aneignung und Auslegung des vierten Evangeliums in christlicher und christlich-gnostischer Literatur*. Arbeiten zur Bibel und ihrer Geschichte, no. 2. Leipzig: Evangelische Verlagsanstalt, 2000.

Najman, Hindy. *Past Renewals: Interpretative Authority, Renewed Revelation, and the Quest for Perfection in Jewish Antiquity*. JSJSupp, no. 53. Leiden: Brill, 2010.

Najman, Hindy. *Seconding Sinai: The Development of Mosaic Discourse in Second Temple Judaism*. JSJSupp 77. Leiden: Brill, 2003.

Najman, Hindy, and Irene Peirano Garrison. "Pseudepigraphy as an Interpretative Construct." In *The Old Testament Pseudepigrapha: Fifty Years of the Pseudepigrapha Section at the SBL*, edited by Matthias Henze and Liv Ingeborg Lied, 331–58. Early Judaism and Its Literature, no. 50. Atlanta, GA: SBL, 2019.

Najman, Hindy, and Tobias Reinhardt. "Exemplarity and Its Discontents: Hellenistic Jewish Wisdom Texts and Greco-Roman Didactic Poetry." *JSJ* 50, nos. 4–5 (2019): 460–96.

Neirynck, Frans. *Jean et les synoptiques: Examen critique de l'exegese de M.-E. Boismard*. Leuven: Peeters, 1979.

Neirynck, Frans. "John and the Synoptics: 1975–1990." In *John and the Synoptics*, edited by Adelbert Denaux, 3–62. BETL 101. Leuven: Leuven University Press, 1992.

Neyrey, Jerome H. *The Gospel of John in Cultural and Rhetorical Perspective*. Grand Rapids, MI: Eerdmans, 2009.

Neyrey, Jerome H. "'I Said: You Are Gods': Psalm 82:6 and John 10." *JBL* 108, no. 4 (1989): 647–63.

Neyrey, Jerome H. "The Sociology of Secrecy and the Fourth Gospel." In *"What Is John?,"* vol. 2: *Literary and Social Readings of the Fourth Gospel*, edited by Fernando F. Segovia, 79–109. SBLSymS, no. 7. Atlanta, GA: Scholars Press, 1998.

Ng, Wai-Yee. *Water Symbolism in John: An Eschatological Interpretation*. Studies in Biblical Literature, no. 15. New York: Peter Lang, 2001.

Nickelsburg, George W. E. *Resurrection, Immortality, and Eternal Life in Intertestamental Judaism and Early Christianity*. Harvard Theological Studies 56. Cambridge, MA: Harvard University Press, 2007.

Nicklas, Tobias. "Revelation and the New Testament Canon." In *The Oxford Handbook of the Book of Revelation*, edited by Craig R. Koester. Oxford Handbooks, 361–75. Oxford: Oxford University Press, 2020.

Nicol, W. *The Semeia in the Fourth Gospel: Tradition and Redaction*. Leiden: Brill, 1972.

Niehoff, Maren R. *Philo of Alexandria: An Intellectual Biography*. ABRL. New Haven, CT: Yale University Press, 2018.

Nongbri, Brent. *God's Library: The Archaeology of the Earliest Christian Manuscripts*. New Haven, CT: Yale University Press, 2018.

Nongbri, Brent. "Maintenance." In *Writing, Enslavement, and Power in the Roman Mediterranean*, edited by J. Coogan, Joseph A. Howley, and Candida R. Moss. New York: Oxford University Press, 2025.

Nongbri, Brent. "The Use and Abuse of P52: Papyrological Pitfalls in the Dating of the Fourth Gospel." *HTR* 98, no. 1 (2005): 23–48.

North, Wendy E. Sproston. "John for Readers of Mark? A Response to Richard Bauckham's Proposal." *JSNT* 25, no. 4 (2003): 449–68.

North, Wendy E. Sproston. *The Lazarus Story within the Johannine Tradition*. JSNTSupp 212. Sheffield: Sheffield Academic Press, 2001.

North, Wendy E. Sproston. *What John Knew and What John Wrote: A Study in John and the Synoptics*. Interpreting Johannine Literature. Lanham, MD: Lexington Books, 2020.

Olsson, Birger. *Structure and Meaning in the Fourth Gospel: A Text-Linguistic Analysis of John 2:1–11 and 4:1–42*. Coniectanea Biblica, no. 6. Lund: Gleerup, 1974.

Orlov, Andrei A. *The Enoch-Metatron Tradition*. Texts and Studies in Ancient Judaism, no. 107. Tübingen: Mohr Siebeck, 2005.

Orr, Peter. *Exalted above the Heavens: The Risen and Ascended Christ*. New Studies in Biblical Theology 47. Downers Grove, IL: IVP Academic, 2018.

O'Sullivan, Jeremiah F. *The Writings of Salvian the Presbyter*. Fathers of the Church Patristics Series, no. 3. Washington, DC: Catholic University of America Press, 2008.

Pagels, Elaine H. *Revelations: Visions, Prophecy, and Politics in the Book of Revelation*. New York: Viking, 2012.

Painter, John. *1, 2, and 3 John*. SP, no. 18. Collegeville, MN: Liturgical Press, 2002.

Painter, John. "1, 2, and 3 John." In *Eerdmans Commentary on the Bible*, edited by James D. G. Dunn and J. W. Rogerson, 1512–14. Grand Rapids, MI: Eerdmans, 2003.

Painter, John. "The Johannine Epistles as Catholic Epistles." In *The Catholic Epistles and Apostolic Tradition*, edited by Karl-Wilhelm Niebuhr and Robert W. Wallace, 239–308. Waco, TX: Baylor University Press, 2009.

Painter, John. "The Johannine Literature." In *Handbook to Exegesis of the New Testament*, edited by Stanley E. Porter, 555–90. Leiden: Brill, 1997.

Painter, John. "Johannine Symbols: A Case Study in Epistemology." *Journal of Theology for Southern Africa*, no. 27 (1979): 26–41.

Painter, John. "John 9 and the Interpretation of the Fourth Gospel." *JSNT* 9, no. 28 (1986): 31–61.

Painter, John. "The Prologue as an Hermeneutical Key to Reading the Fourth Gospel." In *Studies in the Gospel of John and Its Christology: Festschrift Gilbert Van Belle*, edited by Joseph Verheyden, Geert Van Oyen, Michael Labahn, and Reimund Bieringer, 37–60. BETL, no. 265, Leuven: Peeters, 2014.

Painter, John. *The Quest for the Messiah: The History, Literature, and Theology of the Johannine Community*. 2nd edition. Nashville, TN: Abingdon, 1993.

Parker, Floyd. "The Terms 'Angel' and 'Spirit' in Acts 23,8." *Biblica* 84, no. 3 (2003): 344–65.

Parsenios, George L. *Departure and Consolation: The Johannine Farewell Discourses in Light of Greco-Roman Literature*. NovTSupp, no. 117. Leiden: Brill, 2005.

Parsenios, George L. *First, Second, and Third John*. Paideia. Grand Rapids, MI: Baker Academic, 2014.

Parsons, Mikeal C. "A Neglected ΕΓΩ ΕΙΜΙ Saying in the Fourth Gospel? Another Look at John 9:9." In *Perspectives on John: Method and Interpretation in the Fourth Gospel*, edited by Robert B. Sloan and Mikeal C. Parsons, 145–80. NABPR Special Studies Series, no. 11. Lampeter: Edwin Mellen Press, 1993.

Patterson, Stephen J. "Twice More—'Thomas' and the Synoptics: A Reply to Simon Gathercole, 'The Composition of the Gospel of Thomas,' and Mark Goodacre, 'Thomas and the Gospels.'" *JSNT* 36, no. 3 (2014): 251–61.

Peirano Garrison, Irene. *The Rhetoric of the Roman Fake: Latin Pseudepigrapha in Context*. Cambridge: Cambridge University Press, 2012.

Peppard, Michael. "Adopted and Begotten Sons of God: Paul and John on Divine Sonship." *CBQ* 73, no. 1 (2011): 92–110.

Perkins, Pheme. *The Johannine Epistles*. New Testament Message, no. 21. Dublin: Veritas, 1979.

Petersen, Silke. "Die Evangelienüberschriften und die Entstehung des neutestamentlichen Kanons." *ZNW* 97, nos. 3–4 (2006): 250–74.

Petersen, William Lawrence, Jan Krans, and Joseph Verheyden. *Patristic and Text-Critical Studies: The Collected Essays of William L. Petersen*. New Testament Tools—Studies and Documents 40. Leiden: Brill, 2012.

Peterson, Dwight N. *The Origins of Mark: The Markan Community in Current Debate*. Leiden: Brill, 2000.

Piovanelli, Pierluigi. "What Has Pseudepigraphy to Do with Forgery? Reflections on the Cases of the Acts of Paul, the Apocalypse of Paul, and the Zohar." In *Fakes, Forgeries, and Fictions: Writing Ancient and Modern Christian Apocrypha. Proceedings from the 2015 York University Christian Apocrypha Symposium*, edited by Tony Burke, 50–60. Eugene, OR: Cascade, 2017.

Pleše, Zlatko. *Poetics of the Gnostic Universe: Narrative and Cosmology in the Apocryphon of John*. Nag Hammadi and Manichaean Studies, no. 52. Leiden: Brill, 2006.

Poirier, John C. "The Roll, the Codex, the Wax Tablet and the Synoptic Problem." *JSNT* 35, no. 1 (2012): 3–30.

Poplutz, Uta. "Paroimia und Parabolē: Gleichniskonzepte bei Johannes und Markus." In *Imagery in the Gospel of John: Terms, Forms, Themes, and Theology of Johannine Figurative Language*, edited by Jörg Frey and Gabi Kern, 103–20. WUNT, no. 200. Tübingen: Mohr Siebeck, 2006.

Porter, Stanley E. "Jesus and the Ending of John's Gospel." In *John, His Gospel, and Jesus: In Pursuit of the Johannine Voice*, 225–45. Grand Rapids, MI: Eerdmans, 2015.

Porter, Stanley E. "When and How Was the Pauline Canon Compiled? An Assessment of Theories." In *The Pauline Canon*, edited by Stanley E. Porter, 95–127. Pauline Studies, no. 1. Leiden: Brill, 2004.

Porter, Stanley E., and Andrew Pitts. "Manuscripts, Scribes, and Book Production within Early Christianity." In *Christian Origins and Greco-Roman Culture*, edited by Stanley E. Porter and Andrew Pitts, 13–40. Leiden: Brill, 2013.

Prince, Deborah Thompson. "The 'Ghost' of Jesus: Luke 24 in Light of Ancient Narratives of Post-mortem Apparitions." *JSNT* 29, no. 3 (2007): 287–301.

Puskas, Charles B. *Hebrews, the General Letters, and Revelation: An Introduction*. Eugene, OR: Cascade Books, 2016.

Puskas, Charles B., and C. Michael Robbins. *The Conceptual Worlds of the Fourth Gospel: Intertextuality and Early Reception*. Eugene, OR: Cascade, 2021.

Rahner, Johanna. *"Er aber sprach vom Tempel seines Leibes": Jesus von Nazaret als Ort der Offenbarung Gottes im vierten Evangelium*. Bonner biblische Beiträge 117. Bodenheim: Philo, 1998.

Rasimus, Tuomas. *The Legacy of John: Second-Century Reception of the Fourth Gospel*. NovTSupp, no. 132. Leiden: Brill, 2010.

Reardon, Michael M. C. "Becoming God: Interpreting Pauline Soteriology as Deification." *CBR* 22, no. 1 (2023): 83–107.

Reed, Annette Yoshiko. "Pseudepigraphy, Authorship, and the Reception of 'the Bible' in Late Antiquity." In *The Reception and Interpretation of the Bible in Late Antiquity: Proceedings of the Montréal Colloquium in Honour of Charles Kannengiesser, 11-13 October 2006*, edited by Lorenzo DiTomasso and Lucian Turcescu, 467–90. The Bible in Ancient Christianity, no. 6. Leiden: Brill, 2008.

Reed, Annette Yoshiko. "The Construction and Subversion of Patriarchal Perfection: Abraham and Exemplarity in Philo, Josephus, and the Testament of Abraham." *JSJ* 40, no. 2 (2009): 185–212.

Reichert, Angelika. "Durchdachte Konfusion: Plinius, Trajan und das Christentum." *Zeitschrift für die neutestamentliche Wissenschaft* 93, nos. 3–4 (2002): 227–50.

Reim, Günter. "Johannes 21—ein Anhang?" In *Reim, Günter, Jochanan: Erweiterte Studie zum alttestamentlichen Hintergrund des Johannesevangeliums*, 389–96. Erlangen: Evangelische-Luth. Mission, 1995.

Reinhartz, Adele. "'And the Word Was Begotten': Divine Epigenesis in the Gospel of John." In *God the Father in the Gospel of John*, edited by Adele Reinhartz, 83–103. Semeia 85. Atlanta, GA: SBL, 1999.

Reinhartz, Adele. "Building Skyscrapers on Toothpicks: The Literary-Critical Challenge to Historical Criticism." In *Anatomies of Narrative Criticism: The Past, Present, and Futures of the Fourth Gospel as Literature*, edited by Tom Thatcher and Steven D. Moore, 55–76. Atlanta, GA: SBL, 2008.

Reinhartz, Adele. *Cast out of the Covenant: Jews and Anti-Judaism in the Gospel of John*. Lanham, MD: Lexington Books-Fortress Academic, 2018.

Reinhartz, Adele. "'Children of God' and Aristotelian Epigenesis in the Gospel of John." In *Creation Stories in Dialogue: The Bible, Science, and Folk Traditions: Radboud Prestige Lectures in New Testament*, edited by R. Alan Culpepper and Jan G. van der Watt, 243–52. BINS 139. Leiden: Brill, 2016.

Reinhartz, Adele. "The Lyin' King? Deception and Christology in the Gospel of John." In *Johannine Ethics: The Moral World of the Gospel and Epistles of John*, edited by Christopher W. Skinner and Sherri Brown, 117–34. Minneapolis, MN: Fortress, 2017.

Reinhartz, Adele. *The Word in the World: The Cosmological Tale in the Fourth Gospel*. SBL Monograph Series, no. 45. Atlanta, GA: Scholars Press, 1992.

Rhoads, David M., Joanna Dewey, and Donald Michie. *Mark as Story: An Introduction to the Narrative of a Gospel*. 3rd edition. Minneapolis, MN: Fortress, 2012.

Richards, E. Randolph. *The Secretary in the Letters of Paul*. WUNT/2, no. 42. Tübingen: Mohr Siebeck, 1991.

Riley, Gregory J. *Resurrection Reconsidered: Thomas and John in Controversy*. Minneapolis, MN: Fortress, 1995.

Robinson, John A. T. *The Priority of John*. London: SCM Press, 1985.

Robinson, Will, and Stephen R. Llewelyn. "The Fictitious Audience of 1 Peter." *Heythrop Journal* 61, no. 6 (2020): 939–50.

Rosenmeyer, Patricia A. *Ancient Epistolary Fictions: The Letter in Greek Literature*. Cambridge: Cambridge University Press, 2001.

Rothschild, Clare K. *Hebrews as Pseudepigraphon: The History and Significance of the Pauline Attribution of Hebrews*. WUNT, no. 235. Tübingen: Mohr Siebeck, 2009.

Rothschild, Clare K. "The Muratorian Fragment as Roman Fake." *NovT* 60, no. 1 (2018): 55–82.

Rothschild, Clare K. *The Muratorian Fragment: Text, Translation, Commentary*. Studien und Texte zu Antike und Christentum, no. 132. Tübingen: Mohr Siebeck, 2022.

Ruckstuhl, Eugen. "Zur Aussage und Botschaft von Johannes 21." In *Jesus im Horizont der Evangelien*, 327–53. Stuttgarter biblische Aufsatzbände, no. 3 Stuttgart: Kath. Bibelwerk, 1988.

Runia, David T. *Philo in Early Christian Literature: A Survey*. Compendia Rerum Iudaicarum ad NovT, no. 3. Minneapolis, MN: Fortress, 1993.

Salier, Willis H. *The Rhetorical Impact of the Sēmeia in the Gospel of John*. WUNT, no. 186. Tübingen: Mohr Siebeck, 2004.

Sanders, Ed P. *Paul and Palestinian Judaism: A Comparison of Patterns of Religion*. 40th anniversary edition. Minneapolis, MN: Fortress, 2017.

Schäfer, Peter. *The Origins of Jewish Mysticism*. Princeton, NJ: Princeton University Press, 2009.

Schäferdiek, Knut. "The Acts of John." In *New Testament Apocrypha*, vol. 2, edited by Wilhelm Schneemelcher, translated by Robert McLachlan, 152–212. Louisville, KY: Westminster John Knox, 1992.

Schenck, Kenneth. *A Brief Guide to Philo*. Louisville, KY: Westminster John Knox, 2005.

Schenke, Gesa. "Das Erscheinen Jesu vor den Jüngern und der ungläubige Thomas: Johannes 20,19–31." In *Coptica—Gnostica—Manichaica: Mélanges offerts à Wolf-Peter Funk*, edited by L. Painchaud and P.-H. Poirier, 893–904. Louvain: Peeters, 2006.

Schenke, Hans-Martin. "The Function and Background of the Beloved Disciple in the Gospel of John." In *Der Same Seths: Hans-Martin Schenkes kleine Schriften zu Gnosis, Koptologie und Neuem Testament*, edited by Gesine Schenke Robinson, Gesa Schenke, and Uwe-Karsten Pilsch, 598–613. Leiden: Brill, 2012.

Schenke, Ludger. "The Johannine Schism and the 'Twelve' (John 6:60–71)." In *Critical Readings of John 6*, edited by R. Alan Culpepper, 205–19. BINS, no. 22. Leiden: Brill, 1997.

Schlatter, Adolf. *Der Evangelist Johannes: Wie er spricht, denkt und glaubt*. Stuttgart: Calwer, 1975.

Schlüsser Fiorenza, Elizabeth. "The Quest for the Johannine School: The Book of Revelation and the Fourth Gospel." In *The Book of Revelation: Justice and Judgment*, 2nd edition, 85–113. Minneapolis, MN: Fortress, 1998.

Schnackenburg, Rudolf. *The Gospel According to St. John*. 3 vols. Translated by Kevin Smyth. New York: Crossroad, 1982.

Schneiders, Sandra Marie. "The Foot Washing (John 13:1–20): An Experiment in Hermeneutics." *CBQ* 43, no. 1 (1981): 76–92.
Schneiders, Sandra Marie. "History and Symbolism in the Fourth Gospel." In *L'Evangile de Jean: Sources, Rédaction, Théologie*, edited by M. de Jonge, 371–76. BETL, no. 44. Leuven: Peeters, 1977.
Schnelle, Udo. *Das Evangelium nach Johannes*. THKNT, no. 4. Leipzig: Evangelische Verlagsanstalt, 2016.
Schnelle, Udo. "Die Reihenfolge der johanneischen Schriften." *NTS* 57, no. 1 (2011): 91–113.
Schnelle, Udo. "Johannes und die Synoptiker." In *The Four Gospels 1992: Festschrift Frans Neirynck*, vol. 3, edited by Frans Van Segbroeck and Frans Neirynck, 1799–814. BETL, no. 100. Leuven: University Press, 1992.
Schoedel, William R. *Ignatius of Antioch: A Commentary on the Letters of Ignatius of Antioch*. Hermeneia. Philadelphia: Fortress, 1985.
Schrader, Elizabeth. "Was Martha of Bethany Added to the Fourth Gospel in the Second Century?" *HTR* 110, no. 3 (2017): 360–474.
Schultz, Alexandra. "Collection." In *Writing, Enslavement, and Power in the Roman Mediterranean*, edited by J. Coogan, Joseph A. Howley, and Candida R. Moss. New York: Oxford University Press, 2025.
Schunack, Gerd. *Die Briefe des Johannes*. Zürcher Bibelkommentare NT, no. 17. Zürich: Theologischer Verlag Zürich, 1982.
Schwankl, Otto. *Licht und Finsternis: Ein metaphorisches Paradigma in den johanneischen Schriften*. HBS, no. 5. Freiburg im Breisgau: Herder, 1995.
Schweizer, Eduard. "What about the Johannine 'Parables'?" In *Exploring the Gospel of John: In Honor of D. Moody Smith*, edited by R. Alan Culpepper, Dwight Moody Smith, and C. Clifton Black, 208–19. Louisville, KY: Westminster John Knox, 1996.
Scott, Alan. *Origen and the Life of the Stars: A History of an Idea*. OECS. Oxford: Clarendon Press, 1991.
Shelfer, Lochlan. "The Legal Precision of the Term 'παράκλητος'." *JSNT* 32, no. 2 (2010): 131–50.
Shellard, Barbara. "The Relationship of Luke and John: A Fresh Look at an Old Problem." *JTS* 46, no. 1 (1995): 71–98.
Siegert, Folker, and Siegfried Bergler. *Synopse der vorkanonischen Jesusüberlieferungen: Zeichenquelle und Passionsbericht, die Logienquelle und der Grundbestand des Markusevangeliums*. Schriften des Institutum Judaicum Delitzschianum, no. 8/1. Göttingen: Vandenhoeck & Ruprecht, 2010.
Sim, David C. "The Family of Jesus and the Disciples of Jesus in Paul and Mark: Taking Sides in the Early Church's Factional Dispute." In *Paul and Mark: Comparative Essays. Part 1: Two Authors at the Beginnings of Christianity*, edited by Oda Wischmeyer, David C. Sim, and Ian J. Elmer, 73–99. BZNW, no. 198. Berlin: De Gruyter, 2014.
Sim, David C. *The Gospel of Matthew and Christian Judaism: The History and Social Setting of Matthew's Community*. Studies of the New Testament and Its World. Edinburgh: T&T Clark, 1998.
Smith, Dwight Moody. *John*. Abingdon New Testament Commentaries. Nashville, TN: Abingdon, 1999.
Smith, Dwight Moody. *John among the Gospels*. 2nd edition. Columbia: University of South Carolina Press, 2001.
Smith, Dwight Moody. "The Problem of John and the Synoptics in Light of the Relation between Apocryphal and Canonical Gospels." In *John and the Synoptics*, edited by Adelbert Denaux, 147–62. BETL, no. 101. Leuven: Leuven University Press, 1992.
Smith, Tyler. "Deception in the Speech Profile of the Johannine Jesus (John 7.1–10)." *JSNT* 40, no. 2 (2017): 169–91.
Smith, Wesley D. *Hippocrates: Pseudepigraphic Writings: Letters—Embassy—Speech from the Altar—Decree*. Leiden: Brill, 2018.

Spencer, Patrick E. "Narrative Echoes in John 21: Intertextual Interpretation and Intratextual Connection." *JSNT* 22, no. 75 (1999): 49–68.

Speyer, Wolfgang. *Bücherfunde in der Glaubenswerbung der Antike*. Göttingen: Vandenhoeck & Ruprecht, 1970.

Speyer, Wolfgang. *Die Literarische Fälschung im Heidnischen und Christlichen Altertum: Ein Versuch ihrer Deutung*. Handbuch der Altertumswissenschaft: Abteilung, no. 1. Munich: Beck, 1971.

Spicq, Ceslas. *L'Épître aux Hébreux*. 2 vols. 3rd edition. Études Bibliques. Paris: Libraire Lecoffre, 1952–53.

Spittler, Janet E. "The Acts of John 87–105 (Vienna hist. Gr. 63 fol. 51v–55v): Is It a 'Fragment'?" *Ancient Jew Review* May 6, 2019. https://www.ancientjewreview.com/read/2019/4/30/is-vienna-hist-gr-63-fol-51v-55v-a-fragment.

Stang, Charles M. *Apophasis and Pseudonymity in Dionysius the Areopagite: "No Longer I."* OECS. Oxford: Oxford University Press, 2012.

Starr, Raymond J. "The Circulation of Literary Texts in the Roman World." *Classical Quarterly* 37, no. 1 (1987): 213–23.

Stemberger, Günter. *La symbolique du bien et du mal selon saint Jean*. Collection "Parole de Dieu." Paris: Seuil, 1970.

Stibbe, Mark W. G. "The Elusive Christ: A New Reading of the Fourth Gospel." *JSNT* 14, no. 44 (1991): 19–37.

Stibbe, Mark W. G. "A Tomb with a View: John 11.1–44 in Narrative-Critical Perspective." *NTS* 40 (1994): 38–54.

Stimpfle, Alois. *Blinde sehen: Die Eschatologie im traditionsgeschichtlichen Prozeß des Johannesevangeliums*. BZNW, no. 57. Berlin: De Gruyter, 1990.

Stowers, Stanley K. *Christian Beginnings: A Study in Ancient Mediterranean Religion*. Edinburgh Studies in Religion in Antiquity. Edinburgh: Edinburgh University Press, 2024.

Stowers, Stanley K. "The Concept of 'Community' and the History of Early Christianity." *Method & Theory in the Study of Religion* 23, nos. 3–4 (2011): 238–56.

Stowers, Stanley K. "The Dilemma of Paul's Physics: Features Stoic-Platonist or Platonist-Stoic?" In *Christian Beginnings: A Study in Ancient Mediterranean Religion*, 231–53. Edinburgh Studies in Religion in Antiquity. Edinburgh: Edinburgh University Press, 2024.

Stowers, Stanley K. *Rereading of Romans: Justice, Jews, and Gentiles*. New Haven, CT: Yale University Press, 1994.

Stowers, Stanley K. "What Is Pauline Participation in Christ?" In *Christian Beginnings: A Study in Ancient Mediterranean Religion*, 181–94. Edinburgh Studies in Religion in Antiquity. Edinburgh: Edinburgh University Press, 2024.

Strecker, Georg. "Chiliasm and Docetism in the Johannine School." *Australian Biblical Review* 38 (1990): 45–61.

Strecker, Georg. *The Johannine Letters: A Commentary on 1, 2, and 3 John*. Hermeneia. Minneapolis, MN: Fortress, 1996.

Streeter, B. H. *The Four Gospels: A Study of Origins, Treating of the Manuscript Tradition, Sources, Authorship, and Dates*. New York: Macmillan, 1924.

Stuckenbruck, Loren T., and Wendy E. S. North, eds. *Early Jewish and Christian Monotheism*. London: T&T Clark, 2004.

Sturch, R. L. "The Alleged Eyewitness Material in the Fourth Gospel." In *Studia Biblica 1978*, vol. 2: *Papers on the Gospels*, edited by E. A. Livingstone, 313–27. Sheffield: JSOT, 1980.

Sullivan, Kevin P. *Wrestling with Angels: A Study of the Relationship between Angels and Humans in Ancient Jewish Literature and the New Testament*. Arbeiten zur Geschichte des Antiken Judentums und des Urchristentums 55. Leiden: Brill, 2004.

Sundberg, Albert C., Jr. "Canon Muratori: A Fourth-Century List." *HTR* 66, no. 1 (1973): 1–41.

Sykutris, Johannes, and E. J. Bickerman. *Speusipps Brief an König Philipp: Text, Übersetzung, Untersuchungen*. Leipzig: S. Hirzel Leipzig, 1928.

Syme, Ronald. "Fraud and Imposture." In *Pseudepigrapha I: Pseudopythagorica—Lettres de Platon—Littérature pseudépigraphique juive*. Entretiens Sur l'Antiquité Classique, no. 18. Vandoeuvres-Genève: Fondation Hardt, Entretiens sur l'antiquité classique, 1972.

Talbert, Charles H. *The Development of Christology during the First Hundred Years, and Other Essays on Early Christian Christology*. NovTSupp, no. 140. Leiden: Brill, 2011.

Theobald, Michael. *Das Evangelium nach Johannes. Kapitel 1–12*. Regensburger Neues Testament. Regensburg: Friedrich Pustet, 2009.

Theobald, Michael. "Der Jünger, den Jesus liebte." In *Studien zum Corpus Iohanneum*, 493–529. WUNT, no. 267. Tübingen: Mohr Siebeck. 2010.

Theobald, Michael. *Herrenworte Im Johannesevangelium*. HBS, no. 34. Freiburg im Breisgau: Herder, 2002.

Thiessen, Matthew. *Paul and the Gentile Problem*. New York: Oxford University Press, 2016.

Thompson, Marianne Meye. *1–3 John*. IVP New Testament Commentary Series. Downers Grove, IL: InterVarsity Press, 1992.

Thompson, Marianne Meye. *John: A Commentary*. New Testament Library. Louisville, KY: Westminster John Knox, 2015.

Thompson, Michael B. "The Holy Internet: Communication between Churches in the First Christian Generation." In *The Gospels for All Christians: Rethinking the Gospel Audience*, edited by Richard Bauckham, 49–70. Grand Rapids, MI: Eerdmans, 1998.

Thyen, Hartwig. *Das Johannesevangelium*. 2nd edition. Handbuch zum Neuen Testament, no. 6. Tübingen: Mohr Siebeck, 2015.

Thyen, Hartwig. "Entwicklungen innerhalb der johanneischen Theologie und Kirche im Spiegel von Joh 21 und der Lieblingsjüngertexte des Evangeliums." In *Studien zum Corpus Iohanneum*, edited by Hartwig Thyen, 42–82. WUNT, no. 214. Tübingen: Mohr Siebeck, 2007.

Thyen, Hartwig. "Johannes und die Synoptiker: Eine redaktionsgeschichtliche Analyse von Joh 18–20 vor dem markinischen und lukanischen Hintergrund." *Theologische Literaturzeitung* 126, no. 4 (2001): 397–402.

Tomson, Peter. *If This Be from Heaven: Jesus and the New Testament Authors in Their Relationship to Judaism*. Biblical Seminar. Sheffield: Sheffield Academic, 2001.

Tops, Thomas. *Paroimia and Parresia in the Gospel of John: A Historical-Hermeneutical Study*. WUNT/2, no. 565. Tübingen: Mohr Siebeck, 2022.

Trebilco, Paul. "John's Apocalypse in Relation to Johannine, Pauline, and Other Forms of Christianity in Asia Minor." In *The Oxford Handbook of the Book of Revelation*, edited by Craig R. Koester, by 183–201. Oxford Handbooks. Oxford: Oxford University Press, 2020.

Trobisch, David. *Paul's Letter Collection: Tracing the Origins*. Bolivar, MO: Quiet Waters, 2001.

Tuckett, Christopher. *The Gospel of Mary*. OECT. Oxford: Oxford University Press, 2007.

Turner, John D. "5. The Johannine Legacy: The Gospel and Apocryphon of John." In *The Legacy of John*, edited by Tuomas J. Rasimus, 105–44. Leiden: Brill, 2010.

Ullucci, Daniel. "The Anonymity of the Gospels κατά Pac-Man." *Annali di Storia dell'Esegesi* 36, no. 1 (2019): 95–116.

Uusimäki, Elisa. *Lived Wisdom in Jewish Antiquity: Studies in Exercise and Exemplarity*. Education, Literary Culture, and Religious Practice in the Ancient World. New York: Bloomsbury Academic, 2021.

van Belle, Gilbert. *The Signs Source in the Fourth Gospel: Historical Survey and Critical Evaluation of the Semeia Hypothesis*. BETL 116. Leuven: Leuven University Press, 1994.

van Belle, Gilbert, Michael Labahn, and P. Maritz, eds. *Repetitions and Variations in the Fourth Gospel: Style, Text, Interpretation*. BETL, no. 223. Leuven: Peeters, 2009.

Van der Watt, Jan G. *Family of the King: Dynamics of Metaphor in the Gospel According to John*. BINS, no. 47. Leiden: Brill, 2000.

Van der Watt, Jan G. *A Grammar of the Ethics of John: Reading John from an Ethical Perspective*. Vol. 1. WUNT/2, no. 431. Tübingen: Mohr Siebeck, 2019.

Van der Watt, Jan G. *A Grammar of the Ethics of John: Reading John from an Ethical Perspective.* Vol. 2. WUNT/2, no. 502. Tübingen: Mohr Siebeck, 2023.

Van de Weghe, Luuk. "The Beloved Eyewitness." *NTS* 68, no. 3 (2022): 351–57.

Van Kooten, George H. *Paul's Anthropology in Context: The Image of God, Assimilation to God, and Tripartite Man in Ancient Judaism, Ancient Philosophy and Early Christianity.* WUNT, no. 232. Tübingen: Mohr Siebeck, 2008.

Vanni, Ugo. *Apocalisse: Libro della Rivelazione esegesi biblico-teologica e implicazioni pastorali.* Testi e commenti. Bologna: EDB, 2009.

Viviano, Benedict T. "John's Use of Matthew: Beyond Tweaking." *Revue Biblique* 111, no. 2 (2004): 209–37.

Von Harnack Adolf. "Das 'Wir' in den Johanneischen Schriften." *Sitzungsberichte der preussischen Akademie der Wissenschaften Philosophisch-historische Klasse* 31 (1923): 96–113.

Von Wahlde, Urban C. "Archaeology and John's Gospel." In *Jesus and Archaeology*, edited by James H. Charlesworth, 523–586. Grand Rapids, MI: Eerdmans, 2006.

Von Wahlde, Urban C. *The Gospel and Letters of John.* 3 vols. Eerdmans Critical Commentary Series. Grand Rapids, MI: Eerdmans, 2010.

Von Wahlde, Urban C. "The Pool of Siloam: The Importance of the New Discoveries for Our Understanding of Ritual Immersion in Late Second Temple Judaism and the Gospel of John." In *John, Jesus, and History*, vol. 2: *Aspects of Historicity in the Fourth Gospel*, edited by Paul N. Anderson, Felix Just, and Tom Thatcher, 155–74. SBLECL, no. 2. Atlanta, GA: SBL, 2009.

Von Wahlde, Urban C. "The Pool(s) of Bethesda and the Healing in John 5: A Reappraisal of Research and of the Johannine Text." *Revue Biblique* 116, no. 1 (2009): 111–36.

Vorster, Willem S. "The Growth and Making of John 21." In *Essays on Biblical Language, Gospel Narrative and the Historical Jesus*, edited by Willem S. Vorster and Eugene J. Botha, 199–215. NovTSupp 92. Leiden: Brill, 1999.

Vouga, François. *Die Johannesbriefe.* HNT, no. 15/3. Tübingen: Mohr Siebeck, 1990.

Waldstein, Michael, and Frederik Wisse. *The Apocryphon of John: Synopsis of Nag Hammadi Codices II, 1; III, 1; and IV, 1 with BG 8502,2.* Nag Hammadi and Manichean Studies, no. 33. Leiden: Brill, 1995.

Wallace, Daniel B. *Greek Grammar beyond the Basics: An Exegetical Syntax of the New Testament.* Grand Rapids, MI: Zondervan, 1996.

Wallace, Daniel B. "John 5,2 and the Date of the Fourth Gospel." *Biblica* 71, no. 2 (1990): 177–205.

Walsh, Matthew L. *Angels Associated with Israel in the Dead Sea Scrolls: Angelology and Sectarian Identity at Qumran.* WUNT/2, no. 509. Tübingen: Mohr Siebeck, 2019.

Walsh, Robyn Faith. "The Epistle to the Laodiceans and the Art of Tradition." In *Authorial Fictions and Attributions in the Ancient Mediterranean*, edited by Chance Bonar and Julia Lindenlaub, 13–38. WUNT/2. Tübingen: Mohr Siebeck, 2024.

Walsh, Robyn Faith. *The Origins of Early Christian Literature: Contextualizing the New Testament within Greco-Roman Literary Culture.* Cambridge: Cambridge University Press, 2021.

Wassen, Cecilia. "Angels in the Dead Sea Scrolls." *Deuterocanonical and Cognate Literature Yearbook 2007* (2007): 499–524.

Wasserman, Emma. *The Death of the Soul in Romans 7.* WUNT/2, no. 256. Tübingen: Mohr Siebeck, 2008.

Wasserman, Emma. "Paul beyond the Judaism/Hellenism Divide? The Case of Pauline Anthropology in Romans 7 and 2 Corinthians 4–5." In *Christian Origins and Hellenistic Judaism: Social and Literary Contexts for the New Testament*, edited by Stanley E. Porter and Andrew Pitts, 259–79. Texts and Editions for New Testament Study, no. 10. Leiden: Brill, 2012.

Watson, Francis B. *An Apostolic Gospel: The "Epistula Apostolorum" in Literary Context*. SNTSMS, no. 179. Cambridge: Cambridge University Press, 2020.
Watson, Francis B. "A Gospel of the Eleven." In *Connecting Gospels: Beyond the Canonical/Non-canonical Divide*, edited by Francis Watson and Sarah Parkhouse, 189–215. Oxford: Oxford University Press, 2018.
Watson, Francis B. *Gospel Writing: A Canonical Perspective*. Grand Rapids, MI: Eerdmans, 2013.
Watson, Francis B. "Is John's Christology Adoptionist?" In *The Glory of Christ in the New Testament: Studies in Christology in Memory of George Bradford Caird*, edited by L. D. Hurst and N. T. Wright, 113–24. Oxford: Clarendon Press, 1987.
Welck, Christian. *Erzählte Zeichen: Die Wundergeschichten des Johannesevangeliums Literarisch Untersucht: Mit einem Ausblick auf Joh 21*. WUNT, no. 69. Tübingen: Mohr Siebeck, 1994.
Wengst, Klaus. *Bedrängte Gemeinde und verherrlichter Christus*. Neukirchen: Neukirchener, 1981.
Wengst, Klaus. *Das Johannesevangelium*. 2 vols. ThKNT, no. 4. Stuttgart: Kohlhammer, 2004.
Wengst, Klaus. *Der Erste, Zweite und Dritte Brief des Johannes: 16*. Orig.-Ausg. Ökumenischer Taschenbuchkommentar zum Neuen Testament 16. Gütersloh: Mohn, 1978.
Wheaton, Gerry. *The Role of Jewish Feasts in John's Gospel*. SNTSMS 162. Cambridge: Cambridge University Press, 2015.
Williams, Catrin H. "Faith, Eternal Life, and Spirit in the Gospel of John." In *The Oxford Handbook of Johannine Studies*, edited by Judith M. Lieu and Martinus C. de Boer, 347–62. Oxford Handbooks. Oxford: Oxford University Press, 2018.
Williams, Catrin H. *"I Am He": The Interpretation of "Anî Hû" in Jewish and Early Christian Literature*. WUNT/2, no. 113. Tübingen: Mohr Siebeck, 2000.
Wilson, Brittany E. *The Embodied God: Seeing the Divine in Luke-Acts and the Early Church*. New York: Oxford University Press, 2021.
Wilson, J. Christian. "The Problem of the Domitianic Date of Revelation." *NTS* 39, no. 4 (1993): 587–605.
Windisch, Hans. *Johannes und die Synoptiker: Wollte der vierte Evangelist die älteren Evangelien ergänzen oder ersetzen?* Untersuchungen zum Neuen Testament, no. 12. Leipzig: Hinrich, 1926.
Winston, David. *Logos and Mystical Theology in Philo of Alexandria*. Cincinnati, OH: Hebrew Union College Press, 1985.
Winston, David, ed. *The Wisdom of Solomon: A New Translation with Introduction and Commentary*. AB, no. 43. Garden City, NY: Doubleday, 1979.
Wischmeyer, Oda, David C. Sim, and Ian J. Elmer, eds. *Paul and Mark: Comparative Essays. Part 1: Two Authors at the Beginnings of Christianity*. BZNT, no. 198. Berlin: De Gruyter, 2014.
Witetschek, Stephan J. "Ein weit geöffnetes Zeitfenster? Überlegungen zur Datierung der Johannesapokalypse." In *Die Johannesapokalypse: Kontexte—Konzepte—Rezeption*, edited by Jörg Frey, James A. Kelhoffer, and Franz Tóth, 117–48. WUNT, no. 287. Tübingen: Mohr Siebeck, 2012.
Witherington, Ben, III. "What's in a Name? Rethinking the Historical Figure of the Beloved Disciple in the Fourth Gospel." In *John, Jesus, and History*, vol. 2: *Aspects of Historicity in the Fourth Gospel*, edited by Paul N. Anderson, Felix Just, and Tom Thatcher, 203–12. Atlanta, GA: SBL, 2015.
Witulski, Thomas. *Die Johannesoffenbarung und Kaiser Hadrian: Studien zur Datierung der neutestamentlichen Apokalypse*. Forschungen zur Religion und Literatur des Alten und Neuen Testaments, no. 221. Göttingen: Vandenhoeck & Ruprecht, 2007.
Wolter, Michael. "Die anonymen Schriften des Neuen Testaments: Annäherungsversuch an ein literarisches Phänomen." *ZNW* 79, nos. 1–2 (1988): 1–16.

Wolter, Michael. *The Gospel According to Luke*. Translated by Wayne Coppins and Christoph Heilig. 2 vols. BMSEC. Tübingen: Mohr Siebeck, 2017.
Wyrick, Jed. *The Ascension of Authorship: Attribution and Canon Formation in Jewish, Hellenistic, and Christian Traditions.* Cambridge, MA: Harvard University Press, 2004.
Yee, Gale A. *Jewish Feasts and the Gospel of John.* Zaccheus Studies. Wilmington, DE: Michael Glazier, 1989.
Zamfir, Korinna, and Joseph Verheyden. "Reference-Text-Oriented Allusions." In *Exploring Intertextuality: Diverse Strategies for New Testament Interpretation of Texts*, edited by B. J. Oropeza and Steve Moyise, 242–53. Eugene, OR: Wipf and Stock, 2016.
Zelyck, Lorne R. "Irenaeus and the Authorship of the Fourth Gospel." In *The Origins of John's Gospel*, edited by Stanley E. Porter and Hughson T. Ong, 239–58. Johannine Studies 2. Leiden: Brill, 2016.
Zimmermann, Ruben. *Christologie der Bilder im Johannesevangelium: Die Christopoetik des vierten Evangeliums unter besonderer Berücksichtigung von Joh 10.* WUNT, no. 171. Tübingen: Mohr Siebeck, 2004.
Zimmermann, Ruben. "Imagery in John: Opening Up Paths into the Tangled Thicket of John's Figurative World." In *Imagery in the Gospel of John: Terms, Forms, Themes, and Theology of Johannine Figurative Language*, edited by Jörg Frey and Gabi Kern, 1–43. WUNT, no. 200. Tübingen: Mohr Siebeck, 2006.
Zumstein, Jean. "Bildersprache und Relektüre am Beispiel von Joh 15,1–17." In *Imagery in the Gospel of John: Terms, Forms, Themes, and Theology of Johannine Figurative Language*, edited by Jörg Frey and Gabi Kern, 139–56. WUNT, no. 200. Tübingen: Mohr Siebeck, 2006.

Index of Bible References

For the benefit of digital users, indexed terms that span two pages (e.g., 52–53) may, on occasion, appear on only one of those pages.

Genesis
  1, 147
  1:3, 56
  2:7, 34–35
  28:10–22, 51–52
Exodus
  7:1, 56–57
  20:18, 58
  24:16–17, 47–48
  33:18–2, 47–48
  34:29–30, 47–48
Deuteronomy
  18:19, 28
  34:5, 55
  34:6, 55, 56–57
1 Kings
  3:5–10, 152
  4:32, 152
  7–8, 152
  21:8, 28
1 Chronicles
  21:19, 28
Esther
  8:8, 28
Job
  1:6, 51
  2:1, 51
  38:7, 51
Psalms
  82:6, 49–50
Ecclesiastes
  1:1, 152
  12:9, 152
Jeremiah
  44:16, 28
Daniel
  12:2–3, 33
Zechariah
  9:9, 18, 91
Wisdom
  9:7–12, 152

Matthew
  3:17, 96
  4:18–20, 70
  4:23–5:1, 19
  5:14, 126
  6:9, 126
  7:17–19, 126
  8:5–13, 76
  8:9–10, 76
  8:10, 76
  9:1–8, 76–77
  9:37–38, 126
  10:24–25, 18
  10:39, 125
  11:2–7, 12
  12:36–42, 43
  13:13, 106
  14:6–12, 12
  14:22–33, 75
  14:34, 78
  15:29, 18
  16:13–16, 70–71
  16:21, 83
  16:25, 125
  16:28, 84
  17:5, 96
  17:11–13, 127
  18:3, 126
  18:8, 40–41
  18:10–14, 81, 126
  21:1–11, 91
  21:5, 18
  21:12–17, 71
  22:7, 25
  22:30, 34
  24:2, 25
  25:31, 40–41
  25:46, 40–41
  26:6, 89
  26:6–13, 16
  26:6–16, 89

248 INDEX OF BIBLE REFERENCES

Matthew (*cont.*)
  26:29, 97–98
  26:32, 97–98
  26:36–46, 93
  26:38, 97–98
  26:45, 97–98
  26:61, 71–72
  27:15, 18
  27:40, 71–72
  27:55–56, 119–20
  27:57, 18
  27:60, 18
  28:2–5, 19
  28:8–10, 101–2
  28:9–10, 18
Mark
  1:1, 147
  1:3, 15
  1:7, 15
  1:8, 15
  1:11, 96
  1:14, 12
  1:16–18, 70
  1:16–20, 71, 119
  1:19, 119
  1:19–20, 164
  1:21, 70
  1:29, 70
  1:29–31, 119
  2:1, 76–77
  2:1–12, 76–77
  2:9, 16–17
  2:11, 16–17
  2:19, 126
  2:22, 126
  2:23–3:6, 77
  3:13–19, 119
  3:17, 119, 164
  3:17–18, 166
  3:31–35, 83
  4:11, 124
  4:11–12, 106
  4:20, 126
  5:35–43, 119
  5:27, 164
  5:37, 166
  6:3, 166
  6:17–29, 12
  6:34, 126
  6:37, 16–17
  6:45–52, 75
  6:53, 78
  7, 12
  7:3–4, 12
  8:22–26, 83–84
  8:22–30, 131
  8:27–29, 70–71
  8:34, 42
  8:35, 125
  8:38, 124–25
  9:1, 45, 76–77, 84, 126
  9:2, 166
  9:2–8, 119, 164
  9:7, 96
  10:30, 40–41, 124–25
  10:32–33, 83
  10:35–41, 119
  10:46–52, 83–84
  11:1–11, 91
  11:12–20, 131
  11:15–19, 71
  12:25, 34
  12:27–28, 17
  13:2, 25
  13:3, 119, 164, 166
  13:30, 45
  14:3, 16–17, 89, 117
  14:3–11, 20, 89
  14:4–7, 16
  14:12, 127
  14:12–31, 93
  14:13–21, 74
  14:25, 126
  14:25–26, 97–98
  14:27, 126, 182–83
  14:28, 97–98
  14:31, 17
  14:32–42, 93, 119
  14:33, 164, 166
  14:34, 17, 97–98
  14:35–42, 127
  14:36, 17
  14:41, 97–98
  14:42, 17
  14:54, 116
  14:58, 71–72
  14:62, 124–25
  15:29, 71–72
  15:40–41, 119–20
  16:5, 19
  16:8, 8–9
  16:24, 41–42
  18:10–11, 17
  18:11, 17
Luke
  3:8–9, 126

INDEX OF BIBLE REFERENCES

3:19–20, 12
3:22, 96
4:28–30, 83
5:17–26, 76–77
6:40, 18
6:43, 126
7:1–10, 76
7:2, 76
7:7–8, 76
7:9, 76
7:11–17, 89
7:18–25, 12
7:36–38, 117
7:36–50, 16, 20, 89
7:37, 89
7:38, 19–20
7:44, 19
8:10, 106
9:9, 12
9:12–17, 74
9:24, 125
9:27, 84
9:35, 96
9:52–53, 72
10:2, 126
10:14, 43
10:22, 126
10:25–37, 72
10:38, 19–20
10:38–42, 19, 90
11:1, 19–20
11:2, 19–20, 126
11:31–32, 43
13:9, 126
15:3–7, 126
16:19–31, 90
16:31, 90
17:11–19, 72
17:33, 125
18:30, 40–41, 124–25
18:35, 90
19:28, 90
19:28–44, 91
19:45–48, 71
20:35–36, 34, 40–41, 46
21:6, 25
21:20, 25
22:3, 19
22:7–13, 119
22:14, 97
22:17–22, 97
22:26–27, 19, 97
22:39–46, 93
22:50–54, 19
22:55, 116
23:21, 19
23:49, 19
23:53, 19
24:4, 19
24:12, 19, 119–20
24:13–49, 19
24:24, 19
24:36–51, 101–2
24:49, 101–2
John
  1, 60
  1–4, 65–72
  1–20, 5–7, 9–10, 109–11, 121, 149–50, 153
  1:1, 22, 28, 46, 49–50, 57–59, 147, 182–83
  1:1–2, 136–37
  1:1–18, 123, 144
  1:2, 120
  1:3, 22–23, 29
  1:4, 54, 57–58, 81
  1:9, 30–31, 57–58
  1:9–11, 65
  1:10, 29
  1:12, 36, 75–76
  1:12–13, 32, 46, 60
  1:14, 6, 28, 30, 47, 49–50, 53–54, 60, 61, 109, 110, 111, 115, 120, 148–49, 179–80, 183
  1:15, 70–71
  1:16, 57–58
  1:16–20, 65
  1:17, 22, 30
  1:18, 28, 29–30, 48, 53–54, 93–94, 101, 126
  1:19–34, 15
  1:19–51, 65–67
  1:21, 127
  1:21–10:52, 65
  1:23, 15
  1:26–27, 15
  1:28, 24–25, 116–17
  1:29, 30–31, 182–83
  1:30, 30, 70–71
  1:31–33, 66
  1:32, 66
  1:32–34, 30
  1:33, 15, 69
  1:37, 66
  1:38, 24, 66
  1:39, 66, 116
  1:40, 174–75
  1:41, 66–67, 70–71
  1:41–42, 24
  1:42, 66–67

INDEX OF BIBLE REFERENCES

John (*cont.*)
  1:43, 66–67
  1:44, 70, 116–17
  1:46, 66–67
  1:47–48, 67
  1:49, 70–71
  1:50, 67
  1:51, 51–52, 59, 67, 82
  2, 97
  2–4, 71
  2:1, 24–25, 67
  2:1–11, 67–68
  2:3, 67
  2:4, 67, 68
  2:5–7, 41
  2:6, 13, 116
  2:6–9, 36–37, 67
  2:7, 68
  2:9, 36–37, 67
  2:10, 68, 126
  2:11, 4, 30–31, 47, 48, 67, 73, 109
  2:12, 68
  2:13, 13, 69, 174–75
  2:13–22, 125
  2:13–25, 69
  2:14, 70
  2:14–16, 69
  2:16, 69, 96
  2:18, 69
  2:18–19, 99
  2:19, 68, 69, 71–72, 124
  2:20, 116
  2:21, 22–23, 69, 99, 123
  2:21–22, 64–65
  2:22, 122–23
  2:23, 4, 116, 174–75
  3, 60, 69, 72, 114
  3:1–4:42, 69–70
  3:2, 4, 30–31
  3:2–3, 124
  3:3, 124
  3:3–6, 43–44, 45, 59–60, 69
  3:3–7, 36, 41
  3:4, 124
  3:5, 124–25
  3:5–6, 100
  3:6, 32–33, 41–42
  3:8, 36, 37, 68
  3:10–12, 50–51
  3:11, 114, 182–83
  3:11–13, 112
  3:12–13, 36
  3:13, 29–30, 52
  3:15, 73
  3:16, 41, 61, 84, 86, 94–95
  3:17, 177–78
  3:18, 41, 99–100, 114
  3:19, 30, 43
  3:21, 96
  3:22–23, 69
  3:23, 24–25, 116–17
  3:23–24, 12
  3:24, 127
  3:27, 36
  3:29, 68
  3:29–30, 126
  3:31, 29, 36
  3:32, 114, 183
  3:34, 49–50, 69
  3:36, 41, 124–25
  4, 60, 72–73, 97
  4–6, 72–76
  4:5, 24–25, 70
  4:6, 116
  4:9, 13
  4:10, 70, 80–81, 124
  4:11, 124
  4:14, 41, 68, 99, 182–83
  4:20, 70
  4:24, 28, 36, 41–42, 54, 58
  4:29, 70
  4:32, 43–44
  4:35–38, 126
  4:36, 74–75, 96
  4:36–38, 70
  4:40–41, 70
  4:41, 72
  4:46, 76–77
  4:46–47, 72–73
  4:46–54, 125
  4:46–5:47, 72–74
  4:48, 72–73
  4:49, 72–73
  4:50, 72–73
  4:51, 76–77
  4:51–53, 72–73
  4:52–53, 116
  4:54, 4, 72–73
  5, 43, 60, 72–73, 97
  5:1, 4
  5:1–3, 76–77
  5:1–5, 72–73
  5:2, 24–25, 77
  5:7, 99–100
  5:8, 16–17, 72–73
  5:11–12, 16–17

5:14, 70
5:16–47, 72, 73
5:20–21, 77, 94–95
5:20–25, 52
5:21, 73, 99
5:21–30, 124–25, 135–36
5:24, 30, 32, 41
5:24–25, 22–23, 52–53, 73, 86
5:25, 66, 87
5:26, 32, 54, 99
5:28–29, 87
5:29, 43
5:32, 61, 114, 115
5:33, 114
5:36, 30–31
5:37, 114
5:38, 54, 73
5:40, 73
6, 41, 60, 97
6:1, 4, 5–6, 76–77
6:1–5, 74
6:1–14, 74–75
6:1–15, 74
6:1–21, 125
6:3, 18
6:4, 13, 116, 174–75
6:7, 16–17
6:8, 41
6:8–11, 74
6:9, 116
6:12, 74–75
6:12–13, 74
6:13, 116
6:15–17, 75
6:15–21, 75–76
6:17, 75, 76–77, 78
6:19, 75–76, 116
6:19–21, 75
6:20–21, 75
6:21, 75
6:22, 75
6:25, 76–77
6:25–71, 72, 74
6:27, 43–44, 74
6:28–29, 96
6:32, 29
6:33, 74
6:35–59, 124–25
6:39, 44, 74–75
6:40, 44, 86
6:41–42, 124
6:44, 44
6:47, 73, 86, 124–25

6:50, 86
6:50–51, 86
6:52, 30–31
6:53, 32, 41, 43, 73
6:53–56, 126
6:54, 44
6:56, 74, 124
6:58, 86
6:59, 76–77
6:60, 124
6:61–62, 74
6:63, 41, 43–44, 54, 57–58, 74, 94, 124
6:66, 124
6:68, 54
6:70, 30
6:70–71, 95
6:71, 116–17
7–8, 83
7–10, 78–83
7–8, 60
7:1–13, 79
7:1–8:59, 79–80
7:2, 13, 116
7:3–5, 79
7:4, 79
7:7, 80
7:8–9, 79
7:8–10, 124
7:10, 79
7:11, 79, 81
7:14, 70, 80
7:15, 30–31
7:27–28, 30–31
7:28, 36
7:30, 80
7:32, 80
7:33, 31
7:33–34, 79
7:34, 66–67, 68, 79, 81, 124
7:35, 30–31
7:35–36, 124
7:37, 116
7:37–39, 75–76, 80–81, 94, 182–83
7:38, 109–10
7:38–39, 41, 68, 99, 124
7:39, 123
7:44, 80
7:44–47, 97
7:53–8:11, 7
8, 42
8:12, 81, 126
8:14, 37, 68, 79, 80, 114
8:17–18, 114

252 INDEX OF BIBLE REFERENCES

John (*cont.*)
- 8:18, 114
- 8:19, 126
- 8:21, 41, 79, 80
- 8:23, 29, 30–31, 36
- 8:24, 41, 114
- 8:31, 54
- 8:32, 48
- 8:34, 42
- 8:35, 42, 96
- 8:37, 54
- 8:39–40, 22
- 8:43–44, 114
- 8:44, 25, 30, 95
- 8:45–47, 22
- 8:47, 49–50, 92, 114
- 8:51, 84, 86, 114
- 8:51–52, 41, 52–53
- 8:51–53, 84
- 8:52, 84, 85, 126
- 8:54, 47
- 8:56, 30
- 8:58, 30–31
- 8:59, 50–51, 80
- 9, 60, 97
- 9:1, 80, 130
- 9:1–41, 80–81
- 9:3, 96
- 9:5, 57–58, 80
- 9:7, 24–25, 80
- 9:12, 81
- 9:16, 30–31
- 9:22, 25
- 9:24, 81
- 9:29, 30–31, 81
- 9:38, 81
- 9:39, 80–81
- 10, 49, 60
- 10:1, 30, 83
- 10:1–2, 77
- 10:1–3, 98
- 10:1–6, 124
- 10:1–42, 81–83
- 10:2–3, 82
- 10:3–4, 77
- 10:3–5, 66–67
- 10:4, 82, 100–2
- 10:6, 64–65, 81
- 10:7, 77, 82
- 10:8–9, 82, 83
- 10:9, 52, 59, 67, 77, 82
- 10:10, 30, 74–75, 83
- 10:11, 77, 82, 126
- 10:12, 83
- 10:14–16, 66–67
- 10:15, 82, 126
- 10:17, 93–94
- 10:17–18, 82
- 10:18, 143
- 10:22, 116
- 10:22–39, 82
- 10:23, 70
- 10:25, 30–31
- 10:27, 67
- 10:27–28, 77, 82
- 10:28, 41, 42, 74–75, 83, 86
- 10:29, 28, 42
- 10:30, 49, 59
- 10:30–36, 60
- 10:31, 50–51
- 10:32–33, 49
- 10:35, 58–59
- 10:35–36, 49–50
- 10:38, 58–59
- 10:39, 83
- 10:40, 83
- 10:41–42, 83
- 11, 60, 85, 88–89
- 11–12, 84–89
- 11–15, 181
- 11:1, 88–89, 116–17
- 11:1–2, 127
- 11:1–3, 85
- 11:1–44, 90
- 11:1–53, 84–87
- 11:1–57, 84
- 11:2, 12, 90
- 11:3, 87, 119
- 11:4, 84, 85
- 11:5, 97, 119
- 11:7, 119
- 11:8, 119
- 11:9–10, 57–58
- 11:10, 58, 95
- 11:14, 85
- 11:16, 119
- 11:18, 116–17
- 11:20–27, 122
- 11:21, 85
- 11:23, 85
- 11:24, 85
- 11:24–25, 44
- 11:25, 41–42, 85, 86
- 11:25–26, 86
- 11:26, 41, 86
- 11:32, 85

INDEX OF BIBLE REFERENCES   253

11:37, 85
11:40, 47, 48, 62, 109, 115
11:43, 87
11:44, 87
11:47, 44
11:47-53, 84
11:48, 25
11:54, 119
11:55, 13
11:55-12:11, 88-89
11:56, 70, 116
12, 42, 60
12-17, 91-96
12:1, 88, 90, 116-17
12:1-2, 88
12:1-3, 117
12:1-8, 19
12:1-11, 84
12:2, 88, 90
12:2-5, 88
12:3, 16-17, 88, 90
12:4-6, 90
12:4-8, 16
12:5, 90
12:7, 88
12:9, 88-89
12:10, 88-89
12:10-11, 87, 119
12:12, 91
12:12-19, 91
12:12-50, 91-93
12:13, 91
12:14-15, 91
12:15, 18
12:16, 64-65, 91-92, 100, 122-23, 125
12:17-18, 96
12:20-21, 116-17
12:20-22, 92
12:23, 31, 91-92, 100
12:23-24, 92
12:24, 60, 69
12:24-26, 42
12:25, 60, 74-75, 125
12:25-26, 60, 87, 88, 92
12:26, 60, 88
12:27, 31, 68
12:27-28, 92, 127
12:28, 29, 126, 177-78
12:29, 92
12:31, 30, 43, 45, 68, 91-92
12:32-33, 31
12:35, 95
12:35-36, 58, 92-93

12:36, 58
12:37, 92-93
12:38-41, 30
12:39, 92-93
12:41, 47
12:46, 57-58, 95
12:47, 88
12:49-50, 92
13, 93, 94-95
13-17, 60, 122
13:1, 31, 43, 59, 68, 93
13:1-3, 79
13:1-4, 127
13:1-17, 19
13:1-35, 93-95
13:2, 19, 30, 89, 93, 116-17
13:3, 31
13:3-5, 93
13:3-6, 93
13:4, 93-94
13:7, 64-65, 93, 94
13:8, 93, 94
13:9, 94
13:10, 94
13:10-11, 95
13:12, 93-94
13:14, 94
13:14-15, 94-95
13:14-16, 18
13:16, 94-95
13:20, 75-76
13:23-24, 173
13:23-25, 173
13:23-26, 109
13:25, 93-94
13:27, 19, 30, 89, 95
13:30, 130
13:31, 31
13:31-17:26, 37, 93
13:33, 124
13:34, 22, 94-95, 147, 156
13:36, 37, 66, 82, 87, 94-95, 124
13:36-38, 42, 60
14, 22-23, 37, 42
14:1-3, 124, 177-78
14:1-31, 52
14:2, 38, 69, 88-89
14:2-3, 22-23, 69, 75-76, 92
14:2-4, 37
14:2-29, 44
14:3, 42, 52, 82, 100-1, 124-25, 135-36
14:4, 38
14:5, 66, 124

254 INDEX OF BIBLE REFERENCES

John (*cont.*)
  14:6, 52, 66, 82
  14:6-7, 38
  14:7, 48, 126
  14:8, 38, 66, 124
  14:9, 48
  14:9-11, 38
  14:10, 38, 59, 69
  14:10-11, 58-59
  14:12, 31, 37, 52, 59, 94-95, 100-1
  14:15, 88, 182-83
  14:16, 123
  14:16-17, 22
  14:17, 36, 39, 41, 48, 66, 75-76
  14:18-19, 124-25
  14:18-20, 135-36
  14:18-21, 39
  14:19, 45, 47-48, 66-67, 68, 79, 80, 92-93
  14:19-20, 41, 42, 85, 101
  14:20, 58-59, 66, 69
  14:20-21, 39
  14:21, 81, 94, 123, 182-83
  14:22, 39, 66, 79, 124
  14:23, 9, 39, 42, 52-53, 66, 81, 82, 88-89, 94, 97-98, 123
  14:23-24, 88
  14:25, 181
  14:25-26, 122
  14:26, 80-81, 133
  14:28, 28, 31, 37
  14:30, 4, 30, 83
  14:31, 5-6
  15-17, 4
  15:1, 96, 126
  15:1-4, 97-98
  15:1-7, 124
  15:1-8, 95-96
  15:2, 69, 95-96
  15:2-5, 95-96
  15:3, 94, 95, 96
  15:4, 39, 70, 97-98
  15:5, 126
  15:6, 69, 94, 95-96
  15:7, 54, 96
  15:8, 94-95, 126
  15:10, 182-83
  15:11, 88-89
  15:13, 22, 93-95
  15:15, 120, 124
  15:18-16:4, 83, 88-89
  15:20, 18, 94-95
  15:24, 72
  15:26, 114, 123
  15:27, 114, 120, 122
  16:2, 25
  16:4, 122
  16:5, 31, 68
  16:7, 32, 69, 101
  16:8-9, 30
  16:10, 37
  16:11, 30, 45
  16:12, 50-51, 181
  16:12-14, 133
  16:13-14, 123
  16:16, 80
  16:16-24, 68, 75-76, 82
  16:23, 66
  16:24, 88-89
  16:25, 124
  16:26, 66
  16:28, 31, 37, 100-1
  16:32, 109
  17:1, 29, 31, 84, 94-95
  17:3, 27, 48, 114
  17:5, 31, 47, 68, 84, 91-92, 93-94
  17:11, 31, 91-92
  17:11-13, 91-92
  17:12, 88
  17:13, 31
  17:14, 32-33, 57-58
  17:15, 39, 59, 83
  17:16, 32-33, 36
  17:18, 59, 94-95
  17:20, 66-67
  17:20-22, 114
  17:20-23, 49
  17:21, 39, 58-59
  17:22, 47
  17:22-23, 94-95
  17:23, 39, 58-59
  17:24, 39, 47, 52, 59
  18-19, 60
  18-20, 98-101
  18:1, 24-25
  18:1-19:27, 70-99
  18:10, 116-17
  18:10-12, 19
  18:15, 98, 109, 120
  18:15-16, 119
  18:16, 98
  18:18, 116
  18:20, 70
  18:36, 43-44, 45, 91-92, 100, 122, 124-25, 136
  18:39, 18
  19, 109-10

INDEX OF BIBLE REFERENCES

19:6, 19
19:11, 29
19:14, 116
19:25, 19
19:26, 98–99, 120
19:26–27, 109, 119–20
19:27, 98–99
19:30–34, 99
19:34, 109–10, 147
19:35, 61, 99, 109–10, 111, 113, 114, 115, 119, 145, 148–49, 151, 183
19:38, 18
19:40, 13
19:41, 18, 19, 116
19:42, 13
20, 60
20:1–2, 68
20:1–10, 109
20:1–21, 99–101
20:2, 98, 101, 109, 119
20:2–3, 173
20:2–10, 119–20
20:3–10, 19
20:6–7, 116
20:8, 119
20:9, 125
20:11–12, 100
20:11–16, 100–2
20:12, 19, 116
20:13, 101
20:14, 100
20:14–18, 18
20:17, 31, 68, 98–99, 100–2
20:18, 101
20:19, 100, 101
20:19–22, 43
20:19–29, 19
20:20, 99
20:21, 59, 66–67
20:22, 68, 101–2
20:24–26, 101
20:25, 101, 119
20:26, 100
20:27, 99
20:28, 101–2
20:29, 99, 100
20:30–31, 8, 9, 44, 64–65, 121
20:31, 8–9, 60, 61, 91, 99, 110, 111, 145
21, 6, 9–10, 111–13, 121, 141, 153
21:1, 9
21:1–25, 7–8
21:18–19, 10
21:21–22, 120
21:22, 9
21:23–24, 153
21:24, 6–7, 145, 148–49, 183
21:24–25, 6–7, 8–9, 11, 111, 112, 113, 148–49
21:25, 8, 121

Acts
1:5, 101–2
1:13, 164
2:1–42, 101–2
3:1–4:31, 164
4:13, 164–65
6:15, 51
8:4–25, 72
8:14, 164, 173–74
8:14–24, 164
12:1–2, 173
26:16, 182–83

Romans
5:8, 22
6:14, 22
6:15–22, 42
8:9–10, 39–40
8:10–11, 35–36
8:11, 39–41
8:17, 100
8:23, 35–36
12:4–5, 39–40
13:9–10, 22

1 Corinthians
1:8, 35–36
4:18–21, 160–61
5:3–5, 39–40
5:5, 35–36
8:4–13, 166–67
10:16–17, 39–40
12:12–31, 39–40
13, 22
15, 100
15:8–9, 166–67
15:35, 34–35
15:37, 34–35
15:40, 35, 100
15:42–47, 35
15:43–44, 100
15:44, 34–35
15:45–48, 99–100
15:48, 100
15:48–49, 35
15:48–51, 99–100
15:50, 34–35, 43–44
15:50–54, 40–41
15:51–52, 34–35

1 Corinthians (cont.)
  15:51–53, 35–36
  15:52, 44
  15:53–55, 44
2 Corinthians
  3:12–18, 47–48
  3:17–18, 47–48
  4:16, 35–36
  5:4, 44
  5:5, 35–36
  12:1–7, 166–67
  13:1–2, 160–61
  13:10, 160–61
Galatians
  1:11–16, 166–67
  2:1, 164, 173–74
  2:9, 164, 166, 173–74
  2:11–14, 23
  2:12, 23, 166
  2:16, 22
  3:6–7, 22
  5:6, 22
  5:14, 22
  7:5, 23
Ephesians
  1:3, 22–23
  2:1, 40
  2:6, 40
  2:18, 40
  2:6, 22–23
  2:21–22, 22–23
  2:22, 40
Philippians
  2:6, 22
  3:20–21, 35–36
  3:21, 35
Colossians
  1:15–18, 24
  1:19, 57–58
  2:9, 57–58
  3:1, 22–23
  4:16, 158
1 Timothy
  1:2, 157
2 Timothy
  1:2, 157
  2:18, 44–45
Titus
  1:1, 167–68
Hebrews
  1:2, 22–23

  13:20, 182–83
  13:22–25, 152
James
  1:1, 166
1 Peter
  1:1, 151, 167–68
  2:25, 182–83
  5:1, 151
  5:4, 182–83
2 Peter
  3:1, 183–84
  3:2, 167–68
  3:3–4, 45
1 John
  1:1, 148–49
  1:1–3, 183
  1:1–4, 144, 149, 150, 151, 180
  1:2, 183
  1:3–4, 156
  1:5, 155–56, 183
  2:1, 148–50
  2:7, 143, 146, 149–51
  2:7–8, 147
  2:12–14, 149–50
  2:16, 156
  2:18, 150–51, 156
  2:18–19, 150–51
  2:19, 156
  2:21, 149–50
  2:22, 143
  2:26, 149–50
  2:28, 143
  3:6, 155–56
  3:9, 155–56
  3:11, 143
  3:15, 155–56
  3:17, 156
  3:23, 156
  4:1–3, 143, 150–51
  4:6, 156
  5:3, 143
  5:6–8, 147
  5:13, 145, 149–50
  5:18, 155–56
2 John
  1, 146
  3, 157
  5, 148–49
  5–6, 146, 148, 150–51
  7, 148, 150–51, 157–58
  8, 148–49

  10–11, 157–58
  12, 148–49, 159, 162
  12–13, 146
3 John
  1, 146
  5–8, 161
  6, 159
  9, 148, 161
  9–10, 159, 160–61
  10, 160–61
  12, 145, 151
  13, 162
  13–14, 146
Revelation
  1–3, 183–84
  1:1, 165, 167–68
  1:2, 182–83
  1:2–5, 166–67
  1:3, 165

  1:4, 165, 173–74
  1:9, 165, 166–67, 173–74, 183
  1:11, 165, 173–74
  1:12, 168
  2:2, 166–67
  2:14, 166–67
  2:20, 166–67
  5:6–10, 182–83
  7:9–10, 37
  7:17, 182–83
  12:17, 182–83
  14:12, 182–83
  18:20, 167–68
  19:13, 182–83
  21–22, 183–84
  21:6, 182–83
  21:14, 167–68
  22:1, 182–83
  22:17, 182–83

Index of Subjects

For the benefit of digital users, indexed terms that span two pages (e.g., 52–53) may, on occasion, appear on only one of those pages.

Abraham, 22, 90
access, celestial, 26–27, 37–40, 42, 46, 52, 57, 59, 63, 65, 66–67, 77, 81, 82, 103, 122
    walking on the sea as, 75–76
Acts of John, 185
Acts of John in Rome, 185
Acts of John of Prochorus, 185
Acts of the Apostles, 155, 164–65
Acts of Timothy, 170
Adam, 34–35
additions, scribal, 7–11
adoptionism, 30
Aenon, 12, 116–17
Alexandria, Egypt, 24, 117–18
Alexandrian school, 14
allegory, 81
Allison, Dale, 18, 167–68, 183–84
ambiguity, xx–xxi, 112, 124, 132, 135–36, 152
anachronisms, 70, 77–78
Anaxemenes of Lampsacus, 128
Anderson, Paul, 115–16, 172
Andrew (disciple), 66–67, 70–71, 78, 107–8, 116–17, 118, 170, 175, 179–80
angelification, 51
angels, 19, 28, 32–34, 46, 51–52, 54–55, 67, 100, 116, 165
anointing at Bethany, 89–90, 97, 117
antichrist, 150–51, 156, 184
Antioch, 24–25, 117–18
Antonine Plague, 179
apocalyptic, 26, 34, 43, 164–65, 167–68, 173–74, 183–84
apocryphal gospels, xvii, 9, 14–15, 103, 104, 121
    John's Gospel as, xxiv, 103–37
1 Apocryphal Apocalypse of John, 185
3 Apocryphal Apocalypse of John, 185
Apollonius of Tyana, 120, 160
aporiae, 4–6, 8–9, 76–77, 131–32
Apostolic Constitutions, 185
Aquarian Gospel, 133
archaeology, 83–84, 115–16
Aristobulus, 27
Asia Minor, 117–18

asterification, 33
Athenodorus Cananites, 128–29
Athens, 128
Attridge, Harold, xiv, 6, 21, 24, 28–29, 97, 118–19
audience, intended, 11–12, 13, 24, 25, 77–78, 103, 105, 132, 133–34, 135–36, 148–49. *See also* readers, initial
authenticity, xix, xxi, 113, 159, 162
author of John's Gospel, reconstruction of, 24–25, 130–32
authorial claims, xviii–xix, xx, xxiv, 109, 113, 114, 118, 136–37, 148–54, 158
authorship, single, xxii–xxiii, 3, 4–11, 24, 26, 110, 111, 150, 152, 171

Bach, Johann Sebastian, xvii
baptism, 69
    of Jesus, 96
Barker, James, 131
Bauckham, Richard, 12
Baum, Armin, 8, 9
Bethany, 85, 89–90, 116, 117
Bethsaida, 70, 116–17
bibliography, xx–xxi
birth, new, 36, 52–53, 68, 103, 155–56
blind man, healing of, 80, 81, 85
body, the, 41–42, 54–55, 84
    celestial, 33–36
    fate of, 43–44
    of Jesus, 13, 22, 27, 39–40, 57–58, 99–100, 116, 158, 181
    pneumatic, 69, 100–1
    psychic, 34–35
Boer, Martinus de, 4, 6
borrowing, literary, 141, 142, 158, 180
Boyarin, 147
Bread of Life discourse, 74–75, 87
Brown, Raymond, 9, 51–52, 150
Buch-Hansen, Gitte, 54
Byers, Andrew, 49–50
Byrskog, Samuel, 117

Caesarea, 24–25

INDEX OF SUBJECTS

Caesarea Maritima, 117–18
Cana, wedding at, 36–37, 67–68, 71, 72–73, 76–77, 109, 116
Capernaum, 70, 72–73, 76–77
centurion's slave, healing of, 76
chief priests, 87
children of God, 32, 36, 46–47, 48–49, 60
Christology, 22–23, 57–58
chronology, 71, 127, 169, 174–75
Cicero, 128
Clark-Soles, Jaime, 43, 85
Clement of Alexandria, 169, 171–72, 174–75, 176
2 Clement, 44–45
Codex Sinaiticus, 161
Codex Vaticanus, 161
Collins, John, 44
Coloe, Mary, 71, 94
compression, literary, 148
context, xxiii, 11–24, 61, 108, 128, 130, 131, 143, 154
Coogan, Jeremiah, xiv, 131–32
copyists, 7, 9–10, 11
cosmology, 36, 107
Crates, 153–54
creation, cosmic, 28–29, 147, 178
credibility, impression of, 20, 117, 120
criticism, literary, xx–xxi, 6, 7, 102
crucifixion (of Jesus), 16, 20, 31, 50–51, 71–72, 91, 98–99, 101, 109–10, 116, 119–20, 181
    spear, piercing by, 99
cryptic speech, xvii, xxi, xxiv, 51–52, 64–65, 67, 71–72, 74, 81, 94, 103, 106–7, 108, 122–23, 124–25, 136, 159
Culpepper, Alan, 6, 61

Da Vinci, Leonardo, xvii
Damascus, 24–25, 117–18
Damis, 120
Daniel, Book of, 184
dating
    of *Gospel of Thomas*, 104–5, 136–37
    of John's Gospel, 25, 136–37
    of 1 John, 156–57
    of 2 John, 159
    of 3 John, 148, 161
    of Revelation, 166, 182
'deification', 46, 49–50, 56–57, 58–59, 60–61, 64, 81
dependence, literary. *See under* Epistles of John
devil, the, 19, 30, 83, 89, 95, 114, 142–43
Dialogue of the Revealer and John, 185
dialogues, xvii, 10, 39, 41–42, 59–60, 63, 69, 71, 72, 74, 77, 79, 82, 83–84, 85, 99, 101–2, 107, 108, 117, 121, 178, 179, 181
Dictys the Cretan, 120

Diogenes the Cynic, 152, 153–54
Diogenes Laertius, 128–29
Dionysius of Alexandria, 161, 165, 171, 173, 176–77
'disciple whom Jesus loved', the, xvii, xviii, xxiv, 10, 20, 98–99, 101, 103, 108–10, 111–12, 114, 118–21, 123, 133–34, 136–37, 153, 162, 163, 173, 179–80, 185
    arguments against John the son of Zebedee, 119
    arguments against Lazarus, 119
    as author of Epistles, 151–53
    as invented character, 119–20
discourses, xxi, xxiii, 6, 26–27, 36, 37, 38, 39–40, 41–42, 43, 50–51, 58, 60, 63, 65–66, 68, 69, 70, 71, 73, 74–76, 77, 79, 81, 82–83, 85, 88, 93, 94, 95, 97–98, 102, 103, 109, 114–15, 121–22, 123, 124–25, 126, 131, 133–34, 178, 181
disguised authorship, xvii, xviii, xx–xxi, xxiv, 7, 11, 127, 141, 163
    definition of, xviii–xix
    motivations for, xix–xx
dissemination (of texts), xxiv, 127, 128–29, 132, 134–36, 179, 181
    of John's Gospel, xxiv, 127–29, 134–35
    via correspondence, 128
    via tampering with library collections, 128–29
divine being, Jesus as, xvii, xxiii, 26–32, 46, 56, 60. *See also* Logos
divinity, 27–29, 30–31, 33, 46, 47–48, 49–50, 58–59, 81, 169–70
Dodd, C. H., 65
Domitian, emperor, 182
Dormition of the Virgin by the Apostle John, 185
doublets, 5, 8–9

Ecclesiastes, Book of, 152
Ehrman, Bart, xiv, 129, 150, 166, 181
'Elder, the' (claimed author of 2 and 3 John), 146, 150, 151, 159, 160–61, 185
Engberg-Pedersen, Troels, 36
Enoch, Epistle of (*1 Enoch*), 33, 44
Enochian literature, 184
Ephesus, 165, 169, 170–71, 173–74
Epicureans, 33
Epistles of John, xviii, xx–xxi, xxii–xxiii, xxiv, 141–62, 163, 164–65, 168, 177, 182, 185
    common authorial claims of the Gospel and Epistles of John, 148–53
    1 John, xxiii, xxiv, 141, 142, 143, 144–45, 147–48, 149–50, 155–57, 172
    2 John, xxiii, xxiv, 141, 142, 143, 145–46, 147–48, 150–51, 157–59
    3 John, xxiii, xxiv, 141, 142, 143, 145, 146, 147–48, 150–51, 159–61
    literary dependence on John's Gospel, 142–48
    motivations for writing, 154–55

INDEX OF SUBJECTS

similarities in form to John's Gospel, 144–46
verbal similarities to John's Gospel, 142–44
Epistula Apostolorum, xviii, xxiii, xxiv, 163, 179–81, 184, 185
Epistula Petri, 153–54
eschatology
    future, 45, 124–25, 184
    realized, 43, 44, 82, 86, 124–25
ethics, xix, xx–xxi, 22, 156, 161
Eurell, John Christian, 167–68
Eusebius, 147–48, 156–57, 161, 169, 171, 172, 173, 174–75, 176
exaltation, human, xvii, xxiii–xxiv, 46–52, 54, 57, 60, 63, 64, 67, 92, 103, 114
eyewitness account, John's Gospel as, xvii, xx, xxiv, 20, 78, 103, 104–5, 108–26, 132, 133–34, 135, 136–37, 141, 148–49, 150, 155–56, 157, 158, 160–61, 162, 163, 164, 171–72, 173, 176, 179–80, 184, 185

false authorship. *See* disguised authorship
Farewell Discourse (John 13:31–17:26), 37, 39–40, 50–51, 65–66, 68, 69, 70, 73, 75–76, 77, 81, 82, 83, 85, 93, 95, 97–98, 109, 123, 124, 181
feeding of the 5000, miracle of (loaves), 18, 74, 75, 78, 87, 117
feet, washing of, 18, 93, 94–95, 97
Final Chapter (John 21), 7–10, 153
first-person speech, 112, 151, 153, 177–78
Fisher, David Hackett, xix, 133–34
flesh and spirit, theme of, 36–37, 67–68
Forger, Deborah, 27–28, 53–54
forgery, literary, xxi, xxiv, 128, 134–35, 150
Fredriksen, Paula, 27
Frey, Jörg, 4, 15, 21, 25, 183
Friedman, Richard Elliott, 5

gematria, 184
Gethsemane, Garden of, 17, 97–98, 119
glorification, 31–32, 35, 84, 91–92, 94–95, 100, 126
glosses, explanatory, 12–13, 68, 96, 151
gnosis (knowledge), 44–45
Gnostics, 176, 177, 178, 179
godhood, 28–29, 50
'gods', human beings as, 49–51, 52–53, 58–59
Goodacre, Mark, xiv, 14–15, 16, 20, 105
Greek language, 6, 24–25, 51, 130, 164–65, 177, 179, 182–83

Hadrian, emperor, 182
Hakola, Raimo, 143
Hancock, Peter, 132, 134
Hanukkah, 82
harmonization, 135
Hebrew language, 24, 51, 171–72

Hengel, Martin, 172
Herodotus, 110
Hippocrates, 153–54
Hippolytus of Rome, 44–45
historical Jesus, 34, 62, 102
historicity, 109–10, 114, 117–18
hoaxes, 132

'I am' statements, 30–31, 38, 52, 77, 81, 85, 96
idols, food offered to, 166–67, 184
Ignatius of Antioch, 129
imagery, 28–29, 51–52, 67, 71, 77, 97–98
immortality, 34, 40–42, 44, 45, 46, 53, 63, 74–75, 84, 103
immortalization, 54–57
incarnation, 30
indwelling, divine, 39–40, 42, 47–48, 52–53, 64, 74, 75–76, 85, 101–2, 122, 123, 155–56. *See also* participation, divine
    as 'love', 93–95
    mutual, 58–59, 66, 82, 88–89, 101
inferences, textual, 143, 171, 172–75
influences, textual, 14–24, 26
insight, spiritual, 123, 136
'invention', definition of, xviii, xxi–xxii
Irenaeus of Lyons, 159, 168–69, 171–72, 173, 174, 176

Jacob's Ladder, 28–29, 51–52
James (brother of Jesus), 23, 155, 164, 166–68, 173, 179–80
James, Apocryphon of, 121–22
James, Epistle of, 166
Jericho, 90
Jerusalem, 4, 19, 24–25, 49, 69, 72–73, 76–78, 79, 82, 83, 89, 90, 117–18, 152, 164, 166–67
    Jesus' entry into, 18, 31, 91–92, 96
    Temple, 25, 69, 70, 71–72, 80, 116, 152, 174–75, 177–78
Jesus traditions, xxii, 11–12, 24–25, 70, 97–98, 102, 117–18, 125, 126
Jewish-Roman War, First, 25
'Johannine Community' hypothesis, xxii–xxiii, 10, 130, 142, 154, 170–71
'Johannine literature', xviii, xxiii–xxiv, 147–48, 159, 163, 171–72, 182, 184
John, son of Zebedee (disciple), xviii, 119, 177–78, 184
    early traditions of, 164–76
    identification as author of John's Gospel, xx–xxi, xxiv, 163, 177, 185
John the Baptist, 12, 15, 65, 66, 68, 69, 70–71, 114, 116–17, 170–71
'John the Elder', 170–71, 172
Joseph of Arimathea, 18, 99
Josephus, 110, 112

INDEX OF SUBJECTS

Judaism, Second Temple, 27
Judas, Gospel of, 121–22
Judas Iscariot (disciple), 19, 88, 89, 90, 95, 116–17, 179–80
Jude, 141, 157, 166–68
judgment, 40–41, 43, 45, 73, 80–81, 91–92
Justin Martyr, 165, 171

Kells, Book of, xvii
Kerygma Petri, 153–54
King, Karen, 178
kingdom, spiritual, 22, 34–35, 36, 43–45, 59–60, 91–92, 100, 104–5, 122, 124–25, 130, 136
Klauck, Hans-Joseph, 145
Kloppenborg, John, 24–25
Koester, Craig, 6, 63

Lamb, Jesus as the, 182–83
Last Supper, xvii, 93, 95, 97–98, 173
Lazarus, 12, 19–20, 44, 84, 85, 87–89, 90, 96, 99, 116–17, 119, 133–34
Letters of John. *See* Epistles of John
library collections, tampering with, 127, 128–29
Lieu, Judith, 143, 148, 150
life, eternal, 28–29, 32, 40–42, 43, 45, 59–61, 68, 70, 73, 74–75, 77, 80–81, 82–83, 84, 86–87, 88, 94–95, 96, 99, 104–5, 114, 122, 124–25, 149–50
Lincoln, Andrew, 26, 114
literacy, 12, 13–14, 22, 24, 61, 129, 130, 131–32, 134, 164–65
literary criticism. *See* criticism, literary
Litwa, M. David, 49–50, 56, 103, 117, 118, 120
logia, 104, 106
Logos, 26–33, 46, 47, 48, 50, 52–54, 57–60, 63, 73, 96, 123
  ascent of, 29–30
  descent of, 30–31
  immortalization through, 54–57
  Philo's theory of, 27–28
Luke, Gospel of, xxii, xxiii, xxiv, 3, 14–15, 16–17, 21, 24–25, 26, 34, 40–41, 46, 51, 60–61, 70, 72, 76, 97, 101–2, 104, 120, 130, 132, 135, 136–37, 162, 164, 169–70, 171–72, 174–75
  similarities to John's Gospel, 19–21, 89–90

Magness, Jodi, 77
maps, 24–25
Marian and James, Martyrdom of, 120
Mark, Gospel of, xxii, xxiii, xxiv, 3, 12, 14–15, 21, 26, 34, 40–41, 45, 60–61, 64, 65, 70, 71–72, 78, 89, 90, 91, 104, 108, 119, 120, 124, 130, 131, 132, 135, 136–37, 147, 162, 164, 170, 171, 174
  endings of, 9, 10

Markan Priority, 171–72
  similarities to John's Gospel, 16–18, 20
Martha of Bethany, 19–20, 85, 88–89, 90, 116–17, 122
martyrs, 51
Mary (mother of Jesus), 67, 68, 98–99, 158
Mary, Gospel of, 14, 21, 106–8, 115, 118, 121–22, 125, 135–36
Mary Magdalene, 31, 100–1, 119
Mary of Bethany, 12, 19–20, 85, 88, 90, 97, 116–17
Matthew (disciple), 179–80
Matthew, Gospel of, xxii, xxiii, xxiv, 3, 14–15, 16–17, 19, 20, 21, 26, 34, 42, 60–61, 70, 72, 76, 78, 89, 90, 101–2, 104, 120, 130, 132, 135, 136–37, 162, 164, 169–70, 171–72, 174–75
  similarities to John's Gospel, 17–19
memory, xvii, 83–84, 131, 137, 141, 155, 160–61, 171, 173–74, 186
  problems with, 171–72
  supernaturally retrieved, 122–23
metaphor, xxii, 43, 44–45, 57–58, 59, 74, 82, 124, 125
metastory, 29
Metzger, Bruce, xxi
Middle Platonism, 23
'Misdirection-Delay-Secret Action' pattern, 67, 68, 71, 75–76, 79
Mitchell, Margaret, 155
monad, God as, 54–56
monotheism, 27
Montanists, 176
Moses, 47–48, 55–57
Moss, Candida, 131–32
mountains, 18, 19, 152, 177–78
mundane details, use of, 116
Muratorian Fragment, 170, 175
Mysteries of John, 185

Nag Hammadi manuscripts, 177
Nain, 89
Najman, Hindy, xix, xx–xxi
name of God, 5, 28–29, 92, 158
narrative, xvii, xviii–xix, xxiii–xxiv, 4, 6, 12, 14–15, 19–20, 21, 26, 29, 36–37, 50–51, 63, 64–65, 68, 72–73, 79, 80, 81, 84, 89, 92–93, 96, 100, 102, 103, 108, 109, 114, 115–16, 124, 127, 130, 133–35, 136–37, 141, 144, 164, 169–70, 174–75, 178–79
  continuous, 5
  design, xxi
  framing, 71
  pseudo-historical, 117
Nathanael (disciple), 66–67, 70–71, 179–80
Nerva, emperor, 182

INDEX OF SUBJECTS 263

networks, literary, xxii, 11–12, 13–24, 130, 135
Nicodemus, 36–37, 41–42, 50–51, 59–60, 68, 69, 99, 114, 117, 122
non-Jews, 11–13, 25, 76
noncanonical gospels. *See* apocryphal gospels
North, Wendy Spronston, 98
novelties of John's Gospel, 26, 103, 107, 115, 121, 123, 131, 179

Oahspe, 133
oneness with God, 48–50, 53, 56–57, 58–59, 60–61, 94–95, 114, 122
Origen, 51, 147–48, 161, 169, 174

Papias, 151, 156–57, 168–69, 170–72
parables, 81–82, 90, 106, 124
Paraclete, the. *See* Spirit, divine
paratextuality, xviii–xix
Parsenios, George, 142, 144, 145
participation, divine, 22–23, 27–28, 32–33, 46, 49–50, 56–57, 58–59, 74–75, 99. *See also* indwelling, divine
Passion Narrative, 15, 17, 71–72
Patmos, 165
Paul, xxiii, 14, 22–23, 24–25, 26, 34–36, 37, 39–41, 42, 43–44, 48, 61, 99–100, 130, 133–34, 141, 155, 157, 164, 166–67, 173–74, 184. *See also* Pauline and Deutero-Pauline works
Pauline and Deutero-Pauline works
  Apocalypse of Paul, 154
  Colossians, 22–23, 24, 154
  1 Corinthians, 34–35, 100
  2 Corinthians, 47–48
  3 Corinthians, 44–45, 153–54
  Ephesians, 22–23, 40, 153–54
  Epistle to the Laodiceans, 153–54, 158
  Hebrews, 22–23, 24, 99–100, 129, 152, 153–54, 182–83
  Letters of Paul and Seneca, 153–54
  Romans, 39–40
  2 Thessalonians, 153–54
  1 Timothy, 157
  2 Timothy, 44–45, 157
  Titus, 157, 167–68
Pausanias, 128
Peirano, Irene, xix, xx–xxi
Pentateuch, 5, 8–9
Peppard, Michael, 46–47
perfectionism, 155–56
Pergamum, 128–29
Pericope Adulterae, 7
pericopes, 16, 90
Peter (disciple), 19, 23, 66–67, 70–71, 78, 94, 98, 107, 116–17, 119–20, 141, 155, 164–65, 168–69, 171, 173, 179–80
  crucifixion of, 10

Peter, works ascribed to
  Apocalypse of, 154, 164–65
  Coptic Apocalypse of, 154
  Gospel of, 9, 118, 136–37, 164–65
  1 Peter, 100, 151, 157, 162, 164–65, 182–84
  2 Peter, 153–54, 157, 162, 164–65, 167–68, 183–84
Philip (disciple), 38, 66–67, 78, 116–17, 179–80
Philo of Alexandria, xxiii, 21–22, 23–24, 27–29, 47–48, 54–59
philosophy, 30, 33, 35, 107, 130, 182–83
  Hellenistic-Jewish, xxiii, 14, 21–22, 23–24, 26, 57, 58
Philostratus, 120
pilgrim itineraries, 24–25
Polybius, 110, 112–13
Polycarp, 51, 131
polytychs, 131
private exchanges, xxi, 104, 107, 121–22
prologue (proem), 6, 30–31, 32, 57–58, 60, 108–9, 144, 147, 149, 174–75, 180
prophets, 53, 165–66, 167–68
proto-Catholicism, 176, 179, 181
Protoevangelium, 108–9
provenance, 24, 134–35, 154
pseudepigrapha, Jewish (literary collection), xix
pseudepigraphy, xx–xxi, 120, 127, 128–29, 133–34, 152, 154, 162, 164–65, 166–68, 177–78, 183–84
  primary, xx–xxi
  responses to, 176
  secondary, xx–xxi
pseudonymity, 22–23, 133–34, 136–37, 151, 152, 153–54, 157, 159, 160, 162, 165–66, 167–68, 179–80
Pseudo-Clementine Homilies, 154
Pseudo-Dionysian corpus, xix
pseudo-historical letters, 40, 155, 160, 161, 177
Ptolemy (Valentinian teacher), 168–69, 176
publication, ancient. *See* dissemination (of texts)

Questions of John (*Interrogatio Iohannis*), 185

readers, initial, xx–xxi, 11–13, 127, 134–35
reception, 135–36, 141, 147–48, 154, 161, 185
redaction-criticism, xxii
resurrection, 19, 34–35, 40–41, 43–45, 46, 68, 69, 71–72, 82, 84, 90, 93–94, 96, 98, 99–100, 101–2, 119, 135–36, 179, 181
  spiritual, 84–87, 88–89, 122
Revelation, Book of, xxiv, 164–68, 171–72, 173–74, 176, 178–79, 182–84, 185
  dating of, 182
  relationship to John's Gospel, 182–84
Revelation of John about Antichrist, 185

INDEX OF SUBJECTS

Roman Empire, 24
Rome, 120, 173–74
Rosenmeyer, Patricia, xix, 160
Rothschild, Clare, 129
Runia, David, 23–24, 28–29

Salvian, 133–34
Samaritans, 13, 70, 72, 122
Satan. *See* devil, the
Schnackenburg, Rudolf, 150
Schneiders, Sandra, 64
Scott, Alan, 33
Secret Book (Apocryphon) of John, xviii, xxiii, xxiv, 163, 177–80, 181, 183–84, 185
Serapis (deity), 77–78
Sethians, 176, 177, 178, 179
Sheep Gate, healing at the, 72–73, 77
sheep imagery, 52, 81–82, 83, 100–1, 126
Shepherd discourse, 98, 100–1
shepherd imagery, 28–29, 77, 82, 83, 126, 182–83
'sight', spiritual, 47–48, 80–81
'signs' (miracles), 4, 5–6, 8, 9, 30–31, 44, 45, 47, 59, 60, 63–102, 104–5, 109
Simon the Leper, 89
Smith, Dwight Moody, 108, 119
Solomon, 152
source-criticism, xxii
spirit (*pneuma*), 22, 26–27, 32–33, 34–35, 40–42, 43–45, 46–47, 52, 55–56, 69, 74, 84, 86, 87, 99–100, 124–25, 130
  birth from, 37, 60–61, 63, 66, 68, 100
  contrasted with the flesh, 36–37
  God as, 28
Spirit, divine, 9, 22, 30, 32, 35–36, 39–42, 47–48, 52, 55–56, 57, 66, 69, 75–76, 77, 80–81, 94–95, 98–99, 101–2, 114, 133, 135–36, 155–56, 169–70
  coming of, 43, 44, 86, 122, 123
  within Jesus, 99
Stang, Charles, xix
Starr, Raymond, 128
stars, 28, 32–34
Stibbe, M. W. G., 124
Stoicism, 23, 128–29
Stowers, Stanley, 13–14
Streeter, B. H., 16–17, 19
survival, celestial, 42–45
symbolism, xvii, xxi, xxiii–xxiv, 6, 36–37, 63–102, 105, 125, 131
Syme, Ronald, 160
Synoptic Gospels, xxiii, 20, 21–22, 23, 24, 25, 26–27, 37–38, 39–40, 41, 43–44, 46, 60–61, 63, 70, 71–72, 74, 75, 76–77, 78, 81, 83–84, 89, 92, 93, 96, 97–98, 101–2, 105, 106, 107, 108, 116–18, 119, 121, 122, 123, 124–25, 126, 130, 135–37, 164, 169, 171–72, 173, 175, 176
  as literary influences on John's Gospel, 14
  generic similarities to John's Gospel, 14–15
  strategic overlaps of John's Gospel with, 125–26
Syriac Bibles, 147–48

Tatian, 9–10, 21
Temple, Jewish. *See under* Jerusalem
Tertullian, 51, 165, 171
testimony, 6, 15, 61, 66, 70, 103, 110, 113–14, 115, 118–19, 136–37, 145, 148–49, 151, 180, 183
theology, 3, 6, 26, 51–52, 60–61, 62, 63, 64–65, 78, 84, 91, 97–98, 102, 105, 106–7, 115, 122, 125, 134, 135, 162
theophanies, 30–31
Theopompus, 128
third person speech, 104, 110, 153, 177–78
Thomas (disciple), 101, 119
Thomas, Gospel of, xvii, 14–15, 21, 44–45, 104–6, 107, 108, 115, 118, 124–25, 126, 129, 135–37, 179
Thomas the Contender, Book of, 179
Thompson, Marianne Meye, 72–73, 88
Thucydides, 110, 112
Timothy, Acts of, 170
topography, 24–25, 115–16, 117–18
tradition criticism, xxii
Trajan, emperor, 169, 182
transfiguration, 96
Transjordan, 24–25
Twelve Apostles, Gospel of the, 185

unfalsifiability, 117, 120
unity of John's Gospel, 3, 6, 26, 102
unrecorded moments, 72, 93, 103, 104, 107, 108, 121

Valentinians, 44–45, 168, 176
verisimilitude, 117, 120, 126, 161
vine discourse, 95–96, 97–98, 124, 126
voice, divine, 58, 92, 96
Vouga, François, 147

walking on water, miracle of, 75–76, 78
'we' language, xvii–xviii, 6–7, 111, 113, 141, 149–50, 154–55, 175, 179–80
wine, 28–29, 36–37, 68, 126
Wisdom, Book of, 152
witness, role of, 65–66, 71, 114, 151, 182–83

Xenophon, 110

Zeno of Citium, 128–29